Education Reform in Postwar Japan

Education Reform in Postwar Japan

The 1946 U.S. Education Mission

Gary H. Tsuchimochi/Foreword by Carol Gluck

UNIVERSITY OF TOKYO PRESS

Publication of this book was partially supported by a Grant-in-Aid for the Publication of Scientific Research Results from the Ministry of Education, Science and Culture of Japan.

This volume is an English translation of *Beikoku Kyoiku Shisetsudan no Kenkyu* (Tamagawa University Press, 1991).

ISBN 4-13-057200-8
ISBN 0-86008-496-5

Printed in Japan

Dr. Gordon T. Bowles, one of the architects of postwar Japanese education reform, died of heart failure on November 10, 1991. This book is dedicated to him with deep appreciation for his generous support.

CONTENTS

FOREWORD

Carol Gluck
George B. Sansom Professor of History, Columbia University

Sometimes history is told as a tale with a happy or tragic ending, sometimes as a drama, whose characters drive the plot toward its climax, and sometimes as a fable that points to the moral of the story. "Sour grapes," said the fox, who could not reach them anyway; "slow and steady wins the race," read the citation to the tortoise after he defeated the hapless hare. More often than not, the occupation of Japan is told as a fable, whose moral depends on the teller's point of view.

Here are some examples: Tanaka Kakuei is quoted here as complaining that "postwar education reform, particularly the 6–3–3–4 system, was forced on us by America, and was so experimental that it was implemented by only one state [in the U.S.]."[1] In 1987 Gordon Bowles, who accompanied the 1946 U.S. Education Mission, wrote a reminiscence specifically for this book, in which he denied "the recent cries from various quarters that the 6–3–3 system was forced on the Japanese people. The matter was throughly debated and decided by the Japanese educators themselves and their decision coincided with the majority opinion expressed by the Mission members."[2] Nambara Shigeru, the chair of the Japanese Education Committee who delivered opinions to the Americans while they were in Japan, spoke more of manipulation than coincidence: "We not only cooperated with the Mission, but also used it to actualize our opinions."[3] Or, as Aesop has it, "appearances often are deceiving."

It is this series of deceptive appearances that Gary Tsuchimochi illuminates in his detailed study of the 1946 U.S. Education Mission to Japan. Like so many other postwar reforms during the occupation, education reform had a longer and more complex history than the fables usually reveal. Marlene Mayo has examined the elaborate presurrender planning that took place in Washington during the war. When it came to education, the Americans called for the repeal of the "obnoxious laws" by which Japanese students were indoctrinated in military drill and ultranationalistic ideology. They suggested mostly negative measures such as revision of the "mythological claptrap" that cluttered the textbooks and "the elimination of restrictions on liberal education."[4]

Modesty of purpose were the watchwords of the State Department planners until mid-1945. They felt that military government could not itself accomplish positive reforms. These must await the appearance of "cooperative Japanese, themselves proponents of liberal ideas," who could reconstruct the framework of Japanese education. In a pattern that affected other policy areas as well, more aggressive plans for reform took shape in the summer of 1945, influenced partly by planning for Germany and partly by concerns of the army and navy in the face of imminent operations. Bowles drafted the document that outlined the reforms, including a purge and decentralization as well as the earlier negative measures concerning textbooks, history and morals instruction, and the like. The paper recommended that an advisory group visit Japan, but nothing was said about either the Rescript on Education or language reform. Mayo concludes that Washington had set the direction of education reform on track before the Civil Information and Education Section (CI&E) of SCAP began its real work. And as before, the burden of constructive reform was to lie with the Japanese themselves.[5]

Tsuchimochi continues the story, showing that the reforms had a long and deep history among Japanese educators, who did indeed take up the postwar project, although not always in the form that CI&E officials ordained. The thesis of the book has two parts: first, that the postwar education reform was based on Japanese initiative, and second, that it "originated in the dynamic correlation" between prewar and postwar movements in Japanese education.[6] Using new materials, many of which he has unearthed, Tsuchimochi traces the history of the Mission, from its inception through its Report to its outcome. In the process he weaves a tangled skein of social, political, and ideological cross-purposes that operated both among the Japanese and Americans themselves and then between the two sides as they "cooperated" on the matters at hand.

Separate the skein, take one strand at a time, and it seems a nicely typical instance of the so-called cultural encounter that characterized the early part of the occupation. First, the Americans: SCAP requested a Mission in October 1945, and suggested the names of appropriate members, including some solicited from the Ministry of Education. (Minister of Education Maeda Tamon immediately thought of John Dewey, and then of Charles Beard, perhaps partly on the principle that Beard had helped

Japan out after the earthquake and might be disposed to do so again.) SCAP now argued that the Japanese authorities could not manage the reforms without outside support, but demurred when the Japanese included other Allied names in what it planned as an American show. When James Conant, president of Harvard, was recommended as Mission Chairman, the General objected to him as "politically inappropriate." Tsuchimochi suggests that MacArthur feared that Conant might have in mind another presidency, that of the United States, a position to which the General, too, aspired. In response to this not entirely public-spirited objection, Conant's name was removed.

American insistence on fair representation resulted in calls for the addition of a Catholic educator, to acknowledge "the status of Catholic education and the competence of Catholic educators." MacArthur responded as if he were ordering room service: "Send two Catholic educators on Mission, President of Georgetown University and President of Notre Dame, or educators of equal calibre."[7] To meet similar objections, the State Department appointed four more women and a black American. A distance from Dewey or Beard, the selection process had proceeded on hallowed American principles, which had little to do with Japanese education. Equally typical was the official telegram from SCAP requesting the mission: "ESTIMATED 18,000,000 STUDENTS, 400,000 TEACHERS, 40,000 SCHOOLS PRESENT MAJOR MEDIUM FOR INFLUENCING JAPANESE LIFE THROUGHOUT, AND ACTION IN ACCOMPLISHING OCCUPATION MISSION."[8] In the autumn of 1945, the soldiers of SCAP laid no little plans.

When the Mission arrived the following March, CI&E officials were ready with their own views of Japanese education, which they presented during the Mission's first week. For just as Washington had pre-planned the occupation reforms, so, too, did SCAP officials pre-plan the agenda for the Mission. And there were many cooks at work on the broth. Robert King Hall, a CI&E officer obsessed with the need for language reform, introduced his pet project of abolishing Chinese characters and writing Japanese entirely in romanized script. "It will be easier for foreigners to read Japanese" and for the "common people to read laws and newspapers and become thereby really literate." Hall argued his case in the strongest terms, evoking everything from democratization to the fact that romanization had succeeded in Turkey after World War I, an argument that Nambara, not unreasonably, sniffed at.

Hall had already been rebuffed by the State Department, on the grounds that such a reform would have serious consequences, "not only in drastically limiting intellectual and cultural pursuits, but in impeding in most drastic form the operation of the normal economy of the country."[9] Eugene Dooman had stated his rebuke in terms of the victor's national interest, but Bowles added a reason that his fellow Americans may have found even more persuasive: "such drastic reform of the Japanese language is not only undesirable, but in the event of failure, would be our fault."[10] After much debate, the final Report recommended that a phonetic system be adopted, and that some form of romanization be introduced, to be decided by a commission of Japanese scholars.

Having administered the coup de grace to Japan's national writing system, out of their "sense of responsibility to the children of Japan," the Mission members completed their work and left for home. Tsuchimochi reveals that their view on the need for language reform was taken a step further by the U.S. Scientific Advisory Group, which visited Japan in August 1947. "Why shouldn't Japan lead the way in reducing the number of world languages?" the Group asked. "That would be a great contribution toward peace."[11] Ironically, the linguistic narcissism of these Americans abroad later came true, as U.S. power and science drew postwar scientific publication everywhere into an English orbit.

The 27 American educators had spent one week in briefings after they arrived in Japan, one week listening to SCAP and Japanese educators, less than one week observing, and one week compiling their Report, which became the basis for a good part of the subsequent reforms. The time may seem short, until one recalls that the Americans in Government Section were ordered to draft Japan's postwar Constitution within seven days.

Considering the good intentions but sometimes errant proposals of the U.S. Education Mission, it was fortunate that the Japanese side was as active as it appears in Tsuchimochi's portrayal. Like the Americans, the Japanese ran true to their own form, conditioned both by prewar positions and by the changed circumstances of defeat and occupation. Most important was the fact that Japanese educators had already proposed significant reforms before the war, in a pattern shared by the prewar proposal and postwar implementation of other measures such as land reform. So it was that the Ministry of Education scooped the occupation by announcing its "Educational Policy for the Construction of a New Japan" on September 15, 1945, days before the CI&E was even established.

Maeda, the new Education Minister, was not shy about stating that "we ourselves dealt with every single matter independently, without any connection with GHQ."[12] This was not quite true, since what Hall later described as "the most dramatic educational somersault in modern times" had not been executed in a vacuum. Anticipatory acrobatics, one might say, were the educational order of the day. The Ministry had figured SCAP's probable intentions and jumped early to land on its feet. Even so, Tsuchimochi quotes a CI&E official as saying that Maeda, like other immediate postwar bureaucrats, had missed his footing at two places: he assumed the continuity of the *kokutai* and invoked religion as the basis for a new morality. Neither position proved acceptable to SCAP.

The imperial conservatism of this prewar liberal showed itself in his attitude toward the Rescript on Education, which he and the subsequent two Education Ministers, Abe Yoshishige and Tanaka Kōtarō, continued to advocate as a valid basis for the new democratic education. One scholar has written that this constant evocation of the Rescript made the Americans newly suspicious of the document itself, not merely of its ritual uses.[13] The Japanese Education Committee, which had been formed at SCAP's request to cooperate with the Mission, proposed a different view of the Rescript. The Committee chairman was Nambara Shigeru, the noted liberal president of Tokyo Imperial University. Tsuchimochi points out the existence of a written recommendation, in English, stating the Committee's "firm conviction that a New Imperial Rescript will be the most useful instrument that encourages initiative of Japanese educators and realizes the democratization of Japan, thus resulting in the establishment of peaceful Japan."[14]

As a result, the Mission's Report softened the original recommendation of "permanent discontinuance" of the Rescript to a discontinuation only of the ceremonial use of the Rescript, though nothing was said about promulgating a new one. The Mission subcommittee reporting on the Rescript labeled it their "hardest battle," since some Americans thought that condemnation "might be considered an attempt upon our part to destroy Japanese culture."[15] The divergence of views between Japanese and Americans did not end there, however, since the Japanese Committee's own report used different and far less democratic language to describe the desired new Rescript. *This* report, Tsuchimochi writes, was later submitted only to the Japanese government, not to SCAP, which was chagrined to learn about it from an article in the *Shinano Mainichi Shimbun.*

Once again, the alchemy of translation from one language to the other had served to disguise real difference of opinion. As for the Rescript on Education, it soon became and then remained a point of dispute between CI&E and Japanese conservatives who, from Education Minister Tanaka in 1946 to Prime Minister Yoshida in 1949, continued the quest to reestablish an imperial basis for moral authority. The Rescript was ultimately abolished by the Diet in 1948, and no new version was ever issued.

On language reform as well, the Committee had had its influence. There was an active minority in the Japanese lobby for language reform who, like Hall, favored romanization. The Japanese Education Committee, however, argued against it in favor of other forms of simplification. Nambara knew of Hall's enthusiasm, commenting that "we had already learned of his intention, and therefore were able to oppose it."[16] As proof of his statement, Tsuchimochi points out that when the State Department drafted its 1947 policy statement on the basis of the Mission's Report and submitted it to the Far Eastern Commission, it omitted all mention of language reform, the only recommendation of the Mission that was dropped. Meanwhile, the Ministry of Education had responded to CI&E by beginning instruction in romanization in the lower grades, although its "romance with *rōmaji*" was shortlived.[17] The mirror of mutual manipulation between the Japanese, who disagreed among themselves, and the Americans, who did the same, thus reflected many faces.

Some of these faces were liberal, in SCAP terms, others were conservative. Minister of Education Abe greeted the Mission with a speech designed to disarm the visitors: "The war and the Japanese defeat were caused by defects in Japanese education and the low educational standards among the common Japanese. However, you educators, who are visiting Japan now, must not try to impose ideals on the Japanese educational system which are not yet realized, even in your own country."[18] One member of the Mission summarized Foreign Minister Yoshida Shigeru's speech to the group as asking them to "consider the fact that Japan has its own culture and may want to be democratic in a way different from America."[19] Such guarded remarks might seem relevant to proposed structural changes of the sort represented by the recommendation of the 6–3–3 system, but here Tsuchimochi has a surprise.

For this American-style reform seems to have originated not with the Americans but with the Japanese. The Mission had originally proposed a 6–5 system, six years of elementary followed by five years of secondary school. It was the Japanese Education Committee that insisted on the 6–3–3 division, and for the express purpose of introducing a single-track school system. Although they disagreed among themselves, Nambara and others held sway in favor of what he called "the American system." Kaigo Tokiomi, a leading Japanese educator, similarly argued for the democratization of education in terms of equal opportunity. Against the objection of the Ministry of Education, the Committee recommended abolishing the higher elementary schools and youth schools, which constituted the non-elite track, and establishing a single course of six years of elementary school, three years of middle school, and three of high school for all students. This basic plan had been put forward by the Kyōiku dōshikai in 1937, and Abe Shigetaka had proposed a 6–3–3 structure one year before that. Hence the imposed school reform was imposed from within, with the help of the U.S. Education Mission.

Although Bowles commented that about 60 percent of the Mission's Report came from the "pro-American" members of the Japanese Education Committee, when it came to higher education, liberals like Nambara proved less cooperative. In general, CI&E was more concerned with primary and secondary education than with universities. One of their number did consider the reform of higher education a high priority, since as he later put it, "all the civilian war crimes defendants are Teidai graduates."[20] Tsuchimochi suggests that he wielded some influence. But in the end the Mission bowed to the Japanese Education Committee, whose university professors were less intent on radical reform of their own institutions than of the elementary and secondary school system.

Tsuchimochi contrasts the experience of educational reform in occupied Japan and Germany, about which he has also written.[21] Unlike for Japan, re-education policy for Germany had been included in the Potsdam Agreement. An educational mission, though discussed before the surrender, was sent to the American zone in Germany only after the Mission to Japan, in August 1946. This delay meant that it had less effect on reforms already begun, so that where CI&E treated the Mission's Report as "gospel," in Germany the report had less impact. The Bavarians resisted the equalization of educational tracks, which did not in fact take place, while the Japanese, who some portray as having caved in to the Americans, proposed such equalization, which soon occurred. In each case, Tsuchimochi argues, it was the reformed, not the reformers, who won the day, though not by themselves. The Fundamental Law of Education of 1947 in Japan embodied the result of the interaction between prewar and postwar educational visions, between American and Japanese educators in contest with their own sides and with each other. Horio Teruhisa has called the Law "a new constitution for education," which signified "a complete transformation of the entire structure of Japan's educational enterprise."[22]

But this returns us to the world of fable. Before the Mission left for Japan, the British diplomat George Sansom remarked that the Americans seemed "to think that Japan can be supplied with a new system of education as a tailor might furnish a new suit."[23] Years later, Herbert Passin of CI&E remarked of the mechanical application of American ideas to Japan's education system that "we opened a Pandora's box, and since we did it through inadvertence, we would have been wiser to leave it to the Japanese to open it themselves."[24] Not a complete transformation, or a new suit, or a Pandora's box—or perhaps a bit of each—the process of educational reform that Tsuchimochi delineates here has a moral of its own: "By the work one knows the workman." The occupation bears the marks of many.

Notes

1. See below, p. 6.
2. See below, p. 432.
3. See below, p. 107.
4. Marlene Mayo, "Planning for the Education and Re-education of Defeated Japan, 1943–1945," *The Occupation of Japan: Educational and Social Reform* (Norfolk, Va: The MacArthur Memorial, 1982), pp. 25–32.
5. Mayo, pp. 57–72.
6. See below, p. 7.
7. See below, p. 37.
8. See below, p. 29.
9. See below, p. 109.
10. See below, p. 118.
11. See below, p. 159.
12. See below, p. 89.
13. Toshio Nishi, *Unconditional Democracy: Education and Politics in Occupied Japan, 1945–1952* (Stanford: Hoover Institution Press, 1982), pp. 151–54.
14. See below, p. 83.
15. See below, p. 80.
16. See below, p. 116.
17. Nishi, pp. 205–6.
18. See below, p. 69.
19. See below, pp. 103–4.
20. See below, p. 149.
21. Gary H. Tsuchimochi, *Senryoka Doitsu no Kyoiku Kaikaku: Amerika Taidoku Kyoiku Shisetsudan to Amerika Taidoku Shakaika Iinkai* (Tokyo: Meisei University Press, 1989).
22. Teruhisa Horio, *Educational Thought and Ideology in Modern Japan: State Authority and Intellectual Freedom* (Tokyo: University of Tokyo Press, 1988), p. 129.
23. See below, p. 54.
24. Herbert Passin, *The Legacy of the Occupation* (New York: East Asian Institute, Columbia University, 1968), p. 11.

PREFACE

This study originated in my doctoral dissertation, "A Study of the First United States Education Mission to Japan and Its Report," for which I received the Ph.D. in Education from the University of Tokyo in 1990.

My interest in postwar Japanese education reform began during the period when I was compiling my Ed. D. dissertation at Teachers College, Columbia University, in 1980—"The Rapid Expansion of Universities in Postwar Japan with Particular Reference to the Private Universities." Visiting Japan in 1981 as a foreign visiting researcher, at the National Institute for Educational Research of Japan, gave me the opportunity to learn of the extent of Japanese studies on postwar education reform. At the same time, it also allowed me access to primary historical materials relating to postwar education reform on the Japanese side, which are kept at the Section for Historical Documents on Education, the National Institute for Educational Research of Japan.

All these documents, including the dissertations of Mark T. Orr ("Education Reform Policy in Occupied Japan," Ph.D. dissertation, University of North Carolina, 1954), and James I. Doi ("Educational Reform in Occupied Japan, 1945–1950: A Study of Acceptance of and Resistance to Institutional Change," Ph.D. dissertation, University of Chicago, 1952), both of whom were on the staff of the Education Division of the CI&E, stimulated my interest in education reform under the Occupation. At the same time, when I examined the Report of the First United States Education Mission to Japan, which became the blueprint for postwar education, I realized that many of the recommendations made by the Mission had never been implemented. The question of why these recommendations were not carried out led me to investigate the whole process of the drawing up of the Report, from historical sources. Following the advice of Dr. Hiroshi Abe, of the National Institute for Educational Research of Japan, to "write your dissertation with your feet," I discovered many historical documents, including the Pearl A. Wanamaker Papers, in the Henry Suzzallo Library, University of Washington. In other words, the initial groundwork for this study was an extensive search for historical materials relating to postwar education reform, to corroborate the recorded facts.

Some important works have been published on the postwar education reform in Japan, but due to the restriction on historical documents, these works have referred only to the official GHQ documents. My intention here is to describe the details of the drawing up of the Report of the Mission, by using not only the GHQ documents but also personal papers and interviews with Mission members and others involved.

In 1985 and 1986 I was given the opportunity to join the Preliminary Survey (1985) and Actual Survey (1986) of Historical Materials Held in the U.S.A. Concerning Education Reform Under the Allied Occupation of Japan, under the Grants-in-Aid for International Scientific Research Programme sponsored by the Ministry of Education. These surveys not only gave me the chance to obtain important materials, but also allowed me to participate in a collaborative study, based on these surveys: "A Comprehensive Study of the Report of the United States Education Mission to Japan, with Particular Reference to the Preparation." I would like to express my appreciation to Professor Hideo Sato, College of Humanities and Sciences, Nihon University, who was in charge of this collaborative project, and also to Professor Eiichi Suzuki, Faculty of Education, Nagoya University, who was a member of the research delegation. It should be mentioned that the present work discusses the same issues as does the above collaborative study. However, it is based on new material and is written from my own viewpoint.

Professor Masao Terasaki of the University of Tokyo encouraged me to complete this study, and suggested that I submit it to the University of Tokyo for a doctoral degree, as an external applicant (*ronbun hakushi*).

It has been several years since the exclusive nature of the Japanese university system was first internationally criticized, but only recently, in February 1991, was the necessity for a reexamination of the degree system emphasized in a report of the Council on the University. I believe that my success in obtaining a degree from the University of Tokyo as an external applicant is more than a personal matter; it is also an encouragement to future external applicants.

Without the encouragement and advice of Professor Terasaki, this study would never have been completed in this form. I would like to express my special appreciation to him.

I also thank the members of the dissertation examination committee: Teruhisa Horio (chairman), Masao Terasaki, Tadahiko Inagaki, Kosaku Miyasaka, and Masao Nagasawa. Their comments on the main discussion in the dissertation resulted in changes in part of the structure of this book.

I am indebted to many other individuals, without whose assistance this study would never have been completed. Their names are too numerous to mention, but I am particularly grateful to Dr. Herbert J. Wunderlich and Dr. Mark T. Orr, both of whom were on the staff of the Education Divison of the CI&E during the Occupation period.

Dr. Gordon T. Bowles, who acted as a bridge between the U.S. and the Japanese side, as a secretary of the Mission, kindly wrote his memoir especially for this study, as a living testimony concerning postwar Japanese education reform. It is no exaggeration to say that without his assistance this study could not have been completed.

It was Dr. Bowles's help that made it possible for me to interview Mrs. Pearl A. Wanamaker. Due to her state of health, visitors were not normally allowed to see her at that time. But on the appointed day, she came out to meet me in her wheelchair. I introduced myself to her as "a child who was brought up within the 6–3–3 school system," and it seemed to me that a faint smile played around her lips. The prearranged fifteen-minute interview actually lasted for one hour, and Mrs. Wanamaker's smile still remains fresh in my mind. A few months after this interview she passed away.

Dr. Philip H. Stoddard, the son of Chairman Stoddard, offered much material and also information about his father during the course of several interviews. He was the very image of his father, whom I had seen in photographs, so that I had the illusion of interviewing Chairman Stoddard in the early postwar days. I was particularly moved by seeing "Last Copy" in Stoddard's own handwriting, with his signature, on the front page of a copy of the Report. The memoir by Dr. Philip Stoddard, entitled "George D. Stoddard and the U.S. Education Mission to Japan: A Brief Appreciation," which was especially written for this study, is included as an appendix to this volume.

The Japanese edition of this book was published by Tamagawa University Press in August 1991. Tamagawa has a special connection with the Mission: members Trow, Hilgard and Diemer, along with Capt. John W. Barnard of the Education Division of the CI&E, visited Tamagawa Gakuen (Principal, Kuniyoshi Obara) in 1946 because of their interest in the school's progressive methods of education.

Interest in, and studies of, postwar education reform have been increasing, even outside Japan, since an international symposium, "The Occupation of Japan: Educational and Social Reform," was held in 1980 at the MacArthur Memorial, Norfolk, Virginia. However, not many books on Japanese education have appeared in English or other European languages. In order to understand the development of present Japanese education from its origins, study of the U.S. Education Mission is essential. My intention in this English edition is to present more information to non-Japanese readers, and also to show my gratitude for the generosity of the American people, who helped me with advice, time, and materials. The publication of this study is supported by a Grant-in-Aid for Publication of Scientific Research Results of the Ministry of Education, Science and Culture.

The present study, which includes a comparison of the U.S. Education Missions to Germany and to Japan, stimulated the establishing in Tokyo of the Microfiche Collection of the Occupation of Japan: "Educational Reform in Japan, 1945–1952" and "U.S. Occupation of Germany: Educational Reform, 1945–1949" were copied, to form the nucleus of the collection, from the primary historical materials in the U.S. National Archives. I hope that this collection will help future comparative studies.

I owe a special debt of gratitude to Professor Carol Gluck (George Sansom Professor of History, Columbia University), who honored me by accepting my invitation to write the Foreword to this book. I was one of Professor Gluck's students at Columbia University, and she is one of the scholars I most respect.

I would also like to express my special appreciation to Mr. and Mrs. Malcolm Ritchie for their intensive efforts in the translation of this study. Mrs. Masako Hagiwara Ritchie, in particular, showed her interest in this study when I was working on it as a doctoral dissertation.

A portion of this study was published in English in *Toyo Eiwa Journal of the Humanities and Social Sciences*. In the translation and editing of that article, I obtained the cooperation of Dr. Eleanor Tejirian, who has assisted me since my days at Teachers College, Columbia University. I would like to take this opportunity to thank her for her invaluable help on many occasions.

I also wish to thank Wataru Izumi, the manager of the International Publications Department, University of Tokyo Press, and Susan Schmidt, editor at the Press, for their support and editorial work.

Finally, I would like to quote from the words on the marble plaque at the entrance to the National Archives in Washington, D.C.: "What is past is prologue." It tells us of the importance of the study of history, in terms of the continuity of time, by saying that the past is tied into the present and the present will be tied into the future.

June 1992   GARY H. TSUCHIMOCHI

Education Reform in Postwar Japan

The 1946 U.S. Education Mission

INTRODUCTION

I. Subject

This book discusses postwar Japanese education reform, focusing on the First United States Education Mission to Japan. It describes the organization of the U.S. Education Mission to Japan and the drawing up of its Report, by using primary historical documents which have only recently been discovered.

The U.S. Education Mission made two visits to Japan, the first in March 1946 and the second in August 1950. The Reports that were produced on each of these occasions were submitted to the Supreme Commander for the Allied Powers, General Douglas MacArthur. The first Report, which was submitted on March 30, 1946, was entitled *Report of the United States Education Mission to Japan,* and the second was entitled *Report of the Second United States Education Mission to Japan.* Since the Mission in 1950 was officially named the Second United States Education Mission to Japan, the Mission of 1946 has become known as the First United States Education Mission to Japan, for convenience.[1]

These missions were not actually separate organizations or groups as such; each was part of the "United States Education Mission to Japan."[2] All five members of the Second Mission had been among the 27 members of the First Mission, and the aim of the Second Mission was mainly "to study the results and progress of recommendations" made by the First Mission. George D. Stoddard, who had been chairman of the First Mission, was also, up until the last moment, supposed to have chaired the Second Mission. A letter to Gen. MacArthur from Williard E. Givens, who subsequently became chairman of the Second Mission, mentions that the Report of the Second Mission was drawn up and submitted to "supplement" the *Report of the First U.S. Education Mission to Japan*. In other words, the aim of the Second Mission was to examine the results of, and also supplement, the recommendations made by the First Mission.

As a matter of fact, Givens made a distinction between the two Missions, stating: "1946—Members of the First United States Education Mission to Japan, which surveyed the Japanese program of education and recommended to General Douglas MacArthur how the schools and colleges of Japan could be most effectively used to help democratize that country," and "1950—Chairman of the Second United States Education Mission to Japan, which reported to General Douglas MacArthur an evaluation of the Japanese education program."[3]

A further distinction between them is political. The former was organized by the State Department, and the latter planned by the War Department and General Headquarters, Supreme Commander for the Allied Powers, Civil Information and Education Section (GHQ/SCAP/CI&E), Education Division.[4] One of the statements supposed to have been made by the Second Mission was: "One of the greatest weapons against Communism in the Far East is an enlightened electorate in Japan."[5] In reality, this statement was not made by the Mission at all, but was prepared by the CI&E, in advance of the Mission's visit. Thus, the Report of the Second Mission carries political implications, as it indicates the rapid change of the Japanese political situation under the American Occupation.[6]

This study focuses on the First U.S. Education Mission to Japan of 1946, because its Report is a historical document which greatly influenced the planning and implementation of education reform, thus shaping the history of present-day Japanese education. The Report only took the form of a statement of recommendations. However, on April 7, 1946, GHQ released the Report, with Gen. MacArthur's "Statement" approving it as its education reform policy for Japan. It became a practical guideline for the implementation of postwar education reform and was regarded as "gospel" by the CI&E in carrying out education reforms under the Occupation.[7] In other words, "postwar Japanese education reform was carried out along with the plan designed in the Report of the U.S. Education Mission."[8]

Today, with regard to the Report, opinions in Japan are divided into two main groups. One accepts and supports the Report as the source of postwar education, and believes that Japanese initiatives assisted in the reforms. The other believes that the postwar education reform was "forced" on Japan by the U.S. side, and demands its revision. The latter's attitude is highly political in its assertion that the Report was a "recommendation" forced on Japan by the U.S., as a result of the Japanese surrender and the Occupation by the Allied Powers. Eventually, this opinion developed into criticism of the new education system and its teaching methods and contents, which had been based on the Report.[9]

Debate between these opposing groups is still continuing today. There are many who support the view of "forced reform" among those who were government officials of education at that time, and who were under the strict supervision of the Occupation Forces. For instance, they make the point that it would have been impossible for 27 American educators who had almost no knowledge of Japanese education to draw up a Report recommending a radical reform of postwar Japanese education in such a short time, only twenty days or so. Accordingly, they point out, the Report must have been "prepared" by the CI&E in advance.

One of the supporters of this view states it thus:

> The statement of recommendations was not produced by the Mission. Of course, for the sake of form, the Mission took about half a month to complete the Report. However, the CI&E never let them have contact with the Japanese side, in order to complete it. It was officers of the CI&E or the Occupation Forces that discussed the making of the policies. This means, that prior to the invitation of the Mission, or its arrival, they had already made arrangements as to how to draw up the Report. In order to force these arrangements on the Japanese side, they brought a Mission composed of first class American educators. Then, following these arrangements, the Mission democratically made what they called "recommendations" for Japanese education policy.[10]

Another sharply criticizes the recommendations of the 6−3−3 school system as being subtly "forced" by the U.S. side, and says:

> The Mission's visit was, I think, a clever ploy, of the American Occupation policy. They organized a plan, by which education matters were dealt with by a Mission of educators, and not by military officers, and arranged for the Japanese Education Committee to cooperate with them in order to produce a Report, that would be voluntarily accepted by the Japanese side.
>
> If I may say so, the recommendation of the 6−3 system had already been decided before the Mission's arrival. The Mission's task was only to camouflage that advanced decision. If it had been made too obvious that they had forced the Japanese side to accept the 6−3−3−4 system, it would have reflected badly on American democracy. Therefore, they needed to arrange that a Mission, consisting of a group of scholars, came for discussion with the Japanese side. Although this is my own understanding, I don't think I am wrong.[11]

Another view, often expressed, is that the Report was only an "endorsement" of the ideas of the Occupation Forces.[12]

One of Japan's later prime ministers, Kakuei Tanaka, stated: "Postwar education reform, particularly the 6–3–3–4 system, was forced on us by America; it was so experimental that it was implemented by only one state [in the U.S.]."[13]

It is assumed that criticism of the Report originated from an intention to maintain the politically conservative status quo. But it also came from Japan's own colonial policy of the past, as reflected in the statement that "after the war, the Japanese tended to come to the hasty conclusion that the American Occupation Forces forced reforms on them, just as the Japanese themselves had forced their own systems and ways of thinking on their colonies."[14]

Another cause for criticism was the lack of attention paid in the Report to the work done by the Japanese Education Committee, and its active cooperation with the Mission. One reason for this was that the role actually played by the Japanese Education Committee has been underestimated until now, due to the restrictions on historical materials. It was also due to the fact that, in spite of its participation, and for fear of "reactionary" criticism, the Japanese Education Committee itself assumed a "negative" attitude, claiming that recommendations were made only by the U.S. side. Consequently, studies of postwar education reform tended to describe the system developed by the Committee as having been "forced" by the U.S., or having been a product of the Occupation.

At the same time, there is no doubt that some education researchers held the opposite point of view, from the beginning—that the postwar education reform was based on Japanese initiative. However, their difficulty lay in proving their arguments, due to the abovementioned restricted access to historical documents. Nevertheless, Tokiomi Kaigo, in his book *Nihon no Kyoiku no Shinten* [The Development of Japanese Education], describes the continuity of a prewar movement advocating education reform in Japan, such as the reform proposals of the Kyoiku Kaikaku Doshikai.[15] In *Nihon Kindai Kyoikushi* [The History of Modern Japanese Education], Shuichi Katsuta points out: "All the primary factors, even of what was called 'New Education' after the war, were already in existence before the war."[16]

Needless to say, the Occupation policy for Japan entailed not only education reform but also drastic political and social reforms, which varied considerably according to the field in which they were implemented. Some Japanese prewar structures were continued on agreement between the Occupation and the Japanese side, and others were discontinued under the directives of the Occupation. In the field of education, some prewar structures were continued and others discontinued.

The author has always held the firm opinion that the postwar education reform was based on Japanese initiative in accordance with the Potsdam Declaration, which specifies "the revival and strengthening of democratic tendencies among the Japanese people."[17] The purpose of this study is to discuss the significance of Japanese independent reform under the Occupation, in order to clarify the origin of postwar education reform. For this purpose it illustrates the process of organizing the Mission and also the drawing up of the Report. In addition, the author defines the Japanese initiative through observing the role of the Japanese Education Committee. The task of this study, then, is to verify, using primary sources, that the postwar education reform originated in the dynamic correlation between prewar and postwar movements in education, within the context of the history of Japanese education.

At the same time, this study refers to the case of the U.S. Education Mission to Germany, where education reforms under the U.S. Occupation were also carried out. The U.S. Education Mission to Germany (USEMG) was dispatched in August 1946, and it made recommendations on German postwar education reform. Sending these Missions to Japan and Germany was part of the U.S. Occupation policy, and the organization and selection of personnel for the two Missions by the State Department were interrelated. It is therefore important, in studying the Japanese case, to compare it with the German. In other words, for a comprehensive study of the Mission to Japan, it is necessary to reexamine the German case as part of U.S. Occupation policy.

II. *The Method*

1) HISTORICAL MATERIALS

This study is based on Occupation documents relating to education which are held in archives in the U.S.: the Records of the State Department, the Records of the War Department (CAD), the Records of SWNCC, the Records of the Far Eastern Committee, the Records of SCAP, and Executive Branch records.

As basic historical materials, the personal papers of 18 members of the Mission were consulted: George D. Stoddard, Gordon T. Bowles, Virginia C. Gildersleeve, Willard E. Givens, Thomas V. Smith, Pearl A. Wanamaker, Charles S. Johnson, E. B. Norton, Emily Woodward, Mildred McAfee Horton, David H. Stevens, William C. Trow, George W. Diemer, Harold Benjamin, Roy J. Deferrari, Kermit Eby, Frederick G. Hochwalt, and Charles H. McCloy.

Most of the above materials were collected as part of the "Research Study of Existing Documents in the U.S. on Japanese Education During the Occupation Period," under Grants-in-Aid for International Scientific Research from 1985-1987, sponsored by the Ministry of Education. Most of these documents and papers are primary sources which were restricted until recently.

In addition to these documents, materials were included originating from interviews with members of the Mission to Japan, such as the late G. T. Bowles, Ernest R. Hilgard, the late P. A. Wanamaker, M. M. Horton, and E. B. Norton; with sons of the late G. D. Stoddard (Philip H. Stoddard), W. C. Trow (Donald B. Trow), and W. E. Givens (Stuart R. Givens); and with Mrs. William C. Trow. These interviews were important to the development of this study.

Furthermore, the author makes use of personal papers and interviews with the people in charge of the Education Division of the CI&E at the time of the planning for the Mission to Japan, in order to investigate details of the organization of the Mission. These materials include the papers of Joseph C. Trainor, Herbert J. Wunderlich, Mark T. Orr, Eileen R. Donovan, and Robert K. Hall, and interviews with M. T. Orr, H. J. Wunderlich, E. R. Donovan, and James I. Doi.

In order to define the significance and characteristics of the Mission to Japan, it seemed important to compare the Japanese case with the details of the U.S. Education Mission to Germany. For this purpose, efforts were made to locate the personal papers of members of the Mission to Germany, such as T. V. Smith, Earl McGrath, and Helen White. The study also refers to, and quotes extensively from, exclusive interviews with people concerned with German education at that time: John W. Taylor, Chief of Education and Religious Affairs Branch in the Office of the Military Government for Germany; Herman B Wells, educational and cultural adviser to General Lucius Clay, Military Governor of the Office of the Military Government for Germany; and William G. Carr, Secretary of the National Education Association.[18]

Historical documents on the Japanese side are relatively few. The Sanji Aruga Papers and the Chikara Tsujita Papers are referred to as main sources, along with the records of the Japanese Education Committee and the Ministry of Education.

Words omitted or misspelled, and the lack of punctuation in some documents, have been left as in the originals.

2) THE MAIN AIM OF THIS STUDY

In order to bring objectivity to this study, which relies substantially on historical documents, the author has referred to as broad a spectrum of material as possible, including interviews with people involved at the time. Throughout, he has used the following methods and objectives:

a) To demonstrate how the First U.S. Education Mission to Japan was organized and how it drew up its Report.

b) To show how U.S. Occupation policy toward Japanese education was based on provisions in accordance with the Potsdam Declaration, which specified "the revival and strengthening of democratic tendencies among the Japanese people." This was the Mission's basic policy, as well. In other words, Occupation officials had the greatest regard for the inclinations and initiatives of the Japanese side, from the beginning.

The task is to testify to this fact with evidence drawn from historical documents from the U.S. side. At the same time, material is used from representatives of the Japanese side, who themselves conformed to the Potsdam Declaration—especially Article 12, which specified: "The occupying forces of the Allies shall be withdrawn from Japan as soon as these objectives have been accomplished and there has been established in accordance with the freely expressed will of the Japanese people a peacefully inclined and responsible government"—and strove to create their own independent reforms. This is to say, the aims of both sides were in agreement within the limits set by the Potsdam Declaration.

c) In accordance with the sentiments expressed in the Potsdam Declaration, the Mission left the initiative with the Japanese side. Hence, the Japanese Education Committee was able to express its opinion on education reforms, and as a result played an extremely important role. The drafting of the Mission's Report, especially the parts pertaining to the reforms of the Japanese language, the school system, and higher education, testifies to this fact.

d) Postwar Japanese education reform was based on a dynamic correlation between the continuity in the ideological and methodological areas and the discontinuity of the structure of prewar Japanese education. This is demonstrated by referring to the 6–3–3 school system which originated in prewar Japan; the "conversion" of the system under the Imperial Rescript on Education to that under the Fundamental Law of Education; and the Social Studies curriculum, which was introduced after the war. Thus, the content, structure, and ideology of postwar education reform did not follow the same process.

e) In order to locate the Mission within the whole structure of the U.S. Occupation policy on education, the Japanese case is compared with the German.

3) THE LIMITATIONS OF THIS STUDY
The limits to this study should be acknowledged, which at the same time point in the direction of future research.

a) This study is restricted to the First U.S. Education Mission to Japan.

Japanese education reform under the Occupation was implemented during the period between 1945 and 1952, and education reforms introduced by the First Mission of 1946 were carried out in the early part of the Occupation. Estimations of the effects of the Occupation varied from period to period. For example, in the final period, criticism of the Mission emerged, and the Occupation policy was changed to a large degree. For this reason it is essential, for the study of education reform under the Occupation, to study it comprehensively, including the Second U.S. Education Mission to Japan in 1950.

b) Due to the restrictions on historical documents, this study depends on U.S. archives and the personal papers of the Mission members. As an inevitable result, it has a bias toward the U.S. side. For future studies, it will be necessary to reexamine and analyze postwar Japanese education reform as a whole, by referring to historical material from the Japanese side.

It should be noted, however, that postwar Japanese education reform was carried out, strictly speaking, by the Allied Powers, especially the U.S. It therefore goes without saying how important it is to define the Mission's evaluation of Japanese education.

c) The main object of this study is to analyze the organization of the Mission and the drafting of its Report, on the basis of historical materials. Hence, it does not analyze the substance of the Report.

d) In consideration of the fact that Japan was occupied not only by the U.S., but by the Allied Powers, comprehensive studies including the education policies of the other Allied Powers are essential.

e) In order to locate education programs within the structure of U.S. Occupation policy as a whole, this study also embraces a comparative study with the German case. However, a more comprehensive study should be attempted in the future. For example, Germany was divided and governed by the Allied Powers, while Japan was controlled by the U.S. alone, indirectly, through the Japanese Government. For this reason, it is necessary to define the differences between the education policies of the Allied Powers and also to study pre- and postwar German education.

f) This study recognizes the Report of the First Mission as an important, influential document for drawing up, as well as implementing, education reform in the modern and present history of Japanese education. An important future study will be to locate the Report within the history of U.S. education.

4) PREVIOUS STUDIES

Previous studies of the First Mission can be classified into two main types. The first type values the Report highly, while the other's attitude is critical, based on a negative judgment of the Report made at the end of the Occupation.

An example of the first type is a book published in 1950, during the late period of the Occupation, *Amerika Kyoiku Shisetsudan Hokokusho Yokai* [Study by Japanese Educators of the Report of the U.S. Education Mission to Japan], edited by Hiroshi Sugo, Seiichi Miyahara, and Seiya Munakata (Tokyo: Kokumin Tosho Kankokai, 1950). A significant point of this analysis of the Report is that it gave direction to Japanese postwar education as well as influencing educational studies. The editors' foreword states:

> We think that the historical Report of the U.S. Education Mission is one of the most valuable documents on education ever written, and it should be considered the highest form of this kind of document in the world. This is a model of the excellent achievement of democratic ideas in education which were developed by the middle of the twentieth century. We can see particularly how the best of the orthodox tradition of American democracy is given expression in an ideal form. We would like to express our extreme happiness for their effort in producing such a valuable document for Japanese education.

In contrast, during the 1950s, when education policies were aimed at the revision of postwar education reform, critical studies of the Report became noticeable. In 1953, for example, Tokumitsu Yagawa sharply criticized the Report, stating that it was "only lubricating oil" to facilitate democratization by American imperialism.[19] This view is still strongly held in Japan, as a result of the reconsideration of postwar education reform within education policies.

Studies of the history of Japanese education in postwar Japan began with "Senryoka no Kyoiku" (Education Under the Occupation) by Seiya Munakata, Akira Igarashi, and Eiichi Mochida, in *Nihon Shihonshugi Koza* [Lectures on Japanese Capitalism], Vol. 2 (Tokyo: Iwanami Shoten, 1953). Full-scale studies of postwar education reform followed. Despite the restriction on historical materials, the 10-volume *Sengo Nihon no Kyoiku Kaikaku* [Postwar Japanese Education Reform], edited by Tokiomi Kaigo (Tokyo: University of Tokyo Press), which was published between 1969 and 1976, was a remarkable ongoing collaborative series between the Faculties of Education at Stanford and Tokyo Universities, led by Paul R. Hanna and Tokiomi Kaigo, respectively. Volume 1, *Kyoiku Kaikaku* [Education Reform], written by Kaigo himself on the basis of his research in the U.S. and published in 1975, is important as the first corroborated study concerning the circumstances surrounding the organizing of the Report of the Mission.[20]

Volume 2, *Kyoiku Rinen* [Educational Ideology], by Masami Yamazumi and Teruhisa Horio (1976), takes a serious view of the Japanese initiative in education reform, which the Japanese set into motion at the time of the surrender. The authors make the point that postwar education reform was neither forced by the Occupation, as the conventional view asserted, nor carried out on the basis of the Report alone. Their study is important for its emphasis on a dynamic correlation between the continuity and discontinuity of prewar Japanese education. In chapter four, "Beikoku Kyoiku Shisetsudan Hokokusho to Nihon Gawa no Taio" [The Report of the U.S. Education Mission and the Response of the Japanese Side], they discuss the problems that the Mission experienced. They also describe the Mission's expectation of an active attitude on the part of the Japanese toward their own independent reforms, and its efforts to obtain democratic freedom, quoting from the Foreword of the Report: "We can do this without presumption, for if we did not have faith in the democratic potential of the Japanese and did not trust their capacity to reestablish a sound culture, we should not be here."[21]

Masao Terasaki describes the background to the educational ideas expressed in the Report as follows:

> It is based on the idea of "New Education" which was established by John Dewey at the beginning of this century and became the mainstream of modern American education. And it is also backed by the educational ideas of American democracy, which were supported and developed through a sense of crisis in American society after the Great Depression. The two aspects of educational philosophy in the Report, which are the child-centered ideas of Pragmatism and Realism in the New Deal, can be understood as the direct reflection of American educational ideas at the time of World War II.

It is worth noting that the First U.S. Education Mission has been given a place within the history of American education. Terasaki also makes the point that "the Report was backed with the confidence of American educators for its twentieth-century educational ideas and system rather than through the power of a victor." In his comparative study of the Japanese and German cases, Terasaki states that "there is a great resemblance between both Missions in terms of their structures." At the same time, he points out, "the Mission to Germany showed a high appraisal of German learning and culture, which differed from the Japanese case."

He emphasizes the efforts of the Japanese: "It was the only way for the Japanese to properly understand and develop the modern Western educational values which were embodied in the Report [for Japan]."[22]

Taking a general view of the trends in the studies of postwar education reform, we see that it was only in the 1970s that studies were made in depth in the U.S., due to the access given to the general public to the U.S. archives relating to the Occupation of Japan. On the other hand, it was only in the 1980s that studies in the educational field commenced in Japan, much later than studies in politics, economics, and labor. What facilitated the study of Japanese education reform under the Occupation were projects to collect U.S. historical sources inaugurated by the National Diet Library, the National Institute for Educational Research of Japan, and the Research Center of History of Education under the Occupation, Meisei University.

The first full-scale study of the Report of the Mission based on U.S. sources was "Beikoku Tainichi Kyoiku Shisetsudan Hokokusho no Seiritsu Jijo ni Kansuru Sogoteki Kenkyu" [A Comprehensive Study of the Report of the U.S. Education Mission to Japan, with Particular Reference to the Preparation] by Eiichi Suzuki, Hideo Sato, Gary H. Tsuchimochi, and others. This study illustrates the process of drawing up the Report, and is based on primary sources discovered only recently.

As an individual study, Hideo Sato gives the entire picture of the plan, structure, and activities of the Mission, analyzing the details of the G.D. Stoddard Papers in the Hoover Institution Archives, Stanford University. On September 16, 1983, Sato gave a lecture on this study entitled "A Study Concerning the United States Education Mission to Japan, USEMJ," at the National Institute for Educational Research of Japan.

Eiichi Suzuki has also focused on study of the Mission, and has produced important works that take into account his research in sources: "Senryo Bunsho kara Mita Sengo Kyoiku Kaikaku" [Postwar Education Reform Based on Occupation Documents), *Kyoiku* (April, May, June, and September, 1981); "Gakusei Kaikaku no Seiritsu Jijo" [Circumstances of the Organization of the School System], *Bulletin of the Faculty of Education, Department of Education, Nagoya University*, No. 29 (1982); *Nihon Senryo to Kyoiku Kaikaku* [The Occupation of Japan and Education Reform] (Tokyo: Keiso Shobo, 1983); "Kenpo: Kyoiku Kihonho to Sengo Kaikaku" [The Constitution: The Fundamental Law of Education and Postwar Reform], *Kikan Kyoikuho*, 50 (1984); and "Rengokoku no Tainichi Senryo Kyoiku Seisaku" [The Allied Powers' Occupation Policy Toward Japanese Education], *Koza Nihon Kyoiku Shi* [Lectures on the History of Japanese Education], vol. 4. (Tokyo: Daiichi Hoki, 1984).

In addition to the above, *Kyoiku no Ayumi* [The Course of Education], edited by the Postwar History Group, Yomiuri Shinbun (Tokyo: Yomiuri Shinbunsha, 1982), broke new ground for the study of the Mission, as well as postwar education reform, in discovering important historical sources, such as the Gordon T. Bowles Papers, the Sanji Aruga Papers, and the memoirs and diary of Jiro Arimitsu, and including interviews with G.T. Bowles.

In addition, the following previous studies were helpful in this study: Yoshizo Kubo, *Tainichi Senryo Seisaku to Sengo Kyoiku Kaikaku* [Occupation Policy Toward Japan and Education Reform] (Tokyo: Sanseido, 1984); Yotaro Mohri, "Tainichi Kyoiku Shisetsudan no Riron: 'Stoddard G. D.' no Ronri Kozo" [The Philosophy of the Members of the Education Mission to Japan: The Thoughts of G. D. Stoddard], parts 1 and 2, *Bulletin of the Faculty of Education, Yamanashi University*, 29–30 (1978–79); Hiroshi Takuma, "Education in Japan no Kenkyu: Beikoku Kyoiku Shisetsudan Hokokusho to no Kanren" [A Study of Education in Japan in Relation to the Report of the U.S. Education Mission], part 1, *Bulletin of the Faculty of the High School Affiliated with the Department of Education of Kyoto University of Education*, No. 23 (1978); and Toshio Nishi, *Unconditional Democracy: Education and Politics in Occupied Japan, 1945–1952* (Stanford: Hoover Institution Press, 1982).

Nishi in particular makes free use of recently released Occupation documents. However, his viewpoint differs basically from the present author's when he asserts that "the most remarkable achievement of the Mission as a group of scholars was to confirm the political reform which SCAP had been carrying out."

Until now, studies have concentrated on historical facts, based on archival material from the U.S. side, such as the Joseph C. Trainor Papers. They are recognized for verifying the organizational process of the First U.S. Education Mission. However, these studies are limited, owing to the fact that they had to depend entirely on GHQ documents because of the restrictions on historical documents. In reality, matters concerning the drawing up of the Report of the Mission were discussed outside the CI&E Section. Therefore, details are not recorded in the GHQ documents. For this reason it became essential, in studying the First U.S. Education Mission, to collect and examine Mission members' personal papers, which had not been sufficiently researched in previous studies.

It is the author's intention to use this new historical material to focus further studies on the First U.S. Education Mission.

For the last few years I have been concentrating on studies relating to the First U.S. Education Mission to Japan, and he has used the following works of his own as the foundation for the present study:

1. "Daiichiji Beikoku Kyoiku Shisetsudan no Seiritsu Keii ni Tsuite: Senryoki ni Okeru Amerika no Tainichi Kyoiku Seisaku no Kenkyu (Sono 1)" [Circumstances of the Formation of the First U.S. Education Mission: A Study of U.S. Educational Policy Toward Japan in the Occupation Period

(Part I)], *Transactions of the Academic Society of the Humanities* (Kokushi-kan University) 16 (1984)

2. "Daiichiji Beikoku Kyoiku Shisetsudan Hokokusho no Sakusei Keii ni Tsuite: Senryoki ni Okeru Amerika no Tainichi Kyoiku Seisaku no Kenkyu (Sono 2)" [Circumstances of the Drawing Up of the Report of the First U.S. Education Mission to Japan: A Study of U.S. Educational Policy Toward Japan in the Occupation Period (Part 2)], *Bulletin of Japan Comparative Education Society*, No. 10 (1984).

3. "6–3–3 Sei to Amerika Kyoiku Shisetsudan Hokokusho" [The 6–3–3 System and the Report of the U.S. Education Mission], *Kyoiku* 445 (November 1984).

4. "Beikoku Tainichi Kyoiku Shisetsudan Hokokusho no Seiritsu Jijo ni Kansuru Sogoteki Kenkyu" [A Comprehensive Study of the Report of the U.S. Education Mission to Japan, with Particular Reference to the Preparation] (collaboration), *Bulletin of the Faculty of Education: Department of Education, Nagoya University* 31 (1985).

5. "Beikoku Taidoku Kyoiku Shisetsudan no Seiritsu Keii: Daiichi Beikoku Tainichi Kyoiku Shisetsudan to no Hikaku Kosatsu" [Circumstances of the Formation of the U.S. Education Mission to Germany: A Comparative Study with the First U.S. Education Mission to Japan], *Kyoikugaku Kenkyu* [Japanese Journal of Educational Research], 52, No. 2 (1985).

6. "Daiichiji Beikoku Kyoiku Shisetsudan Hokokusho no Sakusei Keii ni Kansuru Kosatsu: Nihon Gawa Kyoikuka Iinkai no Yakuwari" [The Preparation of the Report of the U.S. Education Mission to Japan: The Role of the Japanese Education Committee], *Journal of the Society for Educational History*, No. 28 (1985).

7. "Taidoku Amerika Kyoiku Shisetsudan Hokokusho" [The Report of the U.S. Education Mission to Germany] (joint translation), *Research Bulletin of Educational History of the Allied Occupation of Japan* (Educational History of the Occupation, Research Center, Meisei University) 4 (1987).

8. "Amerika Taidoku Shakaika Iinkai Hokokusho no Sakusei Keii ni Kansuru Ichi Kosatsu: Amerika Taidoku Kyoiku Shisetsudan to no Kanren Kara" [A Study of the Process of Drafting the Report of the U.S. Social Studies Committee to Germany: With Particular Reference to the U.S. Education Mission to Germany], *Journal of Social Studies*, No. 58 (1987).

9. "Amerika no Tainichi oyobi Taidoku Kyoiku Shisetsudan no Hikaku Kosatsu" [A Comparative Study of the U.S. Education Missions to Japan and Germany] (translation), *Research Report of the National Institute for Educational Research of Japan*, No. 16 (1988).

10. *Senryoka Doitsu no Kyoiku Kaikaku: Amerika Taidoku Kyoiku Shisetsudan to Amerika Taidoku Shakaika Iinkai* [Educational Reforms Under the

American Occupation in Germany: The U.S. Education Mission to Germany and the U.S. Social Studies Committee to Germany] (Tokyo: Meisei University Press, 1989).

11. "Senryoka no Kyoiku Kaikaku: Daiichiji Beikoku Tainichi Kyoiku Shisetsudan Hokokusho to Koto Kyoiku Kaikaku" [Education Reform: The Report of the First U.S. Education Mission to Japan and the Reform of Higher Education], *Daigaku Ronshu* [Research in Higher Education] (Research Institute for Higher Education, Hiroshima University), No. 18 (1989).

12. "Senryoka no Kyoiku Kaikaku: Daiichiji Beikoku Tainichi Kyoiku Shisetsudan Hokokusho to Kokugo Kaikaku" [Educational Reform: The Report of the First U.S. Education Mission to Japan and the Reform of the Japanese Language], in *Taga Shugoro Hakushi Kiju Kinen Ronbunshu, Ajia no Kyoiku to Bunka* [Education and Culture in Asia] (Tokyo: Gennando Shuppan, 1989)

13. "Senryoka Doitsu no Kyoiku Kaikaku: Amerika Taidoku Kyoiku Shisetsudan Hokokusho to Koto Kyoiku Kaikaku" [Education Reform Under the American Occupation in Germany: The Report of the U.S. Education Mission to Germany and Reform of Higher Education], *Daigaku Ronshu* [Research in Higher Education] (Research Institute for Higher Education, Hiroshima University), No. 19 (1990).

14. *Taidoku Amerika Kyoiku Shisetsudan Hokokusho* [The Report of the U.S. Education Mission to Germany] (joint translation) (Tokyo: Meisei University Press, 1990)

15. "Beikoku Gakujutsu Komondan Hokokusho to Sengo Nihon no Koto Kyoiku Kaikaku: Adams Bunsho o Chushin Ni" [The Report of the U.S. Scientific Advisory Group and Postwar Japanese Higher Education Reform: With Particular Reference to the Adams Papers), *Daigaku Ronshu* [Research in Higher Education] (Research Institute for Higher Education, Hiroshima University), No. 20 (1991).

1
THE ORGANIZATION OF THE MISSION

The Foreword to the *Report of the U.S. Education Mission to Japan* describes its organizing process as follows:

> Early in January of this year the Supreme Commander for the Allied Powers requested the War Department to send to Japan, for a period of approximately one month, a group of twenty or more American educators to advise and consult with General Headquarters and with Japanese educators on problems relating to education in Japan.
>
> In view of discussions then in progress in Washington relating to the responsibility for long range planning in the education and reorientation of Japan, the War Department requested the Department of State to undertake the final selection of the personnel of the group. After consideration of a wider range of factors in addition to individual qualifications, and with full regard to the preferences expressed by General Headquarters, a group of twenty-seven persons was selected, and Dr. George D. Stoddard was appointed chairman.
>
> Before starting for Japan the majority of the Committee met in Washington for preliminary conferences. Here they were given a large amount of valuable background information about Japan, both past and present, by members of the State Department and by others with special knowledge. Similar conferences were held by other members of the Committee. On the trip out, helpful consultation was held with a number of well informed persons at Honolulu. Also the group was able, during its stay at Guam, and through other interim conferences, to make a preliminary analysis of the task that confronted it.
>
> The group arrived in Tokyo in two sections by plane on March 5 and 6 and constituted itself as the United States Education Mission to Japan. The Mission has remained in Japan through the month.[1]

Although in this statement we can see the outline of the organizational process for sending the Mission, the details of this process have not been studied corroboratively until now, due to the restrictions involving historical documents.

1. *The Plan of the Civil Information and Education Section, General Headquarters, Supreme Commander for the Allied Powers*

1) THE PLANNING STAGE

Discussions concerning the Mission were instigated by the CI&E, which directed Japanese education reform under the Occupation. The CI&E was originally set up at the General Headquarters, U.S. Army Forces, Pacific (GHQ/USAFPAC), Special Staff Section, on General Order No. 183, September 22, 1945. When the General Headquartes, Supreme Commander for the Allied Powers (GHQ/SCAP), was set up on General Order No. 4, October 2, 1945, the CI&E was incorporated within its Special Staff Section.[2]

According to the Trainor Papers, the plan for the Mission was first discussed within the CI&E on October 18, 1945, only one month after the CI&E was established. On that same day, Major Edward H. Farr, Assistant Chief of the Education Division of the CI&E, ordered Lieutenant Robert K. Hall to commence a staff study of the invitation to the Mission to be sent from the United States. On the following day, October 19, R. K. Hall, surprisingly, submitted the first draft of a list of candidates for the Mission to Colonel Kenneth R. Dyke, Chief of the CI&E, through E. H. Farr and Major Harold C. Henderson, Chief of the Education Division.

In this staff study R. K. Hall stated that the role of the Mission was "to assist and advise the Civil Information and Education Section, Supreme Commander [of] the Allied Powers." He then listed the following eighteen candidates as its members:

1. Dr. David Stevens, Director of Division of Humanities of Rockefeller Foundation
2. Dr. Henry Allen Moe, Director of the John Simon Guggenheim Memorial Foundation
3. Dr. Howard Mumford Jones, Former Dean of Graduate School, Harvard University
4. Dr. William Clark Trow, Outstanding Expert on Education Psychology, School of Education, University of Michigan
5. Dean Frank Freeman, Dean of School of Education, University of California, Berkeley
6. Dr. Frank Aydelette, Director of the Institute for Advanced Study at Princeton
7. Dean J. B. Edmonson, Dean of the School of Education, University of Michigan

8. Dr. Edward Thorndyke, Dean of Teachers College, Columbia University, American Educational Psychologist
9. Dr. John Dewey, Dean of Teachers College, Columbia University, American Educator
10. Dean Ralph Tyler, Dean of the School of Education, University of Chicago
11. President Robert Hutchins, University of Chicago, Leading Educational Administrator and Exponent of Classical Education
12. President James Bryant Conant, Harvard University, Leading Educational Leader of America
13. Dr. Guy Stanton Ford, Chancellor of University of Minnesota
14. Senator Elbert Thomas, Expert on International Relations with Special Study of Japan and Constitutional Law
15. President Frank Graham, the University of North Carolina
16. Dr. John Studebaker, Chief of the U.S. Office of Education, Office of Education, Department of the Interior
17. Dr. Gordon Bowles, Director of Far Eastern Section of Cultural Relations Division, State Department
18. Col. Francis Trow Spaulding, AUS, Former Chief, Special Service Division, War Department[3]

As can be seen above, he nominated university presidents, such as James B. Conant of Harvard University and Robert Hutchins of the University of Chicago; well-known educators, such as John Dewey and Edward Thorndyke, who were deans of Teachers College, Columbia University; and John Studebaker and Gordon Bowles, who were government officials and who were later to take part in organizing the Mission members.

There is no doubt that soon after the CI&E was set up it started to actively discuss the plan for inviting the Mission, even though it seems impossible for the study to have been completed within one day.

As a matter of fact, historical documents obtained recently reveal that before the first draft was produced, the CI&E had unofficially suggested its plan for the Mission from the United States to the Japanese Ministry of Education and had requested the Ministry to submit a list of the American educators it would prefer as Mission members. In reply to this request, the Ministry of Education secretly submitted a list to the CI&E on October 8, 1945.[4]

The *Asahi Shinbun* (Tokyo edition) published a four-part article entitled "A Round-table Discussion: American Democracy" from October 2 to October 5, 1945, which described details of the Mission. In the second installment, on October 3, a discussion between Tamon Maeda, Minister of Education, and Tsutomu Nishiyama, Deputy Director, Central Liaison Office, Tokyo, Maeda said: "The Americans mentioned their idea to us for inviting educators from the U.S. who can advise us, and they want to know our preferred candidates, if we have any. Dewey came to mind instantly. This really coincides with your view [referring to Nishiyama]. If he is not available, then someone recommended by him, and second, Charles Beard or someone recommended by him. But Dewey would be my first choice."[5]

This indicates that at an early stage the Education Division of the CI&E required the Japanese side to cooperate with it in inviting the Mission. This is also endorsed by historical documents of the Occupation, such as the CI&E's *Weekly Reports* dated October 8, 1945, which reported under the title "Educational Advisers":

> The Minister of Education has tentatively appointed his own group of advisers. He has also submitted a list of names of foreign advisers with whom his advisers would like to consult. The Educ Section [*sic*] (CIE) has completed preliminary plans for the procurement of a body of prominent educators from the U.S. and Allied countries who will be brought to Japan for varying periods. This body will (1) Act as advisers to the Ed Sect, CIE. (2) Be available for consultation with a similar body of Japanese educators who will act as advisers to the Ministry of Education.[6]

The "List of Foreign Advisers" suggested by the Ministry of Education consisted of the following eighteen people:

Mr. Perry Burgess, President of the Leonard Wood Memorial (American Leprosy Association)

Dr. Arthur Kennedy, Professor of Bacteriology of Rochester University

Dr. Payson Jackson Treat, Professor of History of Stanford University

Paul Monroe, President of the World Federation of Education Association (came to Japan in 1937)

Galen M. Fisher, Former General Secretary of the YMCA Union, Japan (now in California)

Edmund Blunden, University of Oxford (Lecturer), Former Lecturer of English Literature at Tokyo Imperial University 1924 to 1927

Ernest Harold Pickering, Ex-member of Parliament, Former Lecturer of English at Tokyo Imperial University (now at Karuizawa)

C. G. Fink, Professor of Elect[r]ochemistry of Columbia University

Charles E. Locke, Professor of Mining and Ore Dressing of Mass. Institute of Technology

Rear Admiral Emory Scottland, USN (Retired), Chairman U.S. Maritime Commission

Professor Moreland, Dean of Engineering School of Mass. Institute of Technology

E. L. Thorndike, Professor of Teachers' College, Columbia University

W. S. Monroe, Formerly Professor of Teachers' College, Columbia University

Professor Bovet, Director of Institute Jean Jacques Rousseau, Geneva, Switzerland

John Dewey, Or somebody recommended by him.

Charles Beard, Or somebody recommended by him.

Professor Scott, Professor of Yale University

K. T. Compton, President of MIT (now in Japan)

This list included Britons and Europeans as well as Americans. As a whole, the Americans were selected from the same universities, and natural scientists from medical and engineering departments rather than from departments of education-related areas; some also had visited Japan before the war. It seems probable that they were chosen by Minister of Education Maeda, with the support of professors from Tokyo Imperial University.

The *Asahi Shinbun* editorial of October 4, 1945, reported the following names as advisers to the Japanese Ministry of Education:

Advisers to Education Mission

SCAP decided to organize the education advisers' group around the concern with educational problems in the reconstruction of Japan. For this purpose, it required the Ministry of Education to recommend a group of people to support the education advisers' group. Complying with this request, the Ministry of Education recommended the following 12 people: Shozo Uchida, Shinzo Koizumi, Yoshishige Abe, Tsuraki Yano (President of Meiji Gakuin), Hideko Inoue (President of Nihon Women's University), Yonekichi Akai (Principal of Myojo Gakuen), Yosaburo Miyauchi (Principal of Bancho Kokumin Gakko), Masaharu Anesaki, Hideji Yagi, Hiroshi Nasu, Yasaka Takagi, and Setsuko Hani.

Later this group became the core of the Japanese Education Committee. As a matter of fact, the "Memorandum of Jiro Arimitsu" reveals that the Japanese side was informed, prior to all these official procedures, that a group of education specialists was coming from the U.S., and was required to organize the Japanese Education Committee as its counterpart. This memorandum, which was recently made available to the public, records that the matter was discussed on September 24, 1945.

September 24, 1945 (Tuesday)

1. Briefing of Undersecretary's meeting

2. Yesterday Major Henderson from the Information Dissemination Section (IDS) visited the Minister.

[1.] His visit was on behalf of Gen. Fallers. He reported that their policy on education reform was not to be enforced by directive orders. They have set up a Section of E and I (Education and Information), with a General Brigadier at its head, and *education specialists will be coming in the future*. In planning the organization of their advisory committee, they inquired whether we have any intention of organizing an advisory committee of our own to correspond to theirs. We replied that we had no immediate intention of doing so. [Therefore] he requested us to nominate some advisers. In response to this request, we nominated 12 people: Shozo Uchida, Shinzo Koizumi, Yoshishige Abe, Hideji Yagi, Shoji Anesaki, Tsuraki Yano, Yasaka Takagi, Hiroshi Nasu, Yosaburo Miyauchi, Yonekichi Akai, Hideko Inoue, and Setsuko Hani.

As a committee member for their side, the Minister recommended Mr. Biard [*sic*]. [Author's italics][7]

We see that only a few days after the CI&E was set up, on September 22, 1945, it commenced planning to invite the Mission, in cooperation with the Japanese side, with the Ministry of Education playing a central role. These preparatory proceedings made it possible for R. K. Hall to immediately produce a first draft list of eighteen candidates for the Mission. However, comparing his first draft with the "List of Foreign Advisers" drawn up by the Ministry of Education, we see that the Japanese requests were not reflected in the list made by the Education Division of the CI&E. Only John Dewey and Edward Thorndike of Columbia University appeared in both lists; all candidates from other Allied countries were excluded. The CI&E seems to have cooperated with the Japanese side in a way, but had already selected its own candidates. The reason for the exclusion of candidates from other Allied countries reflected Gen. MacArthur's intention.

In the early stages of candidate selection the CI&E obtained individual cooperation from Japanese scholars, such as Tokiomi Kaigo (pedagogy), Shoji Ando (Japanese language), and Hideo Kishimoto (religion). Kishimoto in particular, who had studied in the U.S. before the war, had a great influence on the CI&E's selection. Herbert J. Wunderlich, a former staff member of the Education Division of the CI&E, testified to Kishimoto's influence in an interview:

In the process of selection of candidates, I think we got advice from Professor Kishimoto, who studied at Harvard University before the war. In this connection, he recommended J. B. Conant, President of Harvard University, whose prestige could have been compared with that of the officials in the the Ministry of Education, if he had been able to come.[8]

As in this case, some candidates were chosen through personal connections. For example, Professor Trow of the University of Michigan had been R. K. Hall's academic adviser, and Frank Graham, President of the University of North Carolina, was recommended by Major M. T. Orr, who was a graduate of that university.[9]

We cannot, however, find any specific reason in the Trainor Papers for the CI&E's immediate enthusiasm for the Mission. Accordingly, we need to review the U. S. Government's formulation of policies on Japanese education under the Occupation. As a matter of fact, a plan to send education specialists to defeated countries as one of the American Occupation's policies on education had been discussed before the end of the war. The Postwar Program Committee (PWC) drew up an education reform plan titled "Japanese: The Education System Under Military Government" (PWC 287a) on November 6, 1944. It began:

> Careful study of the problem leads to the conclusion that there will not be available to military government that *large number of competent and qualified American and other foreign personnel* which would be required to carry out such fundamental reforms of the Japanese educational system as might seem desirable and to operate it after such reforms have been inaugurated. [Author's italics][10]

Thus, at this point, the government was pessimistic concerning the availability of enough established and qualified Americans to carry out Japanese education reform.

On December 1, 1944, the State-War-Navy Coordinating Committee (SWNCC) was set up, through which the government undertook to draw up postwar policies toward Germany, Japan, and Korea. SWNCC issued "Positive Policy for Reorientation of the Japanese" (SWNCC 162) on July 19, 1945.[11]

Less than a month later, Japan accepted the Potsdam Declaration, and the war was over. Such a sudden change in the situation upset the government's schedule for preparing policies toward Japan. Consequently, the State Department had to implement an immediate review of policy making.

To examine "Positive Policy for Reorientation of the Japanese," and also the need to send advisory groups or consultants Japan, an ad hoc committee was set up within the Subcommittee for the Far East (SFE; E. H. Dooman, chairman) on August 18, 1945. This committee consisted of six members, including Hugh Borton and Gordon T. Bowles from the State Department, with Borton later appointed as chairman.[12]

This committee revised SWNCC 162, producing a more positive document. The revised draft, dated September 3, 1945, stated: "It is possible that selected civilian groups and organizations within the United States will be able to afford assistance in the reorientation process." At this stage, there was no concrete suggestion of forming an education mission to Japan. The draft only suggested encouraging the supportive activities of American civilian organizations (for example, educational charity programs organized by religious or nonreligious groups), which should be assisted by SCAP. It indicated to Gen. MacArthur, however, the necessity for setting up a section made up of experts on Japan and separate from the military government.[13] This idea was one of the positive policies concerned with the reorientation of the Japanese, as stated in the article "Ultimate Objectives" in "The U.S. Initial Post-Surrender Policy for Japan" (SWNCC 150/3), which expressed the intention "to insure that Japan will not again become a menace to the United States or to the peace and security of the world."

In fact, on September 2, 1945, Gen. MacArthur organized a Section of Information and Education and appointed Colonel K. R. Dyke to be in charge; this later became the CI&E.[14] Through the above process, the Subcomittee for the Far East in SWNCC completed "Education in Japan: Conclusion" on October 23, 1945, which made the following recommendation: "*An advisory group of educators of recognized ability should visit Japan at an early date to advise and assist in the formulation and carrying out of the Japanese educational reforms*" (author's italics).[15] This document became crucial to the Education Division of the CI&E in carrying out its plan for the Mission.

Let us examine the way in which the subcommittee arrived at this recommendation. First, it was based on the lessons learned from the failure of policy toward Germany after World War I. In other words, the subcommittee understood that World War II was provoked by the remilitarization of Germany, which resulted from the Allied Powers' negative policies.[16] This experience led to the idea of creating more positive and comprehensive policies for the reorientation and reconstruction of Germany after World War II, based on American democracy. Therefore, soon after the German surrender, the sending of the U.S. Education Mission to Germany was strongly recommended by educators all over America through the National Education Association (NEA).

Likewise, the idea of sending a U.S. education mission was discussed as a part of education policy toward Japan.[17] Meanwhile, demands for sending an education mission to Japan emerged from civilian groups. For instance, on October 16, 1945, A. B. Chapman, an American aerviceman stationed in Japan, sent a letter to his friend Senator John L. McClellan, a member of the Committee on Naval Affairs. In his letter Chapman mentioned the necessity for directing education reforms by sending an education mission to Japan:

> Many of the educators of Japan are anxious to reform the educational system and the way of living in Japan. . . . A committee of educators from amongst the

colleges and high schools in the United States [should] be appointed along with a Congressman and a Senator to come over to Japan and talk with the Japanese educators and Japanese people who are interested in reforming the Japanese educational system and get suggestions and make a study of the needs and possible remedies of Japanese education and return to the United States and make recommendations to Congress and the President for action. This problem should be attended to as soon as possible, because soon the people will become complacent with a situation embodying an army of occupation and the old Japanese regime, in part, and a change will be more difficult and less effective....

The educational system of Japan is the very heart of the evils which caused the suffering and bloodshed during the past four years in the Pacific Area and will undoubtedly be an arsenal for the thriving of those evils in the future.[18]

He stressed the desperate need for education reforms in Japan, and the sending of an education mission as the immediate task.

Receiving this letter on October 31, Senator McClellan forwarded it to Secretary of State James F. Brynes. In replying to this letter on November 23, Brynes stated the view of the State Department: "It is my hope that before long it may be possible to arrange for such a mission to be dispatched to Japan."[19] The draft of this reply was written by Gordon T. Bowles.

The staff of the CI&E which was carrying out the actual Occupation work in Japan, had kept in contact with the Ministry of Education from the beginning. The CI&E was in desperate and urgent need of experts on education in order to reorientate the Japanese side toward education reform. At the same time, the Japanese side was dissatisfied with the lack of experts in the CI&E. Tamon Maeda, Minister of Education, recollected the situation in an article written in English, "The Direction of Postwar Education in Japan": "Many of those who carried out the Occupation administration of education were persons of extremely limited knowledge and experience in the field."[20]

Others also criticized the staff of the CI&E for having neither the experience nor the specialization to carry out education reform. Kazuo Kawai, editor in chief of *The Nippon Times* at that time, pointed out in a book written in English: "The chief of CI&E was a marine corps reserve lieutenant colonel who in civilian life had been a small-town high school principal. The members of his staff, at first wholly military but later predominantly civilian, were mostly people of about the same level of background and experience."[21]

James I. Doi, a Japanese American who was an interpreter in the Education Division of the CI&E, also testified to this situation in an interview: "In order to carry out the postwar educational reform, the experiences and academic backgrounds of the staff of the CI&E differ greatly from those of the officials of the Japanese Ministry of Education and professors of Tokyo Imperial University. Therefore, as one of the means for adjusting these differences, I imagine the idea of an education mission came up."[22] In addition, R. K. Hall persuaded his immediate chief, H. C. Henderson, of the need for a mission. The reasoning, essentially, was that the staff would not have the technical skill and necessary prestige to reform Japanese education.[23]

This sequence of events contributed to active discussion in the CI&E and the soliciting of the opinions of Minister of Education Maeda concerning the invitation of foreign education advisers at an early stage in the proceedings.

According to the Trainor Papers, on October 30, 1945, K. R. Dyke, Chief of the CI&E, approved the first draft of the list of candidates for the Mission and ordered the continuation of the staff study. Two days later, on November 1, R. K. Hall revised the draft, and on November 3 it was approved by K. R. Dyke through a three-man committee consisting of K. R. Dyke, H. C. Henderson, and R. K. Hall. On the same day Hall prepared a draft of requirements to be cabled to the War Department. On November 4 it finally received the approval of Major General Richard J. Marshall.[24] The candidates in this second draft numbered 20, with the addition of Alonzo B. Grace, Superintendent of the State of Connecticut; Alexander J. Stoddard, Superintendent of the City of Philadelphia; and Howard E. Willson of the Carnegie Foundation, and with the subtraction of Senator Thomas.

On November 5 Hall had a meeting with Dyke and submitted a paper entitled "Memorandum to Chief of CI&E, Notes on Presentation of the Plan for Bringing an Educational Mission to Japan,"[25] in which he proposed bringing to Japan a group of experts, as a kind of education mission, in order to impress Japanese educators and be effective in promoting itself to the Japanese public. This was the CI&E's initial plan, and was in contrast to the State Department's plan to discuss a mission comprising a small group.[26]

The second draft of the list of candidates was drawn up on November 10, with the following aim, stated in Dyke's memorandum: " . . . to bring to Japan for a period of approximately thirty (30) days a Mission composed of distinguished American Educators to advise the Education Section of the Civil Information and Education Section and the Japanese Ministry of Education on the rehabilitation of the Japanese educational system."

The CI&E also explained that the Japanese educational authorities were incapable of accomplishing the reforms in accordance with the GHQ/SCAP order dated October 22, 1945, "The Supervision and Policy to Japanese

Educational System," without advice and technical support from foreigners, and added that the staff of the Education Division of the CI&E needed appropriate technical advice, which could not be supplied by the military but was obtainable only from civilian educators in the U.S., in order to carry out the directive indicated by General Order No. 4, dated October 2, 1945.[27]

In drawing up this second draft, the CI&E had meetings with Japanese educators and referred to Embree's study *Order of Eminence of American Universities*, written in 1936 for the Carnegie Foundation.[28] As part of the criteria for the selection of members, internationally famous scholars and the geographical distribution of educational institutions in the U.S. were also taken into account.

J. B. Conant, the President of Harvard University, was nominated as chairman of the Mission. Also nominated were J. W. Studebaker, U.S. Commissioner of Education, as a government adviser and G. T. Bowles, Director of the Far Eastern Section of Cultural Relations at the State Department, as a Far Eastern adviser. The rest of the candidates were divided into the following four subcommittees:

1. Education for Democracy in Japan: H. M. Jones (chairman), H. A. Moe, D. Stevens, J. Dewey, H. E. Willson
2. Psychology in Re-orientation of Japan: W. C. Trow (chairman), F. Freeman, E. Thornd[y]ke
3. Administrative Reorganization of the Educational System of Japan: J. B. Edmonson (chairman), F. T. Spaulding, R. Tyler, A. J. Stoddard, A. C. Grace
4. Higher Education in the Rehabilitation of Japan: F. Adydellotte (chairman), F. Graham, R. Hutchins, G. S. Ford

According to this draft, the Mission was supposed to leave the U.S. on December 1, 1945, and give technical advice for the new academic year commencing in April 1946.

2) REJECTION OF J. B. CONANT AS CHAIRMAN

As recommended in "Education in Japan: Conclusion" (Oct. 23, 1945) by FEC/SWNCC, the CI&E's preliminary plan for the Mission was successfully carried out, with Gen. MacArthur's full support. An unexpected problem emerged, however. According to the Trainor Papers, on November 10, 1945, the second draft was suddenly rejected by the joint signatories, Gen. MacArthur and Maj. Gen. Marshall. The reasons given were the geographic bias in the choice of the candidates' universities and the "politically inappropriate choice of chairman."[29]

It can be considered, however, that the choice of candidates was unavoidably concentrated in specific universities, such as Harvard, Columbia, Minnesota, Chicago, and so on, because of the limited selection of only 20 eminent educators, because it was easier to obtain information about these universities, and because the Civil Affairs Training School (CATS), the Civil Affairs Staging Area (CASA), and the War and Navy Japanese Language Schools were affiliated with these universities and therefore directly connected with the military.

The main reason given for disapproval was the nomination of J. B. Conant as a "politically inappropriate choice of chairman." Conant, as President of Harvard University, was one of the most eminent figures in the American educational world. The phrase "politically inappropriate choice of chairman," which is recorded in the Trainor Papers, has remained unexplained and a subject of controversy. One possible reason for the rejection of Conant was that he was one of advisers to the President on the atomic bomb project and the plan to drop the atomic bomb on Japan.[30] He was also chairman of the National Defence Research Committee.[31]

To the present day, Gen. MacArthur's attitude toward the atomic bombing of Japan remains unclear. It is not impossible to imagine, however, that as a general, and an expert in conventional warfare, he may have opposed the use of the atomic bomb and the inevitable escalation toward nuclear war in the future. As a matter of fact, at the time there was general opposition to the use of the atomic bomb among high-ranking U.S. officers, who believed that Japan's surrender could be brought about through the strengthening and proliferation of conventional warfare, without the use of the atomic bomb.[32] It is possible that as Supreme Commander Gen. MacArthur judged it unwise, for the sake of the Japanese as well as the Allied Powers, to appoint a person who had been involved in the dropping of the atomic bomb as chairman.

Additionally, through an interview with someone involved with the CI&E, the author has been able to confirm that another possible reason for the rejection of Conant was Gen. MacArthur's personal intention of becoming a Republican candidate in the presidential election, in which Conant himself was believed to be a promising rival candidate. H. J. Wunderlich has testified that "Gen. MacArthur supported the idea of inviting the Mission because of his own political ambition to stand for the presidential election, and he intended thereby to arouse the American public's interest in himself. I think by inviting the Mission from the U.S. he effectively showed his leadership in education. In this connection, it was necessary that the selection of members of the Mission should be representative of all parts of America."[33] Furthermore, in his diary entry for November 19, 1945, he wrote: "President J. B. Conant of Harvard University was recommended on the list as Chairman of the Mission. The recommendation was

definitely unsatisfactory because ... of his political, presidential stature."[34]
From these testimonies, it can be confirmed that two reasons for the rejection of the second draft had to do with the presidential election.

Due to this unexpected rejection by the chief executives, on November
12 H. C. Henderson ordered R. K. Hall to revise the list again, and on
November 22 Hall submitted the revised draft to K. R. Dyke. It became the
third draft, dated November 23, 1945. No major changes were made in the
plan's aim, its role, and the four areas of studies in Japanese education,
apart from the names of some candidates. Through careful consideration
of the geographical distribution of candidates,[35] Hall failed to notice the
real reason for Gen. MacArthur's disapproval of Conant. Consequently, in
the third draft, he again proposed Conant as a candidate for membership
of Committee IV, "Higher Education in the Rehabilitation of Japan."
This naturally infuriated Gen. MacArthur. The Education Division of the
CI&E was forced to reorganize, and Hall was reassigned to the Planning
Division.[36]

3) THE FINAL DRAFT OF THE CANDIDATES

As discussed above, disapproval of J. B. Conant caused a delay in the
Mission, which had been expected to leave the U.S. on December 1,
1945.

Sacrificing their Christmas holiday, the staff members of the CI&E
worked hard to revise the third draft. The final draft was submitted to
Maj. Gen. Marshall on December 27, and on December 31 it received final
approval from Gen. MacArthur and Maj. Gen. Marshall. On January 4
1946, CINCAFPAC cabled an official request to the War Department to
send the Education Mission to Japan.[37] The telegram began as follows:

REHABILITATION OF JAPANESE EDUCATIONAL SYSTEM GIVEN HIGH PRIORITY
IN OCCUPATION OPERATIONS. ESTIMATED 18,000,000 STUDENTS, 400,000
TEACHERS, 40,000 SCHOOLS PRESENT MAJOR MEDIUM FOR INFLUENCING
JAPANESE LIFE THROUGHOUT, AND ACTION IN ACCOMPLISHING OCCUPATION
MISSION.

Thus, the telegram expressed the utmost importance of postwar education to the administration of the Occupation. It continues:

BASIC EDUCATION DIRECTIVES HAVE BEEN ISSUED. ENCOURAGING COOPERA-
TION BY MINISTRY OF EDUCATION BUT JAPANESE EDUCATORS TECHNICALLY
UNQUALIFIED TO PLAN AND INITIATE COMPLETE REFORMS AND ACTION ES-
SENTIAL TO SUCCESS OF MISSION MUST BE COMPLETED BEFORE NEXT SCHOOL
TERM STARTING APRIL THIS YEAR.

The authorities emphasized the necessity of support from the Education Mission. Though they issued four negative directives for educational reforms, their own basic policy was not yet clarified sufficiently to enable them to direct postwar Japanese education. They were concerned about the lack of direction in Japanese education, and considered it essential to have the Education Mission dispatched as quickly as possible.

In the final draft, the number of candidates was increased to thirty; the draft proposed choosing eighteen or twenty-one members and appointing a chairman from among them. It committed the Mission to leaving for Japan as soon as possible and remaining there for thirty days in order to advise the staff of SCAP, the Ministry of Education, and Japanese educators, as well as to recommend some education reforms for the new academic year, which was to start in April.

Meanwhile, on the following day, January 5, *The New York Times* published an article about the Education Mission to Japan and included the list of members.[38] According to this article, *"Thirty prominent American educators were invited today by Gen. MacArthur* to come to Japan to assist the Japanese in gearing their educational system to democratic principles"* (author's italics). Following is the list of thirty names that was published:

1. Dr. Frank Aydelotte, Princeton, N.J.
2. Dr. Fred C. Ayer, University of Texas
3. Dr. Gordon Bowles, Director of Far Eastern Section, Cultural Relations Division, Department of State, Washington
4. Dr. Oliver C. Carmichael, President of Vanderbilt University
5. Dr. Ben M. Cherrington, University of Denver
6. Dr. Wilson M. Compton, President, Washington State College
7. Dr. George W. Diemer, President, Central Missouri State Teachers College
8. Dr. Guy S. Ford, Retired Chancellor, University of Minnesota
9. Dr. Frank F. Freeman, Dean of Education, University of California, Berkeley
10. Dr. Virginia C. Gildersleeve, Dean, Barnard College
11. Dr. Willard E. Givens, Executive Secrtary, National Education Association
12. Dr. Alonzo C. Grace, Commissioner of Education, Connecticut
13. Dr. Frank P. Graham, President, University of North Carolina
14. Dr. Rufus C. Harris, President, Tulane University
15. Dr. Howard M. Jones, Administrative School, Fort Getty, R.I.
16. Dr. Mildred H. McAfee, President, Wellesley College
17. Dr. Henry A. Moe, Director, John Simon Guggenheim Memorial Foundation, New York

18. Lieut. Col. T. V. Smith, Administrative School, Fort Getty, R.I.
19. Col. Francis T. Spaulding, Who is to become New York State Commissioner of Education
20. Dr. Robert G. Sproul, President, University of California
21. Dr. David H. Stevens, Rockefeller Foundation, New York
22. Dr. Alexander Stoddard, Superintendent of Schools, Philadelphia
23. Dr. John W. Studebaker, United States Commissioner of Education, Washington
24. Dr. Willis A. Sutton, Superintendent of Schools, Altanta, Ga.
25. Dr. Edward L. Thorndike, Retired Psychologist, Montrose, N.Y.
26. Dr. William C. Trow, Professor of Educational Psychology, University of Michigan
27. Dr. Ralph W. Tyler, Dean of Education, University of Chicago
28. Dr. Earnest H. Wilkins, President, Oberlin College, Ohio
29. Dr. Howard Wilson, Carnegie Foundation for Advancement of Teaching, N.Y.
30. Dr. George F. Zook, President, American Council on Education, Washington

Thirty names were listed in *The New York Times*, whereas SCAP's telegram to the War Department mentioned only twenty-eight, A. J. Stoddard and F. P. Graham having been omitted by mistake.[39] In addition, G. S. Ford (former chancellor of the University of Minnesota) had been misidentified as the president of the University of North Carolina (in reality F. P. Graham). The article in *The New York Times*, however, corrected these errors. This means that the paper must have obtained its information from a source other than the telegram.

How *The New York Times* obtained the material for this article has never been confirmed. According to the Trainor Papers, SCAP gave a press conference at 7:30 P.M. the day the telegram was sent, announcing the Mission of thirty members. *The New York Times* had a special correspondent in Tokyo to report on the Occupation, who heard the news of the Mission at the press conference. In fact, "Tokyo Jan. 4 (AP)" is printed clearly at the beginning of the article. This press conference was so brief that the details of the telegram were not provided. Consequently, the following morning *The New York Times* simply reported the press release as it was, from the original.

This article created confusion not only in the War Department but also in the State Department, as well as among the people organizing the Mission and the educators whose names appeared in the paper, resulting in numerous reactions from various sectors of society. The State Department received the biggest shock, realizing through this article that the plan of the Mission to Japan had been sent to the War Department for the final decision.

Gordon T. Bowles was in charge of the Far Eastern Section of Cultural Relations at the State Department, and was especially concerned with the Mission to Japan. In an inverview with him, he remembered those days as follows:

> That morning I received a call from the Assistant Secretary of State, William Benton, demanding excitedly, "How on earth did the article on the invitation of the Mission to Japan get into *The New York Times*? How did it happen, do you know?"
>
> As I hadn't read it yet, I answered him, "I'm sorry I don't understand what you are talking about."
>
> He then said, "You should know, since your name is listed there as a member, as also is Studebaker, U.S. Commissioner of Education. He might know something. Look into it straight away."
>
> I rang Mr. Studebaker immediately, but he said, "I thought you would know something about it." Eventually we discovered that neither of us knew what had been reported in the newspaper.
>
> Then I visited the Civil Affairs Division of the War Department, to which SCAP had cabled the request. Here I met Major General John H. Hilldring, the director of that division, and asked him about the actual circumstances of sending the Mission to Japan. I said, "At the request of Assistant Secretary of State Benton, I am investigating the matter reported in *The New York Times* this morning. My name is included in the published list, but I've heard nothing about it. Mr. Studebaker is also listed, but he has told me that he hadn't heard about it, either. What is the meaning of all this, may I ask?"
>
> Hilldring replied, "As a matter of fact, we know nothing about it either. It seems that it was a decision made unilaterally by MacArthur's side. To be honest with you, we are equally confused." As it was my responsibility to make inquiries into this matter, before I left I asked him to request SCAP to investigate the details at once and explain them to us.
>
> A few days later I heard from him, and he told me that the officers in the CI&E were in a very difficult situation. They did not have enough preliminary knowledge, training, or preparation for the Occupation of Japan. Consequently, indirect control in order to maintain the Japanese government was the only way for them to achieve the rehabilitation of Japan. For these reasons, the CI&E staff had contact with the Japanese Ministry of Education from the earliest stage of the Occupation. However, in doing so, the young officers in the CI&E especially had difficulties in discussing Japanese educational problems on an equal standing with people in high position and of more profound knowledge, such as the Assistant Secretary of the Ministry of Education and university professors. Because of these difficulties in the CI&E, MacArthur granted their request and approved the Education Mission.[40]

The above testimony clearly illustrates the background to SCAP's request for the Mission and how desperately it needed the Mission. It also indicates the disturbance created in the U.S. by the *New York Times* article. In this interview, Bowles also said that he himself did not know about the Mission. But this is impossible. What does he really mean? Henry P. Leverich, at the State Department, knew of SCAP's request on January 2, 1946.[41] In addition, the plan to send education missions to the defeated countries (Germany and Japan) had been under discussion in their department since June 1945. Therefore, it would appear that Bowles's real reaction in this matter was a protest against SCAP's interference in the authority of the State Department over such an important policy matter.[42]

II. *The Organization of the Education Mission by the State Department*

1) ADJUSTMENTS BETWEEN THE STATE DEPARTMENT AND THE WAR DEPARTMENT

As discussed above, there was an agreement arranged by SWNCC relating to the shared responsibility for Occupied Japan. A document attached to SWNCC 162/D, "Positive Policy for Reorientation of the Japanese," issued on July 19, 1945, stated: "The principal responsibility for the long-range aspect of reorientation will rest ultimately with the Department of State."[43] Thus, it confirmed that the military should not participate in education issues, which should be the responsibility of the State Department. Hence, SCAP's actions involving the Mission were a definite deviation from the above agreement.[44] To reconfirm responsibility, SWNCC issued SWNCC 162/2 on January 8, 1946, attached to SWNCC 162/D, which stated: "Because of the inherent nature of the problem, the basic planning for and continuing development of a U.S. program of reorientation and reeducation is an appropriate responsibility of the Department of State subject to existing arrangements with respect to control machinery for Japan and the channel of command for issuing instructions to SCAP."[45]

This established that the State Department should take all responsibility for the Mission and, at the same time, partially legitimized SCAP's deviation.

In the document of January 12, 1946, J. H. Hilldring, Director of the Civil Affairs Division (CAD) in the War Department, officially acknowledged that the selection of the Mission members was not within the jurisdiction of his office. As official acknowledgement Kenneth C. Royall, Assistant Secretary of War, sent a letter dated January 14, 1946, to James F. Brynes, Secretary of State, which stated:

> As you probably know, State-War-Navy Coordinating Committee Paper 162/2, dated 8 January, 1946, Subject: Reorientation of the Japanese, now in process for final approval, concludes that the long-range character of reorientation and re-education of the Japanese is an appropriate responsibility of the Department of State and that the Department of State should immediately undertake the development of such a program to be implemented by SCAP. It is, therefore, considered that the recruitment and final selection of this mission is an appropriate responsibility of the Department of State.[46]

He also mentioned that the costs of the Mission were to be borne by the War Department, and that in the light of Gen. MacArthur's Christian views, representation of Catholic and other denominations should be considered.

Dean Atchison, Assistant Secretary of State, in a letter dated January 19, 1946, willingly consented to K. C. Royall's proposals.[47] That day, it was finally agreed that the State Department should take the initiative in the selection of the Mission members and give serious consideration to the list of candidates proposed by SCAP.

2) ORGANIZATION OF PERSONNEL UNDER THE INITIATIVE OF THE STATE DEPARTMENT

After the above adjustment, the State Department commenced organizing the Mission members in earnest. Its method of selection was first to obtain acceptance from the candidates who were nominated by SCAP and then to fill any resulting vacancies.

It was considered important to gain acceptance first of all from J. W. Studebaker, U.S. Commissioner of Education, for the future task of completing the organization of the Mission, and it was thought reasonable, because of his status, to ask him to play a central role in the Mission. However, he rejected his nomination for the following reasons: SCAP had not contacted the U.S. Office of Education concerning the nomination of eminent educators for the Mission, and had nominated him as government adviser to the Mission without his prior consent.

Strictly speaking, the Education Mission should have been sent on the initiative of the U.S. Office of Education. In reality, however, it was excluded. Eventually Studebaker demanded that his name be withdrawn from the list of candidates and recommended Harold Banjamin, Assistant Commissioner of the U.S. Office of Education, in his place.[48] Consequently, without the total support of the U.S. Office of Education, but with occasional and personal support from Studebaker, the State Department took charge of organizing the Mission in cooperation with CAD in the War Department and the other divisions concerned, with G. T. Bowles carrying the initiative for the operation.

On January 28, 1946, Bowles drew up a document entitled "Procedure in Organization of Education Mission to Japan,"[49] which set forth the role of the State Department as follows:

On the basis of the arrangement with the War Department, whereby State will assume responsibility for final selection of personnel and for the formulation of the Education Mission the following procedure is proposed:

1. As soon as final selection of the Mission members has been approved by State these should be forwarded to the War Department for clearance.

2. War Department to assume responsibility for arranging for inoculation, exit permits, transportation and facilities enroute.

3. State to request detailing by the War Department of an officer of the rank of Lt. Colonel or Colonel to act as Liaison between the Mission and the Army. Such an officer would travel with the Mission and would assist in making arrangements to smooth the way for the Mission all along the line in matters of transportation, luggage, despatching of telegrams, mail etc., and p[re]ferably he should have an appreciation of the purposes of the Mission. Selection of officer to be approved by State. Prior to departure this officer would assist in seeing that i[n]noculations and military exit permits have been secured etc.

4. State to appoint a Department Officer to serve as general secretary to the Mission. Such an officer could be a young man but should be experienced in drawing together the results of committee discussions and should serve the Mission until the conclusion of operations. He would be responsible for completing of the Mission's reports and recommendations in Tokyo. Prior to leaving Washington he should be made available to assist in the securing of passports and other ne[c]essary papers for the Mission members.

5. The OIC [Office of International Information and Cultural Affairs of the State Department][50] representative would be responsible for the Mission as a whole and would assist in some of the briefing of the Mission with respect to the background of the Japanese educational system and the immediate problems in the field of education in Japan.

6. A selected list of materials to be assembled to provide background briefing for use of the Mission members. These to consist of a few books on Japanese education, the policies of the U.S. Government, and SCAP, with respect to education and a summary of educational news culled from the press and reports from Tokyo.

7. The Mission would be assembled in San Francisco as soon as possible and would be briefed during the period of alert at Hamilton Field so that all members would have an opportunity to consult together and the Mission could be fairly well coordinated and organized into committees before leaving the continent.

First of all, he was concerned with gaining acceptance from the candidates listed by SCAP. He described those days as follows:

> I discussed procedural matters first with Studebaker and Benjamin and subsequently with Civil Affairs. During the initial discussions it was decided that I should first phone all of the persons listed by SCAP, bearing in mind that if there was anyone on the list judged to be qualified to assume the role of chairman of the group he or she should be called into consultation both for completion of the panel's members and for all related procedural matters relating to formation of the Mission. The plan was approved by both State and Civil Affairs and, as I recall it, after telephoning everyone on the original list of thirty, the number was reduced to something like fourteen or fifteen available candidates. Several on the original list could not adjust their schedules to the specified period abroad and at least three were dead.[51]

As a matter of fact, confirmation of the availability of the candidates was an urgent need. For example, W. C. Trow, one of the candidates, received a telegram dated January 18, 1946:

> DEPARTMENT OF STATE IN COOPERATION WITH OFFICE OF EDUCATION DIRECTS ME TO INQUIRE INFORMALLY WHETHER YOU COULD GO ON EDUCATIONAL MISSION TO JAPAN IF OFFICIAL INVITATION WERE EXTENDED WOULD REQUIRE LEAVING UNITED STATES APPROXIMATELY FEBRUARY 15 AND RETURNING ABOUT MARCH 25 PLEASE WIRE REPLY COLLECT HAROLD BENJAMIN U.S. OFFICE OF EDUCATION.[52]

On the following day, Trow replied by telegram: "Am interested and available. Jan. 19." All other confirmations were also by telegram.

Organizing the Mission was not at all easy for the State Department. It was interrupted by the national confusion which had been created by the *New York Times* article. "Hundreds of letters, phone calls and personal inquiries were received from the public at large."[53]

The reactions against SCAP's method of selection are recorded in the CAD Papers, War Department.[54] Among these reactions, there is a letter dated January 8, 1946, from Edward F. McGrady of the Radio Corporation of America, addressed to J. H. Hilldring, Director of CAD.[55] In this letter McGrady criticized the exclusion of experienced classroom teachers who were actively engaged in teaching and emphasized the importance of six major national organizations of teachers, such as the American Federation of Teachers and the Catholic Educational Association. In regard to the proposal to include Catholic educators, he recommended Monsignor Frederick Hochwalt, Chairman of the Education Section of the National Catholic Welfare Conference.

With regard to public opposition to the exclusion of Catholic educators, one magazine, a Catholic review, *America*, published an article entitled "Educators for Japan." The article began by praising the plan to send American educators to support the democratization of Japanese education. Then it drew attention to the complete exclusion of Catholic educators from the list of candidates, complaining that three major foundations—the Rockefeller, the Carnegie, and the Guggenheim—were represented, along with the State Department, the National Education Association, and the U.S. Office of Education, but not one Catholic organization.

The article argued that this omission was due to prejudice and ignored Catholic education in the U.S., at the same time underestimating the status of Catholic education and the competence of Catholic educators. It then emphasized the Catholic contribution to American education, stating that three million students were enrolled in 11,000 Catholic schools; that of 11,300 American private elementary schools, 8,000 were Catholic; that of 3,568 private junior high schools, 2,105 were Catholic; and that there were 195 Catholic colleges and universities. This, the article maintained, indicated that Catholic education was certainly not for a minority. Moreover, there were Catholic educators, who were equally as eminent as the candidates in the list. The article suggested names that should be included, such as Don Thomas Verner Moor, a psychologist at Catholic University, and Robert I. Gannon, President of Fordham University.[56]

It seems that Monsignor Frederick Hochwalt successfully approached the Department of State for Catholic representation on the Mission on behalf of the National Catholic Welfare Conference (NCWC), although Father Patrick O'Connor, a Columban Father and a representative of the NCWC in Japan, independently approached Gen. MacArthur directly on the matter. This resulted in Gen. MacArthur's cabling the State Department to this effect: "Send two Catholic educators on Mission, President of Georgetown University and President of Notre Dame, or educators of equal calibre." By the time this telegram was received, Roy Deferrari, head of the Administration Office at Catholic University, and Monsignor F. Hochwalt, Chairman of the National Catholic Education Association, had already been chosen on the recommendation of the Education Section of the NCWC.[57]

Irvin R. Kuenzli, Secretary-Treasurer of the American Federation of Teachers, criticized restricting the choice of members of administration and college professors, granting no representation to the millions of classroom teachers who were actively engaged in day-to-day teaching in schools.[58]

There was also criticism of the small number of women candidates. For example, Emily H. Hickman of the Committee on Women in World Affairs sent a letter dated January 22, 1946, to President Harry S. Truman. In her letter she complained of the unfair treatment of women educators in terms of the large ratio of female to male educators in America and the nomination of only two women in the list. She demanded an increase in women candidates, in consideration of the number of Japanese women engaged in education. In particular, she recommended representatives of the Committee on Women in World Affairs in the fields of youth education and child education.[59] She also sent letters to the same effect to J. F. Brynes, Secretary of State, and W. Benton, Assistant Secretary of State.

Meantime, on January 30, 1946, Gordon T. Bowles drew up the following list, which consisted of two parts: people who had been nominated by SCAP and accepted their invitations, and experts still to be nominated as substitutes. In order to maintain an overall balance among the candidates' backgrounds, he considered divisions of education, geographical representation, and organizational representation in making his selection.

1) From the list prepared by SCAP

Compton, W. M., President, Washington State College (Professor, Political Science and Economics)

Diemer, Geo. W., President, Central Missouri State Teachers College (Citizenship and teacher training)

Freeman, F. N., Dean of School of Education, University of California (Educational methods and techniques and educational psychology)

Gildersleeve, Virginia, Dean, Barnard College (General and higher education)

Givens, W. E., Executive Secretary of National Education Association (General education)

Harris, R. C., President, Tulane University (General and higher education)

Horton, Mrs., President, Wellesley College (Higher and Women's education)

Smith, Lt. Col. T. V., Department of Education, University of Chicago

Spaulding, Col. F. T., Occupation Forces, Tokyo, formerly Dean of School of Education, Harvard

Stevens, David H., Humanities Division, Rockefeller Foundation (the Foundations, the Humanities, and higher learning)

Stoddard, Alexander, Superintendent of Schools, Philadelphia (Elementary and secondary education)

Trow, W. C., Professor of Educational Psychology, University of Michigan (Educational psychology)

Wilson, Howard E., Carnegie Foundation for International Peace (General and higher education and Internationalism)

Wilkins, F. H., President, Oberlin College (Higher and general education)

Zook, Geo. F., President, American Council of Education (General education and educational policies)

2) Proposed Additions

Bond, Horace Mann, President, Lincoln University (a prominent negro educator who stands on his merits as an outstanding American educational leader)

Carr, W[illia]m., National Education Association (especially prominent in educational policies)

Counts, George, Vice President, American Federation of Teachers (active in all levels of education)

Embree, Edwin, Rosenwald Foundation (informed on Asiatic educational problems and in rural education)

Hochwalt, Msgr., (National Catholic Education Association and Chairman of the Education Section of the National Catholic Welfare Conference)

Joekel, Carlton B., Head, School of Librarianship, University of California (Formerly University of Chicago, School of Library Science)

Kandel, I. [J.], Professor, Comparative Education, Teachers College, Columbia

Leeper, Miss Mary, Executive Secretary, Association for Childhood Education (Especially for nursery school and kindergarten)

Norton, [F.] B., State Commissioners of Education, Montgomery, Alabama

Starr, Mark, Education Director, Ladies Garment Workers Union

Walker, Mrs., President, Department of Classroom Teachers and also a teacher at Spence Junior High School, Dallas, Texas (Recently returned from a tour of British schools made at invitation of British Government)

Woodward, Miss Emily, State Department of Education, Atlanta, Georgia (Specialist in adult education and the use of the forum in education)

Stoddard, George, President designate of the University of Illinois (Commissioner of Education, New York)

Government Adviser

To the above should be added:

Benjamin, Harold, Assistant Commissioner of Education, United States Office of Education (Suggested as substitute by Dr. Studebaker who was requested by SCAP as Government Adviser)[60]

As can been seen, fifteen of the candidates originally listed by SCAP accepted their nominations, and an additional thirteen members were then selected by the State Department, with the following five criteria as guidelines:

1) Demonstrated knowledge of and practical experience in a given field of specialization;

2) breadth or significance of regional or sectional representation on and awareness of culturally and politically conditioned differences in educational policies and practices;

3) willingness to participate in view of the Mission breadth of representational scope and recommendational limitations of its authority;

4) known ability to participate as a member of a team and to compromise constructively in joint decisions;

5) physical fitness to travel and live under military orders without serious medical consequences to the individual or impositions on the military command.[61]

These five criteria were based on more personal considerations, such as individual ability and character, than social and geographical considerations.

On January 31, 1946, it was decided provisionally to name George D. Stoddard chairman of the Mission, and a telegram was sent to Gen. MacArthur for final approval of the list of Mission candidates, with Stoddard as chairman. Five days later, on February 7, Gen. MacArthur's final approval was received.[62]

When the State Department had completed the selection of the Mission members, it replied to the letters criticizing SCAP's nominations. J. H. Hilldring replied to Edward F. McGrady, who had requested representation of the National Catholic Educational Association and the American Federation of Teachers:

> The State Department has selected a number of individuals and has asked the War Department to obtain General MacArthur's approval before proceeding with the actual formation of the mission. Among those included, you will be glad to know, was Monsignor Frederick Hochwalt as well as others of the Catholic faith. Also included was Dr. George Counts, Vice President of the American Federation of Teachers, the group which you so strongly recommended be represented.[63]

And to Emily Hickman, who had complained of the relatively few women represented in the list, W. Benton, Assistant Secretary of State, sent the following reply on February 15, 1946:

> The Secretary of War has referred to this Department your letter of January 22, 1946 concerning the participation of women in the advisory group on

education in Japan. I understand you have already discussed this subject with Mr. Gordon Bowles, who is accompanying the advisory group to Japan. The Advisory group will include approximately twenty members, of whom four are women. The Department of State has added two women to this group, the Commissioner for Public Instruction from the State of Washington and an adult education leader from Atlanta, Georgia.[64]

From these replies, we can see that the appeals had strongly influenced the selection of the Mission members. The final list included four women and one black American; it can be said that the final selection reached a democratic settlement representing more or less all American groups.

Orin E. Long, who was the Hawaii Commissioner of Education and later played an important role in the preparatory meeting of the Mission in Hawaii, praised the choice of members as a well-balanced group of eminent leaders of education. The list included eleven members of Phi Delta Kappa, such as H. Benjamin, G. Counts, G. W. Diemer, F. N. Freeman, W. E. Givens, I. L. Kandel, E. B. Norton, T. V. Smith, A. J. Stoddard and W. C. Trow.[65]

3) THE APPOINTMENT OF A CHAIRMAN

According to Gordon T. Bowles's testimony, G. D. Stoddard was appointed chairman in the following way:

> Three of us, Assistant Secretary Benton, U.S. Commissioner of Education Studebaker, and myself, in the State Department discussed the best way of selecting an additional seventeen members. We eventually decided to choose a chairman first and then select the additional members, with him as the central figure.[66]

The reason they selected him will be discussed below. His name did not appear in SCAP's original list; therefore it is interesting to examine the process by which he was appointed.

Past Japanese studies on the Mission discuss the appointment of Stoddard by referring to his 1942 study "Frontiers for Youth" in *School and Society*,[67] in which he pointed out the importance of reorientation for the Japanese, the Italians, and the Germans. In other words, his views were in accordance with the intention of the U.S. Government document "The U.S. Initial Post-Surrender Policy for Japan (September 22, 1945)": "to insure that Japan will not again become a menace to the United States or to the peace and security of the world."[68] It was also thought that the War Department and the State Department both regarded him, because of the above-mentioned study, as a person who had studied the theory and practice of "reorientation" in enough depth to be nominated as chairman.[69]

Considering the strained situation in the State Department at that time, the above reasons were not enough. It was on January 14, 1946, that the War Department officially requested the selection of members from the State Department, and only two weeks later, on January 31, that Stoddard received a request to become chairman. It is doubtful that there had been enough time to examine his academic record.

The author would like to focus on other factors in Stoddard's appointment. First, the personal connection between Stoddard and the people in charge of the nominations should be noted. In November 1945, Stoddard attended the organizing committee of UNESCO in London as one of the U.S. representatives. Among them were important figures concerned with education reforms in postwar Germany and Japan: William Benton, Assistant Secretary of State, who helped formulate American education policy toward Japan; Archibald MacLeish, former Assistant Secretary of State, who was concerned with education policy toward Germany; W. G. Carr, who had suggested sending an educational mission to Germany as the plan of the National Education Association and had himself been nominated as a member of the Mission to Japan by SCAP; and finally, Stoddard himself. It is possible that this gathering was the most important factor in the appointment of Stoddard as chairman. Additionally, Stoddard had described his own ability as New York State Commissioner of Education so well that he was selected as one of the representatives for the UNESCO inaugural committee and attracted other representatives from the State Department. It is also reported that Benton and Stoddard were old friends and confidants.[70]

As a matter of fact, Benton sent a letter to the Secretary of State approving of Stoddard as a representative on the UNESCO committee instead of Robert M. Hutchins, President of the University of Chicago.[71] In his memoir "The Emperor and I", Stoddard himself admitted Benton's personal influence in the matter of the appointment of a chairman and that Benton was the chief executive during the selection process for the appointment.[72]

In addition to this personal connection through the UNESCO committee, the spirit of the United Nations Charter was inherent in the criteria used for creating a positive policy for the reorientation of the Japanese,[73] as specified, in the article "Ultimate Objectives" in "The U.S. Initial Post-Surrender Policy for Japan," "to bring about the eventual establishment of a peaceful and responsible government which will respect the rights of other states and will support the objectives of the United States as reflected in the ideals and principles of the *Charter of the United Nations*" (author's italics). He was finally selected as chairman on the basis of his having served as a U.S. representative to UNESCO.

Finally, J. W. Studebaker's recommendation should be taken into account, in the light of his having previously had his own nomination as a central figure rejected. At his meeting with Benton and Bowles, Studebaker said, "It would be best to ask Mr. George Stoddard, who is the New York State Commissioner of Education and President of the University of Illinois."[74] Consequently it was decided to appoint Stoddard as chairman. At that time he was unknown in Japan, but in the U.S. he was already well known. He was an active member of the National Education Association and, as the New York State Commissioner of Education, had demonstrated his ability in educational administration. In short, it was a "sweetheart ticket" (that is, an electoral slate that would appeal to a broad spectrum of interest groups).[75] In fact, Stoddard, showed his organizational ability by increasing the number of women candidates and widening the representation of religious groups and geographical regions in response to public criticism concerning representation. And in nominating Charles S. Johnson, a black American, he was responsive to the social problems suffered by ethnic minorities in 1946.[76]

Moreover, it was a lucky coincidence for him that his term as the New York State Commissioner of Education was about to expire and that he had already been appointed president of the University of Illinois.

Eventually Benton sent the following telegram dated February 6, 1946, to Stoddard in Albany:

THE DEPARTMENT OF STATE IN RESPONSE TO A REQUEST FROM THE WAR DEPARTMENT IS INVITING A NUMBER OF DISTINGUISHED AMERICAN EDUCATORS TO SERVE AS ADVISORS TO THE SUPREME COMMANDER FOR THE ALLIED POWERS IN JAPAN. THE PROPOSAL FOR THIS ADVISORY GROUP WAS ORIGINALLY MADE BY GENERAL MACARTHUR TO ASSIST HIS STAFF AND THE JAPANESE MINISTRY OF EDUCATION ON MATTERS RELATING TO THE EDUCATIONAL PROGRAM FOR THE NEW ACADEMIC YEAR COMMENCING IN APRIL AND TO MAKE RECOMMENDATIONS FOR FUTURE PLANS CONCERNING CHANGES IN THE JAPANESE EDUCATIONAL SYSTEM. THE GROUP WILL ASSEMBLE IN SAN FRANCISCO ON FEBRUARY 20, 1946, AND WILL LEAVE AS SOON THEREAFTER AS POSSIBLE [.] TRAVEL WILL BE BY AIR TO TOKYO. IT IS EXPECTED THAT THE PARTY WILL REMAIN ABOUT ONE MONTH IN JAPAN AND IT IS ANTICIPATED THAT THE MEMBERS WILL BE BACK IN THE UNITED STATES BY THE END OF MARCH. IT AFFORDS THE DEPARTMENT SPECIAL PLEASURE AND SATISFACTION TO INVITE YOU TO BECOME CHAIRMAN OF THIS GROUP. YOUR VALUED COUNSEL AND COOPERATION WILL BE MOST HELPFUL. . . . WILLIAM BENTON, ASSISTANT SECRETARY.[77]

In reply to this request, Stoddard cabled the following day:

I AM PLEASED TO ACCEPT THE HONOR OF BECOMING CHAIRMAN OF THE GROUP OF EDUCATIONAL CONSULTANTS INVITED BY THE STATE DEPARTMENT ON REQUEST OF THE WAR DEPARTMENT TO ASSIST GENERAL MACARTHUR AND HIS STAFF CONCERNING THE JAPANESE EDUCATION PROGRAM. YOUR CONFIDENCE IN ME IS HIGHLY APPRECIATED. WILL BE IN WASHINGTON TO-MORROW OFFICE OF GORDON BOWLES. SUGGESTIONS AND STARTING ARRANGE-MENTS CAN BE MADE IN CONFERENCE. GEORGE D. STODDARD[78]

4) ANNOUNCEMENT OF THE FINAL LIST OF THE MISSION

On February 18, 1946, the State Department gave a press conference on the Education Advisory Group to Japan and officially announced the final list of the members, with Stoddard as Chairman. The announcement was as follows:

Education Advisory Group to Japan

Assistant Secretary Benton, in response to a request by the War Department, has invited a number of distinguished American educators to serve as an advisory group on education to Japan. The advisory group was originally proposed by the Supreme Commander for the Allied Powers in the Pacific, General Douglas MacArthur, who requested the assistance of competent authorities in various fields of education to advise his staff and, through him, the Japanese Ministry of Education on technical matters relating to the educational program to be followed under the Allied Occupation.

The group will also make recommendations to the Supreme Commander on the most effective measures to be taken in the process of demilitarization and reorientation of the Japanese educational system. It is expected that the group will depart about February 22 from San Francisco and spend approximately one month in Japan.

In agreement with the War Department and General MacArthur, the Department has named George D. Stoddard chairman of the group. Dr. Stoddard is at present State Commissioner of Education in New York and President-elect of the University of Illinois.

The selection of the other members of the group was based on a list of 28 [*sic*] names which was proposed by General MacArthur and was announced in the press on January 4. Of these 28 persons, all of whom were invited to serve as members, the following accepted invitations:

Wilson M. Compton, President, State College of Washington.
George W. Diemer, President, Central Missouri State Teachers College.
Frank N. Freeman, Dean, School of Education, University of California.
Virginia Gildersleeves, Dean, Barnard College.
Willard E. Givens, Executive Secretary, National Education Association.
Mrs. Mildred McAfee Horton, President, Wellesley College.
Lt. Col. T. V. Smith, Professor of Philosophy, University of Chicago.
David H. Stevens, Division of Humanities, Rockefeller Foundation.

Alexander J. Stoddard, Superintendent of Schools, Philadelphia.

William C. Trow, Professor of Educational Psychology, University of Michigan.

In order to complete the group, the following persons were invited by the Department to participate in the group and have consented to do so:

Harold Benjamin, Director, Division of International Education, Office of Education.

Leon Carnovsky, Associate Dean, Graduate Library School, University of Chicago.

George S. Counts, Professor of Education, Columbia University and a Vice President, American Federation of Teachers.

Roy J. Deferrari, Secretary-General, Catholic University.

Kermit Eby, Director of Research and Education Congress of Industrial Organizations.

Ernest R. Hilgard, Head of Department of Psychology, Stanford University.

Msgr. Frederick G. Hochwalt, National Catholic Education Association and Chairman, Education Section, National Catholic Welfare Conference.

Charles Iglehart, Formerly Professor, Union Theological Seminary and Methodist Episcopal Missionary to Japan, now Adviser to the Civil Information and Education Section, SCAP.

Charles S. Johnson, Professor of Sociology, Fisk University.

Isaac L. Kandel, Professor of Comparative Education, Columbia University.

Charles H. McCloy, Professor of Physical Education, University of Iowa.

E. B. Norton, State Superintendent of Education, Alabama.

Mrs. Pearl Wanamaker, State Superintendent of Public Instruction Washington.

Miss Emily Woodward, State Department of Education, Georgia.

Harold Benjamin will represent the Office of Education as Government adviser to the group replacing the Commissioner of Education, John W. Studebaker, who is unable to go.

Gordon T. Bowles of Area Division V (Occupied Areas) of the Office of International Information and Cultural Affairs of the State Department will accompany the group as representative of the Department of State and Far Eastern Adviser. Paul P. Stewart, also of the same office in the State Department, will serve as Secretary-General.

Col. John N. Andrews will accompany the group as Military liaison. Colonel Andrews has been with Selective Service.

In making its selections, the Department has been in close consultation with the Office of Education of the Federal Security Agency and has also sought the advice of representatives of nationally recognized educational associations as well as of individuals prominent in the field of education, including the chairman of the group. As finally compiled, the list includes authorities from various parts of the country in all levels of education from the nursery school to the university. Various educational organizations, learned societies, and foundations are represented. Specialists are included in such fields as adult, rural, and woman's education; the use of libraries; physical and health education; educational techniques; curricula and administration; teacher training; educational psychology and comparative education.[79]

Charles Iglehart's name was later withdrawn from the list, so that the final list included twenty-seven names.[80] However, six secretaries were added at Chairman Stoddard's request: Lucille Jewett, Mary Booth Frances Vandenberg, Rose Luscher, Lillian Diamond, Helen Smerling, and Ann Pantaleo.[81]

Originally, it had been planned that the Report should be drawn up on the Mission's return from Japan so that the members could spend all their time organizing meetings and carrying out studies and observations. Stoddard's idea, however, was to complete the Report in the last week of their stay in Japan. He made this adjustment to the original schedule drawn up by the CI&E one of the conditions for his acceptance of the chairmanship.

In the selection of members, Bowles personally had a plan to include internationally known educators from the Allied Powers, but he was forced to abandon it. He reviewed the reasons as follows:

> Inasmuch as SCAP represented all of the Allied Powers, it was my personal opinion that at least five or six non-Americans should be included, but this was not approved for a number of reasons:
>
> 1) Such inclusion might set a precedent which could interfere with plans for the panel of judges participating in the military trials or other panel activities;
>
> 2) nations not represented might raise questions;
>
> 3) the non-Americans might well be unintentionally slighted or feel out of place;
>
> 4) much time would have to be spent and effort expended to make special arrangements and interviews during the tour of Japan;
>
> 5) objections were certain to be made because of the biased appointments of a specialist in this, that, or the other field by specialists who had been ignored.
>
> The inclusion ultimately of one Canadian [Isaac Kandel] was approved but mainly because he was directly associated with Columbia University and not because of his nationality.[82]

F. N. Freeman, one of the members nominated by SCAP, was also Canadian. This fact must have escaped the attention of Gen. MacArthur at the time. Behind SCAP's intention of insisting on only American educational representatives on the Mission was the need to show American superiority over the Allied Powers. It was not only Gen. MacArthur's personal ambition in connection with his desire to run for president, that resulted in this chauvinistic attitude, but also consideration of the potential for confusion in a Germany administered by four Allied Powers.

In the matter of the naming of the Mission, the majoriy of educators were in favor of calling it an "Advisory Group" because they thought "Mission " carried diplomatic and Christian connotations. On the other hand, SCAP insisted on "Mission" because it considered that the title "Advisory Group" would not carry enough authority to influence the Japanese. Consequently, it was decided to call it a "Mission,"[83] after which other delegations of experts to Japan were named likewise.

This chapter has discussed the process of organizing the Education Mission in the CI&E, from the initial idea to the Mission's final structure. It has also pointed out the fact that the original idea for the Mission to Japan was discussed and developed in the U.S. before the Japanese surrender, and was developed out of postwar policies for German education reform.

A recent interview with Gordon T. Bowles revealed that the CI&E staff was well aware that the plan for the Education Mission to Germany had already been discussed in America.[84] Moreover, behind the plan for the Mission to Japan was the strong request from the Japanese. As a matter of fact, Tamon Maeda, Minister of Education, felt strongly that Japanese education reform should be achieved by the Japanese themselves rather than through the orders of the Occupation.[85] Accordingly, the Japanese authorities drew up plans to organize the Kyoiku Seido Sasshin Iinkai (Reform Committee for the Educational System) to implement education reform for the new era before receiving the memorandum from GHQ on the Education Mission. However, before this committee could begin to function, GHQ decided on its policy for education reform, assisted by the Mission. Hence the committee never materialized.[86]

In conclusion, the organization of the Mission can be said to have been the joint achievement of the State Department and SCAP.

2
ADVANCE PREPARATIONS

I. The Washington Meetings: Implementation of the Draft for Reform in Accordance with the Potsdam Declaration

As seen in the previous chapter, the Mission requested by SCAP was organized under the initiative of the State Department. Candidates for the Mission who lived on the East Coast and those involved within the government gathered in Washington to commence preparations. These were called the Washington meetings. Similar meetings had been held during the planning stages of the Education Mission and the U.S. Social Studies Committee sent to Germany.

On January 30, 1946, the State Department decided to proceed in accordance with the list of candidates organized by Gordon T. Bowles. Several meetings were held after Stoddard accepted the appointment of chairman of the Mission on February 7. According to the records of the Washington Meeting, which is referred to in all the documents relating to the Mission, such as the Stoddard Papers, meetings were held on February 7, 8, 18, and 20. Thus, preparations began in Washington, before the Mission's departure. These meetings were held to explain the basic policy on Japanese education during the Occupation.

In 1944 and 1945 the basic intention of the State Department was a limited change to the Japanese education system. This approach was based on the views of Joseph Ballantine, Eugene Dooman, and Joseph C. Grew, all of whom had lived in Japan. Their analysis was that liberal and democratic tendencies in Japanese education had slowly developed before the rise of militarism and ultranationalism in the 1930s.[1] The Potsdam Declaration took this into consideration.

The people in charge of policy making in the State Department recognized the existence of democratic tendencies in prewar Japan and therefore attached great importance to "the revival and strengthening" of these democratic tendencies, as stated in the Potsdam Declaration. However, the Potsdam Declaration did not include any article relating specifically to education. On the other hand, in the case of postwar Germany, the Potsdam Agreement concluded on August 2, 1945, by leaders of the U.S. Britain, and the Soviet Union contained an article specifically relating to education: "German education shall be so controlled as completely to eliminate Nazi and militarist doctorines and to make possible the successful development of democratic ideas."

The State Department affirmed that its basic intention in formulating the policy document on Japanese education reform was in accordance with the provisions of the Potsdam Declaration.[2] The basic policy was drawn up by Gordon T. Bowles. On July 30, 1945, he produced a tentative draft, "Politico-Military Problems in the Far East: The Post Surrender of the Military Government of the Japanese Empire, the Educational System," in which he specified and emphasized the necessity of Japanese cooperation:

> Although *changes in the educational system can only become permanent as they are carried out by the Japanese themselves* it should be the purpose of Military Government to initiate reforms through cooperative Japanese to a point where they can be continued without external assistance. [Author's italics][3]

On the basis of this draft, on December 6, 1945, Hugh Borton, a central figure in formulating the Occupation policy toward postwar Japanese education in the State Department, produced "The Educational System in Japan" (known as the Borton Memo). In this memorandum he concluded:

> Through the elimination of objectionable features and introduction of desired reforms, education in Japan should be modified, developed, and utilized as to afford the maximum possible contribution and assistance in the attainment of the basic objectives of the United Nations. . . .
>
> *Since reforms which are considered desirable in Japanese education will not become permanent unless the Japanese pursue them out of a conviction of their desirability, as far as possible they should be instituted in such a manner as to insure their acceptance.* Among the specific reforms which appear most likely to accomplish the purposes listed [above] are the following:
>
> 1. A greater degree of equality in educational opportunities regardless of sex, social position or economic status.
>
> 2. An increase in the number of secondary and higher educational institu-

tions and a modification of the present examination system to permit more opportunities for promotion.

3. Greater decentralization of the educational system and authoritarian governmental controls to stimulate educational freedom and independence.

4. Assistance and encouragement to private education and educational institutions of a liberal character and the raising of their standards so that graduates can receive equal treatment in the securing of Government positions.

5. The establishing of liberal methods of teacher training and special encouragement to institutions training teachers to comprehend the principles of democracy.

6. Progressive and liberal teaching techniques should be encouraged, especially those which will develop an analytical, critical and scientific attitude in learning.

7. Encouragement to coeducation and to a greater employment of women throughout the educational system.

8. Increased opportunities for adult education along liberalized lines. [Author's italics][4]

Thus, Borton warned that the Japanese initiative should be respected and that education reform under the Occupation must not be forced on Japan, as Bowles had also mentioned in his draft.

As can be seen from the above, the effect of the Potsdam Declaration was reflected in the guidelines drawn up for the Mission. According to Bowles, his draft and Borton's memorandum were handed over to the Mission and became the basis for drafting the Report.[5]

This chapter will describe the process of discussion concerning the framework of the Report, as well as the basic policy of the Mission, by examining the agenda of the major preparatory meetings, which are recorded in the records of the Washington Meeting.

The first meeting took place on February 8, 1946, chaired by Bowles, and was attended by six Mission members and four members of the government. The members of the Mission were G. D. Stoddard, W. E. Givens, H. Benjamin, F. G. Hochwalt, R. P. Stewart, and G. F. Zook (who was a candidate at that time but withdrew from the final list on February 18 and later became the chairman of the U.S. Education Mission to Germany). Representing the State Department, in addition to Bowles, were W. Stone, Director, Office of International Information and Cultural Affairs (OIC); E. Anderson, European Affairs Officer, Division of Occupied Areas, Office of International Information and Cultural Affairs (later State Department representative to the U.S. Education Mission to Germany); and H. Borton, Japanese Department, Far Eastern Section. These ten people discussed the basic policy of the Mission.

At this first meeting, Zook stressed the necessity of Japanese cooperation:

> It does seem very clear to me that we must work with some group over there,
> because as has already been said if we were simply to figure out a report and
> leave it behind for them to pick up, it is entirely possible they wouldn't pick
> it up at all, and it is possible they wouldn't pick up in the way they might. I
> should think that we ought to try to secure the organization of a group which
> would be continuing thereafter and would have a function thereafter, because
> neither we nor they are going to do this in a day, and it is going to take a long
> time to put it into practice whatever it is.[6]

Borton stated the aim of the Mission:

> One of the reasons General MacArthur feels that a group of this kind is so
> essential at this time is the fact that up until now a great deal has been done of
> a negative sort [Four Negative Directives Concerning Education]. . . . Now, with
> a school term beginning in April, you are faced with the positive steps that
> have to be taken if this is going to be effective at all.[7]

Benjamin, who had joined the Mission on behalf of J. W. Studebaker,
the U.S. Commissioner of Education, stated the opinion that "if we just
make a statement for conquered peoples, it won't be worth the powder it
would take to blow it to hell."[8] He explained that the aim of the advisory
group to assist SCAP was to provide the necessary materials, advice, and
encouragement to the Japanese to enable them to implement education
reforms themselves, in accordance with their own requirements.

At this meeting it was also agreed that the Mission should be referred
to as an "advisory group."

The second meeting was held on February 18, 1946, when the State
Department announced the final list of members of the Mission at a press
conference. Present at this meeting were J. C. Vincent, Head of the Far
Eastern Section in the State Department, as chairman, five members of
the Mission—G. D. Stoddard (chairman of the Mission), A. J. Stoddard,
I. L. Kandel, C. S. Johnson, and G. T. Bowles—and G. Atcheson (Political
Adviser to SCAP on behalf of the State Department), and Colonel F. T.
Spaulding (former Chief of the Education Bureau of Information and Edu-
cation at the War Department). These men again discussed the basic policy
of the Mission.

First, Vincent stated that the Potsdam Declaration and the SWNCC Papers
were the basic documents relating to the Mission. On the basis of his own
experience of contact with Japanese leaders, he advised that "the main

recommendations or reports would much better come out of Japanese educators with whom you are talking than to come out as something which was a cut and dried plan of this group." Admitting that the basic policy should be decided on by the Mission itself, he expressed his personal opinion:

> You can inspire Japanese educational leaders with whom you come in contact to think on the problem and themselves produce, as a result of the conversations with you people, some kind of a plan for Japanese education in this period. The Japanese, to my mind, have a submerged democratic tendency, but I do not think it is generally recognized. . . . We wouldn't have an ideal educational system to try to transplant in Japan.[9]

Thus he emphasized the necessity of the initiative of Japanese educators. The presence of Col. Spaulding at this meeting needs explaining. On February 5, 1946, the State Department cabled SCAP the following request:

> STATE REQUESTS COMMENT ON PROPOSAL THAT COL. FRANCIS T. SPAULDING NOW TOKYO COME TO WASHINGTON TO ASSIST IN BRIEFING ON MISSION OF COMMITTEE OR IF THIS IMPRACTICABLE SPAULDING JOIN COMMITTEE TOKYO ALONG WITH DR. CHARLES IGLEHART SCAP CIES ADVISER ON EDUCATION AND RELIGION.[10]

In response to this request, a three-man committee was set up: K. R. Dyke (chief of the CI&E), D. R. Nugent (chief of the Education Division of the CI&E), and F. T. Spaulding, who was visiting Japan at that time for the Troop Information and Education Program. He then returned to the U.S. to attend the preparatory meeting in Washington and report the latest information and the intentions of SCAP. At the meeting, he stated:

> The policy has been to make use of the Japanese themselves in making necessary reforms rather than trying to insert those reforms regardless of the Japanese. . . . There are many phases of the Japanese educational system which during the war have been used with extreme potency for propagandistic purposes which might be used with equal potency to democratic ends. It would therefore be of much interest to you to consider whether it would be possible to *reconvert* the Japanese educational system rather than to do away with it and put in another. [Author's italics][11]

This statement can be read as an official request from the CI&E to the Mission to temper its basic attitude. J. C. Trainor assessed the important influence of F. T. Spaulding on the Mission as follows:

The briefings in Washington were most cursory, the most important contribution being made not by any Washington officials but by Colonel Spaulding, himself a national figure in American education, who had just returned from a visit to Tokyo in connection with Troop Information and Education Program. While in Tokyo he had, at the request of General Dyke, Chief of the Civil Information and Education Section, conferred with both General Dyke and Colonel Nugent, then chief of the Education Division and himself later to succeed General Dyke as Chief of the Section. Colonel Spaulding received in Tokyo considerable information regarding the status of Japanese education and the role which the Mission might well play in developments in Japan. It was his clear and incisive reporting to the group prior to its departure from Washington which gave it a sense of direction and mission not possible of acquisition from the vague questions which arose in the minds of the members of the group and the even more vague replies which officials in Washington were able to furnish.[12]

Spaulding described the preparations on the Japanese side for receiving the Mission:

When General Dyke invited the Japanese to set up a commission of their own parallel to this commission, the first move of the Japanese was to name that group entirely from the Ministry of Education. They thought of this group as being concerned with the professional group. General Dyke found that group completely unacceptable, because it was not of decently high caliber. He said they were going to lose face considerably if that was the best they had to name. They withdrew that list and they were retaining about four members from the Ministry of Education. The bulk of their members will be from outside the government entirely and will be largely scholars, businessmen, and lawyers, but prominent citizens who are interested in education, with, I think, a very heavy load of scholarly interest rather than administrative or organizational or democratic interest.[13]

In fact, as one of the conditions for accepting the chairmanship of the Mission, Stoddard strongly recommended setting up a group of Japanese education experts in Japan,[14] and Atcheson described most of the Japanese educators as receptive, including Yoshishige Abe, the Minister of Education.[15] Attention therefore should be drawn to the fact of the existence, so early in the proceedings, of expectations for organizing the Japanese Education Committee as a counterpart of the U.S. Mission.

The next day, February 19, according to the Stoddard Papers, the following items were discussed:

1. A discussion of the mimeographed report which Col. Spaulding brought and of the three secret documents in the possession of Mr. Bowles (the Potsdam Declaration, SWNCC and others). . . .

2. A discussion of the ways of deciding upon the chief or basic questions which this Group will face, e.g., with respect to: language reform, the place of women, the relation between political and educational policy, the meaning of freedom, place of teacher education, the place of vocational education, the effect of the rote memory demand, the effect of a long dependence on rote, the place of the present examination system with its rigid characteristics, analyses of attitudes, the place of youth movements, means of establishing criteria of measurement and evaluation, the place of the family, and the place of religion.[16]

On the following day, February 20, they had another meeting, at which George B. Sansom, who had just returned from Japan, described the problems and characteristics of Japanese education and religion. A former commercial attaché in the British Embassy in Tokyo, he was an authority on the history of Japanese culture. His lecture made the following points:

1. The hard life experienced by students at school and at home.

2. The learning of Japanese language is exceedingly demanding.

3. The existence of a great respect for and interest in learning.

4. The pressure on students and their parents for the students to pass entrance exams for [securing] the limited places in higher education.

5. The lack of academic freedom.

6. Part of educational system can be regarded to be an indoctrination under an authoritarian regime.

7. Particular attention should be paid to private schools.

8. Although the abolition of national Shintoism is correct, the characteristics of the Japanese remain unchanged.

9. The problem is in how to establish increased and better education, in a country faced with economic collapse.

10. Education is too commonly used as an entry into government agencies.[17]

Although details concerning Sansom himself were not recorded in Stoddard's notes on the meeting, Sansom had been in Japan from December 6, 1945, to February 13, 1946, and had kept a diary recording details of the Japanese situation at that time. For example, he wrote that on January 28, 1946, he had a meeting with K. R. Dyke, chief of the CI&E, and H. C. Henderson, chief of the Education Division of the CI&E. Concerning them, he wrote:

I do not think they realized how deeply rooted and how strong is the Japanese intellectual tradition: They seem to think that Japan can be supplied with a new system of education as a tailor might furnish a new suit. . . . I cannot think that his [Dyke] previous career fits him very well for his present post—Director of Advertising—possible preliminaries to a task of such difficulty. . . . I cannot feel that he [Henderson] is really suited for a revision of a national policy of education. In fact, education in the United States today is not of such a quality as to encourage one in feeling that it provides a good model for any other country.[18]

It is easy to conjecture that these impressions, coupled with his criticism, give some idea of the real situation within the CI&E.

We see from the above proceedings that only nine Mission members actually attended the Washington meetings. For this reason skepticism was expressed with regard to the statement in the foreword to the Report that "before starting for Japan *the majority of the Committee* met in Washington for preliminary conferences" (author's italics). However, we should not overlook the statement that those who were not able to attend the meetings did some individual preparation. The foreword also states: "They were given a large amount of valuable background information about Japan, both past and present, by members of the State Department and by others with special knowledge. *Similar conferences were held by other members of the committee*" (author's italics).[19] For example, we see from the case of E. B. Woodward, who received an invitation to join the Mission on February 8, that she visited the State Department on February 20, and worked intensively for the next five days. She recalls that for those five days she studied all the papers given to her and took notes, just like "a university candidate preparing for an examination."[20]

According to her record, it was necessary to travel in Japan by train, first class, and stay at first-class hotels, such as the Imperial Hotel. This was only allowed to ranks higher than that of colonel; the status of the Mission members was therefore temporarily "promoted" to that of "brigadier general." And when the members appeared at the War Department, at the Pentagon, for photographs, vaccination, and registration of fingerprints, they were formally issued with passports and ID cards. In the event, their status was that of both an educator and a "brigadier general," which can be confirmed from the members' personal records.

According to the diary of W. C. Trow, who was staying at the Hotel Martinique for the Washington meetings, on February 22 he was appointed chairman of Subcommittee II by G. D. Stoddard until they were joined by F. N. Freeman from San Francisco.[21] This subcommittee was supposed to discuss "Psychology in the Re-Education of Japan."

Staying in Washington was important for Trow himself; he had a meeting with Spaulding, who played an important role in the second meeting, and obtained important information, especially concerning the internal affairs of the CI&E. Spaulding commented that the idea of sending the advisory group to Japan was significant and that it would be able to make concrete recommendations within a short period. He also said that it would be possible to give liberal Japanese educators the confidence, as well as the position, to implement these recommendations.

As a matter of fact, Trow was a cousin of Spaulding's, who at that time was Dean of the Department of Education at Harvard University and was to assume the office of New York State Commissioner of Education, succeeding G. D. Stoddard, on July 1, 1946. Trow spent the weekend after their meeting studying the materials and drawing up a plan for the subcommittee. His diary states that Stoddard suggested assigning all members to subcommittees in Washington, not on Guam, as generally believed.

As described above, at the three preparatory meetings in Washington the Mission members actively discussed assisting the Japanese in response to Japanese requirements, based on the basic policy of the Mission, in accordance with the Potsdam Declaration, which specified "the revival and strengthening of democratic tendencies." In other words, the basic attitude was to encourage the initiative of the Japanese themselves and respect Japanese independence, rather than deliver one-sided recommendations for education reforms.

Before the Mission members left Washington, Assistant Secretary of State William Benton, who was responsible for organizing the Mission, emphasized to the members that "their task was primarily to provide ideas and suggest ways in which the goals of the Allies as expressed in the Potsdam Declaration could be realized."[22]

II. The Hawaii Meetings: Reform Proposals in the "Hawaiian Notes"

On February 26, having completed the preparatory meetings in Washington, the members left, and the following day the rest of the members joined them in San Francisco. Seventeen members took off for Honolulu that day and arrived there on February 28. The others left San Francisco on February 28 and arrived in Honolulu on March 1.[23]

As stated in the foreword to the Report, "On the trip out a helpful consultation was held with a number of well informed persons at Honolulu." The members had opportunities to hear lectures by Japanese Americans, as well as by pro-Japanese Americans who had lived in Japan, on the characteristics of Japanese education and various areas which needed to be reformed. They also visited schools in Hawaii.[24]

The Hawaiian meetings were organized by Bowles and Givens, who had both lived there, and were mentioned by Givens at the Washington meeting on February 8.[25] Givens had been the Hawaii Commissioner of Education in the 1920s,[26] and Bowles had taught at the University of Hawaii;[27] Bowles's father had also been living there as a missionary at the time.

Until recently, due to the restrictions on historical documents, the details of the Hawaiian meetings were not revealed. In fact, in the opinion of one researcher, these meetings were not influential.[28] The "Hawaiian Notes," consisting of material from the lectures on Japanese education, provided the basis of the preparatory meetings on Guam. Until recently only part of the "Hawaiian Notes" had been discovered, in the Gildersleeve Papers, but due to a recent search for historical documents the entire "Hawaiian Notes" was discovered in the Horton Papers.[29] On the cover page to twenty-five pages of notes is printed the title "Education in Japan: Some Suggestions for Consideration Prepared at the University of Hawaii by Professors with Previous Teaching Experiences in Japanese Schools and Colleges."

In the introduction to the Notes, providing a general overview, we find a piece entitled "Comments on Japanese Education," which analyzes Japanese education, comments on its basic problems, and suggests proposals to be discussed:

> Despite the fact that of recent years Japanese education has been subject to the control of military Ministers of Education, it must be remembered that the Japanese have a fairly old and well-developed educational system. It has been influenced by European, American, and Chinese concepts of education; but has been, as are all school systems, adapted to fit the people's cultural needs. This means that, in addition to teaching reading, writing, and arithmetic, the elementary grades have also stressed Japan's long history, Confucian family ethics and military Spartanism.

The Notes include eight lectures on Japanese education: "Memoranda on Japanese General Education," by Edwin S. Dozier; "Education in Japan," by Yukio Kimura (War Research Laboratory, Department of Sociology, University of Hawaii); "Comments on Education in Japan," by Ernest S. Fujinaga (a Japanese American); "Concerning Education in Japan," by Alberta Tarr (Director of Christian Education, South King Methodist Church, Honolulu); "Notes on the Reconstruction of the Japanese Educational System," by Gilbert Bowles; "Five Suggestions on Most General Policy for Educational Reconstruction in Japan," by E. V. Sayers (a lecturer at the University of Hawaii with experience of teaching English in a Japanese girls' missionary school); "An Approach to the Problem of Education in Japan," by Laura Thompson (a special representative at the Institute of Ethical Problems, Washington, D.C.); and "Comments and Suggestions," by Oren E. Long.

All the suggestions in these lectures are worthy of attention. For example, Dozier explained, at the beginning of his lecture, that it was prepared for the advisory group to Gen. MacArthur and pointed to the problem with the Imperial Rescript on Education by referring to its official English translation. He suggested the necessity for seriously considering the expansion of general education prior to creating specialized courses for the development of individual initiative, at the same time introducing liberal and progressive educational methods, reforming the school calendar, and reconsidering the strict entrance examinations for high schools. He also explained the existing structure of the Japanese education system and summarized the situation of elementary schools, middle schools, girls' schools, technical colleges (*senmon gakko*), and universities.[30] Thus, the members learned about the Japanese 6–5 school system, which became an important subject in discussions of the reform of the education system.

Kimura discussed the Japanese national sentiment against the atomic bombing of Hiroshima and Nagasaki. He explained that the Japanese naturally thought it was wrong, and that some Japanese leaders thought Japan's defeat could have been brought about without it. In regard to the re-education of the Japanese, he suggested the introduction of articles on Japan written by foreigners, which he believed would be effective and important in helping the Japanese to understand themselves objectively and to develop respect for other nations, as well as to value other cultures. In this context he stressed the need to introduce sociology and anthropology. He also referred to the importance of adult education in the achievement of democratic school education, which would inevitably require parents' cooperation in educating their children in the same way at home. From this point of view, he suggested adult education through the use of newspapers and magazines, without the necessity for attending classes. He even mentioned prewar girls' education.[31]

Fujinaga stated that "to offset and possibly neutralize this tendency to return to their old ways are the recent actions of the Emperor, who, more than any other one person, can contribute towards democratizing Japan."[32]

Tarr, who had taught English in Japan (1934–41), pointed out some central problems within Japanese education, such as the neglect of individual differences in ability, skill, or needs, the inappropriate content of physical education, the insufficient number of middle schools, and the reliance on learning by rote.[33]

The most noteworthy suggestion was made by Gilbert Bowles (father of Gordon T. Bowles), who had been sent to prewar Japan as a missionary. He suggested "the need for a bridge between the old and the new— utilization of all that is inherently valuable in the former system of education."[34]

Sayers listed the five suggestions:

1. A positive program of education for democracy
2. Education for a discipline in democratic processes
3. Education for rehabilitation
4. Thorough preparation of teachers for democratic schools
5. A clear policy regarding personnel[35]

His lecture is dated February 23, 1946, which means that all the lectures were prepared in advance of the Hawaii meetings of the Mission.

L. Thompson indicated "three points for the Committee's consideration": the Japanese social system, Japanese individual education, and the Japanese value system. She directed the members' attention to the necessity for recognizing the differences between Japan and the U.S.: "We cannot make Americans out of the Japanese, but we can, if we will, work toward making them into good world citizens and their society into the kind of social structure which fits and ties into the new flexible and democratic world order in process of creation."[36]

Finally, addressing the problems of Japanese behavior patterns and thought, Long advocated the appropriateness of modifying them by formulating an "Education Edict" describing a norm of desirable behavior. Even if based on a democratic foundation, this approach would appear undesirable. Long went on to say that though these problems were present within the Japanese education system, the existing system could be used to a certain degree, and proposed that its reform be carried out after the example of education in Hawaii, with which many Japanese teachers were familiar.[37]

As a matter of fact, an opinion existed that "there would be a distinct advantage in using Nisei," that the Mission should have engaged Japanese Americans more widely, and that the University of Hawaii should have been given the opportunity to contribute to Japanese education reform.[38]

The Horton Papers include another important document, a one-page undated document entitled "Suggestions for the Educational Mission to Japan," which listed fourteen proposals for Japanese education. One of the important proposals was the necessity of obtaining voluntary cooperation from Japanese educational leaders. This proposal stated that the most effective democratic approach to the re-education of the Japanese was through its own school system. The document as a whole emphasized the development of existing Christian institutions and colleges for women in Japan.[39]

At the press conference in Hawaii, W. E. Givens, as the official editor of the report for Committee III, stated the attitude of the Mission toward its visit to Japan: "You cannot impose an educational system on anybody. . . . How Japan administers her schools must be decided by her people." This speech was reported in *The Nippon Times* just before to the Mission's arrival in Japan under the headline, "Japanese to Decide Own School Setup by Dr. Willard Givens."[40]

The preparatory meetings in Hawaii, mainly organized for lectures, differed from the meetings in Washington and Guam. However, it can be said that these lectures contributed greatly to the Mission's need to confirm its basic policy, which had been discussed in Washington, and gave the members information concerning actual Japanese education. Stoddard named the collected lecture notes the "Hawaiian Notes" at the meeting on Guam,[41] and classified them as being as important as the SWNCC document, and as basic to the discussion on Japanese thought and motivation.

III. *The Guam Meeting: Preparation for Drafting the Report and Organizing Subcommittees*

The Mission left Honolulu in two groups on March 1, 1946, and arrived in Guam via Johnston Island and Kwajalein by the evening of the following day (March 3, local time).

One group stayed on Guam until March 5, and the other was delayed until March 7 due to bad weather in the Tokyo area.[42] As described in the Foreword to the Report, "Also the group was able, during its stay at Guam, and through other interim conferences, to make a preliminary analysis of the task that confronted it."

On the basis of the meeting on Guam, Stoddard produced a paper for the members entitled "On Preparing the Report." In this paper he explained eight points concerning the preparatory work for drafting the Report. In particular, he indicated the importance of defining the problems and actual conditions of prewar Japanese education to study of the effects of the defeat and Occupation on the Japanese. He also discussed the need for reviewing SCAP's directives and clarifying and utilizing "the long-time trends that are discernible."[43] This did not mean simply maintaining the Japanese sense of values but discovering qualities of initiative and vision within the Japanese character, in accordance with the Potsdam Declaration. He stated that as the basic document for the Mission, the "Hawaiian Notes" would be helpful in motivating the Japanese.[44]

In addition, it is clear that he wished to avoid coercing the Japanese as much as possible. For instance, in the "Must Items," an article urging the Japanese to implement reforms, he proposed that those items be restricted to a minimum and also that the greater part of the educational program be decided by the Japanese themselves. At the same time, he emphasized that essential items should be cited as clearly and as straightforwardly as possible in the Report.

In regard to the proceedings for drafting the Report, he proposed that the chairman of each subcommittee convene its members as soon as possible in order to study all the notes and materials available at that time and to start drafting a "dummy" report based on these studies.[45] In addition, he proposed a chairman for each subcommittee and its related area of research, as follows:

Committee I (A. J. Stoddard, Chairman)

The general structure, taxes, finance, control, laws, edicts, supervision, construction, types of programs, teacher needs. As I see it, it will be a Ways and Means Committee. How do you get what you want, how do you pay for it, how do you keep it going?

Committee II (F. N. Freeman, Chairman)

The changing attitudes; the conditions of acceptance. This Committee is a *psychological* Ways and Means. It has prepared a tentative draft.

Committee III (I. L. Kandel, Chairman)

This Committee has a draft on the main issues. Language reform is one, together with the types of materials in the curriculum and the underlying philosophy. This Committee may work from the top down. For example, Imperial Rescript. If we need a charter or rescript we should produce one.

Committee IV (G. Diemer, Chairman)

This Committee deals with two great problems (1) teacher education and (2) liberal and advanced education.[46]

In the above list, it should be noticed that Committees II and III had already drawn up their drafts. As indicated by W. C. Trow's memoirs, the draft of Committee II may have been prepared in Washington by Trow himself.

Referring to the drafting of the Report, Stoddard stated: *"The Report will be started at our first meeting in Tokyo."* He added: "In a sense, we could write a report now, but it would be hastily prepared and very bad."[47] Thus, he indicated that the Mission began drafting the Report immediately after its arrival in Japan. He also hinted that the preparation for drafting the Report progressed rapidly at the Guam meeting.

In order to carry out the assigned tasks effectively and organize the members in subcommittee after their arrival, he proposed that each member be responsible for drafting reports on specific subjects as follows:

A. J. Stoddard: organization and administration in the cities

Eby: labor education

Givens: teachers' associations and non-governmental agencies

Hochwalt: private education and religious freedom

Norton/Wannamaker: organization and administration at the prefectural level; how related downward to the cities and towns, and upward to the National System

Freeman/Hilgard/Trow: attitude, methods, motivation, intellectual
 freedom
Benjamin: maintaining (?) new concepts of freedom
Johnson: family studies, race attitudes, vocational education
Woodward: forum, adult education
Kandel/Carnovsky/Bowles/Counts/Smith: language reform, experiences
 in other countries
McCloy: health and physical education
Diemer/Deferrari/Compton/G. D. Stoddard/Stevens: teacher education;
 universities
Gildersleeve/Horton: advanced education for women[48]

As can be seen from this list, preparations for drafting the Report were set
in motion at the Guam meeting. Stoddard's enthusiasm for visiting Japan
was also reflected at this stage of the proceedings.

The Mission arrived in Tokyo by air in two groups, on March 5 and
March 7, at which time it was officially designated the U.S. Education
Mission to Japan.

This chapter has investigated the Mission's advance preparations, focusing on the meetings held in Washington, in Hawaii and on Guam. It
has also pointed out that the Mission's basic attitude throughout these
preparations was that all education reforms should be accomplished on
the Japanese initiative and in accordance with the provisions of the Potsdam Declaration.

3
ACTIVITIES OF THE MISSION AND ITS JAPANESE COUNTERPART

I. The Mission's Arrival

After the preparatory meetings in Washington and Hawaii and on Guam, the first group of the Mission landed at Atsugi Air Force Base on a military plane on March 5, 1946, ten days after leaving Washington.

The Mission members were invited to luncheon parties hosted by Gen. MacArthur at the American Emabassy in Tokyo in two separate groups, on March 6 and March 8. Gen. MacArthur delivered speeches describing the situation in Japan and stating the aims of both SCAP and the Mission.[1] Then he asked the Mission to recommend both long-range and short-range education plans and submit these to him directly in a confidential report before returning to the U.S. He told the Mission members that any immediately applicable recommendations would be implemented in the new academic year commencing in April.

Gen. MacArthur's fluency and eloquence, coupled with his extensive knowledge, made a good impression on many of the Mission members.[2] In a personal record of the party, Woodward wrote that "General MacArthur talked freely, but when asked if he had any suggestions for the group about our assignment, he said, 'No indeed, education is not my field, you make the recommendations—I will look after their implementation.' "[3] D. H. Stevens recorded that Gen. MacArthur told the members that he relied on the Mission entirely on education issues, and expected high-level recommendations in their report, regardless of the financial aspect. He also wrote: "On the proposal for the new constitution, he said they were products of joint Japanese and American work but would be put into Japanese form and language during the debate in the New Diet.

He added that the conferring group had accepted his requests to them on education—to treat women on an equality with men, and to make all compulsory education free."[4]

II. *Preparations within the Education Division of the CI&E*

On February 1, when the Mission was being organized by the State Department, D. R. Nugent, chief of the Education Division of the CI&E, ordered Major E. H. Farr to assign officers in the Education Division to four committees, to correspond to the committee in the Mission. Accordingly, on February 15 he organized the committees as follow:

Committee I: Education for Democracy in Japan (Cmdr. Wunderlich, Office in Charge, OIC)

  Content of Courses: Cmdr. Wunderlich

  Curricula: Cmdr. Wunderlich

  Textbooks: Cmdr. Wunderlich

  Teacher's Manuals: Capt. Griffith

  Visual and Auditory Aids: Major Orr

Committee II: Psychology in the Re-Education of Japan (Capt. Barnard, OIC)

  Methodology: Capt. Barnard

  Language Revision: Cmdr. Hall (Korea)

  Timing & Priority of Education Reforms: Capt. Barnard

  Development of Student Initiative & Critical Analysis: Capt. Barnard

  Reorientation of Teachers (Independent & Teachers College): Capt. Barnard

Committee III: Administrative Reorganization of the Japanese Education System (Cmdr. Hall, OIC, Major Arrowood, Acting OIC)

  Administrative Reorganization of the Ministry of Education: Comdr. Hall

  Elementary School: Lt. Gibson

  Kindergarten: Lt. Gibson

  Middle Schools for Girls: Capt. Donovan

  Middle Schools for Boys: Lt. McBride

  Youth Schools: Major Arrowood

  Koto Gakko (Jr. Coll): Lts. Daly and George

  Physical Education: Major Norivel

  Who's Who in Japanese Education: Major Noviel

Committee IV: Higher Education in the Rehabilitation of Japan (Comdr. Crofts, OIC)

  Universities: Cmdr. Crofts and Prof. Del Re

  Semmon Gakko (Independent Colleges—Education Department): Cmdr. Crofts

Women's Colleges: Capt. Donovan
Libraries: Cmdr. Crofts (Mr. Keeny)[5]

As can been seen, these officers were assigned a considerable amount of work. A memorandum to the officers from Maj. Farr dated February 15 ordered them to prepare one-hour lectures on their assigned subject for the Mission.[6]

The officers prepared their lectures with the cooperation of Japanese Tokiomi Kaigo and other scholars, as well as the Japanese Education Committee. Tetsuichi Sawato, a member of the Japanese Education Committee, recorded that they were invited by the CI&E to assist it almost every day. He recalled those days as follows:

> We were invited to the Office of the Education Division of the CI&E. At the beginning they asked questions about the present situation in each area of education, based on materials which they had collected. In this way, we started to cooperate with them in the preparation of their lectures for the Mission. I was invited by Major Orr of Committee I, Capt. Barnard of Committee II, and Lt. McBride of Committee III to explain issues of secondary education from all aspects.[7]

Another member of the Japanese Education Committee, Sanji Aruga, was also questioned about youth schools and national lower primary schools (*kokumin gakko*), by Major Arrowood on February 28 and March 4. In his answers, Aruga expressed his desire for the promotion of youth schools:

> I hope those who are not able to attend secondary schools after finishing their primary education are admitted to youth schools. I believe it is important that the education of working-class youth be made part of the mainstream within the education system.[8]

As a part of the preparations for the Mission, the Education Division of the CI&E published an important booklet, *Education in Japan*, on February 15, 1946. This was a revised and expanded edition of *Supervision and Control of the Education System of Japan: A Tentative Brochure*, drafted on January 8, 1946.[9]

The contents of *Education in Japan* are as follows:

Part I: The Educational System of Japan (Prior to 15 August 1945)

1. History of Japanese Education; 2. Supervision of Educational System (1937); 3. The School System; 4. Educational Finance; 5. Teachers; 6. Shinto in Schools; 7. Textbooks; 8. Physical Education; 9. School Inspection; 10. Special Education Media; 11. Women's Education; 12. Adult Education; 13. Private Schools; 14. Civil Service and Court Rank; 15. Reform Movements; 16. War-time Changes

Part II: Allied Control of Japanese Education
  1. Organization of GHQ, SCAP; 2. Present Organization of the Ministry of Education; 3. Voluntary Reform by the Ministry of Education; 4. Basic Education Policies; 5. Implementation of Basic Policies; 6. Compliance with Education Directives; 7. Education Mission from the United States[10]

The foreword of the booklet quotes the Potsdam Declaration: "The Japanese Government shall remove all obstacles to the revival and strengthening of democratic tendencies among the Japanese people. Freedom of speech, of religion and of thought, as well as respect for the fundamental human rights, shall be established. (The Potsdam Declaration, 26 July 1945)"

The foreword states that the aims of education are in accordance with the Potsdam Declaration and specifies the purpose of publishing the booklet: "This brochure on *Education in Japan* has been compiled as an information handbook for members of the American Education Mission and for education officers throughout Japan."

This booklet has been evaluated as "one of the source books with which the Mission formulated its Report" and as having "induced the Mission to compile its ideas for the report."[11] However, it is clear from the above statement that the booklet was intended to provide information to the Mission, not to "induce" it.[12] Orr, who, as a staff member of the Education Division, produced the booklet, and Bowles, who used it during the Mission, have testified that it was not the booklet that influenced the ideas of the Mission in formulating the Report.[13]

In producing the booklet, the Education Division of the CI&E obtained support from the Ministry of Education in order to offer the Mission accurate information on education in Japan.[14]

An historical document concerning the staff study was discovered recently among the Robert K. Hall Papers. Hall was on the staff of the Education Division of the CI&E. According to this document, the Education Division commenced preparing *Education in Japan* on November 12, 1945, when the plan to invite the Mission had already been confirmed. Initially, the title of the booklet was *Brochure for Education Commission*.[15] The process of its composition was as follows:

Subject: Brochure for Education Commission
12 Nov.: First outline for brochure completed.

14 Nov.: Conference with liaison person from the Ministry of Education Re: Materials wanted from the Ministry of Education.

15 Nov.: Survey of Materials in office for information that could be used in brochure.

16 Nov.: Conference (Lt. Fisher) with Father Bitter of Catholic Univ. Re: List of outstanding educators in Japan and Japanese education in general.

17 Nov.: Conference (Lt. Fisher) with Prof. Del Re concerning list of educators and materials that he might have about education in Japan.

19 Nov.: Conference (Lt. Fisher) with Prof. Ianaga [Ienaga] of Ministry of Education Re: List of outstanding Japanese educators.

20 Nov.: Outline for brochure revised in conjunction with Maj. Orr.

21 Nov.: Conference (Lt. Fisher) with Lt. E. C. Shirk of Anal. and Research Sec. concerning materials.

23 Nov.: Visited bookstore (Lt. Fisher) Kyobunkan—looking for materials. Some materials published by Kokusai Bunka Shinkokai received.

24 Nov.: Conference (Lt. Fisher) with Lt. Clark of Planning Section Re: Youth movements.

26 Nov.: Conference (Lt. Fisher) with Capt. Williams of Govt. Section Re: Materials on education in Japan. Received a lengthy list of Japanese educators from him. This list along with other information on Japanese educators turned over to Col. Nugent who is com[p]iling the list of Japanese educators.

27 Nov.: Conference (Lt. Fisher) with Cmdr. Wunderlich and Cpt. Barnard Re: Materials on curricula and teacher training.

28 Nov.: In conjunction with Lt. Shirk had conference with Mr. Fukuda and Mr. Teranishi of Ministry of Education Re: Progress of their work relating to tables and statistics wanted for brochure.

29 Nov.: Certain sub-section to be placed in brochure written up in longhand.

30 Nov.: Visited office of Kokusai Bunka Shinkokai in search of materials. Lt. Shirk assigned certain section to "write up."

1 Dec.: Received copy of "Ministry of Japanese Education" by Keenleyside and Thomas, from Prof. Del Re.

3 Dec.: Certain section written up in longhand.
(Preparation of a brochure on Japanese education ... provide material for adequate briefing of the Education Commission)

The above record shows that the booklet was prepared in cooperation with the Government Section of GHQ and the Ministry of Education from an early stage. It also confirms that it was prepared as a reference for the appropriate briefing of the Mission.

Moreover, the draft of part two, "Allied Control of Japanese Education," was taken to the U.S. by F. T. Spaulding for the Washington meetings and is in the Stoddard Papers along with his own handwritten comments.[16] Thus, *Education in Japan* fulfilled its role of providing information on Japanese education even before the Mission went to Japan.

III. Orientation Lectures by the Staff of the Education Division

Day 1 (March 7): At the first general meeting of the Mission in Tokyo, held in the Peers' Club, D. R. Nugent, acting chief of the CI&E, gave an address on behalf of K. R. Dyke, chief of the CI&E, who was on home leave, describing Japanese education under the Occupation and the various problems confronting the CI&E:

> We here have been facing a task that is stupendous by any method of measurement. We are also facing a condition, and not a theory. Many of us have educational training, to be sure. Many of us have some educational experience: not as broad, of course, as that of the members of the Mission. We know something about education, yet in the reform or rehabilitation of the educational system of some 19 million students, between 400,000 and 500,000 teachers and approximately 50,000 schools, we are pretty humble when faced with such a task.

He then stated the method of procedure in general meetings and subcommittees:

> During the first six or seven days, the officers of CIE will attempt to give you such material in the form of lectures, graphs, etc., which will orientate you to those problems as we see them. We offer no solutions. We offer no suggestions. Each of our officers has been assigned the task of collecting materials in [a] certain field. When he presents that [*sic*] materials to you, he is presenting data which has been collected on behalf of the Education Division. Each of these officers will talk to you, not as an individual, but as a representative of the Education Division of CIE.... We are attempting to contribute toward your study not personal opinion but facts, objective data, and counsel where requested....
>
> We feel we cannot superimpose on the Japanese any ready-made, imported educational system. We feel that any ideas we bring with us must be modified and adapted to the Japanese way of life. We hope to modify that way of life into a democratic process.... We must not at any time feel that this is a field for experiment, because, as I see it, what we do now will be reflected for years to come in Japan.[17]

In this manner, he emphasized the importance of long-range education reform and asked for the support of the Mission toward this goal.

After this speech, Maj. E. H. Farr explained the organization of GHQ/SCAP and the task of the CI&E in his speech, "Explanation of Organization of GHQ/SCAP and the Occupation Objectives as They Pertain to the Education Mission." He then introduced the staff of the Education Division.

Day 2 (March 8): 9:00–11:00 A.M.: Yoshishige Abe, the Minister of Education, delivered a speech, "Address to the U.S. Education Mission," after which he introduced the members of the Japanese Education Committee. 11:00 A.M.: Stoddard delivered a speech of thanks.

W. E. Givens summarized Abe's speech in his diary, "Tokyo and Return," as follows:

While war is the most deplorable and abominable for the human race, we cannot overlook the fact that through war people are brought into closer contact with each other. Actually as a result of our defeat a great number of your countrymen, such as was never seen before, have come to our land. We are to be under the control of your countrymen in everything—in our politics, economy, culture, and education. Although we cannot call it an honor for us, it is yet undeniable that it serves to make our contact with your people more frequent and more profound than ever. In fact, our daily life—mentally and spiritually—has come to be unthinkable without taking into account the influence which your country and your people is exercising upon it. . . . We believe that your country is not going to violate truth and justice on the strength of her being a victor. And we pray that the pressure brought upon by this victory—for we cannot help feeling it as pressure—will help to make truth and justice permeate all our country, and serve as a chance for us to eliminate quickly and vigorously all the injustices and defects existing in our society and all the weaknesses and evils underlying our national character and customs. . . . In a word, we wish to render as significantly as possible this opportunity to come in contact with your country and your people—an opportunity that was brought to us through the war—and we shall be happy if we could do this not only through our own efforts but also through the good will and assistance that may still be granted to us by your country, victor as it is. As you may guess, it is a severe trial and a hard task to be a defeated country and a defeated people, but if I may say so, it must also a very difficult thing to be a good victor.[18]

The Mainichi Shinbun of March 9, reported Abe's speech under the headline "The First Conference of Japanese Educators and the U.S. Education Mission: Minister's View to Promote Our Own Virtue, Gave a Good Impression."[19] The article summarized the minister's speech as follows:

We believe that your people do not assume the attitude that the winner is always right and the loser wrong. As Japanese, we will turn our trials to our advantage. The war and the Japanese defeat were caused by defects in Japanese education and the low educational standards among the common Japanese. However, you educators, who are visiting Japan now, must not try to impose ideals on the Japanese educational system which are not yet realized, even in your own country.

This speech was very persuasive. Recalling that time, E. R. Hilgard said that Abe's speech facilitated cooperation between the Mission and the Japanese Education Committee:

In fact, the Minister's speech was truly to "break the ice" in our tension. Even today, after forty years, I still remember his speech very impressively. I remember his point was something like "We here, educators of two countries, are gathering; one is the victor and the other the defeated. Both are shameful. In

breaking off this relationship, we should talk with each other as educators."
From his speech, we just felt that we could talk with Japanese educators. It was
really impressive.[20]

The speech was also reported in *School and Society*. Abe himself wrote
in his autobiography that he had had difficulty preparing the speech.[21]
After Abe's speech, Stoddard gave a speech of thanks:

Mr. Abe has given a warm welcome; as fellow educators he has made us feel
completely at home.

We have not come here to criticize; we have come to study and learn. We
hope that by cooperative endeavor and analysis—by a recognition of the great
educational and social aims which Mr. Abe has so well elucidated—we may
arrive at common understandings. We seek an improved program of education
which will benefit the Japanese people.

In the aggregate, the members of the American Mission embody a wide
educational experience. It is this experience and a search for enlightment that
we bring to you on a cooperative basis.

It may be helpful to reveal a few of our beliefs.

1) We believe in the individual and civil rights of the Japanese people. We
believe that these rights can be widened and strengthened through education.

2) We believe that there is a tremendous potential for freedom and for
individual and social growth in every child, youth and adult.

3) We shall look for what is good in the Japanese educational system. We
shall help our American friends and our Japanese cooperating groups in dis-
carding what is bad in terms of your new declaration of social and civil rights.
In our policy report we shall then try to strengthen what we jointly feel to be
good....

In short, we are here to help in a process of social evolution. We feel that no
group from another country can by itself establish such a program. The Japanese people must carry out these great tasks....

Our hope is that we may study these tasks together, formulating the joint
outcome of our work. We should be able to turn over to Japanese educational
leaders, on a progressive basis, the final responsibility in carrying on a democratic program.[22]

The *Mainichi Shinbun* reported the above speech, which clarified the
basic policy of the Mission, and summarized it as follows:

We have come here not to criticize but to promote that which is good and
discard what is bad, both of which are inherent in the Japanese educational
system. If we succeed in carrying out our "cooperative effort" with Japanese
educators, we may obtain useful lessons not only for Japan but also for the
Allied Powers.

Day 3 (March 10): Morning: The organization of four committees of the Mission was decided. These four committees and two special committees (set up on March 11) were as follows:

Committee I: "Curricula—Textbook[s"]: Chairman, I. L. Kandel; L. Carnovsky; G. S. Counts; C. H. McCloy; T. V. Smith; G. S. Johnson

Committee II: "Teachers' Training—Teaching Methods": Chairmen, G. W. Diemer and F. N. Freeman; H. Benjamin; E. R. Hilgard; W. C. Trow; E. Woodward

Committee III: "General Administration": Chairman, A. J. Stoddard; K. Eby; W. E. Givens; F. G. Hochwalt; E. B. Norton; P. A. Wanamaker

Committee IV: "Higher Education": Chairman, W. M. Compton; R. J. Deferrai; V. C. Gildersleeve; M. M. Horton; D. H. Stevens

Special Committee on Japanese Language: Chairman, G. S. Counts; H. McCloy; D. H. Stevens; W. C. Trow

Special Committee on Drafting: Chairman, G. D. Stoddard; H. Benjamin; G. T. Bowles; V. C. Gildersleeve; I. L. Kandel; T. V. Smith; W. G. Givens[23]

In addition to the above, Stoddard, Andrews, Bowles, and Stewart belonged to all the other committees, in order to support them.

In the afternoon of day three, lectures on the existing situation within Japanese education, which had been prepared by the CI&E staff in cooperation with the Japanese Education Committee, began.[24]

First R. K. Hall presented a lecture entitled "Mombusho" (the Ministry of Education). He explained the administrative system of the Ministry of Education and its history, as well as the Japanese education system. To illustrate the pyramidal structure of Japanese education under the control and supervision of the Ministry of Education, he placed Kyosuke Yamazaki, Assistant Secretary of the Ministry of Education; Governor Uchiyama of Kanagawa Prefecture, people concerned with education, and students from Fujisawa City on one side of the stage. On the other side he placed Shigeru Nambara, the President of Tokyo Imperial University, and students from its Literature Department. Then he outlined the education system in Japan, which was a variant of the French system, revised according to Japanese circumstances. In particular, he pointed out problems in the interpretation of, and approaches to, the Imperial Rescript on Education:

The next great historic milestone in the Japanese educational system was the publication of the Imperial Rescript on Education on 30 October, 1890 by Emperor Meiji. In itself it is an apparently harmless, and even rather progressive and idealistic document. It has, however, been so warped and destroyed by interpretations that the Militaristic tinge clings.

He then explained the organization of the Ministry of Education, along with the diagram reproduced in *Education in Japan,* and listed the following five basic controls exercised by the Ministry of Education:

1) Inspection by national school inspectors of the Ministry of Education.
2) Specific Orders: a) the Imperial Rescript; b) the Law of the Imperial Japanese Government; c) the Imperial Ordinances; d) the Cabinet Order; e) the Bureau Head Order.
3) Finance.
4) [Control] Through services. The Mombusho has provided radio, film, textbook, recordings, and special institutes.
5) Thought control.[25]

Then Lieutenant P. M. MacBride presented a lecture, "Boys' Middle School." He described its position in the Japanese education system, as well as in society:

Only one boy in eight goes to Boys' Middle School in Japan, but the importance of the Middle Schools in the Japanese educational system is much greater than this number would indicate.

Then he stressed:

The importance of the Boys' Middle School lies in the fact that middle school education is almost a pre-requisite for admission to a Japanese school of higher learning. Most of the boys in Japan who go to a college and all the boys who go to a university are graduates of middle school.[26]

At the end of the day Lieutenant G. B. Gibson spoke on the subject "The Yochien and Kokumin Gakko." He explained that kindergarten and elementary schools were similar to their American counterparts in age groups and basic courses of study and methods, as illustrated by the diagram of the education system published in the booklet. He also explained the present situation of administration, finance, the selection of teachers, and so on.[27]

Day 5 (March 11): In the morning Lieutenant Commander Alfred Crofts reported on the subject "Higher Education in Japan." He explained its historical development and geographical distribution in Japan after World War I, using statistical charts and a map of Japan. He also described the methods of university administration used by the Ministry of Education and the varieties of higher education, curricula, facilities, and personnel.[28]

There followed a panel discussion entitled "Curriculum of Japanese Schools" presented by Maj. M. T. Orr and three Japanese (Kotaro Tanaka,

Superintendent of Schools; Tetsuichi Sawato, Headmaster of Toritsu Fifth Middle School; and Toshio Kumura, Superintendent for School Education) and an interpreter, Hideo Kishimoto, an assistant professor at Tokyo Imperial University.[29]

Day 6 (March 12): Capt. Barnard, the only member of the Education Division of the CI&E who had a Ph.D. degree except for R. K. Hall, gave a lecture entitled "Methodology in Japanese Education." He analyzed the present situation of Japanese education in detail and enumerated the following sixteen points in teaching methods:

1) Methods of teaching in Japanese schools are highly standardized.

2) Textbooks form the basis of teaching with the use of a few supplementary materials.

3) Lecturing is a common method used in Japanese schools at all levels.

4) Methods of teaching emphasize the retention of learned subject matter rather than the development of initiative and independent thinking.

5) The nature of the subject matter, coupled with the peculiarities of the written language, make it necessary for teachers to spend too much time explaining the meanings of written passages and individual words.

6) The content of each subject is taught with no conscious effort to correlate it with other subjects.

7) Individual and group discipline are an important aim in the methods of instruction.

8) Japanese children are disciplined to learn and much of their out-of-school time is spent in studying.

9) Copying and learning by rote are common elements in many learning activities.

10) Emphasis is put upon ceremony and form in Japanese education.

11) Attempts have been made to realize the educational value of work activities.

12) Pupil-teacher relations are much more formal than is found in America.

13) Little provision is made for individual differences of students.

14) Learning activities in youth school may be indicative of what can be done when the pressure of standardization is removed.

15) There has been little fundamental experimentation in methods of teaching.

16) There is evidence that, since the end of the war, some teachers have attempted to modify methods of teaching.[30]

After this there was a panel discussion, "Japanese Textbooks." In this discussion Jiro Arimitsu, Chief of the Bureau of Textbooks, Ministry of Education, talked about the jurisdiction of the bureau; the organization, publication, printing, distribution, pricing, and publishers of textbooks; related laws and regulations; the decision-making process, and teachers' manuals.[31]

After the discussion, Comdr. H. J. Wunderlich delivered a lecture entitled "Critique of Textbook Problem," in which he made the following criticism:

> Wartime textbooks used in the schools of Japan have been written and published since 1941. The content and method of organization of these books has been dominated by one central theme, the development of national unity, strength, and expansion. . . .
> All material is organized around the Imperial Rescript on Education of 1890.

As for "the textbook deletion problem," he said:

> SCAP directives have laid down the general pattern for the elimination of militarism, ultra-nationalism, and Shinto Doctrine as a part of the process of achieving the terms of the Potsdam Declaration and the Surrender Terms. The roots of these objectionable materials lie deeply in Japanese legends, myths, and language.

In conclusion, he stated that preparation of new textbooks was urgent, and suggested that "new textbooks, particularly in the field of social studies, will require several years of study and to be written by scholars."[32]

In his lecture, it is worth noting, he used the term "social studies." When he returned to the U.S., he submitted his Ed.D. dissertation, "The Japanese Textbook Problem and Solution," to Stanford University in 1952.[33]

This was followed by a lecture, "The Development of Japanese Textbooks," by Tokiomi Kaigo, an assistant professor at Tokyo Imperial University. He explained the peculiarities of Japanese textbooks as follows:

> In the problem of teaching material, textbooks have a special meaning in Japan. The content of textbooks has an absolute, authoritative position in education. . . . For that reason all educational ideas are concentrated in textbooks for use in the class room. We can find in the text materials, the objectives of curriculum, ideas of instruction, and one can ever see the principles of education. Therefore the main idea on how to educate the youngster is concentrated on the textbook problem, which determines the school education in Japan.

He then enumerated the following five types of textbooks used during the last eighty years:

> 1) Old texts prior to the Meiji Restoration
> 2) Revised modern texts from the ideas of the U.S.A.
> 3) The texts during the period of national policy
> 4) The first national texts of Mombusho
> 5) National texts prior to the war-time revision

Finally, he stated his own opinion:

> I think it is easy to revise the war-time material, in deleting the militaristic, ultra-nationalistic and shintoism parts from the texts, but it is very hard to get new style of texts, which is good enough to develop the Japanese culture and train the youngster for the future.[34]

Day 7 (March 13): In a lecture entitled "Reorientation of Teachers," Captain Harry Griffith pointed out the importance of teacher training and in-service education. He concluded that in-service education was the most important and urgent issue confronting Japanese education.[35] He submitted his Ed.D. dissertation, "Japanese Normal School Education," to Stanford University in 1950.[36]

Lt. Cdr. R. K. Hall presented a lecture entitled "Language Revision," in which he gave examples appealing for the romanization of the Japanese language, but he modestly suppressed his own views.[37] For reasons that will be detailed in chapter 4, Hall was prevented by D. R. Nugent from mentioning any conclusions concerning the reform of the Japanese language in his lecture. In *Education in Japan* he restricted himself to the following comment:

> More than half of the time in the elementary school was spent in teaching children to read and write their complicated language. Even in the history, geography and morals classes, it was necessary for teachers to spend most of the instructional time in explaining the meaning of words and phrases containing Chinese *kanji* characters which were unfamiliar to the students. Since it was necessary for students to memorize the meaning of each *kanji* character before it could be used as part of their reading and writing vocabulary, the process of building vocabulary was extremely slow. Upon completion of the elementary school, the language potential of students was very low compared to graduates of the elementary schools in America.[38]

Finally, Masatsugu Ando delivered a lecture entitled "On Problems Concerning National Language and Its Character," in which he expressed his opinion on the choice of *katakana* (syllabic orthography) or *romaji* (romanized Japanese). He stressed that in considering the potential confusion caused among the Japanese masses, the number of *kanji* should be limited and replaced with *kana* as a tentative solution. He then stated that the Japanese might eventually decide on the use of *kana* or *romaji* as a complete system after a transitional period. He concluded that the aim of language reform is to lighten Japanese pupils' burden and requires the assistance of the Japanese themselves.[39] It seems that his view influenced the Mission in drawing up the Report on the reform of the Japanese language.

Day 8 (March 14): Major John W. Norviel presented a lecture entitled "Physical Education in Japan," whose text extended to sixty-one pages. He began by stating his own view: "It is my belief that the physical education and sports program offers one of the greatest opportunities for the development of leadership and democracy in Japan."[40]

Referring to the historical development of Japanese physical education described in *Education in Japan*, he emphasized that since 1942 military training had been closely bound up with physical education, and pointed out that during wartime it lost its original aim and became an instrument toward winning the war. He went on to say that after the war it had changed from a militaristic to a nonviolent program.

Captain Eileen Donovan then delivered a lecture entitled "Women's Education." She pointed out that it was a historical fact in Japan the ideal of prewar women's education was "to fit girls to become 'good wives and good mothers,'" and that the academic standard of the girls' middle schools was lower than that of boys'. She went on to state:

> In the basic plan for reform of female education outlined by Mombusho in December, 1945, one of the main objectives is equalization of the level of the basic curricula and textbooks of girls' high school and special schools with those of the middle schools and boys special schools....
>
> There is no woman in the Mombusho in any position of advisory or supervisory capacity.... There is only one inspector of girls high schools exclusively.

She then stated the importance of the early Christian mission schools in the liberal education of girls. With regard to women in higher education, she pointed out:

> The Tohoku Imperial University at Sendai has admitted women, as have the Kyushu and Hokkaido Imperial Universities, but the number has been so small.... In 1944, for instance, there were 24,600 men enrolled in Imperial Universities and 40 women.... Women have been automatically excluded from the other Imperial Universities by the law requiring Kotogakko preparation or its equivalent.... The old laws are in the process of revision and now women are eligible to take the entrance examinations for universities. The plan as outlined by the Mombusho is "to alter or cancel the regulations which prevent women from entering men's schools, to put co-education into operation in universities as well as to establish women's universities." The university and the Mombusho men with whom we have talked shake their heads and say: "very difficult." ... Of the twelve government universities, the Bunrikas at Tokyo and Hiroshima are the only ones which have admitted women. The Tokyo Bunrika (University of Art and Science), which had graduated 3,225 men by 1937, had a total of 82 women graduates; usually earlier graduates of Tokyo Higher Normal School for Women. As you know, several of the private

universities, notably Waseda, Hosei, Meiji and Nippon, admit a few women each year.... The three higher normal schools for women are the only government-supported higher institutions exclusively for women.

She enumerated the following points concerning women's education:

1) The problem of teachers' attitude in girls' schools ... the desire of men teachers and principals in girls' schools to transfer to middle schools. 2) The question of co-education, which is no official problem in any sense, yet about which there is a tremendous amount of interest among the students themselves, especially the girl students. 3) The type of education, listed as civic and social, of the type of Mothers' Clubs now ordered by the Mombusho. 4) Whether or not it is desirable to pattern women's education along the same line as the men's,—which is the crux of the basic plan of the Mombusho.[41]

Finally, Donovan emphasized the necessity for a change of Japanese attitude toward women's status and importance, recognition of women's nature, and respect for women's right to knowledge.[42] For this lecture she obtained the cooperation of Ai Hoshino, President of Tsuda Juku College, and Michi Kawai, President of Keisen Women's College of Agriculture. In reference to this lecture, W. E. Givens wrote in his diary that it was well organized. This lecture seems to have been instrumental in the writing of the part of the Report on girls' education. Nevertheless, Donovan herself expressed her disappointment that it was not reflected sufficiently in the Report despite her hard work in collecting historical materials.[43]

As can be seen, this series of lectures on education in Japan, given mainly by the Education Division of the CI&E, lasted seven days (March 7–14). During this week the participants included D. R. Nugent, Chief of the CI&E, and thirteen staff members and, on the Japanese side, Hideo Kishimoto, a scholar of religion; Tokiomi Kaigo, a pedagogist; Masatsugu Ando, a linguist; and staff members of the Ministry of Education.

The proposals made through these lectures presented by the staff of the CI&E and the few Japanese scholars who assisted them enabled the Mission to draw up their Report. Prior to this SCAP, through Gen. MacArthur, had requested the Mission to make recommendations in four areas of Japanese education. Hence the CI&E prepared information and lectures relating to these four areas. That is to say, it was made extremely easy for the Mission to complete the Report within a short time.

IV. Observation Tour of Kyoto and Nara

After the series of lectures by the Education Division of the CI&E, and the conferences with the Japanese Education Committee, the Mission made an observation tour of Kyoto and Nara March 16–19. They had a very full schedule to enable them to include daily conferences with Japanese educators and visits to cultural and educational facilities.

G. D. Stoddard recorded in his memoirs that on the night train to Kyoto he narrowly escaped death when a bullet was fired through a window and went past the back of his head.[44]

On March 16, during the tour, the Special Committee on Drafting, chaired by G. D. Stoddard, drafted a paper entitled "Proposed Outline of the Report." Its structure was as follows:

I. Introduction setting forth the official status and purpose of the Mission in terms of the requests from SCAP. (G. D. Stoddard and Bowles will prepare a draft of this section)

II. A preamble in general language which might form by itself a new basic charter for democratic education in Japan. (T. V. Smith is asked to prepare a draft of this section)

III. A preparatory section endorsing some of the great cultural influences which have been developed by or accepted by the Japanese people. This section would emphasize cultural features which the Group believes should be preserved. . . .

IV. The main body of the report.

Part 1

An evaluation of the basic curriculum in Japanese education with special reference to democratic reform.

Recommendations.

Part 2

An evaluation of the problem of reforming the written language.

Recommendations.

Part 3

An evaluation of the general administration of the tax-supported schools with special reference to plans and proposals for widening educational opportunity.

Recommendations.

Part 4

An evaluation of teacher education and the place of the teacher.

Recommendations.

Part 5

An evaluation of tax-supported and private higher, technical and professional education.

Recommendations.[45]

This "Proposed Outline of the Report" specified the framework of the Report, the writers, the main areas covered, and the points to be emphasized. Each committee in the Mission referred to this outline in making its drafts.

On the morning of March 18, the Mission had a two-hour general meeting, after which the four committees held their own meetings with about thirty Japanese educators. Committee I, chaired by G. D. Stoddard, discussed the elimination of mass education and methods for promoting individualism through education. Committee II, chaired by G. W. Diemer and F. N. Freeman, held discussions on teachers' in-service training. Committee III, chaired by A. J. Stoddard, discussed the promotion of liberalism within general education. Committee IV, chaired by W. M. Compton, discussed methods for maintaining the original character of private religious schools.[46]

Despite this hard schedule, the Mission fully enjoyed the Japanese cultural heritage of Kyoto and Nara, and returned to Tokyo by night train on March 19. The following day three members of the Mission, F. G. Hochwalt, M. M. Horton, and H. Benjamin, returned to the U.S. ahead of the rest of the Mission.

V. Preparations for Drafting the Report and Activities in Japan

On March 20 working cooperation between the Mission members and members of the Japanese Education Committee commenced. The CI&E rearranged the Mission's schedule between March 21 and March 31 in a memorandum dated March 20. According to this memorandum, most of the entertainment programs planned by the CI&E were canceled to allow more extensive discussions and the drafting of reports by the committees and the Special Committee on Drafting. The CI&E also arranged a special audience with the Emperor for the afternoon of March 27.[47]

On March 20, when they began to prepare for drafting the Report, G.D. Stoddard, G. T. Bowles, and J. N. Andrews held a conference with Gen. MacArthur. According to the notes on that conference, they "asked how far we might go in educational demands from the financial or economic standpoint. He suggested that we ask for whatever was necessary—not holding back. It will then be up to the Japanese themselves to strive to get the necessary support of education at all levels."[48] Thus, Gen. MacArthur advised the Mission to make the necessary recommendations freely, without worrying about the financial aspect. Gen. MacArthur's attitude supported and encouraged the Mission to propose the reforms of the education system in the Report.

It is obvious from the interim report of Committee I, the "Committee Concerning Courses of Study, Language and View of Education," that I. L. Kandel, its chairman, took a serious view of the financial considerations. The interim report stated that "in reality, it is doubtful that the Japanese economic situation allows extension of compulsory education up to age fourteen. However, it is desirable to provide compulsory education up to age fifteen for all children, in order to provide three or four years' education after elementary education."[49]

On March 20, all members of Committee III made drafts of their own sections of the report, and in the evening they held a meeting to discuss them. They continued the work of drafting until midday the following day, and again they had a meeting to discuss their work. This process continued, on March 22, and that evening the committee's report was revised. On March 23 the committee re-edited the draft and made thirty copies of the twenty-three-page draft report. The redrafting process was as follows:

> At 7:30 P.M. we made our report. Our committee report was the only one which had sufficient copies for each member to have a copy in his hands as we discussed it. The hardest battle we had was upon our recommendation concerning the Imperial Rescript on Education. Some of our members opposed it because they thought that this might be considered an attempt upon our part to destroy Japanese culture. We also had a considerable battle on the recommendation to markedly curtail the centralized control of the Ministry of Education. Those of us especially interested in public school education on elementary and secondary levels were determined to make recommendations that would guarantee to the great masses of Japanese people some opportunity for a reasonable education. Our report was discussed, sometimes with considerable vigor, until 11:30 P.M. when it was approved with certain suggestions for rewriting, deleting, and expanding, after which it was to go to the Editing Committee to be made a part of the entire report.[50]

One of the members of this committee, P. A. Wanamaker, sent a letter to her secretary in Washington describing the importance of the committee.[51]

On March 24, at a general meeting, a report on teacher training formulated by Committee II was presented by its chairman, F. N. Freeman, and some suggestions for revision were made. Then I. L. Kandel, chairman of Committee I, delivered a long report on the course of study which was criticized as being too academic. In the afternoon the Mission members visited Tokyo Imperial University and the Rockefeller Library, which had been donated by John D. Rockefeller after the Great Kanto Earthquake in 1923. In honor of their visit Shigeru Nambara, President of the university, gave a short but very impressive address in English.[52]

On the evening of the same day the Mission members discussed a report on higher education and, for the second time, the report of Committee I. This was followed by Committee IV's report on ethics, presented by T. V.

Smith, and a report on language problems by G. Counts, both of which were then discussed. It was confirmed that by March 24, the rest of the committees' reports would be brought to a general meeting to be discussed and revised. By that time draft reports by the Special Committee on Japanese Language and by Committees II, III and IV had already been confirmed in general meetings.

Only recently have the second and third drafts of "Language Reform," drawn up by the Special Committee on Japanese Language, been discovered. Both drafts are more or less the same in content, and on the basis of a comparison with the Final Report, it seems that the second draft was submitted as the final report to G.D. Stoddard on March 24. This report will be discussed in detail in Chapter 4.

The report of Committee II, entitled "Report of Committee II: Teaching and the Education of Teachers," consisted of twenty-nine pages. Its contents were as follows:

I. The Problems Involved

II. Teaching Practices in Democratic Education

III. The Re-Education of Teachers

IV. General Overview of the Preparation of Teachers

V. The Normal Schools of Japan

VI. Preparation of Teachers and School Officials in Colleges and Universities

VII. Summary of Recommendations[53]

Committee II's report included analytical, historical, and statistical details and discussed the actual situation of Japanese education. For example, "V. The Normal Schools of Japan" and "VI. Preparation of Teachers and School Officials in Colleges and Universities" supplied abundant information for detailed discussion. In drafting this report, the committee made free use of *Education in Japan* and also obtained information from the Japanese Education Committee as well as the members' own observation of schools.[54]

In the Final Report, only the outlines of Committee II's report were retained. The committee's summary and criticism of past Japanese education were deleted, and some changes were made to the description of teaching methods. However, it should be noted that the section on teacher training showed that considerable attention had been paid to the structure and content of the Committee's report.[55]

E. R. Hilgard, who was a member of Committee II and edited the Final Report, gave the following important testimony:

The committee report itself was written primarily by Frank Freeman and George W. Diemer.... The editing of the committee report in the form in which it was finally submitted was done by D. Stoddard, T. V. Smith, and me. . . . I do remember that those who had labored over reports such as document II were unhappy that they had no opportunity to read and approve the final version.[56]

As mentioned in Hilgard's testimony, the Final Report was not drawn up on the basis of this committee's report but was based on extracts of what was considered necessary.[57] The Final Report, was completed in the early hours of March 30, and as a result there was not enough time to discuss and revise Committee II's report.

G. T. Bowles later described the situation surrounding the Special Committee on Drafting: "Stoddard had to compile the Final Report and consider how all the recommendations made by each committee could be incorporated within a limited number of pages and avoid repetition."[58]

The report of Committee III, "Administration of Education in Japan at Elementary and Secondary Levels," consisted of twenty-five pages. Its contents were as follows:

I. Basic Educational Principles
II. Reorganization of the Japanese School System at the Elementary and Secondary Levels
III. Financial Support
IV. Conclusion[59]

This report made important proposals regarding the school system, and is discussed in detail in Chapter 5.

The draft regarded as the first draft of the report of Committee III contained a two-page section entitled "Adult Education," but it was deleted in the second draft. This indicates that Committee III also discussed adult education. The first draft pointed out the importance of adult education as a supplement to the school system:

> The ultimate success of our effort to build a democratic educational system in Japan depends on the understanding and acceptance of our program by the masses of the people. Our high resolves will collapse if beneath them there is no foundation of public support. Consequently, it behooves us to recommend the development of a program of public adult education which will insure an understanding of our aims by all the people, old as well as young.

It is worth noting that the draft referred to "social studies" in relation to adult education: "Carefully selected teachers would be trained to lead discussion of the pertinent public issues in the higher schools and in public forums. Thus, the vacuum produced by a ban on social studies would be partially filled." It continues: "Youth schools particularly should be utilized as centers of adult education."

This draft is an interesting historical document because it indicates that Committee III discussed youth schools as part of adult education. The final Report included a chapter on adult education, separate from higher education, which began: "A broad program of adult education is essential to any society that looks toward the highest development of its human resources." It is also interesting that the adult education chapter was placed before the higher education chapter and made only brief statements about public libraries, museums, the press, radio, and films. In the Report of the U.S. Education Mission to Germany, which is discussed in a later chapter, the adult education chapter came after the chapter on universities and higher schools, and films, radio, and libraries were treated as separate subjects, like adult education. These differences need to be noted.

Committee III also made important proposals relating to the Imperial Rescript on Education:

> The ceremonial use of Imperial Rescripts and the practice of obeisance before the Imperial Portraits, have in the past been instruments for regimentation of student thought and feelings. They have served the purpose of a militant nationalism. We consider these practices undesirable in the development of personality and incompatible with a proper system of public instruction in a democratic Japan. We strongly recommend that those practices be prohibited in whatever manner will most likely insure their *permanent discontinuance* [author's italics].

Thus, at this stage, Committee III strongly recommended "permanent discontinuance" of the Imperial Rescript on Education. What we should notice here is the existence of a written recommendation in English, entitled "Statement of Japanese Committee No. 3 Concerning the Imperial Rescript of [*sic*] Education," drawn up by the Japanese.[60] This statement is in the Wanamaker Papers, and for this reason it is supposed that it was presented to Committee III of the Mission.

In a draft of Givens's diary, "Tokyo and Return," in fact, he recorded: "Wednesday March 20 met at 11 A.M.—we received the statement from the Japanese members about the Rescript—1890."

The Japanese committee's statement expressed the members' position as follows:

> We the Japanese members of the Committee No. 3, all agree to see a new Imperial Rescript promulgated, along with a new Constitution to be proclaimed in near future.... As a conclusion, it is our fi[r]m conviction that a New Imperial Rescript will be the most useful instrument that encourages initiative of Japanese educators and realizes the democratization of Japan, thus resulting in the establishment of peaceful Japan.

As can be seen, the committees on both sides had contrasting opinions on the Imperial Rescript on Education. However, the Final Report of the Mission, as is generally known, avoided referring to a "New Imperial Rescript on Education":

> The ceremonial use of the Imperial Rescript and the practice of obeisance before the Imperial Portraits, have in the past been powerful instruments for the regimentation of student thought and feeling; they have served the purposes of a militant nationalism. They should be discontinued.[61]

The Final Report only recommended discontinuing the use of the Imperial Rescript on Education and Imperial Portraits in schools, in order to remove the Emperor System from education. On the other hand, the Japanese Education Committee developed its own opinions on this matter when formulating its recommendation based on its own point of view, including the Imperial Rescript on Education. That recommendation differed from the original draft submitted to the Mission in both style and content. It stated:

> Although the former Imperial Rescript on Education unmistakably manifests universal ethics, it is inadequate for the future spiritual life of the people. It is desirable that a New Imperial Rescript on Education make clear a new national education plan and also show a new path for the spiritual life of the people.... The following points are desirable in the Rescript: a) Humanity (full development of the individual and mutual respect) ..., b) Spirit of self-government, c) Logical spirit, d) Social life, e) Family and neighborhood life, f) National life, g) International spirit, h) Peace and culture.[62]

In order to discuss the postwar Japanese education system, Shigeru Nambara, President of Tokyo Imperial University, proposed forming a "Research Committee on the Education System," parallel with the Japanese Education Committee, in February 1946. This committee also dealt with the problem of the Imperial Rescript on Education as an educational policy. Its view was contrary to that of the Japanese Education Committee, chaired by Nambara himself, which urged a New Imperial Rescript on Education. Accordingly, the reports on this matter by the two Japanese committees show contradictions.[63]

G. T. Bowles clarified the Mission's attitude on this matter thus:

> Because we followed the instructions of the State Department, we discussed this matter carefully, as it was an issue concerning the Occupation policy, and the Mission members didn't seem to be altogether in favor of the Imperial Rescript on Education. The main issue was the administration of the Ministry of Education, rather than the Rescript.[64]

E. R. Hilgard, in contrast, stated: "Wonderful things were included in the Imperial Rescript on Education and its ceremony. It was our opinion as the Mission that the issue should be decided by Japanese educators."[65]

The above two statements show the existence of differing opinions among the Mission members on dealing with the Imperial Rescript on Education. The Mission is considered to have been influenced by the opinions of the Japanese Education Committee through their joint meetings. As a consequence, the wording of the Mission's limited recommendations, in such phrases as "permanent discontinuance" in Committee III's report, was moderated in the Final Report.

Givens's diary, "Tokyo and Return," described the debate over this issue in Committee III of the Mission in depth, and also mentioned that there was strong opposition to the Imperial Rescript on Education.[66] The Wanamaker Papers also include details of the situation within Committee III over the issue. The revision of such words as "We strongly recommend" to "They should be discontinued" in Wanamaker's own handwriting clearly illustrate the situation.

Some other recommendations made by Committee III of the Mission, were excluded from the Final Report. For instance, concerning class size the committee suggested:

> It may be possible to carry on a highly centralized type of instructional procedure of the memory-recitation or teacher-lecture type with large classes, but those instructional procedures designed to promote democratic objectives cannot be realized efficiently with large classes. Pupil discussion, the expression of critical judgement, the development of individual initiative and desirable attitudes, appreciations, and ideals, worthy habits of conduct based on intelligent choice, cannot be realized if each teacher is responsible for too many students.
>
> While there is still much research needed to determine the question of class size, because it undoubtedly varies according to different instructional situations, it seems to us that a desirable next step for Japan would be to provide at elementary and secondary school levels for an average pupil-classroom-teacher situation, a ratio of approximately 30 to 1 on an average daily attendance basis.[67]

Thus, the committee recommended thirty pupils as the limit for a class in elementary and secondary education in order to facilitate a democratic structure. The Final Report may have omitted this because it was thought to be too much to ask of Japanese schools, under the existing circumstances.

Furthermore, concerning fees and scholarships, the committee stated:

> We recommend that the payment of fees by the students at both the elementary and secondary levels be discontinued. Free public education throughout

the compulsory school period or through secondary school is essential if schooling is to be regarded on a democratic basis. Scholarships at public expense might be necessary and desirable to provide education to meet individual needs at the secondary school level, especially if desired school facilities are not locally available.

It should be noted that the committee suggested the abolition of fees in elementary and secondary education and the necessity of scholarships for secondary education.

Another draft of Committee III's report comprised six draft documents, including "Adult Education" and "Teacher Growth in Service." These differed in content from the "Adult Education" and "Teaching and the Education of Teachers" sections of the Final Report. For this reason, it can be assumed that they were written early in the drafting process.

Committee IV drew up its draft report on higher education under the title "Aim and Freedom of Higher Learning." It comprised five sections: "The Plan of Higher Learning in a Free Society," "The Organization of Institutions, etc.," "Freedom for the Individual," "Recommendations for Scientific and Professional Training," and "Advancement of International Understanding." Higher education will be discussed in detail in Chapter 6.

As described above, each committee within the Mission drew up its own report and submitted it to the Special Committee on Drafting. In regard to the writers of each chapter of the Report, H. J. Wunderlich testified that the statement of educational principles in the first chapter was written by T. V. Smith,[68] and documents made available recently clarify that the "Health and Physical Education" section was written by E. B. Norton.[69] It has also been confirmed that Chapter V, "Adult Education," was written by E. Woodward.[70]

In February 1946, before the Mission arrived in Japan, R. K. Hall of the CI&E visited Korea to advise the Military Government for Korea on the preparation and selection of members for an education mission to the U.S. which was to consist of six Koreans who were to visit the U.S. the following month.

On March 27, Committee III had two visitors from Korea, Major E. N. Lockard and a Mr. Auh.[71] When R. K. Hall met Maj. Lockard, Lockard told Hall that he was very interested in the U.S. Education Mission to Japan and would visit Japan to attend the meetings of the Mission.[72] In Korea, at that time, there was discussion of an "Educational and Informational Survey Mission to Korea" similar to the Mission to Japan. In the event, its form and procedures were similar to those of the Mission to Japan. In fact, I. L. Kandel and H. Benjamin, who were members of the Mission to Japan, were deeply involved in its organization.[73]

Among the other visitors to Committee III were three Japanese who applied for permission to translate *Learning the Ways of Democracy: A Case Book of Civic Education*, published by the Education Policies Commission of the National Education Association. They subsequently obtained permission for its translation. (A. J. Stoddard, chairman of Committee III, was also chairman of the Education Policies Commission.)[74]

On March 28, when the Special Committee on Drafting was halfway through preparation of the Report, G.D. Stoddard and G. T. Bowles had a second meeting with Gen. MacArthur. At this meeting Stoddard described the content of the Report to Gen. MacArthur, who told him that he would read the completed Report at the earliest opportunity.[75] It is thought that the purpose of this meeting was to confirm that the Mission's proposals conformed to Occupation policies. It should be noticed that Bowles and Stoddard had two meetings with Gen. MacArthur, the first on March 20 and the second on March 28, during the most important stages of the drafting of the Report. However, it is obvious from Gen. Mac-Arthur's speech to the Mission at the luncheon party that the meetings were not held so that Gen. MacArthur could impose his personal views and opinions on the Report. It is quite clear that the Final Report was based on the draft reports presented by the committees.

After the March 28 meeting Stoddard edited each of the committee's reports with Bowles's cooperation. Bowles later recalled how he and Stoddard worked on the Final Report: "Although the draft reports from the committees were already typed, we deleted material where it repeated or overlapped and standardized their composition, rewriting controversial points and correcting misunderstandings about Japanese characteristics and language which were discussed only from an American point of view."[76]

Bowles also described the details of the final stage of drafting the Report in a letter to his wife, Jane. According to this letter, editing of the Report was completed by 4 A.M. on March 30. Six secretaries typed continuously in four-hours shifts finishing at 6:30 P.M. the same day. By 9:00 P.M. the Final Report and a copy were submitted by G.D. Stoddard, G. T. Bowles, and J. N. Andrews to Major General Stephen J. Chamberlain, Deputy Chief of Staff, SCAP, on behalf of Gen. MacArthur, who was absent because of a heavy cold.[77]

According to Bowles's unofficial memorandum to William Benton, Assistant Secretary of State, which was taken to the U.S. by P.P. Stewart after the Report had been submitted, Stoddard and Stewart returned to the State Department with one copy each. J. N. Andrews also took a copy to the Civil Affairs Division of the War Department. The memorandum also stated that the date of the official announcement of the Report would be decided by communication between Tokyo and Washington after the War Department had received the Report.

The memorandum declared that the Report was drafted as a "confidential report" by the Mission members, and that the CI&E staff was not involved in its composition in any way.[78] Bowles went on to state that it was to G.D. Stoddard's credit that he had accomplished the task of drafting the Report despite the difficulty of gaining a consensus among twenty-four members of differing educational backgrounds. He also noted that a paper entitled "A Report of the Minority" had been produced, which, it had finally been decided by common consent, should not be officially submitted.[79]

At 4:00 P.M. on the day of the last meeting of the Mission in Tokyo, the members raised about ¥20,000 at the suggestion of T. V. Smith and V. C. Gildersleeve in order to present a collection of books "to be as widely useful as possible to the children and teachers of Japan," as evidence of the Mission's deep concern for Japanese democracy. Those instrumental in organizing this were T. V. Smith, V. C. Gildersleeve, and L. Carnovsky.[80]

On March 30 the Mission received an official invitation to visit China from the Chinese Government, through Major General Chin Wang of the Chinese Liaison Office, SCAP. However, the members declined for schedule reasons.[81] In this connection, Bowles later said: "The Chinese Government should have made an official request to the State Department for the sending of a mission to China. The purpose of the Mission in Tokyo was solely for reorientation of the Japanese. For sending a Mission to China, it would have been necessary to include experts on China among its members."[82]

On April 1, the remaining Mission members except Bowles left Japan. At Gen. MacArthur's request, and on the acknowledgment of POLAD, Bowles extended his stay in Japan for another two months as a special adviser to the CI&E and to assist D. R. Nugent, acting chief, during the absence of K. R. Dyke, chief of the CI&E.

Bowles's unofficial memorandum to the State Department also mentioned Gen. MacArthur's personal opinion concerning the inefficiency of the CI&E staff and pointed out that "a staff of highly competent, civilian, trained personnel" capable of administrative responsibilities would be necessary to implement the recommendations made by the Mission.[83]

In fact, CAD of the War Department commenced supplementing the CI&E staff at the request of R. K. Dyke. At the request of the War Department, V. C. Gildersleeve recommended F. N. Freeman, a Mission member, as Planning and Policies Chief in the Education Division.[84] Subsequently, a succession of education experts were sent to the CI&E.

As we have seen, the Mission spent a full month studying education plans for Japan and submitted its report to Gen. MacArthur, expressing its desire to assist Japan in building a democratic society, with a view to future participation in the United Nations.[85]

VI. *The Japanese Response: Japanese Initiative and the Organization of the Japanese Education Committee*

1) JAPANESE INITIATIVE AS SEEN IN "THE EDUCATION POLICY FOR THE CONSTRUCTION OF A NEW JAPAN"

At this point, it is essential to clarify how far the Japanese side was able to maintain its own initiative in postwar education reform under the Occupation. We will examine this through "Shin Nihon Kensetsu no Kyoiku Hoshin" [The Education Policy for the Construction of a New Japan] (here after referred to as the "New Education Policy"), issued by the Japanese Ministry of Education on September 15, 1945, which became the basic policy for postwar Japanese education.

The "New Education Policy" was the first official expression of Japanese views on postwar education set forth by the Ministry of Education. It was written even before GHQ issued its first memorandum, "Administration of the Educational System of Japan" (October 22, 1945). The "New Education Policy" played an important role later, when the U.S. government formulated and carried out its education policy for Japan. Tamon Maeda, who was the Minister of Education at that time, wrote of this period: "It should be noted that before setting forth the policy on September 15, we ourselves dealt with every single matter independently, without any connection with GHQ. In other words, September 15 was a crucial turning point."[86]

As is generally known, the "New Education Policy" was composed of the following eleven articles: 1) Policies of new education, 2) Educational system, 3) Textbooks, 4) Measures for teachers and staff, 5) Measures for schools, 6) Science education, 7) Social education, 8) Youth groups, 9) Religion, 10) Physical education, and 11) Organizational reforms of the Ministry of Education.

The "New Education Policy" aimed principally at providing a basis for education during the immediate post-surrender period. At the same time, it sought the actualization of democracy based on the prewar Japanese thinking epitomized by the phrase *kokutai no hongi* (the national polity). There are conflicting views concerning the drafting process of the "New Education Policy." One view affirms the Japanese initiative, and the other does not.[87] However, it is not the author's purpose to present a detailed argument on the subject.

When the "New Education Policy" was issued, Harold C. Henderson of the GHQ Military Government Section, Government Division, Education Branch (the predecessor of GHQ/CI&E), visited Minister of Education Maeda with a newspaper article reporting the "New Education Policy." He said that the policy was very good, and encouraged Maeda to continue on the same course.[88] This suggests that GHQ and the Ministry of Education shared the same views on the implementation of education policy immediately after the war.[89]

Meanwhile, how did the staff of the CI&E perceive the drafting process of the "New Education Policy"? R. K. Hall wrote:

> Perhaps the most dramatic educational somersault in modern times occurred during three weeks following Surrender. By the time the Civil Information and Education Section of the General Headquarters had been established on 22 September 1945 the Japanese Ministry of Education had carried out in principle at least practically every school reform which the Occupation authorities had planned to demand.... So completely had the Ministry of Education foreseen probable Allied directives and forestalled them by voluntary reforms that as late as the first quarter of 1946 there were conducted staff meetings in General Headquarters to analyze systematically the possible omissions of the Japanese and to plan new demands.[90]

And M. T. Orr stated:

> On September [16], although no instruction had been received from the occupation headquarters, the Ministry of Education announced the basic policies which had been adopted to bring about the reconstruction of education in Japan. It is evident from Mr. Maeda's proposed program that he had anticipated the intentions of the General Headquarters fairly well. He missed on two counts. In the first place, he wanted to maintain the structure of the Imperial State.... Fundamental changes were made in the organization of the government and, particularly, in the relationship between the Emperor and the government. Furthermore, Mr. Maeda announced that he proposed to construct a new moral Japan through the cultivation of religious sentiments.... The Supreme Commander insisted upon the separation of Church and State.[91]

Thus, while pointing out where the "New Education Policy" differed from the reform plans of GHQ/SCAP, he acknowledged that as a whole it was based on Japanese originality and initiative. In short, both Hall and Orr suggested that GHQ/SCAP approved the Japanese initiative. They also implied that early in the Occupation the policy of GHQ/SCAP was to promote Japanese initiatives in education reform.

Why did GHQ/SCAP adopt a position of respect and support for the Japanese initiative? The following three factors should be considered.

In the first place, Gen. MacArthur's view of democracy should be clarified. He thought that postwar reforms in Japan should be carried out by the will of the Japanese themselves. Accordingly, he thought that minimum enforcement by GHQ/SCAP was desirable, based on his strong conviction that the idea of democracy should be nurtured from within the Japanese people rather than imposed externally by force. This attitude is illustrated by the following GHQ/SCAP statement:

> From the beginning, Occupation policy has been based upon the principle that the reform of Japanese society should be accomplished by the Japanese people themselves; that SCAP should not impose a blueprint; and that the function of General Headquarters and the Army of Occupation was not to govern Japan, but to supervise the efforts of the Japanese people to reform themselves and their society. This policy rests upon the belief that within the Japanese people an honest desire exists to build a democratic society capable of directing itself in reconstruction and reform to create a Japan worthy of a position of dignity in the community of nations. That this faith was justified tends to be demonstrated by the reforms effected in Japanese education by the Japanese themselves during the two years and a half since the beginning of the Occupation.[92]

It is clear from the above statement that GHQ/SCAP believed in the existence of a serious resolve within the Japanese, capable of reconstructing a democratic society. And, as noted, during the first two and a half years GHQ/SCAP gave the Japanese the initiative to reform Japanese education themselves.

Second, Gen. MacArthur believed that if reforms were forcibly imposed by the Occupation the results would be temporary and there would be no guarantee of perpetuity. Macmahon William Ball described in detail in his book *Japan: Enemy or Ally?* how GHQ/SCAP indirectly controlled the Japanese through the Japanese Government in order to achieve reforms and avoid the impression that they were achieved through the pressure of the Occupation.[93]

Third, the main reason for encouraging Japanese initiative in carrying out reforms swiftly and attaining independence was to enhance Gen. MacArthur's reputation. In fact, *The New York Times* suggested that the speed of reforms in Japan during the first month of the Occupation depended directly upon Gen. MacArthur's abilities of command.[94] Faubion Bowers, who was the adjutant general under Gen. MacArthur, described Gen. MacArthur's strong desire for the early termination of the Occupation from the beginning, and also indicated that the Japanese were made to chart their own course, within the framework of the basic Occupation policy.[95]

The above statements confirm that GHQ/SCAP encouraged Japanese initiative for reform.

How was Japanese initiative created, as demonstrated in the drafting process of the "New Education Policy"? Two factors must be taken into account. To begin with, as James I. Doi, who was on the staff of the CI&E, has pointed out, the "New Education Policy" can be considered to have been based on the Potsdam Declaration. Article 12 states: "The occupying forces of the Allies shall be withdrawn from Japan as soon as these objectives have been accomplished and there has been established in accordance with the freely expressed will of the Japanese people a peacefully inclined and responsible government."

From this point of view, Doi has stated, the Japanese believed that "the sooner they could show that a new order had been established, the sooner 'the occupying forces of the Allies shall be withdrawn,'" which would make it possible for them to gain independence.[96] In other words, the Japanese government cleverly read between the lines of the Potsdam Declaration, which implied that there were limits to the authority of the Occupation. It is not certain how the Japanese took advantage of this in creating the "New Education Policy."[97] However, the appointment of Tamon Maeda as Minister of Education, with his experience in the U.S. and his close relationship with H. C. Henderson, chief of the Education Division of the CI&E, was obviously of great advantage to the Japanese position.

At the same time, the active Japanese attitude shown in the drafting of the "New Education Policy" was viewed very positively by Japanese popular opinion. This reaction was also seen in the Japanese press, which suggested that Japan should take its own initiative for reform rather than be coerced by the victor.[98] This allowed the maintenance of prewar thinking, encapsulated in the phrase *kokutai no hongi* (the national polity).

Next, the Ministry of Education published a communication from the Vice-Minister of Education dated August 28, 1945, "Matters Concerning School Education in Considering Changes in the Current Situation," directing each school to commence classes as usual by mid-September at the latest. In reality, some direction, such as the "New Education Policy," was necessary to reopen the schools.

As can be seen, it is clear that GHQ/SCAP had a high regard for the enthusiastic and energetic attitude of the Japanese in drafting the "New Education Policy" and their eagerness in actively carrying out education reform. However, the State Department showed an extremely negative attitude toward the "New Education Policy." The State Department's analysis was that the views of the Ministry of Education as reflected in the "New Education Policy" contained elements that were contradictory to the Occupation policy on postwar Japanese education. This analysis was based on a report from the Research and Analysis Branch (Interim

Research and Intelligence) of the State Department, "Japanese Postwar Education Policies," dated October 5, 1945. The report sharply criticized the policy of the Ministry of Education as reflected in the "New Education Policy" and gave the following concrete examples. The concept of the national polity (*kokutai*), mentioned in the first article in the "New Education Policy," had been the source of militant nationalism. The second article advocated the abolition of military training and the elimination of wartime education; these measures however, were considered insufficient. With regard to Article 3, "Textbooks," the revision and expurgation of textbooks was insufficient to eliminate the influence of militarism; and *shushin* (moral instruction) and the history of Japan, which had originally established militant nationalism, were not reformed. As for Article 6, "Science Education," the promotion of science education was nothing but an implicit intention to fill the gap in science and technology that had existed between Japan and the U.S. and had been revealed by the development of the atomic bomb.[99]

These State Department criticisms caused GHQ/SCAP to issue the "Four Negative Directives Concerning Education" from October to December 1945, which decisively determined the course of the reform of postwar Japanese education.[100]

GHQ/SCAP's initial response to the Ministry of Education was appreciation of the positive attitude which had resulted in the "New Education Policy" and of the Japanese search for their own means of education reform. It appears that GHQ/SCAP did not refer to its subject matter or substance, because GHQ/SCAP was not yet well enough organized to be able to discuss the content of the Japanese policy in any detail, since the Occupation had just commenced. GHQ/SCAP's implicit respect for the Japanese attitude can be considered to have been a reflection of Gen. MacArthur's philosophy in relation to the Occupation. He had great respect for Japanese initiative, which assisted him in smoothly carrying out the Occupation policy on education reform. For example, even in issuing the first of the Four Negative Directives, "Administration of the Educational System of Japan," on October 22, 1945, which was based on the State Department's severe criticism of the Japanese education policy, Gen. MacArthur never missed an opportunity, through diplomatic language, to praise the Ministry of Education for its voluntary plan of education reform.[101] Moreover, he refrained as far as possible from issuing memorandums and directives, in order to encourage Japanese initiatives in carrying out their reforms. In fact, the Four Negative Directives were focused on the elimination of prewar "negative" ideas, which would prove an obstacle in the implementation of reforms based on democracy. Prior to implementing these directives, GHQ/SCAP held negotiations to encourage

Japanese initiative. These "negative" directives were terminated at the end of December 1945. The only positive measure among the directives relating to education reform concerned the organization of the Japanese Education Committee, which will be discussed below.

2) ESTABLISHMENT OF THE JAPANESE EDUCATION COMMITTEE

As discussed in Chapter 1, SCAP formulated the plan for inviting the Mission to Japan, and GHQ officially requested CAD at the War Department to send the Mission, by telegram on January 4, 1946. On January 9 SCAP issued a memorandum, "Committee of Japanese Educators," addressed to the Japanese Government through the Central Liaison Office, Tokyo. With regard to this memorandum, M. T. Orr of the Education Division of the CI&E stated:

> On January 9, 1946, the Supreme Commander sent the fifth of the basic directives to the Japanese Government. While it did not contain specific policy, this directive was to have significant and far-reaching influence on the future course of educational reform. Heretofore much of the emphasis had been necessarily placed upon the limitation of militarism and ultranationalism which posited negative directives. From this point on education policy was to shift from the negative phase to the constructive work of educational reform and rehabilitation.[102]

In this way, the Education Division of the CI&E considered inviting the Mission as the first step in a long-term re-education plan under the Occupation.[103] In other words, the fifth "directive" became a turning point, shifting the Occupation policy towards constructive reform. It stated:

> In order to facilitate the work of [the] Educational Mission and in order that the Japanese educational system may derive the maximum benefit from its studies and findings, it is suggested: That the Ministry of Education appoint a committee of highly qualified Japanese educators to work with the Educational Commission.

It went on to recommend "that the members of the Committee be selected with particular reference to their qualifications to assist the Educational Commission in the study of problems set forth in paragraph 3 above."

Thus, it indicated that they were to assist the Mission. Paragraph 3 defined the four spheres which the Mission was expected to study and on which it was later to submit its Report to the Supreme Commander. They were as follows:

1) *Education for Democracy in Japan*:
A study leading to recommendations as to the content of courses, curricula, textbooks, teachers' manuals, and visual and auditory aids.
2) *Psychology in the Re-Education of Japan*:
A study leading to recommendations as to the educational methodology, language revision, timing and priority of educational reforms, the development of student initiative and critical analysis, and reorientation of teachers.
3) *Administrative Re-organization of Japan*:
A study leading to recommendations as to immediate and long range administrative reforms, the reorganization of the Ministry of Education, and the problems of decentralization.
4) *Higher Education in the Rehabilitation of Japan*:
A study leading to recommendations in regard to the use of libraries, archives, scientific laboratories, museums in higher education, to student and faculty freedom, to reorientation of the social sciences, and to more active participation in the life of the community and of Japan.

According to this "directive," GHQ occasionally obliged the Ministry of Education to revise its candidates for the committee members. The ministry finally completed the appointment of the twenty-nine members of the Japanese Education Committee on February 2, 1946. A memorandum entitled "The Manual of the Education Committee" enumerated the following particulars:

1) The Education Committee is within the Ministry of Education and cooperates with the U.S. Education Mission.

2) The committee has a chairman, and no more than thirty members: [In fact, however, as noted above, twenty-nine members were appointed.— *Author.*]

3) The chairman is selected by the committee members.

4) The staff of the Ministry of Education is allowed to attend the committee meetings.

According to Sanji Aruga, a member of the committee, he received an official letter dated February 2, 1946, which said: "Entrusting you as a member of the Japanese Education Committee to Cooperate with the U.S. Education Mission."[104] On February 4 Aruga was requested by Kotaro Tanaka, Director General of the School Education Bureau, to draw up a list of the members of the Japanese Education Committee to be submitted to GHQ/SCAP. It is interesting to see that the list included notes on experience of "studying and visiting abroad."

On February 18 the committee held its first meeting, in a reception room in the Ministry of Education. The agenda was as follows:

1. The organizing of the Japanese Education Committee
2. Its office within the Ministry of Education

3. The assignment of each member
4. Research and the collection of materials
5. Other matters

At the second meeting, on February 23, the committee selected Shigeru Nambara, President of Tokyo Imperial University, as chairman and Shunsaku Kawahara, Privy Councillor, as vice-chairman. The other members were assigned to the following four committees:

Committee 1

Chairman: Risaku Mutai* (President, Tokyo University of Humanities and Sciences)
Vice-chairman: Tetsuichi Sawato (Fifth Middle School, Tokyo)
Sanji Aruga* (Headmaster, Tokyo Kodaira Youth School)
Michi Kawai* (Headmistress, Keisen Women's College of Agriculture)
Toshikata Sano* (Professor Emeritus, Tokyo Imperial University)
Naomichi Shiono (Headmaster, Kanazawa Higher Normal School)
Taketoshi Yamagiwa* (Headmaster, Tokyo Nishida National Elementary School)
Muneyoshi Yanagi (Director, Nihon Mingeikan [Japan Folk Craft Museum]) (Additional posts: Kumaki, Kurahashi, Torikai)

Committee 2

Chairman: Masatsugu Ando* (Former President, Taihoku Imperial University)
Vice-chairman: Mantaro Kido* (Education Training Institute)
Manjiro Hasegawa (Jo Zekan) (art critic)
Michio Kozaki (Congregational pastor)
Sumie Kobayashi (Professor, Keio University)
Sozo Kurahashi* (Professor, Tokyo Women's Higher Normal School)
Taro Ochiai* (Professor, Kyoto Imperial University)
Naoteru Ueno* (President, Tokyo Art School)
(Additional posts: Aruga, Komiya, Sano, Sawato, Oshima, Yamagiwa, Yanagi)

Committee 3

Chairman: Shunsaku Kawahara (Privy Councillor)
Vice-chairman: Tsuraki Yano* (President, Meiji Gakuin College)
Teiyu Amano* (President, Daiichi Koto Gakko)
Suteji Kumaki (Headmaster, Tokyo Daiichi Normal School)
Masanori Oshima* (Former Professor, Tokyo Imperial University)
(Additional posts: Aruga, Hoshino, Hayashi, Kawai, Ochiai, Sawato, Shiono, Takagi, Yamagiwa)

Committee 4

Chairman: Toyotaka Komiya* (President, Tokyo School of Music)
Vice-chairman: Teizo Toda* (Professor, Tokyo Imperial University)

Kimio Hayashi (Vice-President, Waseda University)
Ai Hoshino* (Headmistress, Tsuda Juku Senmon Gakko)
Kosaku Kakinuma* (Professor, Tokyo Imperial University)
Yasaka Takagi (Professor, Tokyo Imperial University)
Risaburo Torikai* (President, Kyoto Imperial University)
(Additional posts: Amano, Hasegawa, Kido, Kobayashi, Kozaki, Mutai, Ueno, Yano)

There were twenty-nine members altogether. Names followed by asterisks indicate members who later, along with Nambara, became members of the Education Reform Council.

After changes made at the behest of the CI&E, this committee was composed of liberal educators. The initial list of the education advisory group which the Ministry of Education submitted to the CI&E on October 8, 1945, included Shozo Uchida, Shinzo Koizumi, Yoshishige Abe, Tsuraki Yano, Hideko Inoue (President of Nihon Women's University), Yonekichi Akai (Headmaster of Meisei Gakuin), Yasaburo Miyauchi (Headmaster of Bancho National Elementary School), Shoji Anesaki, Hideji Yagi, Hiroshi Nasu, Yasaka Takagi, and Setsuko Hani. Later, many of these were excluded from the Japanese Education Committee. Twenty-four of the twenty-nine members had visited the U.S. or Europe before the war. Some had received degrees from foreign universities, and most were first-class liberal scholars. In addition, headmasters of national elementary schools, middle schools, and youth school were included, as were seven members who had participated in the Kyoiku Kaikaku Doshikai (Education Reform Fraternity) before the war: Oshima, Kido, Kobayashi, Sano, Toda, Hasegawa, and Hayashi.[105]

The committees discussed the following matters:

Committee No 1 (Important reform issues)

1. Educational aims of each school—revision of the School Ordinance
2. Reform of the quality of education—discussion of the content of courses and curricula
3. Problems of the Imperial Rescript on Education
4. Discussion of the policy on compilation of textbooks
5. Discussion of administration of textbooks
6. Problems of guidance of teachers
7. Study of audiovisual aids, etc.
8. Research and drafting of materials related to reform matters in Committee No 1
9. Art education
10. Physical education
11. Craft education

[The last three items were added in handwriting.]

Committee No 2 (Important problems)
1. Aim and goal of education
2. Japanese language
3. Democratization of teaching methods
4. Evaluation of results
5. Participation of students and teachers in school education
6. Voluntary activities of pupils and students
7. The present situation of Japanese educational institutions
8. Re-education of teachers
9. The relation between religion and education
10. Special education for the deaf and dumb [Added in handwriting]
Committee No 3 (Problems concerning the committee)
1. Establishment of educational authority
2. Reorganization of the school system
3. Reexamination of the general aims of the School Act
4. Reform of the entrance examination system and admission requirements
5. Improvement of teachers' status and salary
6. Teachers' education [Added in handwriting]
Committee No 4
1. The university system
2. The private school system
3. Employment opportunities for graduates
4. Religious education
5. Faculty organization
6. Women's universities
7. School extension
8. Research facilities and libraries

It should be noted that the subjects discussed by these committees were the same as those that later composed the main part of the Report of the Mission.

The Japanese Education Committee merged with the Educational Reform Council in August 1946 under the terms of SCAP's directive "Committee of Japanese Educators," which specified that "the committee, after the departure of the Educational Mission, continue to study the problems set forth in paragraph 3 above and submit periodic reports on its findings and recommendations to the Ministry of Education and to the Education Division, Civil Information and Education Staff Section."

Nineteen of the members, including the chairman, were reappointed to the council. In this respect, it is worth noting that the Japanese Education Committee played a very important role in terms of the continuity and discontinuity of prewar Japanese education.

3) CONFERENCES WITH THE EDUCATION MISSION

On March 9 the four committees on both sides had their first meetings with their counterparts. Tetsuichi Sawato, a member of the Japanese Education Committee, recollected the first joint meeting:

> The Mission arrived. On March 7 a meeting was held by the U.S. side only, but on March 8 at 9:00 A.M. both sides conferred at the Peers' Club. An important address in English was given by Minister of Education Abe, which left a deep impression in all our minds. I also remember being very impressed by an address given by Chairman Stoddard. In the afternoon, a briefing on the four committees within the Mission was given by the staff in charge of the Education Division.
>
> On March 9 the first meeting of each committee was held at the Mitsui Building. The members of Committee I were I. L. Kandel, Professor of Comparative Education, Columbia University (chairman); L. Carnovsky, University of Chicago; G. S. Counts, Professor, Columbia University; C. S. Johnson, Fisk University; C. H. McCloy, Professor, University of Iowa; and Lt. Col. Smith. Dr. Kandel summarized four papers, which were handed to us in the meeting. The first paper, about general principles, discussed recognition of the dignity of individuals; serious consideration of the educational function of social, political, and economic agencies; decentralization of education; tradition in Japanese culture and education reform; and reform of the entrance examination system. The second paper discussed the education system and stated that the principle of the system should be directed toward considering the abilities, inclinations, and interests of pupils, thereby aiming at the development of individuality and freedom of research and thought. The third paper dealt with the diversification of schools and curricula and the extension of compulsory education. The fourth paper concerned the language issue and discussed the fact that the reform of language, which is too great a burden to learning, is the basis for the development of a healthy education system.[106]

These four papers, written in Japanese, were handed to the Japanese members by I. L. Kandel, and together were considered the interim report of Committee I, the "Committee Concerned with Curricula, Language, and Education View." (The members included Kandel, Carnovsky, Counts, and McCloy, with Norton also attending.) This interim report stated:

> Prior to the discussion of any other education reforms in Japanese education, we realize the necessity of studying the Japanese views on education. In accordance with this, the two directives mentioned, document 108, No. 3 [SWNCC-108, "The Post-Surrender Military Government of the Japanese Empire: The Education System"], became our guidelines. These contain proposals and reforms for what needs to be removed from the Japanese education system. . . .
>
> In situations where the freedom of teaching and study needs to be promoted,

the central government should not direct the content of courses and teaching methods but should limit its activities in this area to the publication of outlines, suggestions, and guides. As soon as they have been suitably prepared for their profession, teachers should be left free to adapt content and teaching methods to the needs of society and environment where individuals perform their duties. Decentralization is most desirable in this area. The Administrative Committee will make decisions on jurisdiction between the central government and the regional authorities, as required by the articles of the administrative organization. . . .

It is freedom of study and thought, not knowledge learned by rote for examinations, that should promote the need for responsibility in the use of knowledge and critical judgement based on knowledge and experience. . . .

In reforming Japanese education, at present it is difficult to predict, due to the uncertain economic outlook, how fast and how far the above proposals can be carried out. . . .

The division of elementary and further education generally takes place at about eleven or twelve years of age. However, this is not the time to discuss such an issue, as the pupil should be placed in his or her appropriate course or school. . . . As a matter of fact, it is doubtful whether Japanese economic conditions are capable of allowing the extension of compulsory education up to the age of fourteen or over. However, it is still desirable to provide compulsory education up to the age of fifteen, in order to give three or four years' additional education after elementary education. This is the trend in other countries, such as Britain, France, New Zealand, and Australia. In the U.S., many states have extended compulsory education over the age of fifteen. Under present conditions, where employment opportunities for youth are lacking, it will be possible to extend compulsory education. . . .

We realize that language is one of the most serious problems within Japanese education. None of us in this committee are qualified to make recommendations on language reform. But the Japanese themselves recognize that their language demands much more time to learn than does any other language. We are concerned not only about the difficulties of learning but also problems which might prevent clarity of communication. We also have the impression that the degree of knowledge of characters creates differentiations in social status.[107]

Thus, Committee I discussed Japanese education not only within the areas that concerned it but also within the framework of the Mission as a whole. It is remarkable that such a detailed report should have been given to the Japanese members on March 9, so soon after the Mission's arrival. This clearly illustrates the Mission's very high standard of advance preparation and also that the subject matter of the Report, or at least part of it, had already been prepared even at this early stage. It is obvious that Committee I's interim report had an important influence on the final Report, and it can be assumed that the interim report was what I. L. Kandel, chairman of Committee III at the time of the Guam meeting, was referring to, when he stated that "the Committee is drawing up a draft concerning important issues."

On the same day Committee II, "Teachers' Education and Methodology," also had its first meeting. G. W. Diemer and F. N. Freeman (cochairmen of Committee II), and Masatsugu Ando (chairman of Committee 2 of the Japanese Education Committee) distributed the following paper, which suggested the main points for discussion:

I. Pre-Service Education of Teachers
  1. Philosophy and General Pattern
  2. Admission Procedures: Selection of Students
  3. Educational Program: Course of Study, Extracurricular Activities
  4. Laboratory Schools
  5. Students: Service, Guidance, Health Service, Student Life
  6. Graduation, Certification, and Placement
  7. Preparation and Selection of Faculty
  8. Administrative Organization and Control of Academic Freedom
  9. Physical Facilities: Buildings, Library, Laboratories, etc.
  10. Financial Support
II. In-Service Education
  1. Summer or Vacation Study
  2. Extension and Correspondence Courses
  3. Conferences, Meetings, etc.
  4. Professional Organizations
  5. Study Leaves (Foreign Study)
  6. Travel (Foreign Study)
III. Re-Education of Teachers Now in Japanese Schools
IV. Graduate or Advanced Study
V. Research and Experimentation
VI. Methodology
  1. Psychology of Learning
  2. Methods of Instruction: Activities, Discussions, Lectures, Forums, Work Experience, etc.
  3. Planning (Freedom to Plan)
  4. Guidance: Techniques and Procedures
  5. Teaching Aids: a) Audiovisual; b) Field Trips and Excursions; c) Laboratories; d) Tests

After this presentation, Captain Barnard and the Japanese members were asked to indicate additional problems which they had under consideration. In the discussion, the following topics emerged:

  1. The Language Problem
  2. The Development of Initiative and Critical Thinking

3. Kindergarten
4. Physical Education
5. Cultural Education (Art and Music)
6. Education for the Feeble-Minded and Defective (e.g., Deaf and Blind)
7. Moral and Religious Education
8. Co-Education
9. The Question of Abolition of Normal Schools and Provision for Teacher Education in Other Colleges and Universities
10. The Part Played by the Home in the Education of Children (Parent-Teacher Education)
11. Re-Education of Teachers, with Special Reference to the Role of Inspectors
    It was decided to start the next meeting with a discussion on the pre-service education of teachers.

Ernest R. Hilgard, Secretary, Committee No. 2[108]

From the above, we can conjecture that the Japanese proposed issues for discussion.

According to Givens's diary, "Tokyo and Return," on that day Committee III, the Committee on the Organization and Administration of Education, also had its first meeting with the Japanese Education Committee. The Japanese members were Teiyu Amano, President of Tokyo Daiichi Koto Gakko; Shunsaku Kawahara, Privy Councillor; Suteji Kumaki, Headmaster of Tokyo Daiichi Normal School; Masanori Oshima, former professor of Tokyo Imperial University; and Tsuraki Yano, Headmaster of Meiji Gakuin College. The U.S. members were K. Eby, Director of Research and Education of the Congress of Industrial Organizations (CIO); W. E. Givens, Executive Secretary of the National Education Association (secretary of Committee III); F. G. Hochwalt, Secretary of the National Catholic Education Association; E. B. Norton, State Superintendent of Education, Alabama; A. J. Stoddard, Superintendent of Schools, Philadelphia (chairman of Committee III); and P. A. Wanamaker, State Superintendent of Public Instruction, State of Washington.[109]

In personal correspondence to her family, Pearl Wanamaker wrote that Committee III had discussed the centralization and decentralization of education, teachers' qualifications, and adult and youth programs. She also mentioned that Gen. MacArthur had suggested that the Mission hold its discussion without worrying about the financial aspects.[110]

On the same day Committee IV, the Committee on Higher Education, had a joint meeting, as well. The Japanese participants were Toyotaka Komiya (chairman), Teizo Toda (vice-chairman), Mantaro Kido, Chikara Tsujita, Risaku Mutai, Naoteru Ueno, Risaburo Torikai, Teiyu Amano, Manjiro Hasegawa, Michio Kozaki, Kinji Shimizu, Tsuraki Yano, Ai Hoshino, Kosaku Kakinuma, and Yasaka Takagi. Attending on the U.S. side were W. M. Compton (chairman), D. H. Stevens, R. J. Deferrari, V. C. Gildersleeve, and M. M. Horton. Also at the meeting were Crofts and Donovan of the CI&E staff. That evening the Mission drew up twelve written inquiries relating to higher education in Japan and requested Committee 4 of the Japanese Education Committee to discuss them.[111]

On March 11 W. M. Compton, chairman of Committee IV, read out a letter dated March 10 from Yasaka Takagi, a professor at Tokyo Imperial University, in which he stated his agreement with equality for men and women in liberal higher education. D. H. Stevens later recalled:

The last name on this short list of liberals is that of Professor Takagi, on the Law Faculty in the Tokyo Imperial University and long familiar with higher education practices in this country. Professor Takagi wrote us a letter on higher education for women, using the story of family sacrifice for his own daughters in making his points clear. It sounds to our sub-committee on higher education as if written by any American father in any of our communities. He believes that the future Japan must identify by the intelligence, not by sex, in planning the future general education of its citizens.[112]

On March 12 Commander Crofts of the CI&E submitted two memorandums for discussion to W. M. Compton, chairman of Committee IV, which referred to the problems of imperial and private universities and mentioned the existence of a report of the Private Universities Association.[113] On the same day Compton decided on assignments for each member which reflected their areas of specialization and experience.[114] For instance, one of the female members, V. C. Gildersleeve, had been appointed by President Franklin D. Roosevelt to serve as a member of the U.S. delegation to the Charter Conference of the United Nations. M. M. Horton was a former director of the Women Accepted for Voluntary Emergence Service (WAVES).[115]

It is obvious that the Mission commenced preparations for drafting the Report during the CI&E's orientation sessions. At this stage the preparatory work was carried out through cooperation between the Mission, the Education Division of the CI&E, and the Japanese Education Committee.

In addition to meetings with the Japanese Education Committee, the Mission had opportunities to see other Japanese leaders. For example, on the afternoon of March 13, the members were invited to a Japanese tea ceremony at the official residence of the prime minister, Kijuro Shidehara, who gave a speech which was reciprocated by G. D. Stoddard. On the evening of March 14, they were invited to a dinner party given by foreign minister Shigeru Yoshida, at which he gave a speech. W. E. Givens summarized his speech as follows: "Foreign Minister Yoshida read a two-page speech in which he asked that, in our recommendations, we consider the fact that Japan has its own culture, and may want to be democratic in a way different from America."[116]

4) JAPANESE INITIATIVE AS SEEN IN THE RECOMMENDATIONS OF THE JAPANESE EDUCATION COMMITTEE

The Mission and its Report directed postwar education reforms as well as stimulating and encouraging Japanese initiative in attempting independent reforms.

In regard to independent reforms by the Japanese, Shigeru Nambara, chairman of the Japanese Education Committee, stated:

> In regard to this important issue, first of all, we discussed how we considered it ourselves. The Government was not pleased with our movement at all; nevertheless, we held some meetings in the office of the Ministry of Education, and also at times in other places. We compiled various opinions which emerged during our meetings, and formed a report of the main points for reform. Then we submitted it to the U.S. Education Mission and our own government, as a confidential report of recommendations.[117]

It is very important, for the study of independent Japanese education reforms, to specify when the confidential report of recommendations was actually submitted. However, because the report bears no date, there are two differing opinions as to the time of its submission: during February, before the Mission's arrival, and in April, after the Mission had left Japan.[118]

As a matter of fact, in the section headed "Establishment of Educational Authority" the report stated: "Although there are various methods of considering the establishment of educational authority, *this committee has decided to follow the "Board of Education" system suggested by the U.S. Mission* [author's italics]."

This indicates that the report was submitted after contact with the Mission. Therefore, the suggestion that the date of submission was in February is unlikely. The date of April, after the Mission had left, is equally dubious. As seen in Nambara's testimony, the Japanese made their own proposals in the form of "opinions," and handed them to the Mission during its stay in Japan.

The author cannot accept either of the above suggested dates, since the draft of the report, drawn up as opinions by the Japanese Education Committee, was prepared before the Mission's arrival. Opinions were expressed on the following six subjects:

1. The Imperial Rescript on Education
2. Establishment of Educational Authority

3. The School System
4. Teachers' Association and League of Teachers
5. Educational Methods
6. National Language Question

As described in the previous section, some drafts of these opinions were presented to the Mission during joint meetings. At the beginning of April, after the Mission had left, the Japanese Education Committee compiled these opinions as "Recommendations of the Japanese Education Committee." The draft of these opinions, submitted to the Mission during joint meetings, was only recently discovered among historical documents. Especially significant is the inclusion of an English written recommendation on a New Imperial Rescript on Education, entitled "Statement of Japanese Committee No 3 Concerning the Imperial Rescript [of] Education." As mentioned in the previous section, this statement, submitted to Committee III of the Mission on March 20, urged the Mission to proclaim a New Imperial Rescript on Education. However, the final Report made no mention of the proclamation of a New Imperial Rescript on Education. Even the committee's own initial recommendation of "permanent discontinuance" of the Imperial Rescript on Education was moderated to a recommendation that it be "discontinued." Nevertheless, the report of the Japanese Education Committee still urged a New Imperial Rescript on Education. Accordingly, it is conjectured that the Japanese Education Committee submitted its report, "Recommendations of the Japanese Education Committee," to the Japanese government, including its opinions concerning The Imperial Rescript on Education, after the Mission had left.

The Japanese Education Committee's opinions concerning the school system, which were based on prewar concerns, were also presented to Committee III of the Mission prior to the Mission's presentation of proposals for reform of the school system. This will be discussed in detail in Chapter 5.

The initial opinion on the "National Language Question," which was supposed to have been presented to the Mission, has not yet been found. However, the report of the Japanese Education Committee comments as follows, under the heading "The Problem of Romanization":

> It is all right for elementary school students to study romaji [the Roman alphabet]; but we cannot agree to the system of mixing romaji and kana in horizontal style in elementary school textbooks with a view to eventually replacing all ideographs and kana with romaji. It is still too early for this move.

Thus, the Japanese Education Committee severely criticized the draft of the report "Romanization of the Japanese Language," which was drawn up by the Mission's Special Committee on Japanese Language. This statement shows the Japanese reaction to the draft of the Mission's proposal. In other words, the Japanese received information on the draft on the romanization of the Japanese language drawn up by the Mission.

As already seen, Shigeru Nambara, the president of Tokyo Imperial University, had proposed the formation of a "Research Committee on the Education System" at Tokyo Imperial University to discuss the postwar Japanese educational system. The committee discussed the problem of reform of the Japanese language from their own point of view. This will be discussed in detail in Chapter 4.

Consequently, it can be said that the Japanese were actively concerned with postwar education reform and had an extremely important influence on the Mission in the drafting of its Report. Their proposals in "Recommendations of the Japanese Education Committee" imply a dynamic relationship between continuity and discontinuity of prewar Japanese education. This will be discussed in detail in subsequent chapters.

After the Mission had left Japan, the Japanese Education Committee compiled all the statements expressing its opinions, for its own report. However, this report was not submitted to both "the U.S. Education Mission and our own Government," as Nambara testified. Apparently it was submitted only to the Japanese government. Bowles was shocked by Nambara's testimony because, while an important coordinator with the Japanese side in his capacity as secretary of the Mission, he did not even know of the existence of the report of the Japanese Education Committee.[119]

GHQ and the CI&E had no knowledge of the existence of this report. On June 6, 1946, at the Far Eastern Commission (FEC) in Washington, the supreme authority for occupied Japan, a U.S. government representative revealed that the report of the Japanese Education Committee had been submitted to Minister of Education Abe a few days after the Mission had submitted its Report to Gen. MacArthur. He had obtained an article from the *Shinano Mainichi Shinbun* dated April 4, 1946, which included the petition for a New Imperial Rescript on Education, which had been excluded from the Final Report of the Mission.[120]

The formulation and compilation of the Japanese opinions, without their having been reported to the CI&E, was against the directive contained in SCAP's "Committee of Japanese Educators." This is why "Recommendations of the Japanese Education Committee" is also called "Confidential Report of Recommendations" in Japan.

Eventually, the Japanese translated the entire report into English and submitted it to the Education Division of the CI&E. Two copies of this English translation are in the Trainor Papers. One is a copy of the original report translated by the Japanese; the other had been revised by GHQ, and shows evidence of strict censorship.

This chapter has described how the Mission was entrusted by Gen. MacArthur to make recommendations on postwar Japanese education reform at a high level, regardless of any financial considerations. It was originally understood that the Mission was to submit its Report as a "confidential report" directly to Gen. MacArthur, without any inspection by the CI&E, enabling the Mission to make free and wide-ranging recommendations. Using the booklet *Education in Japan* produced by the Education Division of the CI&E, the Mission prepared a draft reflecting the opinions of the Japanese Education Committee in order to encourage their initiative, in accordance with the Potsdam Declaration.

At the same time, the Japanese Education Committee suggested its own positive education reforms, as Nambara's testimony indicates: "We not only cooperated with the Mission but also used it to actualize our opinions."[121]

4

THE MISSION'S REPORT AND REFORM OF THE JAPANESE LANGUAGE

I. SCAP and the Reform of the Japanese Language

Chapter II of the *Report of the U.S. Education Mission to Japan*, entitled "Language Reform," states:

> ... the Mission believes that in time kanji should be wholly abandoned in the popular written language and that a phonetic system should be adopted. ... In the judgement of the Mission, there are more advantages to romaji than to kana. Furthermore, it would lend itself well to the growth of democratic citizenship and international understanding.

Thus, in taking up the issue of the language reform, the report advocated the total abolition of *kanji* ideographs, instituting instead, the adoption of phonetic notation (*kana*) and *romaji* (romanized Japanese) for general use, and recommended that committees and research institutes should be set up in order to achieve this great national goal.

Until now, owing to the restrictions on historical documents, the drafting of Chapter II, the discussions and research that were carried out, and the identity of those directly in charge have not been revealed. Recently, however, the unpublished draft of Chapter II by the Special Committee on Language was discovered in the David H. Stevens Papers.[1] This draft presents several recommendations, such as the adoption of *romaji* in postwar Japanese elementary schools and the joint use of Japanese with *romaji* in school textbooks.

The purpose of this chapter is to study and verify details of the drafting of Chapter II of the Report, by referring to primary historical documents such as the David H. Stevens Papers, the Joseph C. Trainor Papers, and the George D. Stoddard Papers. The chapter also draws on interviews with G. T. Bowles and H. J. Wunderlich, Textbook Officer, the Education Division of the CI&E.

On the question of the language reform under the Occupation, the account of R. K. Hall is accepted by most researchers, as a leading figure in the CI&E. His enthusiastic attitude towards Japanese language reform was obvious even before the Mission's arrival in Japan. For instance, in the early summer of 1945, when he was still Chief of the Education Section of the Planning Staff for the Occupation of Japan at the Civil Affairs Staging Area (CASA) in Monterey, California, he had already proposed a plan relating to the abolition of *kanji*. In fact, on June 23, 1945, Hall sent Major General John H. Hilldring, (Director, CAD, War Department) a five-page memorandum entitled "The Exclusive Use of Katakana as Official Written Japanese."[2] In this memorandum, he suggested that only *katakana* be sanctioned for use in Japan under the Occupation as follows: "It is recommended that all written communication in the Japanese language during military occupation be restricted to katakana, and that the use of materials in kanji be prohibited."

As the reasons for this sanction, he enumerated the following:

1. Prohibiting kanji would greatly assist in barring access to prewar propaganda.
2. The exclusive use of katakana would ease the problem of censorship.
3. The use of katakana would shorten the time required for children to reach the same proficiency level in schools.
4. Katakana would increase national business efficiency.

Although Gen. Hilldring tended to favor these proposals, on July 3, 1945, he sent Hall's memorandum to Eugene H. Dooman, who was in charge of Japan in the Division of Far East Affairs in the State Department, in order to solicit his opinion. Dooman replied on July 6, 1945, pointing out that Hall's description of the Japanese language was inaccurate, opining that Hall's proposal should not be implemented because it would be extremely restrictive in relation to intellectual and cultural studies, and concluding:[3]

It is our view that the prohibition of Chinese characters could not be enforced. Even if it could be, the elimination of Chinese characters under conditions of military occupation would probably have consequences of a most serious and *far-reaching character*, not only in drastically limiting intellectual and cultural pursuits, but in impeding in most drastic form the operation of the normal economy of the country. (Author's italics)

The War Department officially refused Hall's proposal on July 11, 1945. Thus, his original plan for Japanese language reform was rejected before he was assigned his post in Japan. However, his idea did not die, and this setback did not deter him from working for reform later in Japan and making converts of many members of the Mission in March 1946.[4]

When Hall arrived in Japan, he discovered that debate on the reform of the Japanese language was under way there, but rather than preferring *katakana*, it favored *romaji*. Once again Hall became very enthusiastic about the reforms, but this time he made a complete reversal of his initial proposal, and accepted the change to *romaji*.

On November 20, Hall discussed the romanization of school textbooks, and their revision, with Jiro Arimitsu, chief of the Bureau of Textbooks and an administrative official. These controversial discussions, which resulted in the creation of a new type of textbook, arose from "Administration of the Educational System of Japan," one of the Four Negative Directives for Educational Reform issued by SCAP on October 22. In that meeting, Hall gave the following reasons for demanding the romanization of school textbooks:[5]

> The reasons for asking that textbooks be written in romaji are the followings. It will be easier for foreigners to read Japanese. It will be easier for the Japanese common people to read laws and newspapers and become thereby really literate. You should prepare the romaji in the vernacular and not in the classical style.

After prior consultation of with Tamon Maeda, the Minister of Education, Harold G. Henderson, Chief of the Education Division of CI&E, declared that he had no intention of issuing an order to romanize textbooks. This contradiction between Henderson and Hall shows that views were not entirely consistent within the CI&E. Consequently, Gen. MacArthur had the Education Division of CI&E reorganized, for having conveyed unnecessary confusion to the Japanese people over this issue, and also for nominating James. B. Conant, the President of Harvard University, to be chairman of the Mission against his, General MacArthur's, own wishes.

Hall was forced to hand the textbook matter over to H. J. Wunderlich, as he was himself reassigned to the Planning Division. He was also relieved of operational duties and liaison with the Ministry of Education. In order to resolve the confusion concerning romanization, Lt. Col. Donald R. Nugent was appointed Chief of Education Division of CI&E, succeeding H. G. Henderson, who was to become a Special Adviser, on December 10, 1945. This confusion over romanization continued until D. R. Nugent told Shigeru Fukuda, a liaison officer, that the romanization of textbooks was unnecessary, effective December 14, 1945.[6] Thus, at this point, the issue of the romanization of textbooks was officially settled.

However, Hall, who still advocated the reform of the Japanese language through the adoption of romanization, began to work behind the scenes to have his proposal studied and adopted by the Mission, which was to arrive in Japan at the beginning of March of the following year. On November 12, 1945, a staff investigation and study of the entire problem of simplifying the written language was begun confidentially, but personnel from the Central News Agency, a semi-official Chinese organ, learned of the study and, without consulting any representative of Headquarters, conducted a private investigation of its own through Japanese channels. On January 18, 1946, this agency filed a story, "Plans to Replace Present Way of Writing Nippon Language by Alphabet," which was published widely throughout China. The reaction in Occupation Headquarters, when press clippings from China arrived, was one of alarm.[7] However, on March 4, 1946, two days before the Mission's arrival, some members of the CI&E staff, with Hall, completed a staff study entitled "A Tentative Study: Japanese Written Language Revision Study."[8] It consisted of 44 typed pages, 35 appendices, and 260 references, and was quite a persuasive document. It presented the Japanese language problems as follows:

> An educated and literate citizenry is the fundamental prerequisite of any form of representative government or democratic society. Despite impressive official claims of an extremely high rate of literacy, the majority of Japanese people are actually unable to read anything beyond the simplest level, and accordingly are politically uninformed. The excessive difficulty of the written form of the Japanese language, rather than the absence of an adequate system of compulsory education, is the cause. No extension of the compulsory educational level which is practical in the foreseeable future can resolve the difficulty. The development and adoption of a radically simplified writing system would provide a solution.

The authors of this study emphasize the Japanese language reform, not from the viewpoint of censorship, but from the necessity for democratizing Japan, as "the Occupation have recognized the impossibility of democratizing education and of establishing a truly representative government while the present language system is retained." It is obvious that R. K. Hall focused the study in such a way as to gain support from the Mission.

This time, Hall attempted to mold his ideas in accordance with the aim of Headquarters, which was to accomplish the democratization of Japan, quoting from the provision in the Potsdam Declaration which specified:

" . . . the Japanese government shall remove all obstacles to the revival and strengthening of democratic tendencies among the Japanese people."

In regard to this staff study, D. R. Nugent issued a strict memorandum prohibiting R. K. Hall from supplying the Mission with any conclusions or proposals, except for mention of the problem of romanization.[9] Accordingly, Hall reluctantly was able only to suggest the problem briefly to the Mission in the orientation session.

The reason Hall persisted in his ideas about the Japanese language reform may have been due to the fact that as a graduate student he was strongly influenced by Charles C. Fries, one of his professors at the University of Michigan. Professor Fries was a prominent linguist who contributed to English education in postwar Japan, and his special subject was language simplification.[10]

As a result of the inclusion in the Report of his recommendation for language reform through the romanization of the Japanese language, Hall was promoted at Columbia University. In fact, however, the Education Division staff members in the CI&E were opposed to the language reform he proposed.[11]

II. *The Education Mission and Japanese Language Reform*

We will now focus on the Mission's attitude toward language reform. Before their arrival in Japan, as we have seen, the members of the Mission had preparatory meetings in Washington, Hawaii, and Guam. According to documents, it was at a meeting in Washington on February 19, 1946, that the first description of Japanese language reform appeared. However, they did not discuss it concretely at that time.

How did the Mission touch upon language reform? On January 9, 1946, SCAP issued a memorandum to the Japanese government on the subject of the Japanese Education Committee. It noted that the Mission was expected to study language "revision," and to submit reports and recommendations to the Supreme Commander for the Allied Powers. The original term used was "revision," rather than "reform."

At the Guam meeting on March 3, 1946, Chairman Stoddard prepared a memorandum entitled "Part II on Preparing the Report,"[12] in which he recorded that five members who were interested in Japanese language reform were chosen to form a subcommittee. They were Isaac L. Kandel (appointed as chairman), Leon Carnovsky, Thomas V. Smith, George S. Counts, and Gordon T. Bowles.

On March 9, in Japan, at the subcommittee's first meeting with the Japanese Education Committee, I. L. Kandel mentioned Japanese language reform only to say: "The members of the subcommittee do not possess any abilities to recommend the language reform.... On the issue of the language reform, a responsible authority will be needed."[13]

On March 11 two special committees within the Mission were organized to prepare the draft of the Report. One was a Special Committee on Language, from which T. V. Smith, I. L. Kandel, and L. Carnovsky had been removed and replaced by Charles H. McCloy, David H. Stevens, and William C. Trow, with G. S. Counts appointed as chairman. The other was a Special Committee on Drafting, which consisted of the following seven members: G. D. Stoddard (chairman), Harold R. Benjamin, G. T. Bowles, Virginia C. Gildersleeves, I. L. Kandel, T. V. Smith, and Willard E. Givens.[14] Only Bowles belonged to both special committees.

On March 16, the Special Committee on Drafting prepared a paper entitled "Proposed Outline of the Report."[15] Therein, they formally decided to include Japanese language reform as an official provision in Part II of the Report, under the title, "An Evaluation of the Problem of Reforming the Written Language." On the evening of March 24, 1946, all subcommittees in the Mission gathered for a general meeting to submit their drafts and discuss them. At this meeting, G. S. Counts, chairman of the Special Committee on Language, reported its proposals and submitted a draft by his committee.

III. The Draft by the Special Committee on Language and the Japanese Language Reform

The draft begins with the following statement:

> The question of language reform is basic and urgent. It emerges in almost every branch of the educational program from the primary school to the university. *If this question is evaded, many of the proposals made in this report will be practically impossible of achievement and the development of democracy in Japan will be seriously hampered.* (Author's italics)

As well as pointing out the importance of Japanese language reform, the draft goes on to discuss it, giving detailed examples of how the Japanese language issue interferes with Japanese school education. It also refers to an example of the simplification of *kanji* in China: "It is significant that in the past China has evolved phonetic symbols, acting quite independently, designed to simplify the Chinese language, and that now Chinese scholars are deeply concerned with ways to improve their language for all the purposes of modern communication." This obviously reflects the chairman's view, as a professor of comparative education in Columbia University. In conclusion, it recommends as follows:

With this conviction, *the Mission recommends the introduction of some form of romaji into all elementary schools and the preparation of textbooks in two language forms*. The two forms might appear on the same page, as in several texts now in circulation, or on opposite pages. Choice in this aspect of the plan should be made by printers and specialists in the subjects taught. Also, the Japanese who themselves have the true feeling for the most desirable form of language now in common use should determine what form of romaji and what blend of kanji and kana would best serve the needs of pupils at a given level.

The making of these decisions might be the work of the Japanese language commission and a similar body might determine at what level in the elementary schools the new texts would be made available to all pupils in the country. The textbooks in two language forms might be prepared for the first three, for the last three, or for all six years of the elementary school. Such texts should be made standard for the entire country, at the same time provision should be made for the publication of newspapers, periodicals, and books, in whole or in part, in romaji. An interesting and exciting children's literature in the new language form would be helpful. In order to speed the reform, children and youths might be prepared to give instructions in romaji to their elders in the family and the community. (Author's italics)

However, the above part of the draft was deleted from the final Report (March 30, 1946), which begins, "We come now to a matter which both modesty and ease would counsel us to avoid, if our sense of responsibility to the children of Japan permitted.... From a deep sense of duty, and from it alone, we recommend a drastic reform of the Japanese written language." From this wording, we can deduce that Chairman Stoddard and G. T. Bowles completed this part of the report on Japanese language reform with much hesitation.

Furthermore, the main recommendation was originally: "The introduction of some form of romaji into all elementary schools and the preparation of textbooks in two language forms," which they then changed to more a flexible interpretation of the recommendations:

1) That some form of romaji be brought into common use by all means possible.

2) That the particular form of romaji chosen be decided upon by a commission of Japanese scholars, educational leaders, and statesmen.

3) That the commission assume responsibility for coordinating the program of language reform during the transitional stages.

4) That the commission formulate a plan and a program for introducing romaji into the schools and into the life of the community and nation through newspapers, periodicals, books, and other writings.

5) That the commission study, also, the means of bringing about a more democratic form of the spoken language.

6) That in view of the steady drain on the learning-time of children, the commission be formed promptly. It is hoped that a thorough report and a comprehensive program may be announced within a reasonable period.

IV. *The Draft on Japanese Language Reform by Japanese Educators*

How did the Japanese Education Committee deal with this issue? With regard to The Problem of Romanization,' in the ''National Language Question'' section of the Recommendations of the Japanese Education Committee, they give their views as follows:

> It is all right for elementary school students to study ''romaji'' (western alphabet); but *we cannot agree to the system of mixing ''romaji'' with ''kanji'' and ''kana'' in horizontal style in elementary school textbooks, with the view of eventually replacing all characters and ''kana'' with ''romaji.''* It is still too early for this move.
>
> Even with the study of ''romaji'' it is difficult as well as undesirable to conduct it nationally in a uniform manner. There are differences between cities and villages. Whatever the case may be, it is probably more suitable to let the school principal decide according to local conditions. (Author's italics)

Here, they state their opposition to reforming school textbooks by printing texts in horizontal lines with *romaji*; nevertheless, they present their view that it is appropriate for *romaji* to be taught in elementary schools.[16] As we have seen, because the Central News Agency had released a story on January 18, 1946, the Japanese Education Committee knew of the Occupation's intention to force the romanization of the Japanese language, and they also knew that the Special Committee on Language in the Mission was to prepare a draft report in line with this policy. Thus, this recommendation shows the committee's strong reaction to the above intentions of the U.S. side, and it seems that their views influenced the draft made by the Special Committee on Language in the Mission.

At the time of the Mission's arrival in Japan, Shigeru Nambara, the President of Tokyo Imperial University, proposed forming a Research Committee on the Education System at Tokyo Imperial University, to discuss the need for education reform in parallel with discussions within the Japanese Education Committee. On March 2, the first meeting of this Research Committee was held,[17] at which the reform of the Japanese language and its written form were discussed. On March 12, 1946, a report was submitted to President Nambara, which states:

> The reform of the Japanese language and its written form should be implemented now, for the progress of Japanese culture. The Japanese language

should be a language which is understood on hearing. The written form should be combined with *kanji* as a main structure. Numbers in *kanji* should be limited and letters of homonyms should be rearranged. Restriction on the use of *kanji* should be implemented not only in school education, but also, by the same policy, newspapers, magazines and books should be published within the restrictions on *kanji*. The reform of the written language is intended to promote a use of the phonetic system and encourage the use of *kana* and to spread romaji. Regarding the use of *kana* to express Chinese sounds, *kana* should be used phonetically, and regarding the use of *kana* to express Japanese words, the historical method should be employed. An institution of the Japanese language should be set up in Tokyo Imperial University, in order to reform the Japanese language by studying its problems. It could accordingly, contribute to Japanese language reform with academic proposals, through continuous studies and the cooperation of scholars and other intellectuals.

A summary of this report by the Tokyo Imperial University Committee on the problem of the Japanese language seems, through the Japanese Education Committee, to have been given to the Mission.[18] On the issue of language reform, it influenced the recommendations of the Japanese Education Committee. At the same time, we can see that it offers suggestions for the Mission's final Report.

Chairman Nambara recalls those days:

> In the report of the Japanese Education Committee, we took up the issue of *romaji* in relation to the language problem. Our main concern was that *romaji* could commence to be taught from the new elementary schools level, but we strongly objected to the idea that it should replace the Japanese language. You may know of a man, whose name was Hall, in the CI&E, who was very enthusiastic. He had intended to influence the Mission to recommend the future romanization of the Japanese language. I presume that it was in the light of the U.S. experience in Turkey after World War I that he strongly suggested the adoption of *romaji*. However, we had already learned of his intention, and therefore were able to oppose it, and even expressed our view personally to Mr. Hall. In fact, we argued about this issue a great deal. In the end, Stoddard's report adopted a neutral position, I think. It was fortunate that the Report finally accepted our opinion in the matter.[19]

Summary: An Interview with Gordon T. Bowles

Why was the original draft of the Japanese language reform moderated in the final Report? As a matter of fact, the person who insisted on moderating the content of the draft was Gordon Bowles. He was opposed to the romanization of *kanji* in written Japanese, and he insisted that the reform of the Japanese language should be left strictly to the Japanese side without outside interference.

When he was shown the draft by the Special Committee on Language, he confirmed that it was certainly considered in the process of drafting the Report. He also verified that as an adviser to the Mission, he had given his comments frankly:

1) It was not necessarily correct to assume that the low percentage (10%) of pupils continuing their education beyond the elementary level was attributable solely to the complexities of the written language. The blame should be placed in large part on the elitist type of society and the assumption that learning even at the secondary level should be limited to those designated to enter academic, political or administrative positions.

2) The Japanese written language is already provided with two alternative phonetic scripts. Learning romaji should definitely be required, but the primary purpose should be to provide the child with the basic script of western European languages and westernized Japanese rather than to use it for textbooks.

3) Such a fundamental change as altering the method of writing should be determined by the Japanese themselves. Would it not be more appropriate to demand that serious consideration be given to the adoption of romaji by the newly established Language Commission?[20]

Furthermore, in relation to the second draft of the "Language Reform," which was drawn up by D. H. Stevens and G. S. Counts, Bowles comments as follows:

1) A recognition of efforts toward reform which had already been made, even though "none has had a fair trial in the school nor had any one of the proposals for change been given serious consideration."

2) Mention of China's efforts to simplify its written language and that possibly Japan might wish to promote some form of collaboration. It was Stoddard's strong feeling that the final Report should be limited solely to Japan's problems.

3) A brief that the Mission should support adoption of some form of phonetic script, but not specifying romaji.

4) A proposal also that the Mission recommend use in textbooks of two language forms. The two forms "might appear on the same page, as in several texts now in circulation, or on opposite pages."

Concerning the final Report, Bowles noted:

Strong feelings were expressed by the proponents of romaji, that Item I in the summary recommendations of the final Report, should read: "That some form of romaji must be brought into common use by all means possible." It was my contention that use of the word *must* was more of a command than a recommendation and that the word *should* might be more appropriate. A compromise was reached by dropping both words. I could see no objection to the final wording, since it would certainly be advantageous to every child to be able to cope with romaji.

I remember, also, that in considering the Commission for Language Reform (as given under items 4 and 5), its function came under considerable debate, and that those of us who urged moderation, did manage to have deleted from the final wording, any suggestion that an immediate adoption of romaji in school textbooks should be made mandatory or even given priority consideration.

The flat statement is made in the final Report that there are more advantages to romaji than to kana, but no reasons were given for this pronouncement. Presumably it was because it opened the way to a study of occidental language. No mention was made of the value of kana as a collective phonetic symbol or a syllabic sound grouping as opposed to the alphabetical qualities of romaji. It is my memory that the usefulness of furigana was never understood. It was perceived more as a shortcut or abbreviation rather than a simplified phonetic cluster equivalent. (Author's italics)[21]

At the same time, Bowles described the objections to his suggestions. For instance, William Benton, the Assistant Secretary of State, showed his disappointment with Bowles' assertions and his influence on the draft. Benton strongly supported romanization of the school textbooks as a convenient means of promoting democratization and improving educational standards.

The Mission had been very influenced by the CI&E (and especially by Hall), with respect to the Japanese language reform. H. J. Wunderlich, recalling those days, stressed in an interview that there were no specialists in linguistics in the Mission,[22] and hinted that the Japanese language reform proposal had been originally prepared at the initiative of the CI&E. Quite a number of Mission members were influenced by Hall's views on romanization of the Japanese language. G. S. Counts, chairman of the Special Committee on Language, was one. G. T. Bowles writes that Counts and D. H. Stevens spent much time with Hall in this connection.[23] In the process of completing the section on the Japanese language reform in the final Report, Hall objected in a personal way to Bowles, which the latter describes as follows:[24]

I agreed to teach some form of romaji in elementary school. However, I opposed its romanization, especially a drastic change to the Japanese written language. The matter of the language reform had to be decided by the Japanese themselves, not by outsiders. This is nothing to do with the Occupation nor the war itself. This is a matter of Japanese culture and arts. Such drastic reform of the

Japanese language is not only undesirable, but in the event of failure, would be our fault. That is why I disagreed with it. Robert King Hall was extremely angry and said, "You will come to realize that you are eternally wrong. In the future, all Japanese children will be sacrificed for not being able to learn the romanized Japanese language, that I proposed," which was contrary to my opinion.

And, according to Bowles's memoir, "Reflections on the March 1946 U.S. Education Mission to Japan"[25]:

The majority of the Mission members and especially George Stoddard, chairman of the Mission, as well as my superior, Assistant Secretary of State William Benton, sincerely believed that forcing a child to master between one and two thousand characters would definitely have a crippling effect on the child's education and impose an unwarranted burden on the whole educational process. I can at least take satisfaction in knowing that *the results of my last minute efforts did produce a tempering effect on the wording of the Report and that, instead of recommending that all elementary textbooks be written in romaji, or Latin script, it was simply urged that some form of writing be given careful consideration.* I felt at the time that recommending a committee or commission to study the matter of simplification of writing was a major victory. (Author's italics)

This testimony is important in understanding the process of the drafting of the Japanese language reform recommendations. The Bowles memoir is particularly worthy of attention because it had been written before the draft was discovered in the Stevens Papers.

As we can see from the above, the draft drawn up by the Special Committee on Language was not reflected in the final Report, because of G. T. Bowles's objection. Though the Report of the Mission became the starting point for the postwar education reform in Japan, the "Language Reform" chapter was not implemented, unlike the 6−3−3 school system and many other reforms in education, for the following reasons: First, in releasing the Report of the Mission, General MacArthur gave the "Statement" on April 7, 1946, in which he suppressed the recommendation, commenting: "Some of the recommendations regarding education principles *and language reform* are so far reaching that they can only serve as a guide for long range study and future planning." (Author's italics)

Second, Lt. Col. Nugent, Chief of the Education Division of the CI&E, did not totally agree with all the contents in the chapter on Japanese language reform. On April 30, 1946, Brig. Gen. Ken R. Dyke, Chief of the CI&E, was called to testify before the Allied Council for Japan (ACJ), the Tokyo representatives of the Far Eastern Commission (FEC). During the meeting, he was questioned as to the official policy regarding the elimination of *kanji* characters from the Japanese writing system by China's representative, Lt. Gen. Chu Shih-ming. Dyke had been in the U.S. on leave at the time of the Mission's visit, and had been represented by his deputy and later successor, D. R. Nugent. Although the Report had unequivocally recommended revision and the adoption of *romaji*, Dyke's reply to the question of the Chinese representative, as reported in the May *Pacific Stars and Stripes*, was that language reform was a matter on which the Japanese themselves would have to decide.[26] As a result, the State Department, the Chief of the CI&E, and, above all, Gen. MacArthur himself all believed it unwise to impose such a drastic reform unless it first won widespread support among the Japanese people.[27] In the event, it was due to the objections raised by the Japanese Education Committee, which had strongly opposed the romanization of school textbooks, that the reforms were revised.

This chapter has focused on Chapter II, "Language Reform," in the Report of the Mission and described its drafting process. The Mission had the greatest regard for the intentions of the Japanese Education Committee, and formulated its Report through discussion with Japanese educators, leaving the initiative with them.

However, quite a number of members of the Mission criticized the final Report's modification of the plan for romanization of the Japanese language. For example, W. Compton wrote to Assistant Secretary of State Benton, after his return:

> I think that fundamentally that recommendation is more important than all the rest because *without the language reform the other reforms in my judgement cannot be fully effective.* I personally would have preferred a much stronger statement on language reform in our report and a stronger challenge to the Japanese to do something about it.[28] (Author's italics)

Also, W. C. Trow, one of the members of the Special Committee on Language, in his unpublished memoirs, expresses his dissatisfaction as follows:

> A final question of general interest was that of recommending that romaji be officially adopted and serve as the written language of instruction. Robert King Hall was convinced that now was the time for this change, that it was possible, since Turkey had actually taken the equivalent step ... the head of CI&E was sensitive to pressure and had consistently opposed the change, so we did what I suppose was the most politic thing—recommended that romaji be taught in the schools if so desired, along with the Japanese characters.... I regretted that our committee did not take a definite stand and suggest a possi-

ble implementation that Hall had worked out, and then leave it to the Japanese [to] decide.[29]

It is interesting to note that Trow was a faculty member of the University of Michigan while Hall was a graduate student there, and that they were on friendly terms.

Thus, the language reform was not solely an issue for the Special Committee on Language, but was also of concern to the other committees in the Mission. It can be said that the matter of language reform influenced other recommendations made in the Report. For instance, language reform is the basis for the recommendation in the chapter on "Adult Education."

Finally, G. D. Stoddard, chairman of the Mission, and William Benton, Assistant Secretary of State, were quite favorably inclined toward romanization as a tool for the democratization of postwar Japan. Chairman Stoddard was responsible for a great deal of the desired simplification of the language, and numerous drafts were made, the final copy being submitted to General MacArthur. As a result, we need to study Chapter II of the Report, "Language Reform," which reflects considerable hesitation on the part of those people involved in the process of drafting it.

The State Department drew up a policy statement on educational revisions based on the Report of the Mission. It was submitted to the Far Eastern Commission on March 27, 1947, and was approved and published as "Policy for the Revision of the Japanese Educational System." It included every important recommendation made by the Mission, with one significant exception. On language reform, there was not a single word.[30]

The Mission recommended the introduction of *romaji* into the schools. However, the Japanese only used *romaji* for the simplification of the Japanese language along the lines proposed in the "Recommendations of the Japanese Education Committee."

In accordance with recommendations made in the Report, the National Japanese Language Research Institute was set up as an organ under the Ministry of Education's jurisdiction, in December 1948. The aim of this institute was to establish the basis for scientific research work and the rationalization of the Japanese language. The elementary and secondary schools, which were reorganized within the new school system, on April 1, 1947, adopted *romaji* in their language textbooks. The introduction of *romaji* in compulsory education had also been the desire of the advocates of romanization in Japan, for a long time.

Referring to *romaji*, the Report recommends that "some form of romaji be brought into common use by all means possible," and also recommends the formation of a commission, which would "formulate a plan and a program for introducing romaji into schools, and into the life of the community and nation, through newspapers, periodicals, books, and other writings." In line with these recommendations, the Ministry of Education set up the Romaji Education Council, which compiled guidelines for *romaji* education. Finally, the Japanese Education Reform Committee decided upon the adoption of *romaji* in compulsory education, in accordance with the suggestions in the Report.[31]

5

THE MISSION'S REPORT AND REFORM OF THE SCHOOL SYSTEM

*I. The Draft Report of Committee III on Reform of
the School System: Recommendation of the 6–5 System*

As is generally known, the reform of the 6–3–3 school system was the
biggest reform introduced by the Mission. This chapter examines the
origin of this reform.

As has been previously described, at the orientation meeting held in
Guam, just prior to the Mission's arrival in Japan, Chairman Stoddard
indicated four areas for the study of Japanese education and appointed
four committees for this purpose, with a chairman for each, requesting
that a report be presented by each of them.

Study of the problems in the school system was delegated to Committee
III—"Primary and Secondary School Administration"—with Alexander
J. Stoddard as Chairman; Kermit Eby, Willard E. Givens, Frederick G.
Hochwalt, Ethelbert B. Norton, and Pearl A. Wanamaker as members; and
Charles Iglehart as advisor. This committee completed a 25-page report on
March 23, and thirty copies were made, as recorded in the journal "Tokyo
and Return" by W. E. Givens, who was in charge of the committee's
keeping records.[1]

The existence of Committee III's report on this issue was known, but its
whereabouts was not, until a copy of the report was recently discovered
in the Wanamaker Papers stored in the Archives of the Henry Suzzallo
Library at the University of Washington.[2]

It comes as a surprise to learn that, in fact, Committee III did not endorse the 6–3–3 school system, but instead recommended that the recently
restored Japanese prewar school system, the 6–5 system, be continued. It

was not simply a matter of preserving the existing school system; the recommendation was based on preliminary meetings in Washington, with government officials, and preparatory proceedings in Hawaii and Guam, and rested on the policy of preserving the traditional Japanese school system while taking steps towards its democratization. In accordance with this, Committee III's report made the following recommendations:

> *The six year elementary school should be entirely free* and attendance compulsory. No form of tuition should be charged. The program of instruction should be such as to prepare children to become healthy, active, thinking citizens eager to develop all of their innate abilities and to be prepared to take their places in a society that is becoming more and more free.
>
> We are convinced that girls are the equal of boys mentally. We therefore *recommend that schools be conducted on a co-educational basis. We recommend that the five-year middle schools be made easily available to all the girls and boys on a co-educational basis and that they be free from all tuition costs to children. We recommend that attendance of all children be compulsory during the first three years.*
>
> These middle schools should be adapted to the personal needs of all the children giving opportunity for the development of all talents and preparing all children to live useful and happy democratic lives participating skillfully in all lines of endeavor in Japan.
>
> Counselling help should be made available in order that each child may be helped to prepare for the work which he will do well and enjoy.
>
> *Higher schools should be made free and open to all.* They should be co-educational and expand to include sufficient course offering to serve the needs of all who wish to attend in order that they may develop personally and be better prepared to participate in the varied activities of their country. (Author's italics)[3]

Thus, it is clearly stated that the 6–5 school system must be made free and co-educational, with nine years' compulsory education.

This report is considered very important in the study of the postwar Japanese school system. At the author's request, Gordon T. Bowles has verified this report, and explains it as follows: "This report does not unconditionally recommend the 6–5 system. The Mission's plan was to allow the 6–5 system to remain, by democratizing its existing structure."[4]

In addition, the author sought confirmation on this specific point from Pearl Wanamaker, who was directly involved in the writing of the report.[5] She says: "The Mission was not very concerned about whether the school system should be the 6–5, or the 6–3–3 system, but rather how to make the substance of the system more democratic."[6]

In fact, the "Conclusion" of Committee III's report states: "The essence of a great school system is in its spirit and substance rather than in its form and structure.''

Between the termination of the war and the beginning of 1946, it is said that the CI&E developed its own education reform plan, parallel with the Four Negative Directives for Education Reform which were issued between October and December 1945. They prepared their reform plan for the Japanese education system, by proposing the co-educational and the 8–3–4 school system, i.e., eight years of compulsory elementary school, three years of middle school, and four years of university.[7]

Furthermore, according to the R. K. Hall Papers, which were made available recently, the Education Division of the CI&E carried out numerous staff studies, before the Mission's arrival. One of these studies discussed compulsory education and took up the issue of the effectiveness of education at the upper elementary school levels, in relation to the extension of compulsory education. It suggested that, before extending compulsory education up to the eighth year in all schools, a critical evaluation should be made of the educational effectiveness of the first six years, in terms of the accomplishment of the aims of the Occupation.[8] In other words, the CI&E examined the implementation of an eight-year compulsory education system, which had already been planned by the Japanese during the war but had not actually been established.

In view of the CI&E's draft plan, why did Committee III recommend the 6–5 Japanese school system in a form that already existed? First of all, as we have seen above, the Mission had learned about the 6–5 school system at the preparatory meeting in Hawaii, and it is possible that they also discussed the reform plan for retaining it. Second, the information booklet produced by the CI&E, *Education in Japan*, states that the existing school system was established in 1937.[9] And on the subject of elementary education, it states:

> Elementary education has been compulsory in Japan since 1872. . . . The period of required general education was fixed at four years in 1886, was raised to six years in 1908, and was raised to eight years in 1941. The eight-year rule, however, has never been put into effect.
>
> The elementary schools were divided into two grades: the ordinary elementary school and the higher elementary school. The ordinary elementary schools were for beginners and extended over a six year period. . .

And on secondary education:

> The middle school course extended over a period of five years, and its object was to prepare boys for higher education, or to fit them to be useful members of society, after graduation. Attendance was not compulsory.

In addition, it describes how the youth school was organized in 1935, and severely criticizes the fact that it was used as a means for ultra-nationalistic and militaristic propaganda.

Meanwhile, the State Department produced new material on the prewar Japanese education system, by adding statistics and charts to a paper published by the Japanese Ministry of Education in 1937. In fact, the Eileen R. Donovan Papers confirm that this edition was used for general lectures on education in the Civil Affairs Training School (CATS) attached to the University of Michigan. It describes the prewar Japanese education system as consisting of compulsory, co-educational, six-year elementary education, with an enrollment of 99.59 percent; secondary education in middle schools, girls' high schools, normal schools, technical schools, and youth schools; and higher education in the preparatory courses for college, higher normal schools, and seven Imperial universities.[10]

At the same time, it should be noted that there was an active movement towards the reform of the school system on the Japanese side as well, just prior to the Mission's arrival.

The 6–5 school system preceded the implementation of the Secondary School Ordinance (four years of secondary school), of January 21, 1943. On January 30, 1946, Tadasuke Yamazaki, Vice-Minister of Education, reported to the CI&E that the Japanese government was going to reform the wartime ordinance, and that the old five-year middle school and three-year high school systems would be resurrected, and a budget estimate was to be drawn up.[11] It was these actions by the Ministry of Education that led to the amendment issued on February 22 of the same year as Imperial Ordinance 102—"Revision of Secondary Schools," changing the "four year" to "five year," and implementing the 6–5 school system on the same day. On February 23, the CI&E, Education Division, records that the prewar school system was reinstated by an Imperial Ordinance from the Ministry of Education,[12] which means that they approved it. In other words, the Mission arrived in Japan just after the reimplementation of the 6–5 school system.

Sanji Aruga, Headmaster of Tokyo Kodaira Youth School, who was a member of Committee No. 3 of the Japanese Education Committee, enthusiastically proposed that the Japanese Government should organize the 6–5–3–3 school system, in a paper entitled "A Concrete Plan of the Reform of the School System,"[13] stating as follows:

> The foundation for the construction of a new Japan relies on education, especially in the fulfillment of education for the masses, which deserves a permanent national policy.
>
> With my recommendations on a separate sheet, I request that the *Govern-*

ment immediately implement a thorough reform of the school system, in order to meet the new circumstance.

A Plan for the School System:

1. Implement 11 year compulsory education for boys and girls, from age 6 to age 17.

2. *Kokumin Gakko (National People's School) provides six years education during their juvenescent period and five years for their adolescence in the middle (kokumin) school.*

3. The present middle school and girls' high school system are maintained for the time being, in place of the implementation of compulsory education.

4. In the middle school (*kokumin*), the first three years are full-time for basic subjects, and the latter two years are part-time, or a half-day system, according to regional circumstances, aiming at vocational education as terminal education. This provides the possibility of transferring to the appropriate grade in middle school or girls' high school, after the completion of three years, for those who so desire, depending on their aptitudes.

5. After compulsory education, other six year educational institutions should be established, in which the first three years are spent in Senmon Gakko (technical college) and the second three years in university.

6. Those who finish compulsory education are qualified to go on to a school of higher grade by request, and result of aptitude tests. (Author's italics)

More of the background to the Mission's recommendation in favor of the 6–5 school system may be found in its attitude, at the time of its arrival in Japan, towards the reform of the school system.

As has been previously stated, the basic policy of the U.S. towards postwar Japan was reflected in the provisions of the Potsdam Declaration. At the same time, people in charge of policy-making on the U.S. side held the opinion that democratic tendencies already existed in prewar Japan, and considered the "revival and strengthening" of such tendencies the most important priority. It was only natural that the Mission's attitude should be along the same lines as this basic policy. In fact, the first part of the paper, "Necessary Adjustments," in which Committee III endorses the 6–5 school system, states: "The form and structure of the school system of Japan should be changed so as to *promote democratic tendencies*" (author's italics).

What then was the understanding of the Mission members who made the actual recommendations? First, Gordon Bowles of the State Department, who was in a key position, and well informed on the Japanese school system, testifies: "My understanding was that problems relating to matters of policy, such as, what kind of school system should be recommended, were not the concern of the Mission."[14]

Also, in writing the Report, E. R. Hilgard, who is thought to have held an influential position on the school system issue, states: "The Mission took the attitude that they should not interfere in school system reform. Such issues should have been decided on by the Japanese."[15]

As mentioned above, Pearl Wanamaker also concurred with the Mission's concern—that it was not the school system itself that needed changing, so much as its substance.

Thus, it must be said that not only Committee III but also the Mission as a whole was very negative concerning the reform of the school system itself. As a matter of fact, the subject matter of Committee III's "Administrative Reorganization of the Educational System of Japan" was: "a study leading to recommendations as to the immediate and long range administrative reforms, the reorganization of the Ministry of Education, and the problems of decentralization."

Studies and recommendations for the school system were not the concern of Committee III. It should be noted that the issue of the school system was a subject for the Japanese Education Committee only, as will be described later in this chapter.

Recommendations by Committee III of the Mission were based, accordingly, on the 6–5 school system. As P. A. Wanamaker testifies, it intended to reform the substance of education rather than the school system itself. As a result, its recommendation was to maintain the 6–5 school system, which provided nine years of compulsory co-education with free tuition, in the fulfillment of democratic goals.

It should however, be noted that this recommendation of the 6–5 school system, did not include the entire system, because the Japanese school system at that time was multi-tracked: After *Kokumin Gakko Shotoka* (National Peoples' Elementary School—six compulsory years), one track led on to the five-year middle school, which was the only possible way to enter higher educational institutions, while the other led to *Kokumin Gakko Kotoka* (National Peoples' Higher Elementary School) or to youth school, both of which were dead ends. When the 6–5 school system was mentioned by the Mission, it indicated only the middle school course, which was just a part of the entire system. In this respect, Committee III's report recommends a change-over from *Seinen Gakko* (Youth School) to *Jitsugyo Gakko* (Vocational School), as follows:

> Youth schools are inadequately housed, poorly programmed and lacking in facilities and leadership. We suggest that they be developed into full scale vocational schools. Vocational schools should provide full opportunity for the development of skill and proficiency on the part of those who desire to prepare for specific occupations.

It seems to suggest discontinuing the multi-track system, but there is no explicit statement advocating its abolition. In other words, at this stage, the recommendation of the 6–5 school system by Committee III betrayed its weakness in its inability to resolve all the problems in the Japanese multi-track school system. Furthermore, the nine years' compulsory education, within the 6–5 school system, would create a splitting of the five-year secondary education into three years and two years, which was inconsistent with the Japanese educational idea of providing a consistent curriculum throughout secondary education. It should be noted, that only the 6–3 school system was practical for the synchronous solution of the problem of six years' elementary education, as well as nine years' compulsory education.

II. School System Reform as Set Out in the Final Report: The Change from the 6–5 to the 6–3–3 School System

Committee III's report was drawn up and submitted on March 23, 1946, while the final Report of the Mission was completed on March 30. This means that the Mission changed its position from favoring a 6–5 school system to actually recommending a 6–3–3 school system within the week. How did this change come about?

During the final six-day period for consideration of the contents of the Report, from March 20 to 25, meetings were held between Mission members and members of the Japanese Education Committee. These last six days figure importantly in the process of change from the 6–5 to the 6–3–3 school system.

On March 21, Shigeru Nambara, Chairman of the Japanese Education Committee, met secretly with Chairman G. D. Stoddard. The minutes of this meeting are recorded in a typed 11-page report entitled "Special Report by Shigeru Nambara, President, Tokyo Imperial University and Chairman of the Japanese Education Committee, to G. D. Stoddard, March 21, 1946."[16] The two met as equals, and as educators. Not only was there a complete lack of any regard for their different positions—one as conqueror, the other as conquered—but Nambara was able to sharply criticize the censorship of SCAP at the time, which reflects their close relationship. Nambara freely expressed his opinions on educational problems and on the reform of the Japanese education system. "Model the whole scheme after the American plan, building up elementary schools, high schools, colleges, and universities, in a natural sequence with wide opportunities at all levels," he said, suggesting that the American style of a single-track school system be introduced. Furthermore, he even said,

"The above reforms are being planned, but Mombusho [the Ministry of Education] is hesitating on this [original underlined]. I regard these reforms as crucial, otherwise a revision of the clique system is impossible." Moreover, he suggested decentralization of the education system, improvement of teachers' status and salaries, and establishment of a powerful teachers' association.

On this point, G. T. Bowles gives important testimony:

> On the 6–3–3 issue, when I became aware of the factionalism that existed among members of the Japanese Education Committee concerning the 6–3–3–4 versus the existing 6–5–3–3 System, and that President Nambara was himself in favor of the change.[17]

In fact, Nambara describes the need for the adoption of the American school system:

> Since the Meiji period, Japanese education incorporated many elements of European systems such as the German and French. Therefore, it is only natural, indeed a necessity, that the American system be incorporated in our education system.[18]

Giving his impression of Nambara, J. R. Trainor describes him as a liberal Christian, with great enthusiasm for education reform.[19] D. H. Stevens writes of him: "He too seems perfectly sincere and constructive in his plan for the future. . ."[20] It is presumed that Stevens had a personal meeting with Nambara, in connection with the Library of Tokyo Imperial University, which was built with a donation from the Rockfeller Foundation, with which Stevens was affiliated.

The key issue of postwar education reform in Japan, was resolving the problem of higher elementary schools (*Koto Shogakko*), which provided education for the adolescent masses, and youth schools (*Seinen Gakko*), which catered for the majority of graduates from higher elementary schools. Concerning the dissolution of higher elementary schools, there were two schools of opinion in Japan. One advocated maintaining them for the purpose of extending compulsory education, and the other advocated reorganizing them as part of secondary education. For instance, Shigetaka Abe of the Kyoiku Kaikaku Doshikai (Professor at Tokyo Imperial University, 1890–1939) opined: "Elementary education should cover a period up to 12 years of age, and be the sole purpose of elementary schools, with the result that existing higher elementary schools would be abolished." Thus "the period of secondary education would cover the years between 12 and 18 and be divided into two stages of three year periods."[21]

In this way, he located the higher elementary school as part of secondary education within the 6–3–3 school system. In other words, he developed the idea of organizing higher elementary schools by absorbing them into the lower part of secondary schools, within the 6–3–3 school system.[22]

"A Proposal for the Reform of the Youth School System" (January–March, 1946) in the Sanji Aruga Papers, mentions as follows:

Although the reform of the entire school system is expected sooner or later, there is, inevitably, a preparation period under the postwar situation. Nevertheless, it is not good enough just to leave youth schools as they are. We desire the following partial reform as a tentative step, and its main aim is to *merge existing youth schools into middle schools and girls' high schools* ... (Author's italics)[23]

Tokiomi Kaigo describes the Japanese approach to the Mission, requesting the reform of the school system:

A strong movement toward reform emerged among the people concerned with youth schools, rather than with middle schools. They demanded equal opportunities for youth schools, which historically had not been recognized as proper schools due to their status as supplementary vocational schools. They naturally insisted on equal opportunities in school education during the meeting with the Mission.[24]

Kaigo also gave a lecture entitled "Democratization of Education"[25] at the first lecture meeting after the war, sponsored by Tokyo Metropolis, in November 1945. In this lecture, he dealt with the subject of the reform of secondary education in the U.S., which was reorganized from an 8–4 system to a 6–3–3 system. He pointed out the ways in which the Japanese education system was not democratic. In order to strengthen equal opportunity, he suggested the establishment of new types of secondary education institutions, which would include higher elementary schools and youth schools at the same level as middle schools, in order to give access to equal secondary education to all, after six years of elementary school. Thus, he suggested that the main means for the reform of the Japanese school system was the reorganization of middle schools. The fact that this lecture was given prior to the Mission's visit is worth noting.

As can be understood from the above, reform within the 6–5 school system, in terms of the idea of equal opportunities of education, presented many problems. It seemed that the only way to resolve the problem of higher elementary and youth schools was to adopt the 6–3–3 single-track school system. This could be the background to Nambara's secretly urging Chairman Stoddard to introduce the 6–3–3 school system to Japan, in spite of the economic difficulties at that time.

On the Japanese side, the records of the movement towards the 6–3–3 school system can be seen in the "Report of Committee No. 3 Concerning Youth Schools Et Al." (originally written in English)[26], thought to have been written by Committee No. 3 of the Japanese Education Committee. The report points out at the outset: "The improvement and expansion of youth schools is of the utmost importance as they are the educational institutions of the people at large." Then it makes the following recommendations:

> The present educational system will be completely changed as follows: The elementary school course will cover six years and the secondary school course will last for six years, which will be divided into two stages, three years for each of them and all schools of the same level such as middle schools, girls' high schools, vocational schools will be included in this category, and youth schools will also come under this category. At present youth schools are excluded from the system of schools in general and receive special treatment in many respects. This is a great disadvantage to encouraging the pupils' study and inviting good teachers, and has a very bad effect on their improvement.
>
> With regard to the question whether or not the higher course of the elementary school which admits the entrance of about 70 percent of the graduates of the lower course of the elementary school will remain, we think it suitable that it will be merged in the youth school of the lower stage lasting for three years, and that by changing the names of both, we will establish a new school.

This report of Committee No. 3, a recommendation for the reform of secondary education in order to promote the youth school, is included among the Wanamaker Papers. For this reason, it can be considered that this Japanese proposal strongly influenced the recommendations made by Committee III of the Mission, including those concerning the school system.

Besides this, there is a personal paper by Eiji Ushiyama (Headmaster of Ushigome Seinen Gakko, Ushigome-ku, Tokyo), entitled "Personal Opinions on the School Education System Reform" (March, 1946), [27] in which he proposes the following:

> 1. Foreword
> ... what has been the biggest problem in the present education system in Japan, is the neglect of working class youth and the adherence to the entrance examination system, resulting in careerism.
> 2. The policy toward reform
> ... thoroughly reform the school system, establishing equality of educational opportunity and pledge to promote a national cultural standard as a basis for the construction of a democratic and liberal Japan...

3. A new education system
Elementary school (six years) age 6–12, compulsory
Middle school (three years) age 12–15, compulsory
High school (three years) age 15–18, semi-compulsory
University (four years) age 18–22
4. Main points of the reform

① Compulsory education should be nine years, from the ages of six to fifteen and wholly financed at the expense of the nation. Followed by three years education up to the age of eighteen, which should be semi-compulsory, in order to encourage the students' own responsibility in furthering their education.

a. The present national people's school will be renamed the elementary school.

b. At present, thirteen years compulsory education is imposed throughout the national peoples' schools and the youth schools. Within the new system, actual compulsory education, will be shortened by one year, to twelve years.

c. *The present higher elementary school, the youth school and the middle school will be dissolved and reorganized into a new three year middle school.* (Author's italics)

In this way, he proposed placing the new middle school and the youth school within the 6–3–3–4 school system, abolishing the higher elementary school.

It should be noted that not only the 6–3–3 school system but also the four-year university system was proposed by the Japanese side in March 1946.

Another proposal by the Japanese side was presented by Taketoshi Yamagiwa (Headmaster of Nishida Kokumin Gakko, Tokyo) in the final joint meeting with the Mission on March 25. In his report, entitled "The Problems of Elementary School Education,"[28] he touched on the school system reform, stating: "Six years of elementary school and three years of junior high school should be made compulsory." As reasons, he cited the rising cultural standard of the Japanese people, the difficulty of choosing a future career at the age of twelve, and the elimination of entrance examination pressure.

There followed an active discussion of Yamagiwa's report, with Chairman Stoddard asking questions about tuition fees and co-education, and W. Compton inquiring about tuition for junior high school.

At four o'clock on the same day, Nambara and Yasaka Takagi (Professor of Tokyo Imperial University) met R. K. Hall of the CI&E and presented a report entitled "Education Reform—Official Version of the Japanese Education Committee."[29] The report proposes thirteen points, the main ones being:

(1) A system of education must be adopted, that is designed to reach the masses, to enlighten the people, and to teach them democratic ideas.

(2) Abolish the *Koto Gakko* (Boys' Higher School), which is the cause of an educational clique, and provide a graded system of schools, all of which can lead either to a terminal course or to admission to a university-level institution.

(3) The differentiation between *Semmon Gakko* (colleges for specialized training) and the *Daigaku* (universities with two or more faculties) should be eliminated in order to equalize academic standards.

(4) Post-graduate institutions should be established in all universities.

(5) The diversification of the secondary school should be abolished. All students should undertake the same courses of study for the first nine years, followed by three years in the upper secondary school, which will provide a diversification of subjects, as optional courses.

(6) The education system should consist of three levels: six year co-educational elmentary school; six year secondary school, divided into a three year junior high school and a three year senior high school, which should be preferably co-educational, but perhaps segregated; a university which includes the present *Daigaku* and *Semmon Gakko* and should be co-educational. The whole nine years' education through elementary and junior high school should be compulsory. There should be no entrance examination for senior high school, but examinations for admission to university would be required.

(7) Teachers' qualifications for elementary school, should require that they have finished the upper secondary school and completed a further two years of Special Teacher Training—perhaps in university.

(8) Teachers' qualifications for secondary school, should require that they have finished a higher education institute (not necessarily a post-graduate course), and completed a further two years of Special Teacher Training—perhaps in university.

(9) The normal school should be abolished.[30]

The above plan of reform was based on proposals which had been made ten years earlier by about one hundred business, professional, and educational leaders of Japan.[31] Shigeru Nambara himself initially opposed this plan, for the reason that he felt that the Japanese school system was not yet ready for such drastic change. He later advocated the reform, however, in the light of changing circumstances. In fact, it turns out that the reform plan which Nambara had mentioned to Chairman Stoddard coincided with the above reform plan in general substance.

At the four o'clock meeting between Nambara, Takagi, and Hall, the 6–3–3 school system, which had been suggested by the Japanese Education Committee during the previous meeting with the Mission that morning, was more specifically laid out. Thus the 6–3–3 school system was discussed on the premise that it was a reform plan common to the Mission, the Japanese Education Committee, and the CI&E. It is conjectured that this official version of the Japanese Education Committee was passed to the Mission by Hall. We can see its strong influence on the final Report of the Mission by comparing the two texts.

The official view of the Education Division of the CI&E is that its staff expected the Japanese Education Committee to reform the education system in order to democratize it.[32]

The whole attitude of the Japanese side to the reform of the 6–3–3 school system can be observed in the "Recommendations of the Japanese Education Committee," compiled after the Mission had left, which consists of their own opinions. As an initial plan, the section entitled "The School System" proposes nine years' compulsory education in the 6–3–3–4 or the 6–3–3–5 school system. In addition, as an alternative, it suggests a 6–2–4 school system, in the event that nine years' compulsory education should prove impractical. However, the initial plan was finally adopted as the basis of the reform.[33]

As is evident from the above records, the Japanese side actively lobbied the Mission to recommend the 6–3–3 school system. An editorial in the *Nippon Times* of April 11, 1946,[34] stated: "The 6–3–3 plan is one which had been advocated by progressive Japanese educators long before the American Education Mission was even thought of." As a matter of fact, the 6–3–3 school system had already been set forth in 1936 by Shigetaka Abe in his "Personal Suggestions for School System Reform."[35] Abe himself had been in the U.S. from May to July of 1923 and was deeply impressed by the secondary school education reform movement there.

Furthermore, in 1935, the Ministry of Education published "The Issue of the Middle School System Reform in the West," in which an article entitled "The Issue of the Middle School System in America" was included, and the significance of "Junior High School" was briefly introduced. The following year, the American 6–3 school system was introduced in "Research on the Educational System," published by the Research Section of the Ministry of Education. These developments show the Japanese concern with the 6–3 school system even at the beginning of the Showa Period.[36] Thus, it is certain that all prewar Japanese school system proposals came to have influence on the Mission.

How did the Mission members who made the 6–3–3 recommendation in the Report regard this issue? E. R. Hilgard today gives the following important testimony:

> The Mission members were not necessarily unanimously in favor of the recommendation for the 6–3–3 school system. I personally was opposed to it. That the recommendation for the 6–3–3 school system was made in the Report came

as rather a surprise. As is known, the final version of the Report was put
entirely into Chairman Stoddard's hands, so it was he who made the final
decision. As the person with the final responsibility for the Report, I remember
that in some matters he was rather "undemocratic." In the background of the
6–3–3 school system recommendation is not the desire of the Mission, but
rather the strong influence of the Japanese side.[37]

G. T. Bowles describes the general meeting of the Mission, in which
they discussed the 6–3–3 school system, recalling:

> I was not opposed to the 6–3–3 school system itself, but insisted that the issue
> of the school system should be resolved by the decision of the Japanese. I
> remember Chairman Stoddard was one of those who supported that system. I
> was unhappy with this recommendation, because the Report does not give
> enough explanation concerning the reasons for the necessity of introducing
> this system as the Japanese education system. It is obvious that this system was
> structured according to the stages of the physiological, as well as the psycho-
> logical development of students, although it never specifically refers to this
> point. It might have been thought too obvious to do so, for the Japanese edu-
> cators. However, it was not a familiar system to the Japanese at large. In this
> respect, I strongly believe that more specific reasons should have been given.[38]

It might be thought that the Mission did not take into account the
necessity for explaining the 6–3–3 school system as it was originally
proposed by the Japanese side. In fact, the "Recommendations of the
Japanese Education Committee" clearly states the reason for the necessity of this system. However, the final Report of the Mission, as Gordon
Bowles pointed out, does not touch on this point at all. For example, the
Report of the Mission sets forth the 6–3–3 school system as follows:

> At the primary school level, there has been some uncertainty as to the length
> of the course. We believe that the length of the primary school should be fixed
> at six years. This would carry most boys and girls through the period of
> childhood and to the threshold of adolescence... Beyond the six year primary
> school, the organization is somewhat confused by the addition of one or two
> years for pupils who fail the examinations for entrance into the middle schools
> or who want to extend their education before going to work...
>
> What this proposal intends is that all the tax-supported schools receiving
> graduates of the primary schools might well be merged into a single system.
> These include the higher elementary, the middle, the girls' high, the vocational
> and youth schools, as well as schools preparatory to normal college...[39]

As can be understood from the above, their main reason for recommending the 6–3–3 school system, was not concern for pupils' and stu-

dents' physiological or psychological development, but the intention of changing the multi-track school system over to the 6–3–3 school system, in accordance with the idea of equality of educational opportunity. And its aim was considered as including the higher elementary school, the middle, the girls' high, the vocational, the youth schools and the preparatory courses for the normal school within the single-track school system.

On the other hand, "The School System" in the "Recommendations of the Japanese Education Committee," states as follows:

> In establishing a nine year compulsory school system it is desirable to have a two level system ... a six year elementary and a three year lower Secondary School. The reason for this is that *physically* and *psychologically* a student will change greatly during this period and to retain a student in a one level system for this period of time will result in difficulties. After graduating from the elementary school, a student will receive a new stimulus by entering the Lower Secondary School. (Author's italics)[40]

It is interesting that this statement by the Japanese Education Committee emphasizes physiological and psychological aspects, which, as G. T. Bowles pointed out, should have been mentioned in the Mission Report.

III. *The Reform Plan for the School System in Japan*

As we have seen above, the Japanese Education Committee played a distinguished role in the drawing up of the Report of the Mission. Not everything discussed by the Mission and the Japanese Education Committee, however, was reflected by the final Report. As has been discussed in previous chapters, complete agreement could not be reached on the Imperial Rescript on Education or the reform of the Japanese language. Consequently, the Japanese Education Committee compiled their own proposals in the "Recommendations of the Japanese Education Committee,"[41] after the Mission had left.

There is also evidence that a "Minority Report" was produced by the Mission, separately from the official Report, and that it contained some members' dissenting views on matters such as the 6–3–3 system and language reform, although no copy of such a report is extant.[42]

The section on "The School System" in the "Recommendations of the Japanese Education Committee" outlines a system in which all graduates of the *kokumin gakko* (national school) must pass through one of three school systems: 1) Secondary, College Preparatory, and University; 2) Secondary, College, and 3) National School Higher Elementary, Youth School. They then propose their own type of 6–3 school system, in which a three-year Lower Secondary School (or Secondary School) would be provided after a six-year Elementary School, and then a three-year Youth School or a three-year Higher Secondary School. Graduates of the latter would be admitted directly to a four- or five-year University. At the same time, graduates of the three-year Experimental Course attached to the Youth School would have the same qualifications to enter the University as the graduates of the Higher Secondary School.

This report states:

> Mr. Tairoku Kikuchi also gave an opinion, and later in 1937 the Education Fraternity proposed a plan. They all agreed upon the unification of the first and second of the present systems. The plan of the Education Fraternity was discussed by the Educational Investigation Committee in 1937. It was supported by many educational leaders, but its adoption was defeated by one vote.

Thus, the report specifically states that the plan for the 6–3 school system originated in the prewar proposals. It is certain that the reform plan of the school system was studied by Shigetaka Abe, a leading authority before the war. The accumulation of these prewar studies, influenced the Recommendations of the Japanese Education Committee, which implies that the Japanese themselves realized the necessity for the reform. However, whether the basic principles of reform were the same as those of the postwar education reform or not should be examined in detail.[43]

It should also be mentioned again, as we have seen in a previous chapter, that in March 1946, at about the time of the Mission's arrival, a Research Committee on the Education System at Tokyo Imperial University was formed by President Nambara, independently of the Japanese Education Committee. This committee held its first meeting on March 2, 1946, to discuss "the urgent issue of the education system."[44]

This research committee consisted of eleven members, with Teizo Toda as chairman and Tokiomi Kaigo as secretary, both of whom had a direct connection with the Mission. Additionally, of course, Nambara was also Chairman of the Japanese Education Committee and had a close relationship with Chairman Stoddard, as we have seen. In view of these factors, this research committee can be considered to be another "non-governmental" group, organized to correspond to the Mission and also to play an important role in the Mission's recommendations on the school system, as well.

At the third meeting of the Research Committee, on March 13, a debate on the subject of "Problems of School Years," discussion began of the school system. On April 15, Nambara's Research Committee completed "A

Report on the School System and Years Required for Graduation." Its outline is as follows:

> The school system is organized into elementary, middle, high and youth schools, university and postgraduate courses. The elementary school provides five years' compulsory and general education from the age of six. The first grade to the fifth grade in the present lower elementary school will be retained to form the elementary school in the new system.
>
> The middle school admits graduates from the elementary school, and provides three years' compulsory education.... The middle school will be reorganized with the sixth grade of the lower elementary school, the first and second grades of the higher elementary school, and the first and second grades of the middle school, in the present system. The high school admits graduates from the middle school, and provides four years' education.... The youth school is for those who plan to work after middle school and provides four years of education, and also a further three years' course.... This is organized within the present youth school.
>
> The university admits graduates from the high school and the further education course in the youth school, and provides four years of education.... However, there is a minority opinion that the system of a five-year elementary school, three-year middle school, three-year high school, and four-year university should be shortened in total by one year.
>
> April 15, 1946.

In short, the committee renamed the "people's school" the "elementary school," and shortened the period of attendance to five years, with a three-year middle school following elementary school, providing eight years of compulsory education in total. This reform appears to adopt a plan for a two-year extension of compulsory education (six-year lower and two-year higher elementary education), which had been introduced by Ordinance in March 1941 but had never been implemented due to the conditions of wartime. However, a more important point in this proposal is the indication that it is based on a single-track school system. In other words, secondary education institutions—which had been organized into a complicated structure of higher elementary, middle, girls' high and vocational school, and special higher education institutions such as *Semmon Gakko* (technical college), normal school, and teacher training school— were all abolished.[45]

The above "Report on the School System and Years Required for Graduation," produced by the Research Committee on the Education System at Tokyo Imperial University, agrees with the Recommendations of the Japanese Education Committee on the names for each category, such as "elementary school," "middle school," "high school" and "youth school," "university and postgraduate course." But in terms of the five-year elementary school and the four-year high school, differences exist between them. Nevertheless, on the basic idea of the reform of the multi-track school system, the Research Committee report agrees with the reform plan of the Japanese Education Committee.[46]

It should also be noted that several members of the Japanese Education Committee—Nambara, T. Toda, K. Kakinuma, Y. Takagi and T. Sano—were associated with Tokyo Imperial University. Thus the Research Committee at Tokyo Imperial University may have been an important influence on the Japanese Education Committee.

As stated above, the reform of the school system was the main concern of the Japanese side, as examined through records of the discussions held by Committee No 3 of the Japanese Education Committee, which are included in the Aruga Papers. They are listed as:

1. A matter concerning the establishment of the educational authority.

2. A matter concerning the reorganization of the school system.

3. A matter concerning reconsideration of the general aim of the School Ordinance.

4. The reform of the system concerning the entrance examination and requirements for admission.

5. Improvement of teachers' status and salary.

6. Teacher education.

From the above, it should be noted that the reorganization of the school system was one of their top priorities.

The final recommendation for the 6–3–3 school system in preference to the 6–5 system, was directly motivated by active lobbying from the Japanese side. The Japanese educators came to the conclusion that only the 6–3–3 school system could resolve the problems presented by the Japanese multi-track system. Other factors, however, also contributed to this final recommendation: the original version of the 6–5 system presented by Committee III of the Mission contained aspects conducive to the adoption of the 6–3 system (nine years of free compulsory, co-educational education); Chairman Stoddard himself supported the 6–3–3 system; and in the preliminary discussions between Stoddard and Gen. MacArthur, the financial aspects of the plan were endorsed by Gen. MacArthur in making recommendations on the reform.

As a matter of fact, Chairman Stoddard, after his return to Washington, testified on May 8, 1946, before the Special Sub-committee on Education of Committee No. 4, "Strengthening of Democratic Tendencies of the Far Eastern Commission": "Many of the recommendations that had been made in the report of the U.S. Education Mission to Japan were actually held by many Japanese leaders in education a long time ago."[47] The same kind of statement was also made by Mission member I. L. Kandel.[48] M. M. Horton also noted:

> My impression was that the Mission was truly free to get the opinions of the Japanese educators, and the best we could hope to do on short notice and brief acquaintance, was to try to put the weight of the Mission behind those projects which were already proposed by the Japanese leaders who could implement them.[49]

On this point, Gordon Bowles has said: "We considered the contents of the Report carefully, always discussing them with the Japanese Education Committee. . . . Probably about sixty per cent of the content of the Report comes from the Japanese Education Committee."[50]

The Education Division of the CI&E mentioned that the Report was strongly influenced by the Japanese Education Committee, and that they intended to utilize it to facilitate the Japanese education reforms.[51] E. R. Hilgard testifies: "The Mission's attitude towards the Japanese educators, was very amicable. And we always tried to avoid simply recommending an American system to them, regardless of the Japanese situation. We gave priority to whatever Japanese educators desired."[52]

With regard to the role which the Japanese Education Committee played, Bowles regarded it highly:

> The Japanese Education Committee aimed to cooperate with the Mission in order to help us to understand Japanese education. Its members were selected by the CI&E in serious consideration of their profound knowledge of English language and experience. Eventually, the Committee consisted, I think, of pro-Americans educators. Without their support, I don't think the Mission could have made recommendations on Japanese education. In a way, these members might have not been accepted very favorably in Japan, but they had deep knowledge as well as experience of American education, so that we were confident in our discussion with them.[53]

Hugh Borton, of the State Department's Far Eastern Section, who held a central position in the formulation of American policy towards postwar Japanese education remembers that the U.S. Government took the position that the Japanese should come to their own conclusions about postwar education reform.[54] And F. N. Freeman states that the Mission members freely discussed with the Japanese educators the various suggested remedies for the deficiencies in the Japanese education system which they had already recognized. He also says the Mission believed that many Japanese progressive educators were capable of carrying out the reform themselves, with appropriate assistance from the Occupation.[55]

I. L. Kandel, as a member of the Mission, as well as an eminent scholar of comparative education, comments as follows:

> The United States Education Mission devoted its attention to the reform of the whole system and had the advantage of constant cooperation and deliberation with a corresponding committee of Japanese educators.... All that can be said is that the Mission did find a large measure of good-will among Japanese educational leaders, which was due to [the] victor–vanquished relationship, and that many of [the] recommendations are based on the ideas expressed by Japanese educators. The task will have to be undertaken by the Japanese themselves; no recommendations will ever be effective, if imposed on a nation by outsiders. The best help that could be given to the Japanese would be to permit a number of their educational leaders to come to the United States and study the meaning of the Mission's recommendations in the American school system. They may find, perhaps, that the recommendations go beyond what it has been possible to achieve in this country, but they will also learn that democracy does not have a perfect pattern but is always seeking to perfect itself.[56]

The only black American in the Mission, Charles S. Johnson, was said to have contributed greatly in the formulation of the basic education principle in the Report, which says that "... educational opportunity, commensurate with individual abilities, should be equally available for all persons, regardless of gender, race, creed or color. Minority groups should be respected and valued."

Johnson's respect for the Japanese Education Committee can also be seen in the speeches which he gave after his return to the U.S.[57] For instance, he quotes, from the introduction to the Report: "No nation is without some elements of democratic way of life, and no nation has them all.... We believe in the power of every race and every nation to create from its own cultural resources something good for itself and for the whole world." In this way, he expressed his view that a democratic education system could only be created by national cultural resources, not by the coercion of others.

According to Johnson, the basic ideas reflected in the Report owe much to the contribution made by T. V. Smith, who experienced directing the educational reconstruction of Italy.[58] H. J. Wunderlich, of the Education Division of the CI&E, also wrote in his "Reminiscences," that the introduction to the Report was written by T. V. Smith.[59]

This chapter verifies that, in the drawing up of the Report, the Mission respected the intentions of the Japanese Education Committee and received their active cooperation.

Chairman Stoddard wrote in his memoir, "The Emperor and I": "Actually, every major statement in the Report was acceptable to the Japanese Committee, and we took pains to determine that acquiescence was not simply a matter of traditional politeness."[60]

Again Gordon Bowles testifies to the following in his memoir:

Only to the extent that the Mission provided the opportunity to Japanese educators to express themselves and to utilize the Report as a foundation for realizing their hopes and convictions, and strengthening their position, does the Mission itself deserve credit for any lasting results.[61]

In this chapter, the author has substantiated the fact that the 6–3–3 school system originated with the Japanese, before the war. The Japanese Education Committee developed the basic structure of postwar education reform, referring to the prewar reform plan proposed by Kyoiku Doshikai (Education Fraternity) in 1936. In other words, the 6–3–3 school system which was adopted by the Japanese side was really their own idea.

It was at the end of March 1946 that the Mission decided on the recommendation of the 6–3–3 school system in its Report. One year later, in March 1947, the School Education Law established the 6–3–3 school system, in place of the prewar system. For the formulation of this reform policy, Shigeru Nambara, Chairman of the Japanese Education Committee, and other members of the committee played extremely important roles.

6

THE MISSION'S REPORT AND
THE REFORM OF HIGHER EDUCATION

*I. Proposals for Reform of Higher Education in the Report of
Committee IV: The Aims and Freedoms of Higher Learning*

Chapter VI of the Report of the U.S. Education Mission to Japan, entitled
"Higher Education," contained a charter declaring, "The university is the
crown of every modern educational system," thus defining its place in
society, and recommend an emphasis on the importance of freedom in
research and university autonomy. The basic principle that higher education should become an opportunity for the masses, and not just for a
privileged few, was recommended for the postwar Japanese higher education system and its ideals. Because of the restrictions on access to historical
sources, however, little is known about the actual process behind the
drafting of the report, such as the discussions and research upon which
the recommendations were based, and which member of the Mission assumed responsibility for writing the chapter.

Recently, in the David Stevens Papers, preserved in the Archives of
the University of Chicago Library, part of an unpublished draft of the
"Higher Education" chapter, entitled "The Aims and Freedoms of Higher
Learning," and an important personal memo, "Draft Report of the Subcommittee on Higher Education in Japan," were discovered.

Using this unpublished draft from the Stevens Papers, the author will
examine the process of preparing Chapter VI, "Higher Education." At the
Guam meeting (March 3, 1946) held just prior to the Mission's arrival in
Japan, Chairman Stoddard discussed specific procedures for the compilation of the official report. He indicated four areas for research, appointed
a chairman for each subcommittee, and requested a report from each of

them. Thus, it was suggested that Committee IV (chairman: George W. Diemer), take up the two areas of teacher training, and liberal and higher education.[1]

On March 11, after the Mission's arrival in Japan, the establishment and composition of Committee IV and two other special committees were arranged. Committee IV was to study higher education, and the members of the committee were Wilson M. Compton (chairman), Roy J. Deferrari, Virginia C. Gildersleeve, Mildred McAfee Horton, and David Stevens.

On March 12, Chairman Compton selected the following members, to assume responsibility for each of the different sections of the report on higher education:[2]

Mrs. Horton: Women, including co-education. (women)

Miss Gildersleeve: Preservation of international peace and formation of international cooperation in all fields. (peace)

Mr. Deferrai: Public and private institutions, including cooperation between institutions, financial position, and relation to Ministry of Education. (institutional)

Mr. Stevens: Individual professional status and opportunity of teachers and scholars, academic freedom, research, position of students, graduates. (individuals)

Mr. Compton: Sciences, technologies, professions, agriculture, forestry, industry, commerce. (technology)

By carefully comparing these divisions of responsibility with the 14 subheadings in the chapter "Higher Education," the particular field of specialization of each member can be identified in the final Report. The personal memo "Draft Report of the Subcommittee on Higher Education in Japan" in the Stevens Papers[3] begins, "This is decidedly a Univ. of Chicago product, reflecting ideas generated there by George Counts and David Stevens before leaving for duties elsewhere." Both Counts (1926–27) and Stevens (1925–30) were professors at the University of Chicago.

According to Stevens:

Teams of four were set going after two weeks of survey and conference with Japanese specialists—each team to develop a statement for discussion with a view to its approval by the 24 ahead of final draft for the Japanese gover(n)ment and its educators on the future steps at all levels, for the revitalized and modernized programs.

This committee on higher education and research has as members Compton, then a president of...Washington State University and by profession a lobbyist for lumber interests in Washington—excellent personality, quite lacking experience but made chairman; Miss Gildersleeve, of Barnard, who with DHS[David H. Stevens]drafted a few sectors before work with Counts;

Miss McAfee, then president of Wellesley and head of the Waves, who sat in only one brief session before an early departure on a chartered Navy plane; Counts, the strongest generalist in the entire commission, with balance and depth in judgment.

It is also recorded that Stevens and Counts undertook a review of the proposals made by the Japanese side, and drew up the committee report.

That George Counts was a member of the higher education subcommittee had been unknown from previous historical sources. Counts and Stevens were not only key figures in the "Higher Education" committee, but were also key members of the Special Committee on Language Reform. Thus, it is natural to suspect that there was a close relationship between the Mission's Special Committee on Language Reform and the "Higher Education" committee.

The draft report on "Higher Education" is entitled, "The Aims and Freedoms of Higher learning," and is composed of five sections: 1) The Place of Higher Learning in a Free Society; 2) The Organization of Institutions, etc.; 3) Freedom for the Individual; 4) Recommendations for Scientific and Professional Training; and 5) Advancement of International Understanding.

Preserved in the Stevens Papers are drafts of 1) The Place of Higher Learning in a Free Society, and 3) Freedom for the Individual , which were written under the direction of Counts and Stevens. The committee's draft report begins with "The Place of Higher Learning in a Free Society," and presents the ideology of the university, as is also presented in the beginning of the "Higher Education" chapter in the final Report, as follows:

> The university is the crown of every modern educational system. In a free society it discharges with equal concern three great functions. First, it guards as a treasure beyond price the tradition of intellectual liberty, stimulates freedom of thought, perfects methods of inquiry, promotes the advancement of knowledge, cultivates science and scholarship, nurtures love of truth, and serves as a source of perpetual enlightment to society. Second, it prepares young men and women of talent, industry, and devotion through acquaintance with the best thought and finest aspirations of all ages and peoples, for positions of leadership in the improvement of family and community life, in the more efficient and humane conduct of industry and government, and in the fostering of understanding and good will among the nations. Third, it trains selected young men and women for technical competence and proficiency in both old and new professions, being ever sensitive to the changing and emerging needs of society...

Here, the university is seen as the "crown" of every modern education system, and its function in a free society as: (1) the preservation of freedom of scholarship, thought, and research, and contribution to society through its pursuit of truth; (2) general education of young men and women to prepare them for positions of leadership in society; (3) training for technical competence and proficiency in professions.[4] Further, the draft concludes, "all of these things the university does in the spirit of service to all the people."

In the part of the draft of the Report relating to "Past Limitations in Higher Education in Japan," there is a statement that is not included in the final Report:

> Under such a charter the colleges and universities of every country can steadily realize those aims of higher education suited to its social and economic needs. Every country through their strength can reach other countries through the freedom of mind and spirit generated in institutions of higher learning. Any nation can make its influence on mankind beneficent. The process of change in higher education of Japan must begin under difficulties. Traditionally higher education here has been both insular and insulated. In spite of the traditional burden put upon student and teacher and in spite of the restraints of war, the elements of growth have persisted. Her own scholars and scientists have the power to bring the values of higher learning to the unidentified millions of Japan—not today or perhaps tomorrow, but by following the universal patterns of intellectual progress.

The draft presents the three functions of the university in a free society as a "charter," recommending that higher education be conducted from the highest ideals. It further states as follows:

> Clearly, the university system in Japan must rest upon the usual elements in any national program for higher education. The country must have the proportion of young talent continuously and amply provided by colleges.... Recognition of the right of access to higher learning can be made clearer to the people and to administrative powers controlling higher education as prerogatives and special advantages of the few are relaxed and redefined for the many.

It is obvious from the above that the committee believed that the basic principle behind changes in the university system in Japan should be the expansion of opportunities for receiving higher education.

Following in this vein, the official Report itself continues, "Only by such recognition can there be a corrective to the preferential treatment given today to the graduates of Imperial universities." It is not clear what is meant by the specific phrase "a corrective to the preferential treatment," but it has been interpreted as an expression of criticism of the "privilege" of the Imperial University, and that at least one of the

objectives of the Mission's higher education reform plan was the reorganization of the Imperial University structure.[5] It is important, however, to
point out that the draft of Committee IV's report contains quite a different
evaluation of the Imperial universities, and recommends instead that the
excellence of the Imperial University be emphasized, as follows:

> Graduation from an Imperial university is given a special preference. That fact
> is not to be over-emphasized by those who want freer access of graduates to all
> positions of importance. *The leadership of the Imperial universities should be
> maintained and fortified by emphasis on excellence in all processes of selection
> and achievement.* All will agree that the spirit of free thought and action must
> dominate the processes of higher education here as in every country. (Author's
> italics)

Committee IV's report was submitted to Chairman Stoddard in the late
afternoon of March 24, and the final Report was completed on March 30.
In the space of that final week, the draft was revised. The circumstances
behind the revision of the statement "Only by such recognition can there
be a corrective to the preferential treatment given today to the graduates
of Imperial universities" is a mystery. Two interesting memorandums,
however, were presented to Chairman Compton as material for discussion
by Committee IV, by Cdr. Alfred Crofts of the CI&E, on March 12.[6] They
touch upon the contrast between government (*kanritsu*) and private universities, and contain several comments sharply critical of the government
universities, as follows: "Government university professors, by reason of
being civil servants, are not in a position to think freely or express their
opinions. They should therefore be considered in the light of 'scholars
under government patronage.'" Crofts criticizes the fact that "Tokyo
Teidai (Tokyo Imperial University) [was] responsible for the development
of the bureaucracy and for the outbreak of the present war by reason of
having 'conspired with the militarist,'" and goes on to say that "in order
to destroy militarism completely it is therefore necessary to overthrow the
'*teidaibatsu*' (the clique of the Imperial University)" and that "a new
democratic Japan will only be possible when and if 'cultural' Government
universities are abolished." It may well be that the plan to reorganize the
Imperial University structure was initiated by Japanese educators, especially representatives of private universities, with the cooperation of the
CI&E Education Division.[7]

It is interesting to observe that within the Education Division, a variety of opinions existed, with staff members within the Higher Education Branch of the Division in disagreement with each other over many
issues, including the desirable directions in which Japanese higher insti-

tutions ought to evolve. A curious situation resulted. Basically, under the policy of the Occupation, the Japanese were fairly free to make their own decisions regarding the reforms which they wish to introduce into education.[8] The Education Division was directly concerned with problems of elementary and secondary education, but there was a lack of attention to higher education.

At the time, Cmdr. Alfred Crofts was in charge of the Higher Education Branch of the Division, and his influence on the Japanese side and the Mission cannot be overlooked. After his return to the U.S. Crofts became a professor of history at the University of Denver. In a radio program broadcast on April 29, 1947, he gave an interesting lecture entitled "Universities of Japan,"[9] in which he gave the following description:

> Universities were imposed by imperial order, under iron supervision of the Education Ministry. Each is chartered by the state, with its courses of study, the number of its faculty and student body fixed in a written constitution. Enrollment is limited by rigid entrance examinations. Approximately one candidate in twenty ever qualifies for the better university.... Higher education is a luxury denied to women; of five thousand university professors of all ranks, not one is a woman, and of fifty thousand students, there are two hundred coeds....

He further criticized the structure of Imperial universities:

> The hierarchy of universities is like that of the old feudal society. No transfer between schools is possible for students or faculty members; throughout life each graduate is classified by the institution he attended. Highest come to the seven Imperial universities, with Tokyo Imperial, the great *Teikoku Daigakko*, at the apex. Their professors are ranked as high state officials. Their graduates completely control government and upper class society. All the civilian war crimes defendants are *Teidai* graduates. Imperial law school graduates nearly monopolize higher government posts.

Crofts supported the views of the Association of Private Universities and criticized Teidai graduates as civilian war crimes defendants. He sympathized with private universities in Japan, saying: "The handicaps of the private universities are severe. Their financial problems are acute, since they cater to the less privileged classes of students.... Their graduates suffer discrimination at every stage in their later careers." He opined that only the decentralization of power could reduce the amount of bureaucracy in education. He was opposed to elitism, particularly at the Imperial universities, such as Tokyo Imperial University, and strongly supported a system of "one public university in each prefecture."[10]

Behind his critical view of the Imperial universities is the fact that before coming to GHQ/CI&E in Tokyo, he had served as the first *de facto* president of Keijo Teikoku Daigaku (Keijo Imperial University, Korea), beginning on October 7, 1945, just after its liberation from Japanese colonial rule; while working in Korea under U.S. military rule, he had tried to wipe out vestiges of Japanese colonization, by instituting fundamental educational reforms based on democratic ideology.[11]

The draft discovered among the Stevens papers also contains a recommendation on private schools, in the part which corresponds to "Public and Private Institutions" in the Report:

Institutionally the aims and freedoms of higher education in Japan will be realized by giving all possible recognition to the private colleges and universities of the country. Many have broad cultural objectives, others an essentially religious purpose. Both forms of institution contribute to the variety and strength of Japanese culture. Those institutions that seem unworthy of Japan in educational standards or in their impartial concern over higher learning, surely should be discouraged or improved by new standards and new safeguards. In negative ways as well as in positive action the leaders of higher education will elevate the social values of their institutions. (Author's italics)

The Report itself presents a different recommendation:

The aims and freedoms of higher education can only be achieved by giving all possible encouragement to the *maintenance of colleges and universities with high standards* and with broad cultural objectives. (Author's italics)

The important phrase "private colleges and universities" has been deleted. The Report encouraged the maintenance of colleges and universities with high standards, rather than recognizing private institutions.

Because the final Report was influenced by the view of private universities held by Shigeru Nambara, chairman of the Japanese Education Committee and president of Tokyo Imperial University, these views need to be examined. Nambara met secretly with Chairman Stoddard on March 21. The transcript of the meeting is found in an 11-page typed report entitled "Special Report by Shigeru Nambara, President, Tokyo Imperial University and Chairman of Japanese Education Committee to G. D. Stoddard, March 21, 1946."[12] Nambara touches upon the private university issue, and suggests to Stoddard that:

The number of private universities should be reduced, far too many of them are merely money-making business enterprises—proprietary schools. On the other hand, private universities of good standing should be brought to the level of the Imperial universities. For example, Waseda. Hence, they should be given autonomy; they do not have it now. The faculties are too dependent upon the Boards of Overseers.

Hence, for both public and private universities, we should (1) encourage professors' associations; (2) arrange for the exchange of professors to some extent. However, I do not believe that a free exchange of students among the public and private universities is possible. There is a lack of facilities in the governmental universities and a great student demand. Under present conditions, the flow would be only from private to Imperial universities. (Author's italics)

On general education, Nambara says: "I believe that education in special fields is well done, but that general or liberal education is weak. We can improve this by better general teaching, by more synthetic study for both teachers and students. In this way we could achieve a harmony between the cultural courses and the scientific courses. Professors could be employed on a less compartmentalized basis."

The final Report recommends the expansion of general education: " . . . for the most part there is too little opportunity for general education, too early and too narrow a specialization, and too great a vocational or professional emphasis. A broader humanistic attitude should be cultivated to provide more background for free thought and a better foundation on which professional training may be based." This reads as if written in compliance with Nambara's suggestion.

Again, Section 3 of the draft, "Freedom of the Individual," corresponds to "The Status of the Individual—The Faculty" in the Report. It begins with the following crisply worded paragraph:

From the charter for higher education that has been put at the opening of this section, some practical conclusions are to be drawn with regard to the institutions of Japan. The country lacks much more than financial support for both private and public universities. It lacks a full sense of its duties to the individual teacher who strives to serve in such ways as are described here. First in order is academic freedom and second is economic security. Each deserves full emphasis in all studies of university reform in the interests of a democratic society.

Further, it can be seen that Committee IV made suggestions on the philosophical and systematic aspects of the freedom of scholarship, based on the highest ideals. The attitude towards academic freedom is based on Carl L. Becker's 1945 *Freedom and Responsibility in the American Way of Life*.[13] This work had attracted much attention in the U.S. at the time, and it is presumed that one of Committee IV members had brought a copy with him to Japan. In fact, the draft says, "To be sure, the scholar or scientist has deep obligations as an individual—to his students, to his institution, and to society at large." Concerning such obligations, Becker wrote:

> The education of college students for leadership in the community, if it be not constantly based on the results of current critical research, tends to become conventional and dogmatic and to leave the student with a body of information learned by rote and housed in a closed and incurious mind; while research, carried on by professors secure in their tenure under no obligation to concern themselves with the social significance of learning to teaching, tends to run into barren antiquarianism, as harmless and diverting and about as socially useful, as cross-word puzzles or contract bridge.

Furthermore, the members of Committee IV expressed their deep appreciation of these high ideals as follow:

> These sentences were written to American readers, but they are timeless and universal.
> These are words, therefore, useful to Japan today. But where shall beginnings be made with forwarding the use of higher education in Japan through higher regard for the value of the individual? How shall the minds of men and the policies of institutions be turned toward freeing mind and spirit to the highest forms of service to others?

In "Expansion of Opportunities," the draft makes suggestions not seen in the final Report. Due to their significance, the recommendations are quoted here in their entirety, as follows:

> In all these directions the universities must be leaders of the way. They can become so by making every student and teacher a full member in the community of scholars according to his developed powers, and from the first a fellow member with rights of free inquiry and of free expression. The test of any university is in its power to combine generosity of opportunity with intensity of objective criticism toward the members of its community.
> The tools of his trade, briefly noted, are laboratories and library resources. The scientist wants apparatus and journals; the scholar needs the book or scholarly monograph in his hand. Therefore, as a minimum for high endeavor, these inquirers after their own forms of truth must be given better facilities here. This calls for a slow, undramatic process of building up libraries covering the primary categories of knowledge, of developing the laboratories needed by generalists and specialists: the two requirements are first an inventory and then a national program. From the present devastation may come the chance of fundamental reorganization.
> Other tools of the specialists eventually will be made ready in Japan. These are the needs of the humanist plus libraries, museums, galleries of art and

archeology, bibliographies and journals covering special areas. For the social scientist, in addition to the resources to be found in print, are such well-recognized needs as statistical laboratories, mechanisms and centers for gathering data on social change, access to the records of governments and institutions at home and abroad. To arouse interest in comparative studies within the fields of sciences, every country that has developed historical museums of science and industry has benefited; to encourage growth in creative arts, there must be places that become the sources of national expression in design, in all the recognized mediums of artistic expression, and in music.

Such measures for freeing the individual mind in a university setting will depend for success upon the quality of mind received from the semmon gakko and koto gakko. Japan has at this point the problem of every country in devising terminal education for its more general needs of society, at the same time developing under encouragement the powers in individuals who will be ready for the freer growth processes of university life. Specialization in the university should be less consuming of time and less compelling in its drive than today is true in typical universities of the country. The well-developed product of the semmon gakko and koto gakko centers for both men and women must still have freedom in the university to develop individual qualities of mind and spirit. It is entirely clear that the educational planning of Japanese universities is to include reforms that will give to the individual these chances for a greater fulfillment of personal powers. That fulfillment is to come by a use of freedom with responsibility, by a wider contact with the work of other scholars and scientists as a means to his own interpretations of humanity and his own discoveries through nature.

Lastly, the author would like to compare the recommendations for the reform of higher education in the Report of the U.S. Education Mission to Germany with those made in the Japanese case.[14] It is characteristic of the Mission to Germany, as a whole, that its members regarded German tradition with respect, and higher education was no exception. The Report states:

Prior to 1933 German universities represented the highest development in scholarship and other intellectual activities. *Lehrfreiheit* and *Lernfreiheit* made possible and encouraged the untrammelled pursuit of truth. From all parts of the world learned men came to study in these institutions and returned to assume positions of educational leadership in their own country. In the production of scholars and members of the older professions, German universities have been outstanding.

It continues:

It is recommended that all universities and higher schools include within each curriculum the essential elements of general education for responsible citizenship and for an understanding of the contemporary world. It is further recommended that extra-class activities such as informal discussion groups and student government be inaugurated to provide practical experience with the processes of democracy.

The German report, like the Japan report, dealt with the problems of general education and curricula. But a major point of difference between the German case and the Japanese is that whereas in the latter proposals of only a theoretical nature were suggested, in the former we see the actual restoration of German higher education and its curricula.[15]

It is worth noting that an important recommendation was made for including a pedagogical faculty within the German traditional four faculties (Philosophy, Theology, Law, and Medicine), as is seen in the following:

> It is recommended that the universities assume responsibility for the preparation of secondary-school teachers, research workers, and administrative officers for the school system. To discharge these responsibilities fully, it is recommended that universities establish a separate pedagogical faculty for the teaching of the professional subject matter required by the future teachers in the secondary schools.

Common to the Reports of the Missions to both Germany and Japan is the serious consideration given to the re-education of teachers and teachers' training. In the case of Japan, relatively few teachers were purged from their positions, and reform efforts were focused on in-service training and the expansion and reorganization of the normal school, which provides four years of education beyond the middle (or upper secondary) schools. In the German case, on the other hand, due to the lack of teachers, a plan for training temporary teachers was implemented, and many institutions for teachers' training were founded. The Report of the Mission to Germany recommended the preparation of a long-term plan of three, or possibly four, years of training after the middle school.

II. *The U.S. Scientific Advisory Group to Japan and the Postwar Japanese Higher Education Reform Plan*

The U.S. Scientific Advisory Group to Japan visited Japan in August 1947, by invitation of the Economic and Scientific Section (ESS) in GHQ/SCAP, and was chaired by Roger Adams, Dean of Science of the University of Illinois and ex-president of the U.S. Academic Society of Chemistry. The group consisted of six eminent scientists, and they submitted a "Report of the U.S. Scientific Advisory Group to Japan," making recommendations concerning the new postwar Japanese system for science, including higher education, to GHQ, through the National Academy of Sciences.[16] It was GHQ/CI&E that was directly concerned in Japanese education reform under the Occupation; however, it is necessary to point out that the ESS in SCAP was also deeply concerned in educational matters, as well. In other words, while Japanese education reforms were under the direction of the CI&E, other sections were also concerned, because of the recognition that education was important for the democratization of Japan. In this respect, M. T. Orr of the Education Division of the CI&E explains the organization of GHQ at that time as follows:

> There were numerous areas in which the responsibility assigned to the Division and to other Divisions and Sections of the General Headquarters overlapped. For example, the Economic and Scientific Section was interested in scientific research, most of which was carried on by universities and attached research institutes; the Public Health and Welfare Section was interested in medical and public health education; the National Resources Section was concerned with education in the fields of forestry, agriculture, and fisheries.[17]

In this section, the author would like to discuss the U.S. Scientific Advisory Group to Japan, in terms of higher education. The Report of this Group made important recommendations for postwar Japanese higher education. In particular, it was the first report to criticize a great deal of the education and research system in the postgraduate course, within the old education system, and also to give concrete suggestions for its reorganization. It should be noted that the Report of the U.S. Scientific Advisory Group provided a section on ''Private Universities'' for detailed discussion, in order to promote them for democratization, and also proposed setting up a non-governmental advisory committee, in order to weaken the power of the Ministry of Education. It also reemphasized the recommendations made by the U.S. Education Mission, in terms of tax exemptions for gifts made to private universities.

1) THE REPORT OF THE U.S. SCIENTIFIC ADVISORY GROUP TO JAPAN
AND REORGANIZATION OF INSTITUTIONS OF HIGHER LEARNING
As seen above, part of an unpublished draft of the ''Higher Education'' chapter written by Committee IV, entitled ''The Aims and Freedom of Higher Learning,'' is included in the Stevens Papers. However, this draft includes only two sections, 1) The Place of Higher Learning in a Free Society and 3) Freedom for the Individual. The rest of the items, 2) The Organization of Institutions, etc., 4) Recommendation for Scientific and Professional Training, and 5) Advancement of International Understanding, have not yet been located. The personal papers of members of Com-

mittee IV, including Horton, Gildersleeve, Deferrari and Compton, rarely contain materials relating to higher education. Recently, however, material referring to the U.S. Scientific Advisory Group was discovered in the Archives of the Library of the University of Illinois. These are the Adams Papers, which include the missing part of the draft concerning the organization of institutions and the advancement of international understanding. As mentioned above, the Scientific Advisory Group was invited for the purpose of reorganizing science and technology in Japan. Their purpose was not directly concerned in the reform of higher education, though they gave their support in a variety of ways to the reform plan for higher education which was recommended by Committee IV. They also discussed various problems which Committee IV could not resolve satisfactorily. In relation to higher education, therefore, the work of this Group should be taken into account.

"The Reorganization of Science and Technology—The Report of the Scientific Advisory Group" consists of eight chapters altogether, of which "I. Present Status of Science and Technology," and "VI. Comments on University Education," describe education and research at the postgraduate level. The section on 'Research in Universities,' under "I. Present Status of Science and Technology," makes the following observations:

> Following the German tradition, there is a high degree of specialization in a Japanese university. A student is confined to a single faculty and all general education is obtained at pre-university level. A graduate student is attached to a single professor and all his works is research and semi-independent study under the guidance of this one man.
>
> There is a strong transfer of family loyalty to the professor. A professor and his students constitute a "family type" unit that probably exerts an undue influence on the thinking and activities of many scientific men. This leads to concentration of activity in very narrow fields and to a decided lack of breadth in training and interest. It also leads to a competition by the scientists and scientific institutions rather than cooperation, and probably hinders the general development and spread of scientific attitudes.

Thus, the scientists criticized the exclusivity of the research and instructional system within universities. We find the same point criticized in the section "General Aspects of Instruction" in "VI. Comments on University Education":

> In general, graduate study in Japan seems to involve attachment to a single professor and work under his direction almost entirely, rather than exposure in advanced seminars to the competition with other students or to the instruction of other professors.

And the section "Relations with Government," on issues concerning the university and postgraduate course, points out the non-existence of exchanges of personnel between higher institutions:

> A striking feature of higher education in Japan is the infrequency of exchange of instructors between institutions. Both instructors and students obviously suffer unnecessary losses thereby. To what extent this immobility of instructional staff has been due to governmental administration we are uncertain. It seems clear, however, that governmental administration is in a position at least to encourage such exchange of staff. Equally striking is the infrequency of transfer of student, even those proceeding to graduate work, from one university to another. To what extent this is the choice of students, to what extent the existence of administratively-imposed barriers to transfer, we are not clear. But on the assumption that quality of instruction in a given field must differ between universities, we consider that a change of practice might well prove advantageous to scientific progress.

This Report does not refer much to the reorganization of the post-graduate course. Although the above statement mentions the system of transfer between universities, it hardly mentions the terms of study and curriculum. However, the following statement in "General Aspects of Instruction" is worth noting:

> At the graduate and research levels, at least in the fields of natural science and technology, emphasis seems to fall upon work in pure sciences to an extent detrimental to applied science. Such emphasis may reasonably be questioned considering the present desperate condition of the Japanese economy and the need to restore it. The appropriate emphasis in Japan at this stage would seem to be the opposite of that in the United States, where there may be said to be overemphasis upon teaching the application of science to industry. Without abandoning the more romantic research in pure science, there appears to be need in Japan for more study of and instruction in production methods, production quality control, design and construction improvements, safety and maintenance methods, and development of a system of pre-failure testing for such things as machinery, electric circuits, and apparatus used by utilities.

This proposal should be understood in relation to its basic emphasis on the necessity for scientific research within industrial circles, and also of cooperation between industry and scientific and technological research in universities. The following quotation from the section "Research in Universities," under "I. Present Status of Science and Technology," describes the Japanese university administrative system:

> The internal administration of the public universities appears at present to be very democratic. The deans are elected by the professors, and the president

either by all the professors or by representatives of the various faculties. This democracy is probably more apparent than real since all of these elections are subject to approval by the Ministry of Education, and in addition, these officers seems to have very little significant authority. The ultimate decision in all matters relating to appointments, promotions, and budget rests with the Ministry of Education, although the extent to which this authority is exercised is not easy to determine.

With regard to the governmental control of administration of private universities, the following important suggestions are made in "Private Universities," in the section "VI. Comments on University Education":

Our impression is that Japan, if it is to become a peace-loving nation respecting internally the individual freedom of its citizens and externally the rights of other nations, would profit from development of private universities.

In accordance with this impression, we have earlier expressed the view that the private universities might wisely be freed entirely from the control of any national administrative agency, whether the Ministry of Education or a new Commission on Higher Education and Research, except as regards the launching of new institutions. The existing administrative power of granting or denying the formation of new faculties, or of passing upon the addition of new departments or chairs within existing private universities, seems to us a power which might reasonably be removed, regardless of how wisely that power may have been exercised in the past or might be exercised in the future. At the same time we have expressed the opinion that the member or faculties of private universities might well continue to be eligible to receive grants from government funds in aid of research projects.

Relating to the finance of private universities, it recommends that the tax on donations toward educational institutions should be abolished. Here, again they emphasize the same recommendation as had been made by the U.S. Education Mission.

2) THE POSTWAR JAPANESE HIGHER EDUCATION REFORM PLAN
INTRODUCED IN THE ADAMS PAPERS
The Adams Papers, kept at the Archives, Library of the University of Illinois, contain important materials relating to postwar Japanese higher education reform which are not included in "The Report of the U.S. Scientific Advisory Group." In this section, the author would like to introduce their vision of higher education as outlined in the draft materials.

Technical Education Reorganization
Science and technology levels are largely determined by the colleges and universities of a nation. Japan must, as has been stated in the "Report of the

United States Education Mission to Japan" (March 1946) re-examine and re-orient all its technological and professional training.

The Scientific Advisory Group recommends that Japan pattern its university technical education along the lines of American technical colleges. Chapter VI of the United States Education Mission deals with "Higher Education for Japan." The major faults which that report discusses are largely corrected in the American technical education system. However, the major fault of the American system, viz., an over-emphasis upon the teaching of the application of science to industry, is just what Japan greatly needs because its universities have gone to the other extreme and glorified pure science research to an extent detrimental to applied science. That a nation cannot afford, when its immediate need is production that will result in sufficient food, clothing, and housing to satisfy the needs of its citizens.

Research in the Colleges

The Education Commission Report, in discussing research, says in Part VI: "Equipment and facilities should be provided as quickly as possible, and fellowships should be made available for advanced students who have demonstrated outstanding interest and capacity." The Scientific Advisory Group concurs [whole-] heartily with this statement, but adds as recommendations:

1. The elimination of the present "chair" system and the substitution of a plan whereby any faculty member who can present a promising plan of research be encouraged to develop it as a part of a broad university research program. If this is done, duplication of effort and apparatus, some of which under the present chair system is often idle, will be reduced.

2. There should be established regional service shops, limited in number, where instruments and apparatus may be repaired or calibrated. Also there should be on each campus a lesser central shop for such work, thus avoiding the duplication, now extreme because the many chair laboratories in operation try to be self-sufficient.

3. There should be a free exchange of literature among all universities and arrangements should be made for making available to each of the faculties of each university as much information as possible about the work of the other faculties.

4. There should be libraries at all universities and so far as possible other public libraries available to anyone who can use them without regard to membership in any university faculty or organization.

5. There should be a liberal exchange of lecture professors among the universities, both public and private.

6. All language barriers should be reduced as much as possible even to the extent of a plan for changing completely the idea of maintain[in]g a national language. Why shouldn't Japan lead the way in reducing the number of world languages? That would be a great contribution toward peace. The publication of all research papers in one of the more commonly used languages of the world would be a big step in this direction.

7. The technical research program should provide not only for pure science

research but should set up studies in production methods, production quality control, design and construction improvements, the development of a system of pre-failure testing for such things as machinery, electric circuits, and apparatus used by utilities, safety and maintenance methods, etc., also such other programs as may be needed to revive the economy of Japan and apply science more completely and directly to raising the standard of living in Japan and adding to her production of useful consumer goods. Such researches do not provide the romance appeal of the pure science researches which have produced such spectacular results as atomic fission, but they are of great value and moreover can be carried out at far less expense than the romantic researches. Also results are more certain and practical results are what Japan now needs. This emphasis on applied research as compared to pure research should not be taken as a recommendation against attention to pure research, but it does imply that much of the attention now given by the universities to certain phases of research and the laboratory space now used by many research chairs could at the present time be put to better use.

Curricula

The Education Mission report recommends a general plan of education for all, extending over a period of twelve years and set up on a 6–3–3 basis. Science and technological education begins at the place where the 6–3–3 program stops, but it must obtain its students from the 6–3–3 schools. Those schools should prepare the natural science students for their more specific education by having available good basic courses in mathematics, physics and chemistry, as well as in the humanistic studies.

At present Japan needs, for teaching the skills of manufacture operation, etc., schools of the type known in America as junior colleges or technical institutes. The usual length of training in schools of this type is two years. The Scientific Advisory Group recommends:

1. The establishment of a school of this type in every city. These schools should not all be the same, the major emphasis in some places being agriculture, for example, whereas in other cities machine shop practice or business accounting should be the chief course.

2. For another group, the American type of four-year university undergraduate curricula are recommended. These, of course, must be followed by graduate courses varying in length according to the time required for giving the professions involved high standards and Japan's need for men so trained. For example, the need for improved medical care in Japan may well justify reducing the present total time required for that training and even justify a sub-medical training for "health and sanitary engineers."

3. The Scientific Advisory Group recommends that for teaching as well as research the chair system be discontinued in its present form and a general system of faculty appointments made in a way similar to that found in the United States. As in the States, all universities need not have the same system of curricula but provision should be made to remove the assistant professors and assistants from the present dictatorship of the chair holders.

4. Under the new arrangement the service courses, such as the more elementary courses in language, history, mathematics, chemistry, physics, etc., especially those taught in the first two or three years of the university curricula should be made general for all students and not taught by each chair as in the past.

5. Courses should be given in the various universities so students may readily transfer from one university to another or from one division in any given university to another division without loss of credit for the work done wherever that work is applicable to the students new choice of profession. This does not mean that the curricula should be the same in all universities.

6. So far as possible the courses in the Japanese universities should be acceptable for credit in the universities of other countries, particularly the United States.

7. Japan should not rely so extensively as in the past upon foreign universities for the education of its students but should be informed that all the educational facilities throughout England, Europe and the United States are overtaxed and cannot accommodate the students of their own lands.

8. Japan should plan to provide a way for its outstanding students to study in other countries keeping in mind the fact that in the United States only persons with high scholarship records and who can pass entrance transfer examinations are admitted for advanced studies. Some American colleges now require good scholastic records plus qualifying examinations of all first time student admissions.

9. The universities of Japan should reduce the time spent in attending lecture courses and introduce more laboratory and problem solving courses in the undergraduate curricula. Only one university showed any undergraduate instruction laboratories for engineering student instruction, and those were a dynamo machinery and heat engine laboratory patterned after the laboratories of about 1900 found in a United States university. A reduction in the number of chair research laboratories now not efficiently used will provide some space and a small amount of useful equipment for student instruction laboratories.

10. When these student laboratories are available faculty members and students should develop more skill in the manual technique of the laboratories and not rely upon assistants for the manual work involved in laboratory practice.

11. All science and technical subject professors should so far as possible teach some undergraduate courses, some graduate courses, and carry on some research. To encourage this attitude, good teaching should receive the same recognition as good research.

12. University faculty members should keep in touch with the industries of Japan and other nations and correlate their teaching with application but should not prostitute their courses into courses descriptive of manufacturing and operation methods.

13. University faculty members should promote and be members of nationwide professional and learned societies and should encourage arrangements whereby students may have a student membership in these societies.

14. The clique program of learned societies which now number 229 and research societies, now 849 in number, should be discontinued and an effort made to maintain only a few societies of the type mentioned in 13 above. Local activity may be carried on by sections and chapters administered by the national societies.

15. Faculty members should interchange information in every way possible with other faculty members, other faculties, other universities, etc.

The University and Industrial Research

16. The universities should in general limit the magnitude of their research projects to those of a pilot plan often indeed passing on that stage of any development to industry.

17. Private research laboratories should be encouraged in every possible way. These laboratories should cooperate with the universities by establishing in their research fellowships which will provide for apparatus and materials and finance the fellows and graduate assistants.

18. Industrial laboratories should employ faculty members as consultants on important problems. This procedure will be of mutual benefit to both university and industry.

19. Team research (handwritten)

The following recommendations were compiled by the U.S. Scientific Advisory Group as its recommendations for universities, and are based on replies to 14 questions presented by the Japanese Renewal Committee, at a joint meeting.

Recommendations

<u>Universities</u>

1. The veto power by the Ministry of Education of appointments of staff members an deans in the universities should be eliminated and confined exclusively to the president of the university.

2. The president, deans and staff members of a university or institute should have more independence in the creation of new chairs or in the reorganization of the university or institute operations.

3. Salaries of professors should be increased so that only one instructional job will be necessary for the individual to support himself.

4. Salaries for assistant professors and assistants should be increased to provide an adequate living wage. Professors may now supplement their salaries by consulting work. Assistant professors appear to be less able to acquire such an opportunity.

5. Tax-free gifts to government and private institutions should be permitted.

6. Exchange of professors between private, government and other institutions would serve to broaden the viewpoint of the students.

7. Exchange of students between universities and institutes should be encouraged in order to widen the students' experience. With a unit credit system, this should be relatively simple to accomplish.

8. International exchange of professors and students is desirable.

9. Invitations to Japanese professors to temporary or permanent posts in well established institutions in the United States, especially where no financial obligation to the Japanese Government is concerned, should be approved.

10. The curricula for students in science should be liberalized by including instruction in subjects other than science.

11. Rigidity in the curriculum under any one chair should be modified to permit a student to select for credit courses in related fields.

12. Consideration should be given to modification of the relative amounts of advanced course work and research required of candidates for the Ph.D. degree. Advanced instruction in subjects related to the major work is now lacking.

13. The professional training period in universities should not necessarily be uniform, but dependent on the subject.

14. More team research should be encouraged between various departments in a university.

15. Duplication of shop facilities, microanalytical laboratories, glass blowing facilities, sectional libraries, more expensive physical equipment should be eliminated as much as possible between units in the same general field in the same institution.

16. Consideration should be given to the establishment of central service laboratories in certain areas in Japan where scientific work is concentrated. These would provide facilities for glass-blowing, microanalysis, shop-work, repair of physical equipment and might be supported either directly by the government or by the institutions desiring the work.

17. Economies would result, if the facilities for instruction of undergraduates in science were not duplicated in several divisions of a university. Advanced instruction and research in special fields could be kept independent as at present.

18. Provision should be made for exchange of scientific literature and for acquirement of foreign books and periodicals in Japan as soon as possible.

19. Gradual adaptation of American or German terms in place of Chinese characters should be attempted in the medical field as has been satisfactorily accomplished in the physical science fields.

As we can see above, the U.S. Scientific Advisory Group made important recommendations for the reform of postwar Japanese higher education. The Report is formulated from an economic point of view, as a natural result of the proposals made for the Scientific and Technical Division, Economic and Scientific Section, GHQ, SCAP. Needless to say, this Report influenced the Second U.S. Education Mission of 1950, while at the same time it affected the reform of higher education under the Occupation. This Group was the only one to make recommendations for postwar Japanese education reform between the First U.S. Education Mission of 1946 and the Second Mission of 1950.

III. The Higher Education Reform Plan of the Japanese Education Committee

After SCAP's decision to request an education mission and repeated revisions of the list of candidates, on January 4, 1946, an official request for sending an education mission was made to the Civil Affairs Division, War Department by telegram. SCAP then issued a memorandum, "Committee of Japanese Educators," addressed to the Japanese Government, through the Central Liaison Office, Tokyo. As we have seen, the Ministry of Education set up the Japanese Education Committee in accordance with this directive, and twenty-nine members were appointed on February 2, 1946.

At a second meeting on February 23, the twenty-nine members, with Shigeru Nambara, President of Tokyo Imperial University, as chairman and Shunsaku Kawahara, a Privy Councillor, as vice-chairman, were divided into four subcommittees. Committee No. 4 was concerned with higher education and was composed of the following seven members:

Toyotaka Komiya, Chairman; President of Tokyo School of Music

Teizo Toda, Vice-chairman; Professor of Tokyo Imperial University

Ai Hoshino, Headmistress of Tsuda Juku Senmon Gakko

Kimio Hayashi, Deputy President of Waseda University

Kosaku Kakinuma, Professor of Tokyo Imperial University (Medical Department)

Yasaka Takagi, Professor of Tokyo Imperial University (Law Department)

Risaburo Torikai, President of Kyoto Imperial University

According to the Aruga Papers, the subjects deliberated on by this group were: (1) the university system; (2) the private school system; (3) employment opportunities for graduates; (4) religious education; (5) faculty organizations; (6) women's universities; (7) school extension; and (8) research facilities and libraries.

On March 9, when the first joint meeting with the Mission took place, Committee IV of the Mission handed a question sheet, containing twelve topics on higher education, to Committee No. 4 of the Japanese Education Committee. The replies to these questions were presented on March 20, the day on which Committee IV began preparations for writing its draft report. Some of the questions and the responses to them were as follows:

(Question) Should general education be made widely available to both men and women in institutions on the higher level?

(Answer) Assuming that general education is an education which includes "general culture," this answer is written. Although the method of the actual practice of this may differ in the universities and in senmongakko and individuals' opinion may vary, all the members of the committee agreee that we should give such an education in Japan.

(Question) Should positions of leadership for all social, industrial, and civil needs be more widely available to men and women from a greater variety of institutions on the higher level?

(Answer) As regards to the second question we believe it should be so. But up to present with a very few exceptions men took all the possible positions of leadership in Japan. This is because women were allowed in very limited numbers to go into the institutions of higher learning and to specialize in any one subject. Today men and women are given equal opportunity to study. There is no doubt that very soon positions in various fields will be opened to women. Moreover, we must make every effort to give such opportunities.

(Question) Should exploration be made of the possibilities for establishing an association of universities, public and private, to exercise accrediting functions?

(Answer) There is a strong tendency among the committee members to establish an association of the universities to exercise accrediting functions. In order to improve present Japanese universities, these accrediting functions must exist. Especially in Japan, although there is a great number of private universities, their standards are rather low and unfortunately some of them are used as institutions for the owners to earn money.

Selection of private universities and raising the standards of learning of private institutions are the two great projects which this suggested association alone can undertake.

Now the problem we must face at present in Japan is how to organize such an association. This is a rather difficult problem. We shall appreciate very much if you can given us some practical information from your experience in your country as to:

(1) How is the association organized?

(2) In what manner is it put into practice?

We feel that we might be able to form this association in Japan with your kind cooperation.[18]

It can be seen from these examples that both committees were very eager about higher education reforms. It was inevitable that such exchanges would influence the writing of the final Report. Other questions included matters concerning the exchange of professors, students, and facilities; international contact for both study and research; importation of publications from abroad; and other aspects of higher education institutions.

It can be said that these answers and the other suggestions made by Committee No. 4 of the Japanese Education Committee became the foundation of Committee IV's section of the Mission's report.

In the final Report there is no specific recommendation made on the reform of the prewar system of Imperial universities, universities, high schools, and *Senmongakko*. Whether or not the High Schools and *Senmongakko* should be discontinued, how many years should be required for the new university course, and how the graduate school system should be organized were problems debated by the Japanese Education Committee. The Mission hardly touched upon these matters, recommending only, in Chapter IV of the Report, "Teaching and the Education of Teachers," that university education for teachers' training should last four years. The Report specifically recommended a single-track school system of 6–3–3 years for elementary and secondary schools, but there was only a statement concerning the ideals of higher education, with no specific policy as to the number of years, or its organization.

Why did the Mission not make concrete recommendations on higher education? The reason was due to the fact that Committee IV was charged only with discussing the university system at a practical level:

> *Higher Education in the Rehabilitation of Japan*: A study leading to recommendations in regard to the use of libraries, archives, scientific laboratories, museums in higher education, to student and faculty freedom, to reorientation of the social sciences, and to more active participation in the life of the community and of Japan.

Thus, it is not suggested that a study of the reform of the university system be made, nor that recommendations be presented to General MacArthur. Chairman Stoddard's request to Committee IV was for them to study teachers', liberal, and advanced education only.

In contrast, the subjects for discussion by Committee No. 4 of the Japanese Education Committee, were (1) the university system; (2) the private school system; (3) employment opportunities for graduates; (4) religious education; (5) faculty organization; (6) women's universities; (7) school extension, and (8) research facilities and libraries. The university system, was placed as the first topic for discussion.

As we have observed in the Chapter 5 on the Reform of the School System, the Mission initially recommended the Japanese 6–5 school system in putting emphasis on democratization within the school system, but declined to impose its own reforms. However, it finally recommended the 6–3–3 system in accordance with the suggestion of the Japanese side. The recommendation of the 6–3–3 system was decided on only at the last moment. Therefore, the school system below secondary education was the main issue, as noted by Pearl Wanamaker, and this situation prevented any discussion of higher education reform. In light of this, it is possible to conjecture that the Mission members felt that the reform of the university system should be discussed after establishing the 6–3–3 school system. As the Report of the Second U.S. Education Mission to Japan states:

> In making recommendations on higher education, the first United States Education Mission to Japan devoted most of its attention to desirable improvements within the framework of the existing institutions. In attempting to reform these institutions, however, the Japanese have thought it necessary to reorganize the total system of higher education. . . .

The First Mission did not touch on the reform of the higher education system at all.

In this connection, the Japanese Education Committee served an important role. At the meeting on March 21, as can be seen above, Shigeru Nambara, Chairman of the Japanese Education Committee, suggested to Chairman Stoddard, that the recommendation on school reform be to "model the whole scheme after the American plan, building up elementary schools, high schools, colleges, and universities in a natural sequence with wide opportunities at all levels."[19] Further, on March 25, when the last round of discussions was held between the Japanese Education Committee and the Mission, Nambara and Yasaka Takagi met with R. K. Hall of the CI&E, and presented a report entitled "Education Reform—Official Version of Japanese Education Committee."[20] Concerning higher education, suggestions were made as follows:

> Because of the strangle hold that the koto gakko (boys' higher school) has on the education of Japan it is the real cause of the gakubatsu or educational clique. The fate of a boy is decided when he enters the koto gakko, they and only they can become the leaders of Japan. Hence he [sic] would abolish the koto gakko and provide a graded system of schools, all of which can lead either to a terminal course or to admission to a university level institution (originally underlined).

The Japanese Education Committee saw the *Koto Gakko* as a cause of *gakubatsu* and abolished it by providing a graded school system leading up to university. Furthermore:

> The differences between the semmon gakko (college of specialized training) and the daigaku (university of one or more faculties) should be eliminated, and all institutions at the higher level should have the same academic standing. . . . Post graduate institutes should be established in all universities. . . . Normal schools as now organized in Japan should be abolished (originally underlined).

The Japanese Education Committee eliminated the differences in status between the *Semmon Gakko* and *Daigaku* and placed them on the same academic footing, establishing graduate schools in all universities and abolishing the normal schools. Here, for the first time, a direction is indicated for the higher education system. In other words, the reorganization of the higher education system was set forth in clear terms by the Japanese side.

In "The School System" section of the "Recommendations of the Japanese Education Committee,"[21] plans for university reform were set forth. This reform plan was ". . . to be regarded as references and not as decisions," and the first and second plans were presented on an equal basis. However, both plans were identical with respect to university reform. A relevant portion of the first plan reads as follows: "After three years of Higher Secondary School, a four or five year University, and all graduates of the Higher Secondary School, regardless of the type, are to be admitted to the University."

The second plan differs only in the number of years allotted for elementary and secondary education: the first plan has six years of compulsory elementary school followed by three years of lower secondary school, three years of higher secondary school, and three years of *Seinen Gakko* (youth school), while the second plan calls for two years of lower secondary school and four years each of higher secondary school and *Seinen Gakko* (youth school).

Compared with the prewar higher education system, the above differs mainly in (1) the abolition of *Koto Gakko* (boys' higher school) and *Semmon Gakko* (college of specialized training); (2) increase in the number of required years of university from three years to four or five years.[22]

In this way, the "Recommendations of the Japanese Education Committee" proposed the alternative school system of 6–3–3–4 or 6–3–3–5 as their initial plan, which introduced the four-year university system for the first time.

This plan recommended either a four- or five-year university course; how was the four-year university system decided on? As mentioned in the previous chapter, besides discussing the Japanese Education Committee, the Research Committee on the Education System at Tokyo Imperial University also discussed the issue of the mandatory period required for university courses, and produced the "Report on the School System and Years Required for Graduation." This clearly states: "The universities admit the graduates from high schools and also the graduates from the postgraduate course of the youth school, and provide four years education. . ."

J. C. Trainor of the Education Division of the CI&E states that the Education Division focused on elementary and secondary education, but not on the subject of higher education, and that there were disagreements over this issue. He also mentions that the reform of higher education was not an easy matter for the SCAP educators, and that the 6–3–3–4 single-track school system included a four-year university course which had been originally excluded from the Mission's recommendations and was only set forth in the final report of the Educational Reform Council. He also points out that the four-year university system was the original Japanese reform plan.[23]

The CI&E's Education Division actively carried out the reform of elementary and secondary education with the cooperation of Nambara and other university scholars. In terms of higher education reforms, however, they fell into a dilemma as to how to implement them while avoiding creating difficulties in the relationship between university scholars and themselves. In fact, when it came to reform at the university level, those scholars who had previously been supportive tended to oppose it, in order to secure their own positions. In respect of this point, a researcher says, "In fact, university scholars, such as Nambara Shigeru, and the JERC (Japan Education Reform Committee) did support radical reform at the preuniversity level but resisted many changes at their own level."[24]

An official of the Ministry of Education at that time acknowledges that the Ministry of Education had the intention of preserving the old system of three-year *Koto Gakko* (boy's higher school), and university, beyond the 6–3–3 system.[25] It can be said that the postwar higher education reform contained many problems that were inherent within its own system from the beginning.

This chapter has discussed the process of drawing up Chapter VI, "Higher Education," in the Report of the U.S. Education Mission to Japan. The Mission respected the ideas of the Japanese Education Committee to the greatest degree. It was through repeated discussions with the Japanese, allowing them to take the initiative, that the Report was prepared. Committee IV of the Mission advocated in its draft a higher education system based on high educational ideals, stressing the need for higher education in a free society and freedom of the individual. However, during 1949 and 1950, with the change in U.S. Far Eastern policy, the ideals that were recommended by the Mission were to be betrayed by the U.S. Occupation itself.[26]

7
THE U.S. EDUCATION MISSION
TO GERMANY: A COMPARISON

*I. The Office of Military Government for Germany and
the U.S. Re-education Policy towards Germany*

1) THE ADMINISTRATION OFFICE OF THE MILITARY GOVERNMENT
FOR GERMANY

After the unconditional German surrender to the Allied Powers, on May 8, 1945, the Secretary of War, Henry L. Stimson, disclosed the American plan for organizing the Military Government for Germany on May 11, 1945. In conformity with the Yalta Declaration, Germany was divided into four zones, to be governed by the U.S., Britain, France, and the Soviet Union respectively, through the Allied Control Council. The Allied Control Council was set up in Berlin as the organ for coordinating the four military governments, and consisted of the military commanders from the above four countries. The U.S. was represented by Gen. Dwight Eisenhower, as Commander-in-Chief of the U.S. Forces of Occupation in Germany, who governed the U.S. Zone. Besides this Council, a Coordinating Committee was organized, which included the deputy governors of the four respective zones, and to which the Allied Control Council entrusted the discussion of, the proposals for, most of the problems that arose. However, the actual discussions themselves were carried out by ad hoc committees under the Coordinating Committee; educational matters were discussed by the Subcommittee for Education.

The Subcommittee for Education held monthly meetings and discussed the common education policies among the four zones, submitting any decisions made to the Allied Control Council for approval. It was the duty of the Education Division in each military government to act on these decisions, within their respective zones.

In the Office of the Military Government (U.S.) for Germany (OMGUS), these matters were undertaken by the Education and Religious Affairs Branch (E&RA). This branch was part of the Internal Affairs and Communication Division (IA&C), and had its main office in OMGUS in Berlin. At the same time, it had a branch office in each of the self-governing states (*Länder*) in the U.S. Zone, to supervise, as well as assist, the education plans on the German side.

On October 1, 1945, OMGUS was set up in Berlin to represent the U.S. within the Allied Control Council, in order to supervise the control of the military government in the U.S. Zones.

Gen. Eisenhower was Commander-in-Chief of the U.S. Forces of Occupation in Germany until November 21, 1945, when he was succeeded by Gen. Joseph T. McNarney, who served until March 15, 1946. During this period, Lt. Gen. Lucius Clay was Deputy Military Governor, the U.S. representative in the Coordinating Committee, and also the U.S. representative within the Allied Control Council. He then assumed the office of Commander-in-Chief of the U.S. Forces of Occupation and Military Governor, in March 1947. Clay had, in fact, served unofficially as the Military Governor following Eisenhower's departure in 1945.

At the beginning of the Occupation, there were only a few officers in OMGUS who were in charge of education. These included John W. Taylor, a graduate of Teachers College at Columbia University, and Marshall Knappen, a professor of modern European history at the Universities of Chicago and Michigan. These two were actively carrying out democratic educational reforms in line with the principles of the New Deal.[1] J. W. Taylor had studied under Richard Thomas Alexander, a professor at Columbia University, who was an eminent authority on German education. The subject of Taylor's Ph.D. dissertation was "Youth Welfare in Germany."[2] Additionally, he had had experience teaching in a school in Berlin. He was also an early graduate of the School of Military Government (SMG) which was attached to the University of Virginia in May, 1942.

Before being sent to Germany, Taylor had been ordered to assist in the educational reconstruction of Italy. Thomas Vernon Smith, however, who was head of the Education Division in the Military Government for Italy at that time, and later became a Mission member to Germany, as well as to Japan, requested the War Department to send Taylor to Germany, rather than to Italy, in order to put his special expertise in German education to practical use.[3]

In July 1945, Taylor set up the main office of the E&RA Branch in Berlin, which was small, consisting of only six officers. Initially, it was part of the Public Health and Welfare Division (PH&W), and later came under the control of the IA&C. The IA&C was one of 12 major divisions corresponding to the German Central Government, until educational affairs were upgraded to the Education and Cultural Relations Division (E&CR) in February 1948.

It is easy to understand that, due to the situation within and surrounding the E&RA Branch, educational problems were not necessarily taken very seriously at the beginning of the Occupation. This neglect, however, was harshly criticized by U.S. educational circles,[4] and the Report of the U.S. Education Mission to Germany proposed that:

> In view of the vital importance of the work of the Education and Religious Branch ... provisions should be made for the constant recruitment of the staff of the Education and Religious Affairs Branch.... The present staff is not fully recruited to the number allowed by the present budget. In many fields of specialization the staff must be enlarged beyond the present quota. It is our judgement that the staff should be about double its present size if a thorough job is to be done.[5]

On April 23, 1947, J. W. Taylor resigned from the E&RA Branch and accepted the post of President of the University of Louisville. R. T. Alexander, who had been assistant head of the branch assumed the position of acting chief.[6]

Intending to reorganize the branch, Gen. Clay requested the Secretary of War to recruit Herman B Wells as an advisor on education and culture. Wells was at that time President of Indiana University and one of the authorities on higher education in the U.S. Consequently, Wells temporarily left his university for six months and, from November 21, 1947, to March 27, 1948, contributed to the improvement of the E&RA, as a cultural advisor to Gen. Clay. Under his guidance, its status was raised to the E&CR Division, in February 1948.[7]

2) THE U.S. POLICY TOWARD RE-EDUCATION FOR GERMANY

What kind of policy did the U.S. Government carry out in the re-education of Germany? It was during wartime (June 19, 1942) that the Advisory Committee in the State Department first commenced discussing the issue of educational reconstruction in the Occupation zone. In order to expand this committee, William G. Carr of the National Education Association and Geroge F. Zook of the American Council on Education joined forces in June of the following year.[8]

In May 1945, Archibald MacLeish, Assistant Secretary of State (for Cultural Affairs), set up the Advisory Committee on German Re-education[9] with the cooperation of civilians. On May 28 and 29 of the same year, this committee formulated a draft entitled "Long-Range Policy Statement for German Re-education," which was submitted to MacLeish on June 2, 1945.[10]

On August 21, 1946, this statement was accepted as the basis for U.S. educational policy towards Germany. It proposes the following:

1. The re-education of the German people can be effective only as it is an integral part of a comprehensive program for their rehabilitation. The cultural and moral re-education of the nation must, therefore, be related to policies calculated to restore the stability of a peaceful German economy and to hold out hope for the ultimate recovery of national unity and self-respect.

2. In the initial phases of control, Military Government has been concerned with the elimination of Nazi and militaristic doctorines and practices, and the permanent exclusion of objectionable personnel from posts of influence. These objectives will continue to be its concern. At the same time, a program for the reconstitution of German cultural life has been initiated.

3. The political and moral re-education of the German people will foster the reestablishment of universally valid principles of justice.

4. The German people must come to understand that the Nazi repudiation of these principles destroyed all individual rights in the Nazi state, made the effort at world tyranny inevitable and brought Germany to its present disaster. They must come to understand that the present control measures over Germany are not prompted solely by the German violation of the rights of the other people. They were also made necessary by the political chaos in Germany, which was the direct consequence of the Nazi denial of all political rights and destruction of all alternative organized forces within the nation.

5. The primary principles of justice, basic to the program of re-education, are:

a. That men and nation owe obligations to each other; and that these responsibilities are not, as Nazism maintained, limited to a single race, nation or group.

b. That the dignity and integrity of the individual must be respected by society and other individuals; and that the individual is not, as Nazism maintained, merely a tool of the state.

c. That citizens bear their share of responsibility for public policy and that they have the right and duty to participate in government resting on the consent of the governed.

d. That the untrammel[l]ed pursuit of truth is a prerequisite for the maintenance of justice; and that free communication between individuals, groups and nations is a necessary condition for national and international understanding. Experience with Nazism proves what evil consequences flow from the supression and corruption of the truth.

e. That toleration between diverse cultural and racial groups is the basis of national and international tranquility; and that coerced unity of culture, after the manner of Nazism, is the source of both tyranny and anarchy.

6. To be effective, the program of German re-education must make increasing use of those native resources of German civilization which offer promise of the peaceful development of new ideals and institutions. The collapse of centralized authority in Germany has been conducive to the assumption of local and regional initiative and responsibility for such civic enterprises as schools, literary societies, libraries, social agencies and hospitals. But in addition to the mobilization of healthy cultural influence in the locality and in the region, it is essential that the cultural revival be allowed on a national scale. A potential basis for German self-respect is the justifiable pride of Germans in their former great literary, artistic, scholarly, scientific and religious contributions to civilization.

7. The occupation authorities will bear in mind that permanent cultural changes can be effected only as they are developed and maintained by the Germans themselves. Having first eliminated the Nazi elements, they will seek to effect the progressive transfer of authority in re-education to responsible Germans as rapidly as conditions permit.

8. Efforts will also be made to effect the earliest possible restoration of cultural relations between Germany and other nations.

The above policy on the re-education of Germany became part of the Potsdam Agreement, which was concluded by the leaders of the U.S., Britain, and Russia on August 2, 1945, and provides: "German education shall be so controlled as to completely eliminate Nazi and militarist doctrines and to make possible the successful development of democratic ideas."[11] Thus, they reached agreement on "denazification," "demilitarization" and "democratization." However, prior to the Potsdam Conference, the Allied Powers had already developed their own views on educational reconstruction within the framework of their policy for the re-education for the Germany. This situation resulted in the principles of the Potsdam Agreement being interpreted in several different ways.[12]

In the U.S., educational policy towards Germany had been discussed within the State Department from an early stage. Despite the Potsdam Agreement, full accord could not be reached on any concrete plans for the task of demilitarization and democratization.

Several factors created difficulties in reaching an agreement. First, attention should be drawn to the unusual organization of the Occupation Military Government (OMGUS). As mentioned above, Germany was divided and governed by the U.S., Britain, France, and Russia under the Potsdam Agreement. Southeast Germany was occupied and governed by the U.S., the Northwest by Britain, the Southwest by France, and the East by Russia. The Allied Control Zone was based in Berlin, where an Allied Control Council and a Coordinating Committee were set up to carry out their common policies.

In reality, however, ruling by division created complications. It was hard to arrive at a consensus among the representatives within the Allied Control Council. For instance, G. F. Zook, who was chairman of the U.S. Education Mission to Germany, points out details of the complicated situation in the Occupation Military Government organization, in comparison with the Japanese case.[13] And Robert K. Hall, who was on the staff of the GHQ/CI&E in Japan, compared Germany and Japan under the Occupation. He states that in the German case, because of the difficulty of arriving at a consensus among the four countries, on the basic policy for education, the only solution was for them to carry out their own policies.[14] As a matter of fact, it was only on June 25, 1947, two years after the war, that the Allied Control Council reached an agreement on the basic principle for the reconstruction of education, by the Allied Control Authority Directive No. 54.[15]

The following statement describes the educational policies formulated by the four countries:

Perhaps the most marked feature of the British approach was its informal, pragmatic nature. It was deliberate policy on the part of the Education Branch to deploy its members as widely as possible in order to influence German education through personal contact with individuals. . . . As regards the workings of the school system, the thinking of the British was strongly influenced by their own 1944 Education Act, and it is hardly surprising that in the *Länder* which they occupied (Hamburg, Schleswig-Holstein, Lower Saxony and North Rhine-Westphalia) the tripartite structure had been consolidated by the time control was handed over to the German authorities in January 1947. But the precise form which this structure took had by no means been imposed by the Occupation authorities and after the handover, the latter, while continuing to support various reform measures, left the ultimate decisions to the German.

In the United States there was, towards the end of the war, a good deal of public debate on the subject of "re-education," but such a variety of attitudes among the authorities that by the time of the Potsdam Conference no clear conception of aims had been arrived at, let alone agreement reached on specific plans for the development of the school system . . . the reopening of elementary (*Volksschulen*), middle (*Mittelschulen*) and vocational (*Berufsschulen*) schools at the earliest possible date after Nazi personnel had been eliminated. Textbooks and curricula which are not free of Nazi and militaristic doctrine shall not be used. . . . A year of Occupation elapsed before there was any indication of the more positive approach on which the seal was set in September 1946. In specifically educational policy, the new orientation was reflected in the dispatch of an official mission (U.S. Education Mission to Germany) to study the school system in the U.S. zone at about this time.

Of the three Western allies it was the French who approached the "re-education" issue with the greatest precision. . . . The emphasis on purging the system of personnel with Nazi affiliations was less pronounced than in the

> British and American zones and the day-to-day administration of the system
> was handed back to the Germans almost directly.... And since the territory
> alloted to them was smaller and more homogeneous than the others, the policies
> were less difficult to implement.... In the event they were not, any more than
> the British or the Americans, able to extend the duration of common primary
> education but they were more determined than their Western partners to inter-
> vene directly in the drawing up of the curriculum. Thus the study of Latin was
> abolished in the first three years of *Gymnasium*.... A compulsory daily period
> of French was regarded as the appropriate medium for fostering independence
> of mind and clarity of judgement.
>
> It was in the Soviet Union that the most comprehensive planning for the
> reorganization of the German educational system took place before the end
> of the war and it was the Soviet policy which had the most far-reaching
> effects.
>
> Like the French they put the administration of the educational system under
> German control as soon as it was possible to do so. But clearly they were at
> pains to ensure that the key posts were held by Communists or Social Demo-
> crats who were prepared to liaise closely with their own education officers.[16]

A second factor contributing to the difficulties in reaching an agreement should be considered, namely the conflicting attitudes in the U.S.,
towards the reform of German education. In other words, on one side
there was a positive attitude towards a drastic reform of the German
education system and curriculum on the basis of the New Deal, with the
intention of even intended to reform the German way of thinking and
sense of values and the general pattern of German culture. On the other
side, a negative attitude existed, based on the idea of William E. Hocking,
of Harvard University, that the Americans themselves, should learn from
the German education system, since it had maintained the highest standards in the world.[17] The American educational policy towards Germany
was therefore, developed from a mixture of contradictory attitudes, and in
the early period of the Occupation, the former opinion seemed to be the
dominant one. Later on, however, within the reform process, the idea for
maintaining the traditional aspects of the German educational system as
well as its content, gained the consensus.[18]

II. *The Process of Organizing the U.S. Education Mission to Germany*

1) PLAN FOR SENDING THE EDUCATION MISSION
The U.S. sent an education mission to its Occupation Zone in August 1946.
Its organizational process is described in "The Situation of German Educa-
tion under the Occupation"[19] as follows:

In the summer of 1946, the U.S. Government realized the necessity for accurately examining the existing educational situation in her own Occupation zone in Germany, and decided to send the Education Mission. The War and State Departments together assumed responsibility for the selection of its members. They selected G. F. Zook as chairman and ten eminent educators to organize the Mission. In August 1946, the Mission left for Berlin, visiting schools in Berlin and three self-governing states (*Länder*) in the U.S. Zone. After detailed observation over a period of five weeks, they submitted a Report to Gen. Clay, the Deputy Military Governor at that time, which gave various recommendations for each area of education, after which they returned to the U.S.

As described previously, it was very difficult for the U.S. to obtain a general consensus on German educational reform and the means by which to carry it out, such as the sending of the Education Mission. Under such conditions, how was the plan for sending the Education Mission arrived at and implemented?

To begin with, external to the Government departments involved, the activities of civilian organizations such as the National Education Association should be observed.[20] This Association early on proposed sending Education Missions to both Germany and Japan, and it played an important role in organizing the Missions to both countries; Willard E. Givens, Secretary of the Association, was nominated as a Mission member to Japan; Carl Williams and W. Carr were nominated as candidates for the Mission to Germany.

The proposal that the Association should indicate the necessity for sending a U.S. Education Mission to Germany was originally made in June 1945, and W. E. Givens sent the following letter, dated June 14, 1945, to Henry L. Stimson, Secretary of War:

The educators of the United States are naturally interested in the provisions being made for civilian education in that part of Germany occupied by United States troops. We have received a great many inquiries on this subject.... For the period of rebuilding, both during the later stages of occupation and afterwards, a somewhat different approach might be desirable. In view of the lively interest in this question among educators and many other persons, it might be in the public interest if a small committee of about five well-qualified persons selected by our Association in cooperation with the War Department, could be sent to Germany in the next few weeks to make a first-hand study of: (1) the remaining evidence of the disastrous effect of Nazi education upon German youth and adults and (2) the present situation and outlook for German education. It would not be the function of such a committee, as I see it, to offer advice to the Army regarding the conduct of education during the period of military occupation, unless the responsible officers felt that informal discussion could be of some value to them. The primary function of the committee, on the other hand, would be to attempt to secure background and information, which can only be properly gathered and evaluated on the spot...[21]

In reply, the War Department sent a letter dated June 28, stating that the setting up of a committee for sending experts on education was not within their jurisdiction, but that it was within that of the State Department, and that Givens's letter would be forwarded.

Meanwhile, the other civilian education organization, the United States Committee on Educational Reconstruction[22] was also discussing the problem of the re-education of the German people. The committee's report stated that an education advisory committee should be set up immediately, consisting of education experts who could give advice to the Germans on their educational development, and it continued to suggest that the committee members should be selected from the United Nations or neighbouring countries to Germany. Additionally, the Council for a Democratic Germany[23] showed enthusiasm for the re-education of the German people, and proposed the same in its report, "Program for the Reconstruction of the School and Education System in Germany."

At this stage, there was no sign of movement within the State Department or the War Department for sending education experts on an Education Mission. In May 1945, however, Gen. Eisenhower, Commander-in-Chief of the U.S. Forces of Occupation in Germany, requested the immediate nomination of an eminent American educator to serve as a chief of the E&RA Branch in the Control Council for Germany. Eventually, granting this request, the State Department and the War Department recommended Frank P. Graham, President of the University of North Carolina. However, the nomination did not materialize, because F. P. Graham declined it.[24]

On January 23, 1946, while the plans for the Mission to Japan were already being activated, John H. Hilldring, Director of Civil Affairs in the War Department, sent a letter to William Benton, Assistant Secretary of State, stating that the most important and urgent need in the re-education of the German people was the appointment of an eminent American educator as the chief of the E&RA Branch, in order to direct the U.S. education policy.[25]

In March 1946, while the U.S. Education Mission was in Japan, the National Education Association re-requested the State Department and the War Department to send the same level of education mission to Germany. Also, at the same time, the Friends Committee on National Legislation sent a letter, dated May 3, 1946, to James F. Brynes, Secretary of State, suggesting the sending of the same type of education mission to Germany as the one already sent to Japan, and asking for Brynes's opinion on the matter.[26] In response, Eugene N. Anderson, a representative of the State Department, who later became a secretary to the mission to Germany, reflected a more flexible attitude within his department by discussing it more seriously.

Subsequently, William Carr, Associate Secretary of the National Education Association, sent a letter dated May 6, 1946, to David Harris, Assistant Chief in the Division of Central European Affairs, emphasizing again the necessity for the education mission:

> At the meeting sponsored by the Department of State on May 1st, on the subject of "Reeducating Japan and Germany," I asked whether the Department planned to send a mission of educators to Germany comparable to that which has recently returned from Japan. I assure you that I was quite serious in making the suggestion. From all that I can learn regarding the situation of German education in the American Zone, it appears that a mission could give valuable aid to the Government of the United States with reference to its policy toward German education.
>
> This proposal was fully discussed by the Executive Committee of the National Education Association at a meeting in March. In Mr. Givens' absence, I was instructed to present the matter formally to the Department of State and to the War Department. This was done. The proposal was acknowledged with thanks. A similar proposal was made by our Association, and acknowledged by the Department, in July 1945... We are prepared to make every effort to be of assistance to the Department in insuring the success of such a mission. Since it has now been definitely decided that UNESCO will not be concerned with education in former enemy territory, it seems to me all the more important that the United States move forward in this matter. As you probably know, the British Ministry of Education sent a mission to the British Zone in Germany last October. When I was in London in November, I heard many favorable comments from British educators regarding the value of such a mission...[27]

In a positive reply to this letter, dated May 10, D. Harris said that the State Department would discuss sending a U.S. Education Mission to Germany in the near future.[28]

Moreover, on May 22, in a radio discussion, "The State of the World Progam," Frederich G. Hochwalt, who was a member of the Education Mission to Japan, and William Carr gave the activities of both GHQ/CI&E in Japan and OMGUS, high praise, and described Gen. MacArthur's invitation to the Mission to Japan, to assist SCAP and the Japanese Government. F. G. Hochwalt said that he expected that the War Department would send the same kind of mission to Germany as well, in the near future.[29]

It should be emphasized that the crucial factor for the implementation of the Mission to Germany was the favorable impression created by the achievement of the Mission to Japan.

The Mission to Japan returned to the U.S. at the beginning of April 1946, and submitted its Report to the State Department and the War Department. About the same time, Gen. MacArthur's "Statement" was released, and the Report was acknowledged as the official policy for educational reform in Japan. Eventually, the success of the Mission to Japan was publicized in the press, and through the proposals made in the Report, the U.S. demonstrated its power and leadership to the other Allied Powers. Appreciating the Mission's results anew, U.S. Government authorities began discussing the Mission to Germany all over again. In this way, the U.S. attitude began to change to a more positive one.

Reviewing this process in detail, on April 17, Oliver P. Echols, Chief of the Civil Affairs Division in the War Department, sent a letter to Gen. Clay with ten copies of the Report of the U.S. Education Mission to Japan.[30] In his letter, he quotes from Gen. MacArthur's "Statement" concerning the Japanese case, and the necessity for American experts:

> The report will be most helpful to my Headquarters in its further efforts to assist the Japanese government in modernizing the Japanese educational system. The report may well be studied by all educators, regardless of individual aspects.

And he continued to urge Gen. Clay to respond to this matter by saying:

> Several inquiries have been received here and at the State Department relative to a similar Mission to Germany. Since your views on this subject are not known, I have advised waiting until you have had an opportunity to look over the report and indicate whether such a group would be desirable at this time.

Generals MacArthur and Clay, as officers commanding the Occupation in Japan and Germany respectively, readily invite comparison. General Clay was, like Gen. MacArthur, a graduate of the U.S. Military Academy at West Point and had been appointed especially as the Commander of OMGUS by President Franklin D. Roosevelt. Therefore, Gen. Clay was well aware of the likelihood of comparisons between himself and Gen. MacArthur. It is natural that Gen. MacArthur's achievement in relation to the Mission to Japan should have attracted his attention. As a matter of fact, Gen. Clay handed the Report to J. W. Taylor and directed him to work out a similar plan.

Taylor carefully studied the Report and presented the following negative criticism to Gen. Clay on April 29:

> ... Japan is an oriental country, the culture of which never reached a level comparable to that of Germany, the Nazi interregnum notwithstanding. The

Japanese educational system was based on a nineteenth century pattern which provided one type of education for the masses and another for the privileged few.... The so-called negative aspects of present Military Government policy with respect to German educational control, by their application, tend to re-establish an already highly developed and well articulated system of education. Hence, the situation in Germany is not analogous to that in Japan. Further, U.S. policy in Germany requires German state educational authorities to produce plans for new programs as well as for proposed reforms of existing programs in the functional fields of education. These proposals are discussed with German education ministry representatives by Military Government education officers, and it is through such conferences that the positive influencing and reorienting of German education actively takes place.

There are usually only two reasons for conducting educational surveys, namely, setting up a proposed program and evaluating an existing program. This Section plans to request an evaluation of the Military Government program as it is working out in the German educational system at a future date, namely, at the time when the Department of State takes over policy responsibility for education from the War Department. It is believed that such a survey should be made by a commission not to exceed five members, but preferably three, and if possible, from among the membership of the Advisory Committee on Policy for the Control of German Education [constituted by the Department of State in the summer of 1945].

Since a U.S. educational control program has already been set up in Germany by experienced American educators with the aid of the Advisory Committee and the program has not been in operational long enough to warrant an evaluation, it is the view of this Section that the constitution at this time of a U.S. education mission to Germany similar to the mission to Japan is unnecessary.[31]

Taylor's comments show that OMGUS had already discussed bringing education experts from the U.S., by contrast with the inactivity of the U.S. government. In fact, it was in autumn 1945 that they began discussing it for the first time. The idea of bringing education experts to Germany was originally formulated, in autumn 1945, as one of the means of evaluating the education program which was being carried out under OMGUS, in terms of the democratization of the German education system. The plan was to include three to five members from the Advisory Committee on German Re-education.[32] J. W. Taylor joined this committee as a member.

O. P. Echols of the War Department sent a telegram, dated May 5, to Gen. Clay insisting on an answer to his previous letter of April 17:

... BAD PRESS HERE (THE U.S.) ON REORIENTATION PROBLEMS DUE 2 THINGS:

(1) NO DIRECT KNOWLEDGE PART REPRESENTATIVE AMERICAN EDUCA-TORS (IN GERMANY) PROBLEMS, ACCOMPLISHMENTS GERMANY.

(2) LACKING EXPERT OPINION AMERICANS CONSIDER SELVES COMPETENT PASS JUDGEMENTS ON EDUCATIONAL ISSUES. BELIEVE SELECTED MISSION COULD HELP EASE PRESSURE HERE FOR CURRENT MISS INFO IN MINDS US PUBLIC.

IF YOU CONCUR SUGGEST CABLE WARCAD FROM THEATER COMMANDER REQ WAR, STATE INVITE GP. WE WILL INSURE HIGH CALIBRE REPRESENTATIVE GP. GROUP WILL TRAVEL AT WD EXPENSE.[33]

His specific suggestions had a positive influence on the formerly rigid attitude of OMGUS towards bringing the Education Mission to Germany, and finally created a more flexible position of acceptance. The record of documents dated May 7, 1946, of the E&RA Branch, expresses their final view on the Education Mission, as follows:

On the basis of intensive study for ten months the ERA Branch has already set up a proposed program of educational development for the next years. Military Government policy in Germany requires that German authorities themselves produce plans for the reorientation and reorganization of German education. These steps are already being taken under the supervision and with the help of the ERA Branch (OMGUS). An annual report in the form of a yearbook on education in Germany under Military Government is planned to serve as an evaluation of work thus far accomplished and to furnish reliable information to the American public upon the situation. Further, this Branch proposed in its functional program to request an evaluation of its program by a commission every two years.

While a Commission on Education would not be necessary to aid Military Government here to set up a program as was the case in Japan, it is possible that two purposes would be served by an Education Mission a) to give a full and correct interpretation of our program to the American public, and b) to pass judgement for the Military Government upon the soundness of the plan now in operation, with suggestions for improvement or modification.

The opinion is therefore held, that it would be advisable to invite this proposed Education Mission for a period of one month of observation, consultation and study, provided that the visitation be set at the proper time to avoid school vacations, and provided that Military Government be permitted to suggest some of the personnel to be invited. . .[34]

Based on this view, on May 8, they sent an official telegram to the War Department requesting the Education Mission:[35]

REURAD WCL-38807 AND URLET 17 APR WE WOULD BE GLAD TO RECEIVE EDUCATIONAL MISSION FOR PERIOD OF 1 MONTH TO OBSERVE AND EVALUATE OUR EDUCATIONAL PROGRAM. OUR PROGRAM IS QUITE DIFFERENT FROM JAPAN AND A LARGE MISSION IS UNNECESSARY. WE WOULD SUG-

GEST A MISSION OF NOT EXCEED 8 HIGHLY QUALIFIED PERSONS.[36] MISSION SHOULD ARRIVE BY 1 JUNE OR POSTPONE VISIT TO 14 AUGUST AS SCHOOLS ARE CLOSED FROM 1 JULY TO 14 AUGUST.

2) THE PROCESS OF SELECTING THE EDUCATION MISSION MEMBERS AND THE APPOINTMENT OF A CHAIRMAN

On the official request to the War Department for sending the Education Mission, the selection of members for the mission was begun. In selecting members and organizing the Mission, Robert P. Patterson, Secretary of War, suggested to the State Department, on May 14, 1946, the following in reference to the telegram from OMGUS:[37]

A) RECRUITMENT AND FINAL SELECTION WAS TO BE THE RESPONSIBILITY OF THE DEPARTMENT OF STATE

B) CONSIDERATIONS BASIC TO RECRUITMENT AND SELECTION BE IDENTICAL TO THOSE CRITERIA APPLIED TO THE SELECTION OF THE EDUCATION MISSION TO JAPAN

C) THE MISSION NOT TO EXCEED EIGHT HIGHLY QUALIFIED PERSONS

D) COLLATERAL CONSIDERATIONS OF INCLUDING WOMEN, CATHOLIC AND OTHER SECTARIAN ADVISORS, AND PROPER GEOGRAPHIC REPRESENTATION BE GIVEN WEIGHT IN THE FORMATION OF THE MISSION

E) THE ADVICE OF THE U.S. OFFICE OF EDUCATION BE SOUGHT

F) THE MISSION DEPART NOT LATER THAN THE FIRST WEEK OF AUGUST

G) THE WAR DEPARTMENT PROVIDE ALL NECESSARY EXPENSES AND TRANSPORTATION

These suggestions correspond to those of the Mission to Japan in selecting members. In consequence, the State Department sent OMGUS the following names as candidates: Bess Goodykoontz, Edmund Day, Frank P. Graham, Alvin Johnson, Reinhold Niebuhr, Thomas V. Smith, William G. Carr, Felix N. Pitt, George F. Zook and Dave Morse.[38]

OMGUS telegrammed back to the Civil Affairs Division of the War Department, requesting a revision of the list:

TENTATIVE SELECTION FOR EDUCATION MISSION ARE HIGHLY SATISFACTORY. HOWEVER NEITHER OF PROPOSED SUBSTITUTES APPEAR TO BE UP TO CALIBER OF 9 REGULAR MEMBERS. PERMISSION TO MODIFY MEMBER LIST IS GRANTED BUT SUGGEST ANY MODIFICATIONS BE COMMUNICATED BY CABLE TO THIS HEADQUARTERS. IT IS TO BE NOTED THAT THERE IS

A. NO REPRESENTATIVE FROM WEST OF MISSISSIPPI;

B. NO PERSON WITH TEACHER TRAINING BACKGROUND;

C. NO PERSON WITH "GENERAL" EDUCATION (GENERAL COLLEGE) BACKGROUND;

D. NO PERSON ACTIVE IN PUBLIC SCHOOL ADMINISTRATION.

SUGGEST DR. EARL J. MCGRATH, DEAN COLLEGE LIBERAL ARTS, STATE UNIVERSITY OF IOWA, IOWA CITY AS MEETING ITEMS A. AND C. ABOVE. MCGRATH HAS COMMAND OF GERMAN LANGUAGE AND HAS HAD EXPERIENCES WITH INSTITUTIONAL AND STATE SURVEY WITH AMERICAN COUNCIL ON EDUCATION AND HAS WRITTEN NUMBERS OF SURVEY REPORTS. IS ALSO ONE OF FOREMOST MEN IN GENERAL EDUCATION FIELD WHICH IS UNDER DISCUSSION HERE IN CONNECTION WITH PROPOSED REFORMS IN SECONDARY (GERMAN EQUIVALENT TO U.S. JUNIOR AND GENERAL COLLEGE PROGRAMS) AND UNIVERSITY EDUCATION. SUGGEST FURTHER ADDITION OF DR. HENRY HILL, PRESIDENT OF GEORGE PEABODY COLLEGE FOR TEACHERS, NASHVILLE, TENNESSEE, AND FORMER SUPERINTENDENT OF SCHOOLS OF LEXINGTON, KENTUCKY AND PITTSBURGH, PENNSYLVANIA, AS REPRESENTING BOTH TEACHER EDUCATION AND CITY SCHOOL ADMINISTRATION FIELDS (THUS SATISFYING ITEMS B. AND C. ABOVE).

SUGGEST INCLUSION OF SUCH REPRESENTATIVES AS MCGRATH AND HILL EVEN IF NECESSARY TO INCREASE SIZE OF COMMISSION. POSSIBLE ALSO DROP ALVIN JOHNSON DUE TO ADVANCED AGE AND STILL KEEP COMMISSION MEMBERSHIP AT MAXIMUM 10.

APPROVAL IS GRANTED FOR DEPARTMENT OF STATE REPRESENTATIVE DR. EUGENE N. ANDERSON TO ACCOMPANY COMMISSION. ENTHUSIASTICALLY ACCEPT OFFER OF STATE TO SEND 2 SECRETARIES WITH COMMISSION. SUGGEST GROUP ARRIVES IN BERLIN 24 AUGUST.

PERMISSION IS GRANTED FOR HOLDING TELECON ON PROBLEMS AND ARRANGEMENTS REGARDING BRIEFING AND PREPARATION OF MISSION FOR DEPARTURE FROM UNITED STATES WITH DR. JOHN W. TAYLOR, CHIEF EDUCATION AND RELIGIOUS AFFAIRS, INTERNAL AFFAIRS AND COMMUNICATION DIVISION OMGUS.[39]

William Benton, Assistant Secretary of State, considered it important to appoint a chairman first, in order that the planning of the Mission could be carried out smoothly, as in the case of Japan.[40] Accordingly, he sent the following letter to Edmund Day, President of Cornell University, asking him to accept the position of chairman of the Mission:

The Department of State and the War Department are inviting a small number of distinguished American educators to go to Germany for the purpose of observing and evaluating the educational program of the United States Military Government in that country. The proposal to send the group has received the approval of Lieutenant General Lucius D. Clay, Deputy Military Governor, Office of Military Government for Germany in Berlin...

The Department of State and the War Department appreciate the valuable service already performed by you as chairman of the State Department's Advisory Committee on German Reeducation in formulating the Long-Range Policy on German Reeducation of this Government. They wish to avail themselves further of your aid, and in[sic] their behalf I am inviting you to act as chairman of the proposed group of educators. In the hope that you will be able to accept the invitation, I suggest that you come to Washington in the very near future to consult with this Department and the War Department about the plans for the trip.

It is proposed that the group meet in Washington on August 19 for the preliminary briefing, and that it leave by air on August 23, so as to arrive in Berlin on August 24. The Mission will remain in Germany for about one month and it is anticipated that the members will be back in the United States by the end of September.[41]

In reply to the above letter from Benton, Day telegrammed on July 29 declining the position, due to his commitment to his university schedule.[42] The next day, Benton replied to Day, expressing his regret; at the same time he indicated to the person in charge, that they should nominate another possible candidate for chairman.

In a telegram to OMGUS dated August 1st, the State Department informed them that George Zook, Reinhold Niebuhr, Felix Pitt, Earl McGrath, Henry H. Hill, and Bess Goodykoontz had accepted their invitations, and that Edmund Day, William Carr, Alvin Johnson, and Frank Graham had declined. Additionally, it reported that Dr. Dykstra of the University of California at Los Angeles was expected to become chairman, and a representative of an area of labor problem, was in the process of being selected.[43]

In response, OMGUS telegrammed a reply dated August 6, acknowledging the six members who had accepted, and T. V. Smith, who had also been a member of the Mission to Japan, continuing by saying that they only Dykstra and H. White had been accepted as substitute members. As for a candidate for the chairman, they proposed the following selection in order of priority: Zook, Dykstra, and Spaulding. They also requested the inclusion of Paul M. Limbert, who was the president of the YMCA College and an authority on youth activities in the U.S., as a representative concerned with youth problems.[44]

A telegram from the War Department to OMGUS, dated August 10, reported that Limbert had accepted membership, and suggested that the State Department and themselves considered it important to include a representative in the area of labor problems, so that Lawrence Rogin had been nominated.[45]

As for appointing a chairman, according to the proposed selection, in order of priority, made by OMGUS, W. Benton sent a letter dated August

7 to George Zook, in which he says, "Your acceptance of the joint invitation of the Department of State and the War Department to be a member of the Education Mission to Germany has been received with great pleasure. I should appreciate it if you would also serve as Chairman of the group."[46]

This request was extremely simple, and almost only a formality when compared with the request to E. Day. As a matter of fact, OMGUS began to quietly formulate a plan for the Mission in accordance with the idea of J. W. Taylor that the Mission should be organized by Zook.[47] As seen in the above names of candidates listed in order of priority, it had already been planned by OMGUS, that Zook should be chairman; nevertheless the State Department nominated Dykstra. In other words, Zook was appointed by special request of Gen. Clay.

William Benton sent the following official letter to each candidate:

> The Department of State and the War Department are inviting a small number of distinguished American educators to go to Germany for the purpose of observing and evaluating the educational program of the United States Military Government in that country. The proposal to send the group has received the approval of Lieutenant General Lucius D. Clay, Deputy Military Governor, Office of Military Government for Germany in Berlin.
>
> Since the reeducation of the German people from Nazism and militarism toward the acceptance of peace-loving, democratic ideals and ways of life is fundamental for the winning of the peace, the group of educators will be called upon to bear a responsibility of the highest important. Every facility will be placed at its disposal to assure the success of its work.[48]
>
> In behalf of the Department of State and the War Department, I have the honor to extend to you an invitation to become a member of the proposed group of educators.
>
> It is suggested that the group meet in Washington on August 19th for preliminary briefing, that it leave by air on August 23rd, and that it arrive in Berlin on August 24th. The Mission will remain in Germany for about one month and it is anticipated that the members will be back in the United States by the end of September.
>
> I shall appreciated your giving me a reply as early as possible.

Through the above process, the State Department selected eleven members who were acknowledged as well known and well informed in all fields of education, and possessing political ability in educational affairs, and also full comprehension of the relationship between education and society. These members were drawn from all regions of the U.S. and represented a variety of religious groups.

The Mission members were finally approved by Gen. Clay on August 19, 1946, as follows:[49]

1. Chairman of Mission, George F. Zook, Ph.D., Cornell University; Professor of European History, Pennsylvania State College and other institutions between 1925–33; President of the University of Akron; U.S. Commissioner of Education from 1933–34, President of American Council of Education since 1 July 1934. Appointed Chairman of the President's Commission on Higher Education in 1946.

2. Earl McGrath, Ph.D., University of Chicago; Dean of Administration, University of Buffalo, 1940–45; Dean of Arts & Science, University of Iowa since 1945. Served in the U.S. Navy as Lt. Commander and was officer in charge of Educational Services Section, Bureau of Navy Personnel, from 1942–1944.

3. Helen White, Ph.D., University of Wisconsin. Professor of English at University of Wisconsin. Author of numerous books on English poetry and devotional literature. Appointed official advisor to U.S. Representative on the Preparatory Commission of the United Nations Educational, Scientific and Cultural Organization. Recent national president, American Association of University Women.

4. Lawrence Rogin, M.A., Columbia University; onetime instructor of Economics at Columbia University. Education Director of American Federation of Hosiery Workers in Philadelphia. Since 1942 Educational Director of Textile Workers of Union of America. Member of advisory committee to the Department of Labor on publicity for educational materials. Consultant to Adult Education Association.

5. Thomas Vernon Smith, Ph.D., University of Chicago. Since 1927 professor of philosophy, University of Chicago. Illinois State senator 1935–38, member 76th Congress 1939–41. Served in U.S. Army as Lieut. Colonel and was Chief, Educational Branch, U.S. Military Government in Italy. Member of the U.S. Education Mission to Japan.

6. Reinhold Niebuhr, Doctor of Divinity, Amherst, Yale, and Oxford. Professor at Union Theological Seminary since 1938. Representative of Federal Council of Churches of America at the World Council of Churches held in Cambridge, England, 1946. Editor of *Christianity and Society* and of *Christianity and Crisis*.

7. Paul Limbert, Ph.D., Columbia. Professor of Education at New College, Teachers College, 1933–39; Professor of International YMCA College 1939–46, now its president. Outstanding leader of youth work in YMCA and community.

8. Felix Newton Pitt, Ph.D., Freiburg Baden, 1933. Diocesan superintendent of schools in Louisville, Ky., since 1925. Professor of philoso-

phy at Ursuline College in Louisville. Contributor to the *Catholic School Journal*.

9. Bess Goodykoontz, D.Ped., N.Y. State College for Teachers. Assistant Professor of Education, University of Pittsburgh, 1924–29. Assistant Commissioner of Education, Office of Education, since 1929.

10. Henry Harrington Hill, Ph.D., Columbia. Dean, University of Kentucky, July 1941 to 1942; Superintendent of Schools, Pittsburgh, Pa., 1942. President, George Peabody College for Teachers, Nashville, Tenn., since 1942.

11. Eugene Newton Anderson (Representative of the Department of State), Ph.D., University of Chicago. Assistant Professor, European History, University of Chicago, 1932–36; Professor of European History at American University, Washington, D. C. 1936–41. Central European Section, Office of Strategic Services, 1942–45. At present Associate Chief, German-Austrian Activities, Division of Occupied Areas, Office of International Information and Cultural Affairs.

In addition to the above members, two secretaries, Beatrice Braude and Irma L. Coon, were included at the request of OMGUS.

The following day, August 20, the State Department held a press conference announcing the reason for sending the Education Mission to Germany plus the list of Members, as follows:

The Honorable William Benton, Assistant Secretary of State for Public Affairs, in response to a request by the War Department, has issued a joint invitation on behalf of the Department of State and the War Department to a number of distinguished American educators to serve as members of an education mission to Germany. A similar mission recently returned from Japan and a report of its findings has been published. The proposal to send the mission to Germany, which originated with the War Department, received the full approval of Lieutenant General Lucius D. Clay, Deputy Military Governor, Office of Military Government for Germany in Berlin. The members were selected by the two departments in consultation with the United States Military Government in Germany and with the advice of the United States Office of Education. The Mission will observe and evaluate the education program of United States Military Government in that country, and will submit a report setting forth the results of its work. "The sending of the Mission is in keeping with the long-range constructive policy on German reeducation released August 13, 1946 by the Office of Military Government in Berlin," said Assistant Secretary Benton.

It is expected that the group will depart August 22 from Washington and will spend approximately one month in Germany.

The group will be composed of the following educators:...[50]

The members gathered in Washington between August 19 and 23, to complete arrangements for their passage and to hold preparatory meetings.

There was criticism concerning the selection of the members, as recorded in a memo of a telephone conversation between Gen. Echols, Chief of the Civil Affairs Division of the War Department, and Col. Robert McRae of the Reorientation Branch of the same division.[51] According to this memo, Gen. Echols made this criticism with particular reference to the appointment as chairman of G. F. Zook, whom he described as "a high-pressure salesman and not an educator." He added that most of the other members were not experts on German education, and that the aims of the Mission were "not educational but political." He went on to point out that a positive report could not be expected, and that the opposition in the selection of the members should be reported to the State Department through the Secretary of War.

Responding to this criticism, Col. McRae said that he believed that the Mission would produce an excellent report, and that OMGUS in Berlin had expressly approved the selection of members and expressed their deep satisfaction in the matter.

George F. Zook was born in 1885 in Kansas and, as can be seen above, was an historian, government official, and educator. He studied at the University of Kansas (B.A. 1906) and at Cornell University (Ph.D. 1913). He taught at Pennsylvania State, 1912–20. After World War I, he became the chief of higher education in the U.S. Bureau of Education, serving until 1925, and afterwards became president of Akron University, 1925–29. He was professor of European history, Pennsylvania State College, 1925–33. In 1933 President Franklin D. Roosevelt appointed him Commissioner of Education, a post he held for one year. From 1934 on, as Director and President of the American Council on Education, he became the most prominent lobbyist for higher education.

It is obvious that Zook was a distinguished enough figure to be nominated as chairman. It is, therefore, possible to conjecture that the opposition to his appointment was due to a subtle difference of opinion on the appointment of a chairman, among the State and War Departments and OMGUS.

On August 21, 1946, as the Mission was preparing for departure, the first basic policy document concerned with German education, entitled "The Long-Range Policy Statement for German Reeducation," was released to the public. This document had initially been drawn up by the Advisory Committee on German Reeducation on May 28 and 29, 1945; on May 16 of the following year it had been acknowledged as the SWNCC's policy document (SWNCC 269).

Assistant Secretary Benton stated at the press conference that sending the Mission was in keeping with "The Long-Range Constructive Policy on German Reeducation," released on August 13, 1946, by OMGUS. This document can be considered to be "The Long-Range Policy Statement for German Reeducation," and Benton's reference to it indicates that OMGUS adopted this SWNCC policy as of August 13, 1946, before the State Department released it.

On August 23, this document was handed over to the the Mission as a guideline. A copy is kept among the personal papers of H. C. White, and it is referred to in the Report of the Education Mission to Germany as an important policy document.[52]

The Mission left the U.S. by air on August 23 and arrived in Berlin on the following day. They stayed in Germany for about one month to study and observe the situation in elementary, middle, and vocational schools, higher education institutions and social education groups, in the three *Länder* within the U.S. Zone (Greater Hesse, Württemberg-Baden, and Bavaria). After they had held meetings with the officers in charge of education in OMGUS and with officials, teachers, and civilians on the German side, they returned to Berlin and drew up the "Report." On September 20, 1946, they submitted their Report to Gen. Clay, and returned to the U.S. on September 26, 1946.

Their schedule in Germany is shown in Appendix B.[53]

According to the above proposed schedule, they concentrated on studying and observing elementary, middle, and higher education and youth education institutions. Upon their return to Berlin, they had a final meeting with the staff of the E&RA Branch. They took only four days to complete the Report before submitting it to Gen. Clay, who had asked that drafts be completed by September 15.

According to documents kept by H. C. White,[54] major problems of German education that were supposed to be covered by the U.S. Education Mission had already been mentioned at the briefing in Berlin:

1. Educational content of the *Länder* constitutions.
2. Teacher training—should teacher training be on university basis?
3. Control of youth activities—should it reside in education at all or in Army?
4. Control—basic curricula, reforms, opening new types of schools, reopening of new faculties especially those given back to Germans.
5. Denominational school problem—present policy let Germans decide.
6. Study organization of educational headquarters.

A framework of the Mission's Report can be constructed by referring to the briefing in Berlin.

G. F. Zook assigned the outline of the "Report," accordingly, as follows:[55]

VERY TENTATIVE OUTLINE OF REPORT

I. Introduction (Zook) (500 words)

Appointment of the commission; statement of Secretary Patterson and General Clay as to importance of education in present German situation; appreciation for assistance, etc.

II. Basic Facts Affecting the German Educational Situation (Goodykoontz and White) (2000 words)

The Potsdam Agreement; the zones; food; coal; glass; school buildings; children; teachers; crowded housing conditions (expellees, etc.); university teachers and students; etc.

III. Denazification and Demilitarization (Niebuhr and Smith) (1000 words)

Official policy; emergency phase completed; second phase.

IV. Development of Democracy (Smith) (2000 words)

Official policy; relation of education to successful practice of democracy.

V. Status of Education in Germany—as Evaluation with Recommendations (7000 words)

A. The Elementary Schools (Goodykoontz, Hill and Pitt) (1000 words)

B. The Secondary Schools (Hill, Goodykoontz and Pitt) (750 words)

C. Vocational Education (Rogin) (500 words)

D. Youth Organizations (Limbert) (1000 words)

E. Adult Education and Libraries (Rogin) (500 words)

F. Teacher Education; Comprehensive Pedagogical Institute at Frankfurt (Hill and Goodykoontz) (1000 words)

G. Films and Radio; Film Institute at Munich; Use of Radio in the Schools (Rogin and Goodykoontz) (250 words)

H. The Universities and the *Technische Hochuschulen* (McGrath, Nieburh and White) (1500 words)

I. *Land* Ministries of Education (Hill) (500 words)

VI. Recommendations to OMGUS and to War Department; State Department (Niebuhr and McGrath) (3000 words)

Food; Paper; Coal; Buildings; Books (gifts; importation from other countries); Control and/or Advice to German Educational Authorities.

Relations of education in Berlin OMGUS.

Relations of Berlin Section in education to *Land* education offices.

The *Land* staff and relations to German Educational Officials.

Internal cooperation.

Relation of State Department and War Department.

VII. Ways and Means in which the United States Can Help (Limbert) (1500 words)

Federal Government

Continue appropriation of $5,500,000 (experts and films);

I & M books; American Libraries; Fulbright bill; exchange of students and teachers; book situation (gifts; importation from other countries).

Voluntary Agencies

A Committee or Committees; food and clothing; books; teacher and student exchange.

VIII. Conclusion (Zook) (1000 words)

Importance of Regarding the Educational Task in Germany as Long-Time Responsibility.

Need for More Information in the United States Regarding Educational System in Germany.

Need for continuing Advisory Committee.

(Total 18,000 words)

In comparison with the actual Report, the above outline was considerably revised. It can be conjectured that the preparation for drafting the Report and assigning writers to specific subjects was begun some time in advance. In fact, there was a very important handwritten draft on German Reeducation, prepared by H. C. White.

According to the Earl J. McGrath Papers, which were only made available recently, after they submitted the Report, some members of the Mission visited Vienna at the request of Brigadier General Ralph Tate of the Austrian Military Government. They arrived in Vienna on September 21 and stayed until September 26, submitted a report on the Austrian education system, and returned to the U.S. on September 28.[56]

The *New York Times* reported the visit to Austria on September 27, 1946, under the headline "Austria's School Purged of Nazism—6 U.S. Educators Felt Vienna is Capable of Setting Up a Democratic System," as follows:

Vienna, Sept. 25. Six prominent United States educators, who today completed a tour of Austria, felt, according to their chairman, Dr. Earl McGrath, dean of liberal arts at the University of Iowa, that the Austrians are perfectly capable of setting up a democratic educational system without much outside interference. The Austrians, to a greater extent than the Germans, show a good deal of educational vitality, members of the group said.

Three of the visitors, Dr. Thomas V. Smith of the University [of] Chicago, the Rev. Felix Pitt, superintendent of Catholic School in Louisville, Ky., and Dr. McGrath, indicated they did not feel that there was much danger of Nazi ideas playing any serious role in the future development of Austrian education.

The educators, brought here at the invitation of the United States Command in Austria made a rapid survey of the Austrian educational conditions. They had already taken part in a general survey of German educational conditions earlier at the invitation of the War Department.

The general impression gathered from the group was that they had found the educational situation in Austria considerably more encouraging than that in Germany. They will suggest that two or three American educational officers remain here until the end of the occupation to aid the Austrians in promoting such American techniques and ideas of education as can be helpful here. They added that any attempt to force American educational methods on the Austrians would be useless and dangerous.

Dr. Smith said he had been informed by officials in the Ministry of Education that 30 per cent of the elementary school teachers and 40 per cent of the teachers in the equivalent of high school grades had been expelled from their positions because of their connections with Nazism...[57]

Soon after the Mission's return to the U.S., G. F. Zook visited R. P. Patterson, Secretary of War, and officially submitted the Report. Patterson expressed his appreciation to the Mission in a letter to Zook, dated October 8, 1946, and added:

The recommendations of the Mission will be of the greatest assistance both to Military Government in Germany and to the responsible departments of the Government in Washington. In addition, however, I believe that the report should be given the widest possible distribution throughout the United States, in order that the scope of the problem can be clearly understood by the American people. Arrangements have been made for an official release of the report by the State Department...[58]

In his reply dated October 15, G. F. Zook repeated the importance of increasing staff, as recommended in the "Report":

As is brought out in the report, however, we believe that it is exceedingly important that the education staff should be increased very materially in order that it may be fully equal to its responsibility...

When they returned, after having submitting the "Report" to Gen. Clay, it was reviewed by the State Department. Although there were no major changes concerning its substance, the term "Commission," which had been used up to this point, was changed to "Mission," and "State Department" to "The U.S. Government."[59] The War Department telegrammed OMGUS on October 8 requiring that these changes be made. B. Braude, one of the secretaries who typed the Report, admitted that, after their return, the "Report" was reedited by E. Anderson of the State Department and Reinhold Niebuhr of the Union Theological Seminary.[60] These revisions show that the organization of the Mission, as well as the formulation of the Report, did not proceed smoothly.

On October 12, prior to the releasing of the Report, William Benton, Assistant Secretary of State, and George F. Zook gave a press conference, at which Benton expressed his personal dissatisfaction at three recommendations made by the Mission.

His first objection was to the way of increasing the number of teachers, which were extremely short at the time. The Mission's recommendation was to re-employ ex-teachers on a probationary basis, immediately after they were judged innocent by the Denazification Tribunals. Opposing this recommendation, Benton suggested that they should be given priority in special hearings before the official Denazification Tribunals. His second objection was to the integration of vocational middle education with general middle education, within the same building. And his third opposed the establishment of the pedagogical faculty in German universities with the same rank as other traditional faculties, such as law, medicine, and theology. These personal criticisms detracted from the dignity of the Report.[61]

On October 12, the Report was submitted to J. F. Brynes, Secretary of State, with the following long letter from Benton:

> I express the Department's gratitude to Dr. George F. Zook, the Chairman of the Mission, and to the other nine members of the group. It is indeed remarkable that in three weeks of observation and one week of deliberation and writing they were able to gather so much important information and to formulate so many concrete suggestions. . .
>
> To me the most striking and important of the many proposals made by the Mission is its recommendation for the reorganization of Germany's primary and secondary schools along democratic lines. It will be a surprise to Americans who have not studied German education, and who take for granted the ideal of equal educational opportunity, to learn the extent to which caste distinctions have prevailed in the German educational system.
>
> At the end of the fourth grade of elementary school, or about age 10, the small group that is destined for the universities and the professions is set apart in secondary schools which then prepare them for advanced work.
>
> In practice, the financial or social position of the parents is, to an overwhelming extent, the basis of selection for these secondary schools. The overwhelming majority of pupils, a large proportion of whom deserve university education because of their ability, finish elementary school and then go on to vocational education, their adult potentialities frustrated by the early and undemocratic division of the educational stream. . .
>
> A policy Statement for German Re-education, prepared by a distinguished group of educators at the request of the State Department more than a year ago, pointed out, "The re-education of the German people can be effective only as it is an integral part of a comprehensive program for their rehabilitation. The cultural and moral re-education of the nation must, therefore, be related to policies calculated to restore the stability of a peaceful German economy and to hold out hope for the ultimate recovery of national unity and self-respect."
>
> "Nowhere in the world," the Mission says, "has it been possible to erect the structure of successful democratic self-government upon starvation or economic disorder."

It is thus clear that the education of the German people to democracy and to the love of peace involves far more than the educational system, even though that system is democratically inspired and conducted. Indispensible to the success of our effort is a political and economic setting such as you urged in your Stuttgart address...[62]

Submitting the Report, Zook wrote to R. P. Patterson, Benton, and Gen. Clay, and said:

I wish herewith to submit the report of the Education Mission which, in response to the invitation of the Department of State and the War Department, undertook to make a study of the educational program of the United States Military Government in Germany.

The members of the Mission were profoundly impressed with the significance of the educational problem in Germany, not only for the Germans but for all the world. It is hoped that the recommendations contained in this report may aid materially in the solution of these problems.

In its study the members of the Mission were assisted most effectively by the staff of Military Government at the central office in Berlin and in the three *Länder*.

For the members of the Mission I wish herewith to express to you all to all personnel who assisted us in this study our deep appreciation...

The Report was published on October 15, 1946. Its structure is as follows:

Letters of Transmittal
Foreword
I. Factors Conditioning German Education
II. The Basic Undertaking
Denazification
The Development of Democracy
III. German Education
School for Children and Adolescents
Teacher Education
The Universities and Higher Schools
Youth Groups and Activities
Adult Education
Films
Radio
Libraries
The Administrative Structure of Education
IV. The Administration of Education Under Military Government
V. American Aid to Germany

First of all, the Report reveals weaknesses in the old German educational system, and emphasizes the importance of reeducation for the Germans. It also discusses the unfavorable economic and other conditions which were obstructing a sound reconstruction of education.

It presupposes the overcoming of the existing problems in the areas of elementary schools, middle schools, teacher's training, youth groups, and adult education, and proposes direction for future reforms.

Last, it makes recommendations for the administration of education in Germany, as well as the direction which OMGUS should take in the future. Various recommendations in the Report are noteworthy as reflecting the opinion of representatives of the U.S. world of education concerning future German education.

The following are the major recommendations:

1. Give a minimum of six years of elementary education to all children regardless of social class, sex, and their future choices.

2. As much as possible, simplify the middle educational system. Free schools should be established in the place of state middle schools, and an adequate scholarship system should be open to all children.

3. Eliminate traditional subjects in school, especially in middle schools, which have been inclined towards the academic, and create more practical subjects instead, linked directly to actual life, as appropriate education for members of a democratic society.

4. Drastically reform the content of Social Studies, so that it can play an important role in the education of members of a democratic society.

5. Encourage voluntary group activities among students and pupils, such as cooperative programs in the classroom, class committees, discussion groups, student councils, students' clubs, and social volunteer groups.

6. Improve vocational training.

7. Promote the status of teachers in elementary schools and raise educational standards.

8. Develop not only school education for youth, but also facilities for adult education, in homes, labor unions, and so on. Pay particular attention to the activities of youth groups.

9. Help German students and teachers to visit the U.S. for study.

According to the State Department, 30,000 copies of the Report were printed in the U.S. J. W. Taylor described it as creating a "sensation" in Germany, with 20,000 copies of the German translation sold within three hours.[63]

The original Report submitted to Gen. Clay, on September 20, was analyzed thoroughly and reviewed in detail by the E&RA Branch. For instance, on the introduction of related subjects to social science, which became a foundation for introducing "Social Studies" in postwar Germany, the Report recommends as follows:

> The most important change needed in all German schools is a change in the whole concept of the social sciences, both with respect to content and form. The pupils themselves must be the active agents in the learning process. Thus the social sciences (history, geography, civics, and *Heimatkunde*) will contribute perhaps the major share to the development of democratic citizenship.[64]

Responding immediately to this recommendation, the E&RA Branch states, "Provision has already been made in 1946-1947 for the recruitment of the American personnel in many education fields. It is anticipated that before July 1947 forty experts on various fields will have been obtained and utilized in educational activities of all sorts."[65]

In other words, the E&RA had already planned necessary reforms prior to the recommendation made by the Mission. However, the Report was used for supporting the "Program of Sending American Experts to Germany" drawn up by OMGUS, which suggested including American experts in the social sciences. As a matter of fact, Taylor wrote to George Zook on January 3, 1947, saying that the "Program of Sending American Experts to Germany" was proceeding, and suggesting that he contact Dr. Edward D' Arms of the War Department if he had proposals for that program.[66]

In the Japanese case, based on a study of the Report, SCAP/CI&E drew up a comprehensive plan for the "Reorganization and Democratization of the Japanese System of Education"[67] at the beginning of June 1946, and carried out the recommendations in the Report, as "gospel."[68]

On the other hand, OMGUS considered the Report as only a supplement. Thus the responses of the two Occupation Forces show remarkable contrast.

3) A COMPARATIVE STUDY OF THE U.S. EDUCATION MISSIONS
TO JAPAN AND TO GERMANY

In this section, the author sets out to clarify the differences and similarities between the U.S. Education Missions to Germany and to Japan, as their purposes and roles were quite distinct.

First of all, under to the Potsdam Agreement, Germany was divided and directly governed by four countries, the U.S., Britain, France and Russia, and the Allied Control Council was set up for coordinating the military governments of these four Occupation zones. In Japan, there was indirect control by the U.S. alone, through the Japanese government, rather than direct control by a military government. Under the United States Initial

Post-Surrender Policy for Japan, the Supreme Commander for the Allied Powers "will exercise his authority through Japanese governmental machinery and agencies, including the Emperor, to the extent that this satisfactorily furthers United States objectives..." Gen. MacArthur had far more power to control Japan, than Gen. Clay had in divided Germany.

MacArthur had learned extensively from the experience of Occupied Germany in many respects. Like Germany, Japan was originally slated to be divided by the Allied Powers. However, the U.S. Government and Gen. MacArthur rejected the plan. As we saw in previous chapters, the original candidates as members of the Education Mission to Japan included not only Americans but also representatives of the Allied Powers. Gen. MacArthur rejected this arrangement also and insisted on having U.S. educators only.

Comparing these different occupation systems, it can be said that the Education Mission had greater potential for success in Japan than in Germany. In fact, Gordon T. Bowles at the State Department, who was involved in educational issues in both countries at the time, testifies as follows:

> In the German case, there was a constant need among the four countries, the U.S., Britain, France and Russia, for conferring, in order to make policy adjustments. However, it should be noted that in the Japanese case, Gen. MacArthur's title was Supreme Commander *for* the Allied Powers, not Supreme Commander *of* the Allied Powers. His position meant, that he not only received his orders from the Allied Powers, but that he was also authorized to make decisions himself and carried them out. If his position only authorized him to execute the orders of the Allied Powers, it would have been impossible for him to implement his plan for inviting the Mission to Japan, within such a short period.[69]

As a matter of fact, the need for sending a U.S. Education Mission to Germany was discussed before the Japanese surrender. Sixteen months passed, however, before it was actually dispatched, because of the Occupation's complicated administrative system. In the Japanese case, however, it was only seven months after the surrender, that the Mission was sent.

Second, due to the delay in its implementation, by the time the Mission arrived in Germany, education reform had already begun in accordance with the OMGUS program. Elementary schools had reopened in October 1945, and junior and high schools in November and December. This situation naturally created crucial differences between the roles of the two Missions.

The Mission to Japan effectively accomplished its work, which was "to assist and advise the Civil Information and Education, the Supreme Commander for the Allied Powers." However, the purpose of the Mission to Germany, as is stated in the foreword to its Report, was restricted to "observing and evaluating the educational program of the United States Military Government in that country."[70]

Third, there were differences in the professional backgrounds of the officers stationed in the two countries, as Bowles states:

> In the Japanese case, the young officers in the CI&E lacked experience, and their superior officers did not have the specific guidelines for educational reforms. In other words, this situation demanded that they obtain proper advice from educational experts in America. On the other hand, the young officers in Germany were experts on German education and therefore, did not need to consult any of the American experts. The result of the officers in the CI&E having no knowledge of Japanese education became an advantage for them, enabling them to produce an early plan to invite the Mission, and to efficiently carry it out.[71]

Many of the officers in the CI&E obtained their degrees in Japanese education, based on their experiences in Japan, only after they had returned to the U.S.[72]

The aims of the Occupations of both Germany and Japan were the same. With respect to German educational reform, the Potsdam Agreement states: "German education shall be so controlled as completely to eliminate Nazi and militarist doctrine and to make possible the successful development of democratic ideas." OMGUS commenced by purging most of the civil officials, including school teachers and university professors, from their positions.

In the Japanese case, U.S. Initial Post-Surrender Policy stated: "Militarism and ultranationalism, in doctrine and practice, including paramilitary training, shall be eliminated from the educational system." To accomplish this, a purge of the teaching profession was carried out, but on a smaller scale than in Germany.

As previously seen, the basic policy document for the U.S. Education Mission to Japan was consistent with "the revival and strengthening of democratic tendencies among the Japanese people," as stated in the Potsdam Declaration. Consequently, the Report, recommended proposals for education reform by encouraging the initiative of the Japanese Education Committee.

The basic policy document for the U.S. Education Mission to Germany, SWNCC 269/5, "Long-Range Policy Statement for German Reeducation," relates education reform to German economic revival, as follows:

> The reeducation of the German people can be effective only as it is an integral
> part of a comprehensive program for their rehabilitation. The cultural and
> moral reeducation of the nation must, therefore, be related to policies calcu-
> lated to restore the stability of a peaceful German economy and to hold out
> hope for the recovery of national unity and self-respect.

It also expresses their respect for German culture, stating: "A potential
basis for German self-respect is the justifiable pride of Germans in their
former great literary, artistic, scholarly, scientific and religious contributions to civilization."

Moreover, as Zook points out that "the educational system of the United States during the nineteen century received substantial contributions
to its development [from Germany] which we have always been glad to
acknowledge."[73]

The Mission's attitude towards Occupied Germany was hesitant. For
this reason, recommendations in the Report are inarticulate and passive, in
direct contrast to the Japanese case. We can see an example of this in the
first chapter of the Report:

> The difficulty of the task is due in no small part to the special character of
> German culture, with its peculiar defects and virtues. The virulent disease of
> Nazism developed in a culture of very profound dimensions. No country—
> unless it be ancient Greece or Rome—has contributed more generously to the
> common treasures of our civilization. No approach to the German educational
> problem dare be blind to this achievement or lacking in gratitude for it.[74]

The Mission drew up its Report with this attitude, and the details of the
recommendations are exceptionally passive and paradoxical. Perhaps as a
result, they had little effect on German education reform.

In comparing the organizations of the two Missions, some similarities
can be seen, as Zook points out:

> The Educational Mission to Japan was originally requested by General Mac-
> Arthur. Later it was decided that the War Department and the Department of
> State should sponsor it jointly. It consisted of twenty-seven persons under the
> chairmanship of President George D. Stoddard of the University of Illinois. The
> mission left the United States in March, 1946, and spent approximately one
> month in Japan.
>
> The Educational Mission to Germany consisted of ten individuals, again under
> the joint sponsorship of the War and State Departments. The author of this
> statement served as Chairman of the group, which spent one month beginning
> August 24, 1946, in that part of Germany assigned to the United States by the
> Potsdam Agreement, August 2, 1945, for military occupation and government.

The Department of State was rightly concerned in the work of the missions because of its implications for foreign policy; the War Department because education is a part of the responsibility of military government administered by that Department in Germany and Japan respectively. Members of the staffs of the two departments accompanied the missions throughout their entire journeys and were indispensable in facilitating their work.

In each case the members of the two missions were given extensive "briefings" first in Washington and later in the two countries with respect to the general background and with respect to the major policies being pursued. Later the American educational officials on the staffs of military government in the two countries summarized the educational systems under review and described the progress to date in their organization and reorientation. Finally the members of the two missions were given frequent opportunities for conferences with Japanese and German educational officials respectively, both in groups and as individuals. . . .

At the conclusion of the program of visitation in various parts of the two countries, the members of the two missions returned to Tokyo and Berlin respectively where there were further conferences with educational officials, long discussions among members of the missions as to their conclusions and recommendations, and the writing of the reports which were then submitted to the appropriate authorities. Inasmuch as they serve to inform the American people, the reports have now been printed by the Department of State and widely distributed in this country. They have also been translated into German and Japanese respectively and circulated in those countries.[75]

Furthermore, as can been seen above, in organizing the Mission to Germany, Secretary of War Patterson required the Department of State to include seven requirements for the selection of members, corresponding to the Japanese case. With regards to this, W. E. Carr, of the National Education Association, who contributed to the idea of the Mission to Germany in its initial stage, testifies that the Mission was not planned in advance by the U.S. Government, but formulated along with the changing situation. He also suggests that it was influenced by the Japanese case, though indirectly.[76]

The method of appointing a chairman for each Mission was different, however. In the Japanese case, the State Department selected its own chairman with the cooperation of the U.S. Office of Education before the commencement of the final selection of the other members, which they entrusted entirely to the chairman. SCAP left the selection of chairman in the hands of the War Department, which received suggestions from the U.S. Office of Education.

In the German case, the order of priority for OMGUS in the selection of a chairman differed from that of the State Department. In consequence, OMGUS and the State Department compromised and settled for George

Zook as chairman. This caused the appointment of Zook to be delayed long after the selection of the other members. Accordingly, the situation in which he would have taken the initiative in selecting the other members never arose.

While the Mission to Germany was smaller in scale than that to Japan, experts from wider areas of education were selected, with the special inclusion of experts on youth. Therefore, the Report included a chapter on "Youth Groups and Activities," which made important recommendations. Two other chapters were also included, "The Administration of Education under the Military Government," which made recommendations concerning the administrative control of OMGUS, and "American Aid to Germany." The latter says: "It is recommended that this program be supplemented by the provision of funds for bringing carefully selected German students, teachers, and other cultural leaders to the United States for a period of training."

In the Japanese case, a chapter on "The Reform of Language," is included in the Report.

As is described earlier, the initial idea of sending the Mission to Germany was part of the postwar German education reform which had been discussed in the U.S. civilian education organizations since the surrender. It influenced the plan for the Mission to Japan, and made it possible to implement it immediately. The Mission to Germany was then deployed partly in response to the success of the Mission to Japan. Thus, they were affected by each other and were designed as part of American diplomatic policy.

The influence of the Reports on education reform in the two countries, however, was not the same. In the German case, the reforms were carried out differently in each *Land* because of differences in the beginnings of school terms, holiday periods, curricula, and teachers' training. Additionally, in a conservative *Land* like Bavaria, reforms were resisted until the last moment. A liberal *Land* such as Greater Hesse, on the other hand, actively carried out the recommendations made by the Mission, as well as those made by the U.S. Social Studies Committee.

In concluding this chapter, the author will quote two testimonies. One is from Henry J. Kellerman, of the State Department, who was in charge of the preparations for sending the Mission to Germany, and who was present at the meeting when the Report was submitted to Assistant Secretary of State Benton. The other is from B. Braude, one of the Mission secretaries who typed the Report.

Kellerman states as follows:

> ... School reform got off to a rocky start. There was probably some inner contradiction, inherent in the very nature of Military Government, in ordering

democratic precepts by fiat. Reform-minded educators supported the changes, but traditionalists who regarded education as their inner sanctum, off-limits to foreigners whatever their purpose and authority, opposed such outlandish innovations as free tuition, free textbooks, abolition of corporal punishment and, above all, equal educational opportunity for all, as unwarranted intrusion. Successful in some areas, the military authorities saw themselves compelled to fight a rearguard action in others, notably in Bavaria. Their demand to re-structure a school system and to terminate a two-track practice that separated at an early stage the poor kids from the rich and that thus perpetuated the monopolization of higher education by a well-endowed elite drawn from the moneyed brackets of society, became a highly controversial issue hotly con-tested by some and favored by others. To compound matters, the Education and Religious Affairs Branch of the Office of Military Government (OMGUS) was poorly equipped to give battle. Badly understaffed and underfunded and relegated to a relatively low level in the OMGUS hierarchy, it even lacked the money to buy paper to have the new textbooks printed. Whatever funds were available was needed to buy the dire necessaries of life, such as food. General Clay, the chief of OMGUS, insisted that democracy could not be taught on empty stomachs, and he had a point there, but he also refused to request additional funds from the Congress, and there he was in error. Meanwhile reports began sporadically to trickle back to Washington that not only Ger-mans but German education had been placed on a starvation diet. The program, as originally planned, seemed in jeopardy. It was at this moment that upon the urging of the American educational community, a Mission consisting of eleven prominent educators, under the chairmanship of George F. Zook, President of American Council of Education, was sent to Germany to take stock of condi-tions in the U.S. Zone of Occupation.

The Mission did a remarkable job. It identified correctly the major flaws in the German educational system, that is, not only of those caused by the ob-scene corruption of concepts and standards under the Nazi regime but also of the undemocratic features that had characterized the structure, objectives and methods of education dating back to the empire and the Weimar Republic, such as the two-track system. It suggested a number of remedies in critical areas and, to end the isolation of Germany from the outside world, proposed a modest exchange program that involved American experts and German students. But while the recommendations went beyond the pale of OMGUS policies, they went regrettably not far enough. Rather than upgrading and strengthening the cadre of educationists in the Education and Religious Affairs Branch, the Mission recommended that American experts be dispatched to Germany to serve in effect as an auxiliary arm of the OMGUS staff; and, rather than insisting that General Clay request more money from the Congress, the Mission suggested the broad enlistment of the private sector, i.e. of individuals and organizations, such as professional societies, foundations, churches, etc. to augment the meager resources of Military Government. As a result the immedi-ate impact of the Mission's report remained negligible. OMGUS paid lip service to the recommendations, but little, if anything was done to carry them out.[77]

Thus he indicates problems within OMGUS. Furthermore, the Occupation authorities were restricted by their own guideline that "Permanent cultural changes can be effected only as they are developed and maintained by the Germans themselves" ("Long-Range Policy Statement for German Re-education"). As a result, due to their respect for German initiatives, OMGUS gradually became associated with German conservatism, in its efforts to smooth the path of reform. An example of this was their ignoring of the Mission's criticism of, and recommendation for, the abolition of the multi-track school system in German education.[78]

Braude suggests that a negative German attitude was one of the reasons the Report did not have a greater effect on reforms, saying: "It was the fault of the German educators that the report was not completely accepted,"[79] because the Long-Range Policy Statement for German Re-education spells out a major goal, "transfer of authority in re-education to responsible Germans." In other words, in Germany, important elements within OMGUS and among Germans were negative towards the education reforms under the Occupation. This is in direct contrast to the positive Japanese response to postwar education reforms.

In the late 1960s, when education reforms came to be discussed in West Germany, reformers reconsidered, adopted, and implemented many of the recommendations that had been made by the U.S. and Britain during the Occupation period. This suggests that the effects of the ideas for education reform developed under the Occupation need to be reevaluated within a historical context.[80]

CONCLUSION: SUMMARY AND FUTURE STUDIES

I. Summary

The study of the Mission and its Report is important in understanding the history of modern Japanese education and clarifying the origins of postwar education reform. Towards this task, the author has investigated both the organizational processes of the Mission and the drawing up of its Report, by making use of primary historical materials which were discovered only recently. He has also included interviews with the people who were involved at the time. The author defines the significance of the first Mission to Japan by comparing it with the Mission to Germany, as part of the U.S. Occupation policy for education. Each chapter can be summarized as follows:

CHAPTER 1: THE ORGANIZATION OF THE MISSION

The first half of this chapter describes the organizational process, from the commencement of the plan for inviting the Mission, which originated in GHQ/CI&E, to the request for the final list of candidates of Mission members from the War Department. In particular, the author points out that the idea of sending an Education Mission had been discussed in the U.S. as part of the German education reform soon after the German surrender, and that the Mission to Japan was an offshoot from this. He also shows how the Japanese side actively cooperated with the plan of GHQ/CI&E to invite educators from the U.S.

Through the testimonies of the people concerned, the author confirms that the first candidate for chairman of the Mission, James B. Conant, the President of Harvard University, was officially rejected by General

MacArthur as being a "politically inappropriate choice of chairman." The reason for this rejection, was MacArthur's intention to become a candidate in the presidential election, in which Conant was believed to be a promising rival candidate.

The author then describes SCAP's one-sided selection of candidates for the Mission and its request to the War Department for sending the Mission, as a deviation from the original agreement with SWNCC, and as having been based on MacArthur's own political situation.

The second half of the chapter investigates the final selection process of the members, which was carried out at the initiative of the State Department. In the process of selecting members, based on the initial list of candidates drawn up by GHQ/CI&E, the State Department obtained the authority to send the Mission by appointing George D. Stoddard as chairman. William Benton, Assistant Secretary of State, recommended Stoddard, and the final selection of the other members was completed by Stoddard, together with the State Department.

As one of his conditions for accepting chairmanship, Stoddard requested the establishment of a group of educators on the Japanese side to correspond to the Mission, which was evidently in accordance with the Potsdam Declaration. It was also his idea that the Report be completed during the Mission's stay in Japan, and for this purpose he required the inclusion of six secretaries, which exceeded the limit stipulated by the War Department. The personnel organization of the Mission strongly reflected American society at that time: it included four women, representatives of the Catholic church, various organizations, and a black American.

CHAPTER 2: ADVANCE PREPARATIONS

The details of the Mission's preparatory meetings in Washington, Hawaii, and Guam have not been sufficiently studied, due to the restrictions on historical materials. The author, however, reveals the details of these meetings, providing documentary evidence in the form of a complete copy of the "Hawaiian Notes," which record the whole proceedings of the meeting in Hawaii and were only recently discovered among the Horton Papers. The "Hawaiian Notes" show that in Hawaii the Mission obtained extremely important information about the prewar and postwar situation of Japanese education. And the author shows that Chairman Stoddard proposed organizing subcommittees and preparations for the drawing up of the Report based on the "Hawaiian Notes," and that these advanced preparations were all been made within the provisions of the Potsdam Declaration, so that the education reform finally was accomplished through the initiative of the Japanese themselves.

CHAPTER 3: ACTIVITIES OF THE MISSION AND
ITS JAPANESE COUNTERPART

The chapter opens by describing the speech MacArthur made to the Mission as his luncheon party, soon after their arrival, in which he stated that he entrusted the Mission with drawing up a report concerning postwar Japanese education and that he expected the Report to be based on high ideals, and to include both long- and short-term views of education, without being burdened by the considerations of any financial restrictions. The author also shows that the Mission agreed in advance to submit their findings to MacArthur as a Confidential Report, before their departure from Japan.

As part of their own preparations, GHQ/CI&E produced *Education in Japan* prior to the Mission's arrival. This booklet was not intended to direct the Mission in formulating the Report, as has already been pointed out in previous studies, but aimed to offer information and materials concerning prewar Japanese education.

The author then discusses the response of the Japanese side. "The Education Policy for the Construction of a New Japan," which was formulated by the Japanese Ministry of Education shortly after the war, showed that the Japanese side was searching for its own initiative on reform, within the restrictions of the Potsdam Declaration.

The author also observes the Japanese initiative in producing their own report. The report of the Japanese Education Committee was prepared by its subcommittees and submitted to the Mission at a joint meeting of the two groups as the opinions of the Japanese side, with the result that it influenced the Mission's own Report. However, not all of the subject matter in the Japanese report agreed with that of the Mission's. The Japanese Education Committee also compiled its own opinions and views independently, as a separate report. This report, entitled "Recommendations of the Japanese Education Committee," was submitted only to the Japanese government, at the beginning of April, after the Mission had left. These suggestions for postwar education reform included proposals that originated from the prewar movement for education reform in Japan. The author describes the proposals made in this report in terms of the continuity and discontinuity with prewar Japanese education.

The basic idea of the Mission was to encourage the Japanese initiative in accordance with the Potsdam Declaration; this led them to accept the cooperation of the Japanese side in the person of Shigeru Nambara, Chairman of the Japanese Education Committee, and many others.

CHAPTER 4: THE MISSION'S REPORT AND
REFORM OF THE JAPANESE LANGUAGE

The author focuses on the draft drawn up by the Special Committee on Japanese Language in the Mission, in which they discussed the postwar reform of the Japanese language. This draft made a firm recommendation for the adoption of both Japanese and *romaji* in elementary school textbooks. This recommendation, however, was deleted from the Mission's final Report, and the author shows that it met strong opposition both from the Japanese side and from Gordon T. Bowles.

The Japanese Education Committee understood that there was strong opinion in the U.S. that the romanization of the Japanese language should be forced on the Japanese, as a policy of the Occupation, and that the Special Committee on Japanese Language was prepared to propose reforms in line with this policy. The Japanese showed a severely critical attitude towards the draft on the romanization of the Japanese language proposed by the Special Committee on Japanese Language, and later produced their own report on language reform. The Mission was influenced by this Japanese reaction, and moderated this part of their final Report. Consequently, in the matter of language reform, the Mission compromised with the Japanese side.

CHAPTER 5: THE MISSION'S REPORT AND
REFORM OF THE SCHOOL SYSTEM

This chapter focuses on the postwar reform of the 6–3–3 school system. It demonstrates that Committee III's draft recommended democratic education reform based on a 6–5 school system, which had just been restored from the prewar Japanese school system. The Mission's task was only to study the reform of the school system, not to make recommendations on it, which was properly the subject of study of the Japanese Education Committee.

A confidential meeting between Shigeru Nambara, Chairman of the Japanese Education Committee, and George D. Stoddard, Chairman of the Mission, made numerous suggestions as to postwar education reform. In particular, the author confirms, through related historical material, that Nambara confidentially suggested to Stoddard that the American 6–3–3 single-track school system be recommended, which also gives evidence of the independent Japanese attitude toward reform. Instead of accepting the Mission's recommendation of the 6–5 school system, the Japanese Education Committee took the initiative in suggesting the 6–3–3 school system, which had in common with the Mission's own recommendations such democratic ideas as nine years' free compulsory education, coeducation, etc. The main factor in this request was that a 6–5 school system would not resolve problems in reorganizing the system of secondary education, especially the higher elementary school and the youth school. In addition, Nambara himself supported the 6–3–3 school system.

Lastly, the author highlights the role which the Japanese Education Committee played, and compares the report of the Japanese Education Committee with that of the Mission, in terms of the school system. By describing how strongly the Japanese attitude was reflected in the Mission's Report, he defines the continuity of the prewar, wartime, and postwar thinking of the Japanese on school system reform.

CHAPTER 6: THE MISSION'S REPORT AND
THE REFORM OF HIGHER EDUCATION

Focusing on Committee IV, this chapter discusses the principles of the postwar Japanese higher education. The draft produced by the Committee was entitled "Aims and Freedoms of Higher Learning," and it consists of five chapters: 1) The Place of Higher Learning in a Free Society; 2) The Organization of Institutes, etc.; 3) Freedom of the Individual; 4) Recommendations for Scientific and Professional Training; 5) Advancement of International Understanding.

The committee members recommended the establishment of academic freedom as part of the reorganization of Japanese higher education, with the high educational ideals aspired to in the U.S. at that time. Regarding the specific problems of Japanese higher education, the draft reflected the opinions of the Japanese Education Committee. Here again, the author demonstrates the important role of the Japanese Education Committee. He also includes and discusses, the report on the recommendation for higher education reform, formulated by the Scientific Advisory Group, which was invited to Japan in 1947 by GHQ/ESS.

Committee IV's task was to study the reform of the higher education system, but not to make recommendations on it, so the Mission did not propose a concrete reform plan for Japanese higher education. The reform of higher education remained one of the main concerns of the Japanese Education Committee, which in its own report, "Recommendations of the Japanese Education Committee," compiled after the Mission's return to the U.S., set out for the first time the 6–3–3–4 and 6–3–3–5 school systems and the four-year university system. These newly discovered materials document the fact that postwar higher education reform was the product of the initiative of the Japanese side.

CHAPTER 7: THE U.S. EDUCATION MISSION TO GERMANY:
A COMPARISON

The idea of sending an education mission to Germany was one of the first proposals concerning postwar German education reform discussed by

American non-governmental groups, especially the National Education Association. The idea of sending a Mission was also applied to postwar Japanese education reform. The author suggests that these discussions, held, as they were, at such an early stage, made the Mission to Japan possible so soon after it was requested by SCAP/CI&E, and that the success of the Mission to Japan encouraged the revival and implementation of the almost abandoned plan to send a mission to Germany.

Occupied Germany was divided and controlled by four countries, which made it too complicated to reach a consensus on the basic policy for education. It was difficult to reach agreement on postwar German education reform because of the discrepancy among opinions even within the U.S. These circumstances caused the U.S. to miss the most opportune time for sending a mission to Germany, thus limiting its influence on the reforms.

An understanding of the backgrounds of the two missions and their similarities and differences, the author points out, is essential to a more comprehensive study of the Mission to Japan.

The general view in Japan tends to emphasize the differences between the two missions. One commentary, for example, states: "The German Government maintained its own traditional school system and rejected coercion by the U.S. Education Mission. On the other hand, Japanese educators yielded under U.S. pressure, and adopted the 6–3–3 system."[1]

As stated in the testimonies of the people concerned, the Military Government in Germany, as well as the German people, were negative towards education reform. This shows a decisive difference from the active response and initiative of the Japanese on postwar education reform that is observed throughout this study. In both cases, in other words, the fate of postwar education reform rested with the recipients of the reform, and to what extent they themselves were receptive to initiating its implementation.

Through the above chapters, the author demonstrates that the Mission's attitude toward implementation of the education reform was always in accord with the Potsdam Declaration, which specified "the revival and strengthening of democratic tendencies among the Japanese people." In other words, they had the greatest respect for the Japanese initiative.

Later, Chairman Stoddard opposed the "conventional view," which stated that the Report was prepared in advance by the Occupation:

> *We cannot allow such an assumption that states that Mission's recommendations were prepared by GHQ, and that we used them to draw up our Report.* The Mission members are experts in their fields. They had a higher level of knowledge than the staff of the CI&E. It cannot be imagined that they needed others' help... (Author's italics)[2]

Confronted by the seriousness of the undertaking, the Japanese Education Committee actively participated in the postwar education reform, and its members cooperated with the Mission wherever they could be of assistance. It can be said that the Japanese participation originated in the prewar movement for education reform. In other words, there existed a dynamic correlation between the continuity and the discontinuity with prewar Japanese education. The Mission's influence on postwar Japanese education should be understood within this historical context.

Last, the author introduces a memoir by Gordon Bowles, who was actually in charge of the Mission as a representative of the State Department.[3] It was written specifically for this study, in April 1987, and includes the following important testimony:

The Mission's stated purpose was to advise General MacArthur, the Supreme Commander for the Allied Powers, and his staff (both commonly referred to as SCAP), in carrying out overall policy directives with respect to revision of the entire educational system and process, so as to conform to the spirit and objectives of the Potsdam Agreement—the declaration adopted by the Allied Powers as the basic pattern for democratization and re-orientation of the peoples of both Germany and Japan. General MacArthur made it specifically clear to the Mission upon their arrival in Japan that any and all recommendations submitted in their Report were to be couched in terms of the future, and that existing economic and related problems were to be ignored...

The most important point, however, was that although the Report was drafted by the Mission, most of its provisions were the result of careful discussions with the Japanese Education Committee and various SCAP personnel.

Whether or not the Mission met the expectations of the Japanese is another matter. It undoubtedly assisted the more liberal and progressive-minded, who welcomed the Mission's presence and cooperated in its activities. Among the most prominent leaders were such people as the Minister of Education [Yoshishige] Abe, Shigeru Nambara, President of Tokyo University and Chairman of the Japanese Education Committee, and all of the Committee members. In addition, there were hundreds if not thousands of liberal-minded Japanese in all walks of life who were anticipating changes not only in the educational system, but in all aspects of life affecting the public domain...

To say that the Mission and its report had fully met the needs of SCAP personnel or the expectations of liberal-minded Japanese educators would be an exaggeration, but I believe it can be said that, given the circumstances—the shortness of notice and necessity to accomplish its mission and prepare a final report within the space of one month—the Mission deserves high marks. Much of the credit must certainly be given to George Stoddard, who insisted on having a secretarial staff large enough to meet the needs of four subcommittees and on reserving the last week of the Mission's stay in Japan for writing the Final Report. As a result of several years' experience as Commissioner of Education for the State of New York, Dr. Stoddard knew how frustrating it could be to try to re-assemble a group of busy educators once they had disbanded. His insistence, also, that only majority opinions should be expressed was crucial. He knew that ambivalence, or incorporation of differing views would only lead to further debate and confusion.

There is no doubt that a differently worded report would have been forthcoming had it been prepared by a "perfect" Mission with the advice of a "perfect" Japanese committee, and had the collective time at their disposal been extended. It is doubtful, however, if the general content would have differed substantially from the prepared document...

On the 6–3–3 issue, when I became aware of the factionalism that existed among members of the Japanese Education Committee concerning the 6–3–3–4 versus the existing 6–5–3–3 system, and that President Nambara was himself in favor of the change, it seemed to me that there should not be undue pressure from the outside and that the matter should be left to the Japanese themselves to decide...

I certainly cannot support the recent cries from various quarters that the 6–3–3 system was forced on the Japanese people. The matter was thoroughly debated and decided by the Japanese educators themselves and their decision coincided with the majority opinion expressed by the Mission members...

So far as the long term impact is concerned, it seems to me that in no small part, the remarkable changes which have taken place in the Japanese educational system, can be traced to the recommendations incorporated in the Mission Report. The Report emphasized equal opportunities for all, regardless of sex or economic circumstances, throughout the period of compulsory education. It recommended also de-emphasis on elitism by greatly expanding the number of higher educational institutions and increasing the range and volume of library and other resources...

Only to the extent, that the Mission provided opportunity to Japanese educators to express themselves, and to utilize the Report as a foundation for realizing their hopes and convictions, and strengthening their positions, does the Mission itself deserve credit for any lasting results. Without the Mission, transformations would undoubtedly have occurred, but progress might have been slower and possibly not as far reaching.

II. *The Influence and Significance of the Report*

On April 7, 1946, General MacArthur released the Report, together with a statement in which he praised it highly, saying, "The Report will be most helpful to the Civil Information and Education Section of my headquarters in their further efforts to assist the Japanese government in modernizing the Japanese educational system." This statement stamps the Report with MacArthur's full approval, and it became established as the CI&E's basic policy for education reform.

The Report gave suggestions for drastic education reforms based on democratic ideals, and became a guideline for postwar Japanese education. Later it had a great influence on the establishment of the Fundamental Law of Education and the School Education Law. In particular, the 6–3–3 school system, nine years' tuition-free compulsory education, and coeducation became the centerpieces of the postwar education reforms. An analysis published in 1950, during the later part of the Occupation, *Amerika Kyoiku Shisetsudan Hokokusho Yokai* [Study of Japanese Educators of the Report of the U.S. Education Mission to Japan], edited by Hiroshi Sugo, Seiichi Miyahara, and Seiya Munakata (Tokyo: Kokumin Tosho Kankokai), noted that the significance of the Report was that it gave direction to Japanese postwar education, as well as influencing educational studies:

> We think that the historic Report of the U.S. Education Mission is one of the most valuable documents on education ever written.... [It] is a model of the excellent achievement of democratic ideas in education which were developed by the middle of the 20th century. We can see particularly how the best of the orthodox tradition of American democracy is given expression in an ideal form. We would like to express our extreme gratitude for their effort in producing such a valuable document for Japanese education.

The Report influenced not only the Japanese, but also the Okinawa Occupation. "The Extract of the Report of the U.S. Education Mission to Japan" (1946) produced by the Education Department of the Okinawa Civil Administration suggested in its Foreword that the Report was a guide for Okinawa education reform as well:

> In March, 1946, the U.S. Education Mission to Japan, which was ordered to investigate Japanese education, stayed in Japan for a month to accomplish their mission, and submitted their Report on March 30th, to the Supreme Commander for the Allied Powers. Chairman George D. Stoddard and the Mission members, as might be expected of those who were representing experts in American universities and colleges, produced a significant Report. The subject matter of the Report is instructive in no small measure, for us, as Okinawa educators. Last year, one of the copies of the Report was given to us by Col. Hanna, an officer in charge of education in the U.S. Military Government, from which we made a free translation. We chose part of it, especially as study material for schools, and published it as a supplement to *Bunkyo Jiho* No. 3, March 5th, 1947.
>
> The Education Department.[4]

During the Mission's stay in Japan, educators visited them from Korea to ask their advice about sending an "Education-Information Inquiry

Commission." In the event, its form and procedure were similar to those of the Mission to Japan. It can be said that it was indirectly influenced by the Mission to Japan. In fact, Isaac Kandel and Harold Benjamin, members of the Mission to Japan, were deeply involved in its formation.

As mentioned in an earlier chapter, just before they left Japan, the Mission members received an invitation from the Chinese government through its liaison office in Tokyo. They declined it however, due to the timing of their schedule. This Chinese invitation shows that the Mission to Japan attracted the attention of the Chinese education world. As a matter of fact, it was confirmed recently, that a complete Chinese translation of the Report of the U.S. Education Mission to Japan had been published in Shanghai in 1947.[5] The Chinese government obtained a Japanese translation of the Report through contacts with GHQ, considering it useful for Chinese education reform. Judging from this fact, it seems that the Report influenced not only Japan but also other Asian countries as well.

Moreover, the Report had influence on America, as well as on the Allied Powers. As was described in Chapter 7, the Deputy Military Governor of OMGUS, Gen. Clay, decided under the influence of MacArthur's statement, to bring a U.S. Education Mission to Germany.

Not all aspects of education in Japan today are the result of the education reforms of the Occupation period. The succeeding forty years have seen the education system revised, changed, and reformed, along with the development of national pride and economic development in Japan, after the termination of the Occupation and the recovery of Japanese independence. It can be said, that while the present education system is not the same as the prewar education system, it still retains many aspects of the original U.S. reforms, and can be described as the result of a combination of education reform under the Occupation and Japanese educators' own efforts and initiatives in cooperation.

The apparent ease and enthusiasm with which the Japanese accepted the education reforms under the Occupation should be explained by pointing to the Japanese tendency, after the Meiji period, to actively adopt aspects of Western culture, selecting whatever they could adapt while at the same time maintaining their own traditional culture.

Touching on the present-day assessment of education reform during the Occupation period, the National Council on Education Reform (1985–1988) set forth, in its First Report on Education Reform, "Significance of the Educational Reform" as follows:

> Postwar education reform intended to eliminate militaristic and ultranationalistic education, which was at its peak during wartime, and to establish democracy and ideals of freedom and equality in education, such as the

development of character, respect for the individual, and equal opportunity, as its base.

And it continues,

> In spite of the positive results of the reform, it has unfortunately also created the present crisis in education: fiery zeal for entrance exam competition; school bullying; children's refusal to go to school; school violence, and juvenile delinquency. Also, by way of implication, [it has exacerbated] various problems affecting the development of creativity, respect for the individual, the content of higher education and internationalism, and has resulted in the creation of negative influences through the uniformity and rigidity of the system. We must honestly recognize that, in particular, postwar education reform contained an element that negated certain characteristics and virtues of our traditional culture, resulting in the neglect of moral education, an imbalance between the sense of rights and duties, and also limitations in terms of the development of character and the respect for individuality.

It thus provides a negative assessment of the postwar education reform. However, on closely examining the Report, it clearly states the importance of encouraging individuality and denying uniformity, and warns against superficially imitating the democratic system, as follows:

> We believe in the power of every race and every nation to create from its own cultural resources something good for itself and for the whole world. That is the liberal creed. We are not devoted to uniformity; as educators we are constantly alert to deviation, originality, and spontaneity. That is the spirit of democracy. We are not flattered by any superficial imitation of our own institutions. Believing in progress and social evolution, we welcome cultural variety all over the world as a source of hope and refreshment.

Moreover, the Report states:

> Responsibility is of the essence of this freedom. Duties keep rights from cancelling each other out. The test of equal treatment is the taproot of democracy, whether it be of rights to be shared or of duties to be shouldered.

The controversial aspects of postwar education reform which were pointed out by the National Council on Education Reform had already been mentioned by the Mission, more than forty years earlier. The present situation within Japanese education is not the same as that which the Report had taken aim at. In terms of the school system, coeducation and compulsory education within the 6–3–3 school system, etc., have obviously been the products of education reform during the Occupation period. At the same time, however, teaching methods and educational ideals have remained unchanged within the Japanese tradition. It can also be said that because education reform was taken only halfway during the Occupation period, the negative aspects of postwar education reform emerged, presenting the present serious problems within education. It was this very denial of education reform during the Occupation period, however, that led to the achievement of the highest standards of education in the world. Considering that the progressive educational philosophy in which the Occupation believed caused the lowering of educational standards in the U.S., education reform under the Occupation may need to be judged within its own historical context.[6]

The background against which postwar Japanese education reform was implemented originated in the Japanese traditional pattern of acceptance of Western culture. The Allied Occupation was restricted by the need to give the initiative for the reform to the Japanese side, in accordance with the provisions of the Potsdam Declaration. The Occupation was also in a dilemma due to the fact that the bureaucratic education reform which had been ordered from above contradicted the principles of democracy.

In the final analysis, the characteristics of Japanese postwar education reform resulted from the contradiction between education reform mandated by the Occupation and democratic education. Any examination of Japanese postwar education reform must begin with the study of the U.S. Education Mission.

III. Future Study

There are several areas for future study. The following are the main ones:

1. This study is restricted to a specific subject: the First U.S. Education Mission to Japan. A more comprehensive study of postwar education would investigate how the Report, as the origin of postwar education, affected later Japanese education reforms. In particular, it is important to relate it to the Fundamental Law of Education and the School Education Law.

2. It needs to be fully recognized that the education reform in Japan was accomplished under an occupation, which had never been experienced before in Japanese history. For the majority of materials used in this study, the author has entirely relied on what has been preserved in the U.S., and the testimonies of people concerned on the U.S. side. In order to attain a balance of materials, he has tried to refer to Japanese historical material wherever possible.

3. For the purpose of an objective analysis of the Mission to Japan, the author investigated the consistency of U.S. Occupation policy by including a comparison with the U.S. Education Mission to Germany. However, analytical comparison of the contents of the Reports of both Missions is necessary.

4. It is essential, for a comprehensive study of postwar Japanese education, to analyze the contents of the Report of the First Mission, and to study the relationship between, and compare, the Reports of the First and the Second Missions.

Appendices

APPENDIX A: BRIEF BIOGRAPHIES OF THE MEMBERS OF THE MISSION TO JAPAN AND INFORMATION ON THE COLLECTIONS OF THEIR PAPERS

1. *Harold R. Benjamin* (Born in 1893): Ph.D. Stanford University; Professor of Education and Director, College of Education, University of Colorado 1937–39; Dean, College of Education, University of Maryland 1939–51; Director of International Education Relations, U.S. Office of Education 1945–46; The Second U.S. Education Mission to Japan 1950; and Chairman, Coodinator of Education Team, Korea 1954–55. "New Education for a New Japan," *School Life 28*: 1, 3–4 (June 1946).

[The Benjamin Papers are kept at the Peabody College Library, Vanderbilt University, and the Manuscript Division, U.S. Library of Congress]

2. *Leon Carnovsky* (Born in 1903): Ph.D. University of Chicago; Professor of Library Science, University of Chicago since 1943; President, Association of American Library Schools 1942-49; and Managing Editor of *The Library Quarterly*.

3. *Wilson M. Compton* (Born in 1890): LL.D. Wooster University; Professor of Economics, George Washington University 1934–41; President of Washington State University 1944–57; Vice President of the American Federation of Teachers 1946; and U.S. Delegate 4th General Assembly United Nations.

[The Compton Papers are kept in the Manuscripts, Archives and Special Collections, Washington State University]

4. *George S. Counts* (Born in 1889): Ph.D. University of Chicago; Professor of Education, University of Chicago 1926–27; Professor of Education, Teachers College, Columbia University 1927–56; President of the American Federation of Teachers 1939–42; and Authority on Russian Education. "Can the Schools Build Democracy in Japan?" *American Teacher 31*: 11–13 (Nov. 1946)

5. *Roy J. Deferrari* (Born in 1890): Ph.D. Princeton University; Professor, Catholic

University since 1923; Dean of Graduate School, Catholic University 1930–38; and Secretary General, National Catholic Education Association 1938–67.

[The Deferrari Papers are kept in the Department of Archives and Manuscripts, the Catholic University of America]

6. *George W. Diemer* (Born in 1885): President, Teachers College of Kansas City 1923–37; President, Central Missouri State Teachers College 1937–56; and The Second U.S. Education Mission to Japan 1950. "Educating the Japanese for Peace," *The Educational Forum*, Vol. XI, No. 4 May 1947.

[The Diemer Papers are kept in Ward Edwards Library Archives, Central Missouri State University]

7. *Kermit Eby* (Born in 1903): Executive Secretary, Chicago Teachers Union 1937–43; Director, Education and Research (Congress of Industrial Organizations) since 1945; and Member National Commission for UNESCO, Paris Conference 1946. "Japan and Then and Now" *Christian Century* 63: 750–752 (12 June 1946), and "Re-education on Japan," *Far Eastern Survey* 15: 203–5 (3 July 1946)

[The Eby Papers are kept in the Department of Special Collections, the Joseph Regenstein Library, the University of Chicago]

8. *Frank N. Freeman* (Born in 1880, Ontario, Canada): Ph.D. Yale University; Professor of Psychology, Yale University 1920–39; and Professor of Educational Psychology, Chairman of Department of Education and Dean of School of Education, University of California, Berkely since 1939.

9. *Virginia C. Gildersleeve* (Born in 1877): Ph.D. Columbia University; Professor and Dean, Barnard College since 1911; and U.S. Delegate to the United Nations Conference, San Francisco.

[The Gildersleeve Papers are kept in the Rare Books and Special Collections, The Butler Library, Columbia University. The most note-worthy item in the Gildersleeve Papers is a letter from President Franklin D. Roosevelt, appointing her to serve as member of the U.S. Delegation to the Charter Conference of the United Nations]

10. *Willard E. Givens* (Born in 1886): Ed.D. Miami University; Executive Secretary, National Education Association 1935–52; Chairman, The Second U.S. Education Mission to Japan 1950. "U.S. Education Mission to Japan," *Journal of the National Education Association* Leader Letter #53 (May 7, 1946).

[The Givens Papers are kept in the National Education Association Archives]

11. *Ernest R. Hilgard* (Born in 1904): Ph.D. Yale University; Professor of Psychology, Stanford University since 1933; and Executive Head of Psychology Department, Stanford University 1942–50. "The Enigma of Japanese Friendliness," *The Public Opinion Quarterly* (Fall 1946).

12. (Monsignor) *Frederick G. Hochwalt* (Born in 1909): Ph.D. Catholic University of

America; Director, Department of Education, National Catholic Welfare Conference 1946; Executive Secretary of the National Catholic Education Association 1946; and the Second U.S. Education Mission to Japan 1950.

[The Hochwalt Papers are kept in the Department of Archives and Manuscripts, the Catholic University of America]

13. *Mildred McAfee Horton* (Born in 1900): LL.D. University of Chicago; Dean of College Women, Oberlin College 1934–36; President of Wellesley College 1936–49; and Women's Res., USNR, from Lieut. Cdr. to Capt.

[The Horton Papers are kept in the Margaret Clapp Library, Wellesley College]

14. *Charles S. Johnson* (Born in 1893): Litt.D. Columbia and Harvard Universities; Editor *Opportunity* (a Journal of Negro Life) 1923–29; Director, Department of Social Science, Fisk University 1928–47; President of Fisk University 1946–56; Member of U.S. Delegation 1st UNESCO Conference, Paris 1946; and Author: Pertaining to the Negro).

[The Johnson Papers are kept in the Archives, Fisk University]

15. *Isaac L. Kandel* (Born in 1881, Canada): Ph.D. Columbia University; Professor of Education, Teachers College, Columbia University since 1923; (Author on Comparative Education, Philosophy of American Education); and Editor of *School and Society*. "The Revision of Japanese Education," *School and Society* 64: 134 (24 August 1946), and "Reorienting Japanese Education," *Education Forum* 11: 11–18 (Nov. 1946).

16. *Charles H. McCloy* (Born in 1886): Ph.D. Columbia University; Director, School of Physical Education, National Seern University, Nanking, China 1921–26; Research Professor, Anthoropology and Physical Education, State University of Iowa 1930–59; and Expert Consultant U.S. War Department 1941–59.

[The McCloy Papers are kept in the Special Collections Department, University of Iowa]

17. *Ethelbert B. Norton* (Born in 1902): Litt.D. Birmingham–Southern College; Alabama State Superintendent of Education 1942–46; Director, School Administration; U.S. Office of Education 1946; and Department Commissioner 1947.

[The Norton Papers are kept in the Archives, University of North Alabama Library]

18. *Thomas V. Smith* (Born in 1890): Ph.D. University of Chicago; Dean of University of Chicago 1923–26; Professor of Philosophy, University of Chicago since 1927; Director of Education, Allied Control Commission, Italy 1944; and Member of the U.S. Education Mission to Germany 1946. "Ethics in the Japanese Educational Curriculum," *Ethics* 56: 297–302 (July 1946), "Personal Impressions of Current Education in Italy, Germany, and Japan," *Educational Record* 28: 21–32 (Jan. 1947), "The Re-education of Conquered Peoples," *Proceedings of the National*

Conference of Social Work (1947), and *The Re-education of Germany, Italy, and Japan* (Claremont, Calif.: Friends of the College at Claremont, 1947)

[The Smith Papers are kept in the Department of Special Collections, the Joseph Regenstein Library, the University of Chicago]

19. *David H. Stevens* (Born in 1884): Ph.D. University of Chicago; Professor University of Chicago 1925–30; Associate Dean of Faculties, University of Chicago 1929–30; Vice President, General Education Board, Rockefeller Foundation 1930-38; and Director of Division for Humanities, Rockefeller Foundation.

[The Stevens Papers are kept in the Rockefeller Archives Center and in the Department of Special Collections, the Joseph Regenstein Library, the University of Chicago]

20. *Alexander J. Stoddard* (Born in 1889): LL.D. University of Pennsylvania; President Rhode Island Institute of Instructions 1932–33; President of American Association School Administrators 1935; and Superintendent Schools in Denver, Philadelphia, and Los Angeles 1910–54.

21. *George D. Stoddard* (Chairman) (Born in 1897): Ph.D. University of Iowa; Professor of Psychology and Education, University of Iowa 1929–42; Director, Iowa Child Welfare Research Station 1928–42; Dean of Graduate College, University of Iowa 1936–42; Head Department of Psychology, University of Iowa 1938–39; President, University of State of New York and Commissioner of Education 1942–45; Chairman, American Council of Education 1946–47; President of University of Illinois 1946–53; UNESCO General Conference, London (Active until 1952); and Author: Child Psychology. "MacArthur and the U.S. Education Mission to Japan," *National Parent–Teacher 41*: 22–24 (Sept. 1946), "Education Mission to Japan—A Summary," *Association of American Colleges Bulletin 32*: 347–354 (Oct. 1946), "Reflections on Japanese Education," *Phi Delta Kappan 28*: 40–43 (Oct. 1946), and "The Emperor and I," in *The Pursuit of Education: An Autobiography* (New York: Vantage Press, 1981)

[The Stoddard Papers are kept in the Hoover Institution Archives, Stanford University and University Archives, University of Illinois]

22. *William C. Trow* (Born in 1894): Ph.D. Columbia University; and Professor of Educational Psychology, University of Michigan since 1931. "Democracy vs. Ultranationalism in Japanese Education," *Humanist 6*, No. 2: 73–75 (Autumn 1946), and "Education Mission to Japan," *Michigan Educational Journal 23*: 494–7 (May 1946)

[The Trow Papers are kept by Mrs. W. C. Trow and his son, Dr. Donald B. Trow]

23. *Pearl A. Wanamaker* (Born in 1899): State Superintendent Public Instruction, Washington 1941–57; Advisor U.S. Delegation to UNESCO Conference, Paris 1946; President of the National Education Association 1946–47; and the Second U.S. Education Mission to Japan 1950.

[The Wanamaker Papers are kept in the Henry Suzzallo Library, the University of Washington]

24. *Emily B. Woodward:* Consultant and Lecturer in England and Scotland under Auspices of U.S. OWI and British Ministry of Information 1944; and Author: Georgia & Forums.
[The Woodward Papers are kept in the Main Library, Special Collections and Manuscripts, the University of Georgia, and Special Collections, the Robert W. Woodruff Library, Emory University]

25. *Gordon T. Bowles* (Born in 1904): Ph.D. Harvard University; Assistant Professor, University of Hawaii 1938–42; Visiting Professor, University of Tokyo 1951–58; Professor, Syracuse University 1962–72; and Area Division V (Occupied Areas) of the Office of International Information and Cultural Affairs of the State Department 1942–47 (as Representative of the State Department and Far Eastern Adviser).

26. *Paul P. Stewart*: the State Department, as Secretary–General.

27. *Col. John N. Andrews*: the War Department, as Military Liaison.

[Information for these biographical sketches compiled by the author, based on the following: *Who's Who in America*, Vol. III (1951–1960), Vol. XXIV (1946–1947), Vol. XXV (1948–1949), and Vol. XXXV (1968–1969); and *Official Congressional Directory*]

APPENDIX B: THE SCHEDULES OF THE U.S. EDUCATION MISSIONS IN JAPAN AND GERMANY

THE SCHEDULE OF THE U.S. EDUCATION MISSION IN JAPAN
(March 5–April 1, 1946)

Tuesday, 5th

First Group of the Mission (18 Members) Arrived

Wednesday, 6th

Entertained at Lunch in the American Embassy by Gen. & Mrs. MacArthur. (The Rest of 15 Members Arrived)

Thursday, 7th (1st Day)

General Introduction to Problem (Lt. Col. Nugent)

Organizational & Educational Objectives of SCAP, CIE, Education Division (Lt. Col. Farr)

Introduction of Officers in Education Division (Lt. Farr)

Announcements, Issuing Brochures, Press Responsibilities (Mr. Don Brown). Other Instructions (Lt. Col. Schmitz)

Friday, 8th (2nd Day)

Address by Japanese Minister of Education (Mr. Abe)

Introduced Japanese Committee to U.S. Mission

Response of Chairman of U.S. Mission (Dr. Stoddard)

1/2 U.S. Mission Lunch with General MacArthur

General Scope of Committee No 1 on Curriculum & Textbooks (Cdr. Wunderlich)

General Scope of Committee No 2 on Teacher Education & Methodology (Capt. Barnard)

General Scope of Committee No 3 on Administrative Organization of Ministry of Education & Elementary–Secondary Schools (Comdr. Hall)

General Scope of Committee No 4 on Administration of Institutions of Higher Learning (Lt. Comdr. Crofts and Prof. Del Rey)

Saturday, 9th (3rd Day)

Organization of Sub-Committees

Administrative Organization of Japanese Ministry of Education (Lt. Comdr. Hall and Japanese Representatives)

Administrative Organization of Elementary & Secondary Schools (Major Arrowood et al.)

Boys' Middle School (Lt. P. M. MacBride), the Yochien and Kokumin Gakko (Lt. G. B. Gibson)

Sunday, 10th (4th Day)

Entertained by Japanese Tea Ceremony

Monday, 11th (5th Day)

Administrative Organization of Institutions of Higher Learning (Lt. Cdr. Crofts et al.)

A Panel Discussion, Curriculum of Japanese School (Major Orr, Kotaro Tanaka, Tetsuichi Sawato, and Toshio Kimura)

Tuesday, 12th (6th Day)

Methodology in Japanese Education (Capt. Barnard et al.)

A Panel Discussion, Japanese Textbooks (Cdr. Wunderlich, Jiro Arimitsu, Tokiomi Kaigo et al.)—Critique of the Textbook Problem (Cdr. Wunderlich) and The Development of Japanese Textbooks (Tokiomi Kaigo)

Wednesday, 13th (7th Day)

Language Revision (Lt. Comdr. Hall)

Reorientation of Teachers (Capt. Barnard)

On Problem Concerning National Language and Its Character (Shoji Ando)

Tea with Japanese Premier Shidehara

Thursday, 14th (8th Day)

Physical Education (Major Norviel)

Women's Education (Capt. Donovan)

Dinner Guests of Shigeru Yoshida, Minister of Foreign Affairs

Friday, 15th (9th Day)

Visited Japanese Schools—Elementary, Boys' Middle School, Girls' Higher School, and the First Higher School of Tokyo

Left for Kyoto

Saturday, 16th (10th Day)

Visited Nishi Honganji Temple, Chio-In Monastery, Kinkakuji Temple, Ryuanji, and Arashiyama. Stayed at Biwako Hotel.

"Proposed Outline of the Report" by the Special Committee on Drafting (Chairman: G. D. Stoddard)

Sunday, 17th (11th Day)

Visited Nara—Nara Museum, the Nara Women's Normal School, Kasuga Shrine, and Todaiji Temple (Great Buddha)

Stayed at Biwako Hotel

Monday, 18th (12th Day)

Visited the Kyoto Imperial University

Noh Performance

Tuesday, 19th (13th Day)
 Committee III Visited Schools—the First Middle School in Kyoto, the Third Higher School, the Kyoto Fine Arts School, et al.
 Imperial Palace
 Left for Tokyo
Wednesday, 20th (14th Day)
 Worked on the Committee Reports
 Chairman Stoddard, G. T. Bowles and J. N. Andrews Conference with Gen. MacArthur
Thursday, 21th (15th Day)
 Worked on the Committee Reports
 Committee III Visited Sugamo Prison (War Criminals)
 "Special Report by Shigeru Nambara, President, Tokyo Imperial University and Chairman of Japanese Committee to G. D. Stoddard"
Friday, 22nd (16th Day)
 Worked on the Committee Reports
Saturday, 23 (17th Day)
 Committee III Completed 25 Pages Draft Report—"Report of Committee of USEM—Administration of Education in Japan at Elementary and Secondary Levels"
Sunday, 24th (18th Day)
 Discussion on the Committee Reports
 Visited Tokyo Imperial University and Rockefeller Library
 Tea with President Nambara
Monday, 25th (19th Day)
 Japanese Education Committee Reports—The Problem of Elementary School Education (Taketoshi Yamagiwa), Youth Schools (Sanji Aruga), Religious Education (Rev. Michio Kosaki), and Handicraft Work (Shuetsu Yanagi)
 Committee III met with Representatives of Teachers' Organization and Middle School Teachers
 "Education Reform—Official Version of Japanese Education Committee"
Tuesday, 26th (20th Day)
 Shown the NEA Motion Picture, "Assignment: Tomorrow"
Wednesday, 27th (21st Day)
 Committee III met with the Visitors from Korea: Maj. E. N. Lockard and Mr. Auh.
 Audience with Emperor (Imperial Palace)—Emperor asked for an American tutor for the Crown Prince
Thursday, 28th (22nd Day)
 Chairman Stoddard and Bowles met with Gen. MacArthur
 Dinner Party with CI&E
Friday, 29th (23rd Day)
 Visited the Diet, the War Ministry Building for the Trials for the War Criminals
 Dinner with Mr. Abe, the Minister of Education

Saturday, 30th (24th Day)
> Submitted the Report by Chairman Stoddard, G. T. Bowles and J. N. Andrews, to Maj. Gen. Stephen J. Chamberlain, Deputy Chief of Staff, SCAP, on behalf of Gen. MacArthur who was absent, due to a heavy cold.
> Gift of books to Japanese children and teachers from the Mission Members
> Official Invitation from Chinese Government through Maj. Gen. Chin Wang of the Chinese Liaison Office, SCAP, Tokyo, declined.

Sunday, 31th (25th Day)
> Flight cancelled due to typhoon

Monday, April 1st (26th Day)
> Left for the U.S.A. (except Bowles)

Sunday, April 7th
> Gen. MacArthur released the Report with his Statement

[Schedule compiled by the author, based on the following: "Tentative Schedule of U.S. Education Mission," Wanamaker Papers, and Willard Givens, "Tokyo and Return"]

PROPOSED ITINERARY FOR
AMERICAN EDUCATION MISSION TO GERMANY
(26 August to 26 September 1946)

BERLIN August 24–28, 1946, Headquarters and Offices
Monday, 26th
> 10:00 Meet General Lucius D. Clay, Deputy Military Governor, Director Building, 2051, with Mr. Sumner Sewell, Director of Internal Affairs and Communications Division; General Robert A. McClure, Director of Information Control; Dr. John W. Taylor, Chief Education and Religious Affairs Branch, IA&C Division, OMG(US); Dr. R. T. Alexander, Chief Office of General Education Institutions and Agencies, ERA Branch, OMG(US).
> 10:30 The Organization of Military Government and of the Allied Control Authority—Dr. M. E. Muelder, Chief of Program Control Branch, Control Office.
> 11:30 German Governmental Organization.
> Mr. Henry Parkman, Chief Civil Administration Division, OMG(US).
> 12:00 Military Government and Denazification.
> Major M. K. Wilson, Chief of Denazification Section, Public Safety Branch, IA&C Division, OMG(US).
> 14:00 Military Government Policy with Reference to Control of the German Educational System—Dr. John W. Taylor.
> Philosophy and Development of Education in Germany during last 40 Years—Dr. Fritz Karsen, Chief, Higher Education Section, ERA Branch OMG(US).
> Youth Activities—Mr. W. Hayes Beall, Chief Youth Activities Section, ERA Branch, OMG(US).
> Teacher Training—Dr. R. T. Alexander.

Tuesday, 27th

(Morning unscheduled)

14:00 Conference: Information Control Program.

General Robert A. McClure, Col. W. H. Kinard, Deputy Chief, Information Control OMG(US).

14:30 Conference with ODIC media chiefs (30 minutes each).

Wednesday, 28th

09:00 The Program and Work of Berlin District.

Room 4, 26–28 Ehrenbergstrasse, Major Paul Shafer, Chief, ERA Section, OMG(US).

10:00 Military Government Control Policy (Continued from Monday afternoon).

Religious Affairs—Dr. C. Arild Olson, Chief, Religious Affairs Section, ERA Branch, OMG(US);

Adult Education—Dr. William Van de Wall, Chief, Adult Education Section, ERA Branch, OMG(US).

14:00 Afternoon unscheduled.

18:26 Depart for Frankfurt, Wannsee Station.

GREATER HESSE August 29–September 4, 1945

Thursday, 29th

08:47 Arrive in Frankfurt (*Sudbahnhof*) by train from Berlin.

11:00 Preliminary meeting with the Director of OMG(GH).

Brief orientation and planning session.

12:00 Lunch with Director.

13:50 ~ 15:30

Brief by ERA staff. Topics for discussion:

1. Achievement of Past Year.

2. Teacher Training.

3. Adult and Vocational Education.

4. Youth Organization and Activities.

15:30 ~ 17:00

Conference with Information Control Service staff.

Friday, 30th

School Visitation

a. Higher Education—University of Frankfurt; American Library.

b. Teacher Training Institutions, Elementary and Secondary Schools.

c. Adult and Vocational Schools.

d. Youth installations.

Saturday, 31st

09:00 ~ 12:00

Meet with Hessian Ministry of Education staff in the Conference Room.

14:00 ~ 18:00

Rhine trip with ERA staff and German ministrial officials.

continue discussions.

Sunday, September 1st

Morning:

Catholic Church, Kiedrich.

Evangelical Church, Wiesbaden.

Afternoon:

a. University group leave for Marburg.

b. Youth Meeting in Frankfurt.

c. Music in Eltville by Teacher Training Group.

Monday, 2nd

School Visitation:

a. University—Marburg

b. Teacher Training, Elementary and Secondary—Weilburg/Lahn.

c. Adult and Vocational

d. Youth installations.

Tuesday, 3rd

Morning School Visitation.

a. University—Darmstadt

b. Teacher Training, Elementary and Secondary—Eltville

c. Adult and Vocational—

d. Youth installations.

Afternoon Conference with ERA officers or various functional branches of education.

19:00 Dinner with Director.

WÜRTTEMBERG–BADEN—September 4–10, 1946

Wednesday, 4th

09:00 Depart by auto for Stuttgart via Heidelberg.

12:00 Lunch at Schloss Hotel, Heidelberg with Lt. Col. Irvin.

13:00 Visit Heidelberg University and conference with the Rector.

15:00 Depart for Stuttgart.

17:00 Arrive Stuttgart.

20:00 Dinner with Director OMG(WB)—Graf Zeppelin Hotel, Stuttgart.

Thursday, 5th

09:00 ∼ 10:00

Conference with Director, Deputy Director and Assistant Directors OMG(WB) in Conference Room.

10:00 ∼ 10:30

Visit to Military Government Chart Room.

10:30 ∼ 12:00

Conference with Director and Staff of Education and Religious Affairs Division in Division Director's Office.

Subject: "Organization of OMG(WB)—Personnel, Responsibilities and Facilities of Education and Religious Affairs Division OMG(WB)."

12:15 ∼ 14:00

Lunch at Military Government Officers' Club.

14:00 ~ 15:00

Conference in Division Director's Office.
Subject: "Welfare Problems in Württemberg–Baden."
15:00 ~ 16:00

Conference in Division Director's Office.
Subject: "Health and Nutrition Problems in Württemberg–Baden."
16:00 ~ 17:00

Planning of work for the Remainder of Period in Württemberg–Baden.

Friday, 6th

08:30 ~ 09:15

Group Conference with Chiefs of Branch of Education and Religious Affairs Division.

Subjects: Higher Institutions and Teacher Training.
Elementary, Secondary, Vocational, and Special Schools.
Adult Education.
Youth Activities.
Religious Affairs.

10:00 ~ 12:00

Conference at Württemberg–Baden Kultministerium.
To include:
Minister President Mair
Minister of Culture Houss
Ministerialdirektor Bauorle
Landesdirektor Schnabel (Baden)
Ministerialrat Hagel (Administration)
Ministerialrat Rupp (Higher Institutions)
Ministerialrat Hassinger (General School Questions, Adult Education, Youth Activities)
Ministerialrat Schneckenburger (Elementary Schools)
Oberregierungsdirektor Mack (Secondary Schools)
Oberregierungsdirektor Stroheker (Vocational and Special Schools)
12:00 ~ 14:00

Lunch at Military Government Officers' Club
14:00 ~ 17:00

Individual Conferences with German School Officials and School Visitation in Stuttgart and Vicinity.

Saturday, 7th

14:00 ~ 17:00

Conferences with Rectors of Higher Educational Institutions:
Rector von Camponhausen (University of Heidelberg)
First Senator Ernst (University of Heidelberg)
Rector Waffenschmied (College of Commerce at Mannheim)
Rector Grammel (Technical College at Stuttgart)
Retiring Rector Plank and Rector Poeshl (Technical College at Karlsruho)
Rector Munsinger (Agricultural College at Hohonoheim)
Ministerialrat Rupp.

(Alternatives:)
(08:30 ∼ 12:00)
School Visitation
(08:30 ∼ 17:00)
Group Conferences with Germans not in the Ministry of Culture and or with
  Information Control Officials
(13:00 ∼ 17:00)
Visit to Landesbibliothek.
(13:00 ∼ 17:00)
Visit to Education and Religious Affairs Book Depository at Zeppelin Ober-
  schule in Stuttgart.
18:00 ∼ 20:00
Dinner at Military Government Officers' Club.
20:00 ∼ 24:00
Entertainment of Mission by the Ministry of Culture at Rotenberg.

Sunday, 8th
Church services
Reception given by Landesbishop Wurn
Optional scenic trips.

Monday, 9th
08:30 ∼ 16:00
School visitation in the field.
Additional Interviews or conferences as desired by members of the Mission.
16:00 ∼ 17:00
Final Conference with Director and Staff of Education and Religious Affairs
  Division.

Tuesday, 10th
08:30 Depart by auto for Munich.

BAVARIA

Tuesday, 10th
12:00 Arrive Munich.
14:00 General briefing by Chief and members of Education and Religious
  Affairs Branch.
20:00 Dinner with General Muller, Director, OMG (Bavaria).

Wednesday, 11th
09:00 Conference with Information Control Service staff.
10:30 Conference with officials of the Bavaria Ministry of Education.
14:00 Tour Munich in three groups:
(a) Higher Education Group;
(b) Elementary and Secondary Education Group;
(c) Youth Activities Group.

Thursday, 12th
Arrive noon, lunch with Military Government officer in Garmisch.
Visit rural schools, youth center, and Displaced Persons camp in afternoon
  (DP Center at Mittenwald).

Friday, 13th

Alternatives for three groups:

(a) Drive to Oberammergau—visit schools, attend lecture by one of Military Government staff at German youth center.

(b) Adult and Vocational Education—visit Erlangen or Nuremberg—attend Adult Education Conference.

(c) Visit agricultural school and seminary at Eichstatt or University of Würzburg.

Saturday, 14th

Alternatives for three groups:

(a) Drive to Berchtesgaden to visit youth center.

(b) Adult and Vocational Education—visit Erlangen or Nuremberg—attend Adult Education Conference.

Sunday, 15th

Sightseeing arrangements on request.

Monday, 16th

Alternatives for three groups:

(a) All day trip to Furth—visit schools, see examples of overcrowding in border areas.

(b) Visit Chiemsee—see Boy Scout camp.

(c) Visit Dachau and nearby towns—for youth activities and rural schools.

(d) Visit school for under-privileged children in Ammersee.

Tuesday, 17th

10:00 Final conference with officials of the Bavarian Ministry of Education.

14:00 Final briefing with ERA Branch Chief and members of staff.

Depart from Munich Airport by plane for Berlin.

BERLIN

Tuesday, 17th

16:00 Arrive Tempelhof Airport Berlin.

Wednesday, 18th to 25th

Final conference and writing report.

Thursday, 26th

Depart by plane for the United States.

[Schedule compiled by the author, based on "Proposed Itinerary for American Mission to Germany, 26 August to 26 September 1946," Helen C. White Papers]

APPENDIX C: DRAFT PAPERS OF THE U.S. EDUCATION MISSION COMMITTEES AND THE JAPANESE EDUCATION COMMITTEE

1. Language Reform
Special Committee on Japanese Language, U.S. Education Mission

The question of language reform is basic and urgent. It emerges in almost every branch of the educational program from the primary school to the university. If this question is evaded, many of the proposals made in this report will be practically impossible of achievement and the development of democracy in Japan will be *seriously hampered* (placed in serious jeopardy).

Many believe that a complete change in the form of written Japanese is necessary; others hold that more moderate reforms are sufficient. But whatever solution to the problem is finally adopted, it will be profitable to view the matter through the educational experience of the average Japanese child. The role of language in helping the individual to learn during the school-years and in progressively assisting him to develop during all the later years of life is well known. In Japanese, as in all languages, men and women think through *phonetic and* written symbols (and their associated sounds). It is imperative therefore that the Japanese child be provided with the best possible linguistic symbols with which to learn and think.

Practically all informed persons agree that the time devoted to memorizing the *Kanji* (characters) in which the Japanese language is written places an excessive burden of learning on the pupils. During the elementary school years they are required to give at least one-half of all their study time to the sheer task of learning to recognize and *to* write (language characters) (Kanji). These six years are crucial

---

Note: Words and phrases in italics are corrections made in the final draft. Those in parentheses are deletions.

in the development of the individual. During this period basic habits and attitudes are formed. In addition to acquiring the fundamental verbal and numerical skills, the child makes his first contacts with the more complex natural and social phenomena. At this time, moreover, foundations may be laid for an understanding of economic and political realities and for intelligent citizenship.

The results achieved by the inordinate amount of time alloted to the written language are grievously disappointing. Studies of the abilities of Japanese boys and girls leaving the elementary school show that they very generally lack the linguistic abilities essential to democratic citizenship. They are quite unable to read freely in daily newspapers and popular magazines. As a general rule books dealing seriously with contemporary problems and ideas are beyond their grasp. The fact is that, although one-half of their time and energy during the six years of elementary education is devoted to learning the written characters, they do not acquire a degree of mastery sufficient to make possible steady development through reading after leaving school.

It would be (interested) interesting to know how easily these young people handle a large telephone directory, or how readily they use (a) Japanese dictionar*ies* [dictionary] in search of both (of) the meanings and the forms of Kanji [characters]. Then, too, one would like to be able to estimate their loss in essential fields of knowledge because of the devotion of so much time to the tasks of simple reading and writing. To be a part of this world, the individual should have a clear understanding of the meaning of simple statements of fact touching his daily life. Also, he should (have) possess those elements of general education that can be developed, even outside the school, by personal interest in those circumstances directly affecting his own fortunes. If a child fails to make a beginning in such matters before leaving the elementary school, he rarely will find time or curiosity to make the start for himself. And *approximately* ninety percent of Japanese children terminate their formal education at this time.

For the ten percent going on into the middle school, the language problem remains. They *pupils* continue to labor at the unending task of mastering the symbols of the written language.

In order to overcome the obstacles to learning that inhere in the written language of Japan today, a number of reforms have been proposed. But none has been given a full or fair trial in the schools; nor apparently has such trial even received serious consideration at the hands of the responsible educational authorities. Scholars, to be sure, have devoted much attention to the question. Many influential private citizens, as well as many *editors of* newspapers and book*s* (editors), have helped to explore possibilities. It is said that some thirty Japanese organizations today are deeply concerned with the question of language reform. Broadly speaking, three proposals for *the* reform *of the language* are under discussion [in these organizations] *of the people*: the first suggests a reduction in the number of Kanji; the second, the complete abandonment of Kanji and the adoption of some form of Kana; and the third the complete abandonment of both Kanji and Kana and the adoption of some form of Romaji.

It is fortunate that historically Japan has been as active as other countries in testing ways of language reform, and that today her schools are awake to the need of moving steadily and constructively toward the common goal of a modern written form of national language. It is significant that in the past China has evolved phonetic symbols, acting quite independently, designed to simplify the Chinese language, and that now Chinese scholars are deeply concerned with the ways to improve their language for all the purpose of modern communication.

In the light of the foregoing facts and other data on language analysis, this Mission supports the conclusion that the Japanese people should look toward some phonetic system as their final goal. The language already has an excellent phonetic base which can be utilized in developing a standard written language *for common use*. Such a form would be easy to acquire, would greatly facilitate the use of dictionaries, catalogues, typewriters, linotype machines, and so on. More important still, it would open to the great mass of the Japanese people the knowledge and wisdom to be found in their own writings in philosophy, science, technology, and other aspects of their rich and varied culture.

That the *aesthetic and other values* depth and variety of meaning residing in the *Kanji can* (Japanese characers may) never be fully conveyed by a phonetic system is readily granted. But the common man, if he is to be informed and articulate, must be given entry to knowledge and ideas through a far more simple medium than the current form of writing. Fortunately many Japanese leaders realize that language reform is the surest way of advancing (the) *popular* understanding (of men and women). The achievement of a unified and practicable plan may be slow, but the present is the time for beginning. *Now is the time for the Japanese people to take decisive action.*

[With this conviction, the Mission recommends the introduction of some form of Romaji into all elementary schools. *During the period of transition this would probably involve the* preparation of textbooks in two language forms. The two forms might appear on the same page, as in several texts now in circulation, or on opposite pages. Choice in this aspect of the plan should be made by printers and specialists in the subjects taught. Also, the Japanese who themselves have the true feeling for the most desirable form of language now in common use should determine what form of Romaji and what blend of Kanji and Kana would best serve the needs of pupils at a given level.]

The *taking* (making) of the(se) *necessary practical steps to schools* (decisions) *should* (might) be the work of *the* (a) Japanese language commission. *The commission may* (and a similar body might) determine at what (level in the elementary schools) *appropriate* (the new) texts *for the difficult levels of the elementary schools* (would be made available to all pupils in the country). [The textbooks (in two) language forms might be prepared for the first three, for the last three, or for all six years of the elementary school. Such texts should be made standard for the entire country.] (,but) At the same time (undoubtedly there will be) (provision should be made for the) publication of newspapers, periodicals, and books, in whole or in part, in Romaji *may be expected*. An interesting and exciting children's literature in the new language form would be helpful. In order to speed the reform, children and youths might be prepared to give instructions in Romaji to their elders in the family and the community. *These reforms of the written language may be accompanied by a democratic form of the spoken language.*

The language commission, appointed to launch this momentous undertaking in education, might grow into a national language institute to study the great wealth of data on the learning process that would come from the use of the new methods and forms. Such an institute would attract scholars from other countries working on language problems, for many would discover in the Japanese experience ideas immediately useful to themselves. The problems of China, for example, are somewhat like those of Japan. China too has made useful trials of simpler forms for the written language, and in fact is now beginning discussions of new plans. The Japanese specialists would be the best judges of useful ways for collaboration in such matters, but they would find in every developed society of the world a number of specialists in the study of language ready to cooperate.

In this step toward simplified forms of writing and printing the language in elementary schools, Japanese educators should be encouraged by the clear signs of public interest in phonetic forms for writing the Kanji symbols. The newspapers of Tokyo carried twenty-three editorials during the first two months of this year dealing with the question of language reform. Publishers have watched with deep interest the attempt of certain newspapers to reduce the number of Kanji symbols to a lower and still lower figure. For translations from all other languages into Japanese the book publisher will find Romaji a natural medium—not only to increase the reading of Japanese but also to open the Japanese language to all foreign readers now baffled by the character symbols. Of this last fact, the war has given proof in the success of programs to train for reading and for hearing with understanding the sounds of standard Japanese. The hundreds who have begun in this way to think in the language may follow their reading of Romaji by a learning of the characters. This is the only easy road for a foreigner into the rich cultural heritage of Japan. For the Japanese people themselves, it is undoubtedly the way to rapid and continuous transmission of ideas in both directions across national boundaries.

Insularity and isolation are powerful obstacles to understanding and social progress in the entire world as well as in Japan. In making these recommendations regarding the Japanese language the Mission recognizes that the charge of isolation can be made in this form or in some other form against other nations and against their own country. Every country suffers misunderstanding at times by reason of language differences. Therefore, in calling to Japan to hasten the simplification of her language for reading and writing, the Mission is speaking for the world at large, not for itself. Moreover, it is only repeating after them what the Japanese people themselves have thought and hoped, that their language might assist rather than hamper intercourse among the nations. In every country of the world it is essential that citizens should be able to read without difficulty and that the flow of thought between peoples should be possible for all mankind.

[*Source*: Stevens Papers, Joseph Regenstein Library, University of Chicago]

2. Teaching and the Education of Teachers in Japan
Committee II, U.S. Education Mission

I. THE PROBLEMS INVOLVED

The reconstruction of teaching and of the education of teachers has the same aim as the reconstruction of the education in general. This aim is the re-centering of the life and thought of the Japanese people. This life and thought has hitherto been centered on the nation as the supreme object of devotion, to the exclusion of broader human values, and on the vertical system of duties pertaining to relations in the family, the clan, and the nation. This system has proved to be a ready instrument of militarism. For it must be substituted a system which frees the individual in all the relations of life to develop and express the powers and aspirations of common humanity. We recognize that the leaders of the Japanese people have already reoriented their own thinking, thus making dominant the strains which have existed for a long time. Our mission is to give support to the liberal movement in Japanese education. Only the Japanese people can carry out the proposed reforms, which therefore must be expressed in indigenous patterns.

The effects of the old regime are clearly manifest in the teaching in Japan. It has suffered from severe disabilities. It has been hampered and restricted in both content and form. The teachers have been told exactly what to teach and how to teach it. The content of instruction has been contained in the present textbooks, and the form has been laid down in the teachers' manuals. To prevent any deviation from the prescribed content and form, the inspectors have been charged with the duty of seeing to it that the printed instructions were followed to the letter. This system has put teaching in Japan in a straight-jacket.

As result of this condition, teaching has been, by and large, formal and stereotyped. It has emphasized memory at the expense of thinking; confomity at the expense of originality. It has enforced uniformity to the exclusion of variation, to suit the needs of different individuals with divers interests or capacities, and to meet the demands of communities of different occupational or cultural make-up.

This condition is severely criticized by intelligent Japanese themselves. In fact, a few teachers have managed, in spite of their handicaps, to attain an admirable degree of flexibility in their teaching. A good many leaders of education in Japan have, singly and in groups, striven to break away from the restrictions in which they have been held and to develop freer ways. All honor is due them.They have made progress under great difficulties. This indicates the presence of a spirit of liberality, which, if it were given full opportunity, would soon pervade the main body of teachers.

The first step in our procedure is to further define and describe good teaching so that we may have clearly in mind the result we wish to produce. In so doing, we must emphasize, or even exaggerate, those qualities which are deficient in the schools of Japan. Japanese teachers need no one to tell them how to conduct drill or to develop skill of hand. They are past-masters at this art. Neither would any one detract from the value of this kind of teaching. It is only bad if it shuts out the possibility of developing spontaneity, curiosity, intelligence, and originality in the attack on problems, and judgment in dealing with social and moral questions. The next section of this chapter is a description of the characteristics of good teaching.

After agreeing on what good teaching is, we must mark out the way in which such teaching may be secured in all the schools of Japan. Two groups must be dealt with, the teachers now in service, and those preparing for service. The teachers now in service must be re-educated to the new conceptions, and the new methods. The third section of this chapter, therefore, deals with in-service education, first as a means of re-educating the present teaching staff, and second, as a means of continuing the education of all teachers after they are inducted into service. The fourth and final section of the chapter deals with the reconstruction of the preparatory education of teachers, and other school officials. The teacher is the key to the whole enterprise of education. The reformation of the education of teachers is therefore the key to the reformation of education in general. This section will emphasize the features in the present system of educating teachers which embody its chief evils and will propose new procedures to be substituted for them.

II. *TEACHING PRACTICES IN DEMOCRATIC EDUCATION*
1. *Characteristics of Good Teaching*

The nature of the program for the preparation of teachers is determined by the kinds of practices considered as desirable in the classroom. It may be natural to assume that democratic practices are good practices. But at the outset, it should be pointed out that this is not necessarily the case. Good practices are those which attain the desired objectives most effectively. If the objectives are democratic, a wise use of democratic procedure is indicated. But when they are so employed as to result in wasted time with little learned, or when they afford more freedom than can be profitably used at the stage of individual and social development the pupils have attained, they are not being wisely used. Certain parts of the school program call for direct instructional methods and direct teacher control. The mature, well educated, and well trained teacher, as a part of the practice of his art, will be expected to be able to judge which kinds of method to employ. Hence the tabulation at the close of this section of the report is presented to suggest extremes between which good instruction will be expected to fluctuate.

Desirable practices can be facilitated by having smaller classes and well equipped laboratories, libraries, gymnasiums, playgrounds and special classrooms, and by the use of radios, phonographs and motion picture projectors. But schools with a wealth of equipment are not necessarily good schools, and those with meager equipment may provide rich educational experiences.

If the teacher is given sufficient freedom, it is possible to make use of many facilities outside the school to enrich the learning of pupils. Local farms, factories, offices, libraries and hospitals provide educational opportunities. If classes are too large, a teacher skilled in democratic processes can make good use of student leadership, breaking up the class into smaller groups under student chairmen.

Democratic education can be characterized by its recognition of individual differences in pupils, by its emphasis on the development of the potentialities of the individual, and by its goal of acceptable and effective participation in the social group.

a. *Individual Differences*

Some differences between pupils are properly ignored by the democratic school, such as those of religion, race and social status. Equal educational opportunity should be provided for all in spite of any prejudices which may be found in the adult population. The democratic school, however, through its testing program, and in other ways, seeks to discover the intellectual level of its pupils and adjusts its program accordingly. It tries not to make demands on pupils which they are unable to meet, and further, it broadens its offerings to provide educational experiences for those of differing intellectual abilities. Similarly, it seeks to adjust its program to pupils of differing home background, to those from rural and from urban areas, for example, endeavoring to adapt to individual needs.

Since intellectual differences between the sexes are practically non-existent in the democratic school, the sexes are educated together in the belief that the experience of growing up together is natural and helpful to both boys and girls. Segregation within the school for such activities as sports and physical education and, when desired, certain manual activities, presents few difficulties.

It is believed that insistence on conformity to necessarily arbitrary standards does not produce the most desirable type of development. Methods which are effective for some are not for others, and an atmosphere in which the teacher tells and the pupils listen and then give back what they have been told, or one in which reliance is placed on a single textbook for all, is not effective in stimulating pupil development. Initiative and originality are stifled unless pupils can ask questions, consult different sources, subject their ideas to group criticism, work at solving their problems, and test their solutions in the light of reason and in terms of possible or actual consequences.

A formal examination system emphasizing memorized learning and minimizing the importance of independent thinking exaggerates the condition especially when failure or success is followed by important social consequences.

c. *Social Participation*

The goal of acceptable and effective social participation is sought in the process of education as well as at the end of the pupils' school career. Democratic attitudes cannot be learned from precept alone; they must be learned through the experience of democratic action. Informal pupil-teacher relationships contribute to it, together with a self-discipline based on willing conformity derived from a knowledge of the consequences of behavior for the common good. Training for participation in community life in a democracy calls for experience in the process of group deliberation, in the choosing of leaders and the exercise of leadership, in the toleration of different points of view and in accepting responsibility for the actions of the group.

In the chart below, a number of these points are summarized to indicate the direction of desired change in teaching practices in democratic education.

Less Desirable Practices	*More Desirable Practices*
Pupil penalized for not doing that of which he is intellectually incapable.	Pupil encouraged to work at tasks at which he can succeed.
Highly standardized and uniform methods.	Flexible methods adopted to local and individual needs.
Teacher a lecturer only.	Teacher also a discussion leader and guide.
Teacher asks questions, pupil answers.	Pupil asks questions, answers sought cooperatively.
Textbook sole source of authoritative information.	Textbook supplemented by other sources.
Subject matter organized according to conventional patterns; little inter-relationship between courses.	Subject matter organized meaningfully around a problem to be solved or a project to be completed.
Examinations favor material memorized.	Achievement judged according to initiative and independent thinking.
Pupil-teacher relations formal; little sense of mutuality.	Pupil-teacher relationships informal; genuine sense of partnership in a mutual task.
Discipline imposed by authority or precept.	Self-discipline imposed through acceptance of demands of the social situation.
Group activities initiated and controlled by teacher.	Group activities and controlled in part by pupils under the leadership of the teacher.

2. *Suggested Practices in ''Civic Education''*

In order that the above generalizations concerning teaching methods may have a clearer and more definite meaning, illustrations will be given showing specific practices that may be employed. Undoubtedly many if not all the practices suggested can now be found in operation in one or another of the public or private schools of Japan, and some of them have been tried out experimentally, but they are not generally employed. The field chosen for illustration is that which is referred to as ethics and sometimes ''civics'' in Japan, and is a part of ''social studies'' in the United States. It embraces Political Science, Economics, Sociology, and Ethics, adapted to the age and stage of development of the learner. This subject matter field is chosen because it is of chief concern at the present time in view of the modifications in process of being made in the curriculum.

The several religions have put forward one or another system of ethics, and these systems have merit, but since they are bound to incompatible religious dogmas, the state is wise to exclude religious indoctrination from its schools. This, however, should not be interpreted as the exclusion of the teachings of the different religions, particularly at the higher levels, when each religion is treated impartially, with no attempt to inculcate the dogma of any one of them. The latter should be the responsibility of the home, the religious organizations, and private institutions.

Neither should the exclusion of religious indoctrination be interpreted as excluding ethical and moral instruction. The latter, however, should be taught not alone by precept, but through knowledge, experience, discussion, and practice, and should be reflected in the attitudes and social behavior of the individual.

a. *Knowledge*

According to their age level, pupils should learn about local industry and local prefectural and national government. In the elementary and middle schools they should visit business establishments, banks, stores, police and fire departments, and government offices, and learn how private and public business is carried on. They should be encouraged to ask questions, express opinions and engage in discussions. Responsibilities of employers and government officials should be dwelt on, and the common rights of individuals as employees and as citizens. Questions should be raised as to the means of safeguarding these rights, and ways of improving them. Film strips and motion pictures can supplement the usual methods of instruction to extend the pupil's knowledge beyond the immediate locality.

b. *Experience*

To vitalize the knowledge so gained, certain class periods each week (one or two) can be devoted to problems of the class, or grade, or other school groups and to the school itself as a social institution. A simple type of political organization can be set up, with a flexible committee plan to discuss and work out solutions to such problems as improving the appearance of the school, improving health conditions, developing recreational facilities, obtaining exhibits of books or pictures, planning school parties, introducing new pupils to the school, developing special interest clubs, etc. In all of these, the teacher's role is that of participant, helping the pupils to develop their ideas, not dominating the discussion but giving them the practice in working together toward the solution of common problems. It might be expected that in some schools elected representatives of each class or group would serve as a student council, which would act within its sphere of power as a governing body of the school, and which might forward suggestions or recommendations to the faculty for their consideration.

c. *Discussion*

While group discussion is an important part of the methods suggested above, it is given a separate position here as a way to deal with problems of personal or individual adjustment. Teachers, or pupils, may decide that something that has happened or might happen calls for discussion on the part of the pupils in order that they may understand the situation better or know better how to conduct themselves. For example, a talk on safety by a member of the police department before the whole school might well be followed up by small group discussions on ways to promote safety as they affect individual pupils. The occupying forces present problems for adolescent girls. Democratic processes may be misinterpreted and need clarification. With the impact of other cultures on the traditional Japanese codes of behavior, a number of conflicts will undoubtedly arise between different classes, and between the younger and older generations. Discussions, led by wise and well-educated teachers should help the younger generation to hold to what is good in the old, and at the same time not to oppose, or embrace, the old because it is old, nor to oppose or embrace the new merely because it is new.

d. *Practice*

Besides the experience provided in the regular class period, moral behavior and ethical attitudes can be developed through practice in other school situations. For example:

In musical organizations—choir, chorus and speaking choir, and in band, orchestra and ensemble, when musical instruments are available, in addition to the aesthetic values involved—a pupil may gain practice in individual responsibility for achieving the ends sought by the group. He can likewise obtain individual satisfaction through being a group member and making a contribution to the group product.

In formal or informal dramatic presentations, plays, and marionette shows, a variety of talent is called upon, each contribution having its respected place.

In plan, group games, and team sports, children can learn the simple virtues of sharing, respect for the role of others, and the rules of good sportsmanship under practical and often trying situations. If these attitudes so acquired are generalized to apply to other life situations, they are given meaning and substance which is not apt to follow from purely verbal preceptual methods.

In summary, it may be said in general that well educated, broadly-trained teachers can adapt methods of instruction to suit the varying needs of pupils. There is enough and more than enough to fill the school periods formerly devoted to morals and civics. It remains for Japan, instead of seeking to produce "loyal subjects", to develop instead a free citizenry. In accomplishing this change, a heavy responsibility rests upon the teachers of the young. If they prove equal to their task, the future is assured.

III. *THE RE-EDUCATION OF TEACHERS*

The teachers now at work in the schools of Japan are faced with perplexing tasks—tasks of enormous social significance. They must interpret the events of the past years to the younger generation, while preparing that generation to take its place in the new Japan. They are expected to teach in accordance with new aims, and by democratic methods little familiar to them. If the teachers are to meet the obligations which they have accepted, they need all the help which can be given them.

1. *Emergency Re-Education Programs*

In order to give the needed assistance and guidance to the teachers now in the schools, an emergency training program is required. It is recommended that such programs be undertaken at once, and in many ways. Time will be required for the transition, and it is suggested that the emergency program be planned to cover two years. Within that time, every teacher should have had an opportunity for consultation or training in the newer approaches to teaching.

Among the emergency re-education possibilities, the following are suggested:

a. *Teachers Meetings Within Each School.* Every school should have frequent meetings of its teachers in which new problems and practices are freely discussed without domination by the principal.

b. *Democratically originated practices in ordinary schools, under the guidance of educational consultants.* Wherever feasible, experienced educators qualified to assist the teachers and principal of a school to begin newer practices should select an ordinary school (not a demonstration school connected with a normal school) and, working with its staff, the parents, and the pupils, help in evolving new methods appropriate to the given school. Such demonstrations in real schools will prove helpful to other schools through showing the participation of teachers in planning, and the variety of practices which may be found acceptable.

c. *The mobile unit, or traveling group of teachers.* Selected teachers, skilled in democratic methods, may move about in teams or groups, from community to community, giving encouragement to the local teachers and aiding in obtaining answers to their questions. Such groups should be made up of teachers from various parts of Japan and from communities varying in size. Some plan for multiplying these teams should be arranged so that within the emergency two-year period all schools are reached. The teams may be supplied with motion pictures and other aids to make easier their communication of the newer practices.

d. *Use of the demonstration school in connection with the prefectural normal school.* The demonstration school in connection with each normal school should be quickly revamped to represent the more desirable practices. It may be necessary to transfer teachers out of these schools and to replace them with teachers recruited from among those who have demonstrated their ability to use the newer methods. Perhaps those to teach in the demonstration schools may meet together in regional institutes or conferences to consider ways of modifying their practices.

After the prefectural normal schools have revised the practices in their demonstration schools, teacher representatives chosen by the teachers in rural areas, villages, and cities should be sent, to study in these demonstration centers, to return to their own communities prepared to share with other teachers what they have learned.

The above suggestions are offered as emergency programs. At the same time, other practices for continuing the training of teachers already serving the schools should be begun. These programs may be described as in-service education.

2. *The In-Service Education of Teachers*

The New Japan envisioned by liberal Japanese and by their friends throughout the world will require a dynamic, steadily improving school system. Such a
system must have teachers whose professional education continues as long as
they are in service. A static school is one whose instructors stop learning when
they begin to teach. A dynamic school is one whose teachers start the most
effective part of their professional learning when they complete initial preparation and undertake the full duties of their calling.

There are teachers in Japan today, in overcrowded poorly equipped classrooms, who bring light and warmth and gaiety to dark, cold rooms in temporary
structures set amid deserts of devastated rubble. There are teachers in Japan
today whose knowledge of children and whose wealth of skills make the drama
of cooperative learning sparkle and come alive. It is the aim of in-service education to give every teacher continuing opportunities to get and to develop that
kind of teaching power.

Several suggestions for the in-service training of teachers follows:

a. The first educational necessity for teachers is that they shall be given
   many opportunities to meet with their fellows for the interchange of
   professional counsel and inspiration. The faculty meeting of each school
   is one answer to this need, but it is only a beginning. Professional
   meetings of all teachers of all types of schools in a village, a city, a
   prefecture, or a large region should be encouraged. The university
   professors and the middle school instructors follow the same calling as
   the elementary teachers. If they more often meet with their elementary
   school colleagues, they would be able not only to help other members of
   their profession but also to discover why the teaching in the elementary
   schools of Japan is sometimes superior to that in many schools above the
   elementary level.

   Meetings of groups of teachers with special professional interests should
   also be held. Teachers of a particular subject, administrators of particular
   types of schools, and members of the profession desiring to band together
   for a particular type of school reform furnish examples of the special
   interest meetings that need to be held.

   While the Ministry of Education and the administrative authorities
   in the prefectures and cities should encourage professional meetings and
   give needed assistance to them, it must be emphasized that the most
   effective meetings of teachers are usually those which the teachers
   themselves plan and hold. This is one important reason why teachers'
   associations of all kinds, including teachers' unions, should be allowed
   freedom of organization. No democratic principle is more crucial than the
   right to organize for the extension of ideas, and teachers in a democratic
   society cannot be free men and women without having and holding that
   right.

b. *Institutes and Conferences*

   Teacher-training institutions, such as normal schools, higher normal
   schools, colleges and universities, have a clear duty to provide teachers in

service with those special means of professional education variously called in English by such terms as conferences, workshops, institutes and vacation courses.

It seems clear that the present worthy attempts of certain Japanese teacher-training institutions to continue a program of professional help to their own graduates and other teachers in the field by offering occasional lectures and institutes should be greatly expanded and intensified. The duty of these institutions to teachers in service is fully as important as their duty to the young men and women in their regular classes. For the immediate future, indeed, in view of the pressing re-education task among Japanese teachers, the in-service function may even hold top priority.

c. *Publications for teachers*

Professional publications may be used more widely for discussion of teachers' problems and for reporting successful practices. In connection with professional reading, correspondence courses might well be developed.

d. *Observation by one teacher of the practices of another.*

One of the most effective phases of in-service education is also one of the simplest. It is the observation of another teacher in action followed by a discussion with that teacher of the educational aims and methods involved. This kind of in-service experience can begin with giving each teacher in a school one hour a week to visit another teacher in the same school. It can be extended to include visits to other nearby schools for an entire day or to more distant localities for even longer periods. When the observation-discussion takes a teacher outside his own school building, it becomes increasingly difficult to administer this technique of in-service education. The technique should be employed, however, because it has been proved to be a highly effective method of professional education.

e. *The Supervisor*

The value of good supervision in furthering the continuing education of teachers should not be ignored. Perhaps the outstanding mark of an effective supervisor in the modern school is his faithful adherence to the principal that he is above all a helping teacher whose first function is to aid his fellow teachers in learning their craft better. The professional quality of the present inspectoral staff of the Japanese schools must be decidedly raised and the character of its functions changed to conform more nearly with the modern conception of the work of a supervisor as a professional leader and helper of teachers, if in-service education is to be carried on effectively.

f. *Travel*

We venture to express the hope that in the not too far distant future, Japanese teachers will be able to travel freely again to visit and study in other countries and that many exchanges between Japanese teachers and those of all the United Nations may be arranged to the lasting benefit of education throughout the world.

g. *Improving Teacher Welfare*
In connection with all planning for in-service education, including re-education, we point to the obvious necessity of reducing the present excessive teaching load, providing adequate leaves for study and travel, and establishing an adequate salary scale for teachers. Without these changes, teachers of Japan will have too little time and resources for effective education in-service.

IV. GENERAL OVERVIEW OF THE PREPARATION OF TEACHERS

In considering the education of teachers, it is necessary to include teachers of all types. Attention is given usually to primary school teachers and to the normal schools which prepare these teachers. Equal consideration should be given to teachers in middle schools, higher schools, the normal schools themselves, the vocational schools and youth schools, colleges and universities. The general fact seems to be that special preparation is given mainly to teachers in primary schools and not more than half of these, at the most, are given specific preparation for their work.

The first outstanding fact, therefore, appears to be that preparation for teachers is meager, in that only certain types of teachers receive specific preparation, and that only a minority of this type are specifically educated for their work. Professional preparation should be extended to all types of teachers, and to all teachers within each type.

Other school officials such as school principals, school inspectors, chiefs of educational divisions in the prefectures, and officials in the Ministry of Education, receive even less preparation for their jobs than do teachers.

So far as can be discovered, no institution provides professional preparation for these types of work. In fact, some of them have not even had experience in teaching before they undertook their responsibilities. They have received a university preparation for some other profession such as law, etc., and are given educational positions with no background of either experience or training.

The major task of providing in-service education for teachers and other school officials and for carrying on the re-education of teachers, is performed without definite preparation for this task, and without adequate professional leadership in it. The responsibility for this leadership is not centralized in any institution which is adequately prepared to carry it on. The individual schools are not equipped with the personnel or the training necessary. The prefectural staff have not had the necessary experience or training, and the Ministry of Education has been concerned with other functions. In-service education must be carried on with a conception of education different from that which has animated the activities of the Ministry of Education. It must be carried on, furthermore, by individuals whose education has equipped them both to entertain this newer conception and to carry it out in practical activities.

The education of teachers and of other school officials, as has been stated, must be extended so as to include all persons engaged in education, and it must be reorganized so as to fit the needs of teachers and administrators in a re-organized system of education.

The first requirement is that the work of the normal school shall be reoriented to make it an agency in the development of democratic education, This matter will be dealt with in more detail in the next section.

The reorganization of work of the normal schools is only half the task, because it will touch only those teachers who receive their education in these schools. Unless all primary school teachers are to be required to pass through the normal schools, which would probably be both impractical and undesirable, it will be necessary to set up programs in education of teachers in all institutions in which they receive their training. It will be necessary also to modify the requirements of education of teachers so that, except during an emergency, no teachers may be certificated without having had appropriate preparation in an educational institution. This means, for example, that no teacher shall be certified to teach merely upon graduation from a middle school or a university, without having had systematic preparation in education, i.e. teacher-training. The is a requirement which it may not be possible to meet immediately. It is, however, a goal which should be definitely set up and which should be attained as soon as it is possible to form the necessary organization, develop the necessary faculty, and provide a sufficient number of teachers with the proposed preparation.

The preparation of the teacher should be three-fold:

It should include, first, as broad and as thorough as possible a general or liberal education, i.e. it should include such elements as mastery of language and the means of communication; an understanding of the civilization in which one lives, including both that of one's own nation and that of the other nations of the world; an appreciation of the literature and the art of one's own country in relation to that of other countries; some knowledge of the place of science in the modern world; and some understanding of the distinctive problems of an economic and political nature which confront the citizens of a modern nation.

In the second place, the preparation of a teacher requires a special knowledge of the subject matter which he is to teach. In the case of the primary teacher this field of instruction is varied. In the more advanced schools it becomes progressively specialized.

In the third place, the teacher should have a knowledge of the professional aspects of his job. He should know something of the comparative history of education: of the psychological and sociological foundations of education; of the organization of the educational system in which he is to teach; and what procedures have been found through experimentation and experience to be the most effective. This professional work should include the observation of children and of schools, and teaching under supervision. This professional preparation in its complete form should be extended at least to all teachers in the primary and secondary schools. It is desirable also to provide it for teachers at higher schools and colleges. It is obvious that such preparation is provided for only a part of the primary teachers and for practically no others.

This professional preparation is peculiarly necessary in Japan which is confronted with the task of making a fundamental reorganization of its educational system. Education in Japan has been conducted under minute direction and supervision of a central authority, the Ministry of Education. The procedures in the schools have been narrowly determined by text books, by teachers' manuals, and by inspection. This system must be completely reorganized. The educational procedure must be determined by the teachers, principals, and supervisory officials, on a basis of an understanding of the underlying principles which are derived from a study of the child who is to be educated and of the society in which he is to live. The educators themselves must be free to create their own procedures and the instrumentalities for carrying out these procedures. This requires that they shall be free, but it also require that they shall have the necessary equipment in education to make use of their freedom. This can only be done by an education of the teachers which envisages the enlarged task they are to perform.

If this enlarged education of teachers is to be carried out, all institutions which prepare teachers must participate in it. This means that fully equipped departments or faculties of education must be established in all such higher institutions and must be enlarged and better equipped for their task than those in institutions in which they now exist. Every such department of education should be staffed and equipped to provide the education with the qualities as outlined. The program may be sketched in somewhat more detail.

Assuming that the prospective teacher has had an adequate general education, the department or faculty of education should provide the following types of education:—it should offer work in the history of education which will do two things—first, it will enlighten the student regarding the development of education within his own county. This should be an objective presentation and not an ultra-nationalistic or mythological one. It should include criticisms of the education of the past and a frank statement of its short-comings and of its share in the responsibility for the Imperialistic policy of the country. It should also give perspective for the evaluation of education in the nation by comparing it with systems and philosophies of education in other countries.

Second, the educational courses should include thoroughgoing treatment of the psychological background of education, including the learning process, individual differences, educational measurement, and particularly, child-development and child-psychology. This treatment should include experimentation and observation, not merely theoretical instruction.

Third, the student should be introduced to the study of the community in which the child lives and in which the school operates. The two foundation stones of the curriculum are the child and the community. The curriculum must consider the nature of the developing child and the nature of the community in which the child lives.

Fourth, there should be included a comprehensive and critical study of the curriculum. This study is practically absent in Japan because the curriculum has been completely determined and regimented. The teachers and other school officials must, in the future, study the foundation of the curriculum and the methods or techniques by which the curriculum may be planned and developed. They should be given an opportunity to actually work on some curriculum problem.

Finally, the student must have practical experience in putting into operation, under supervision, the principles which have been studied in the courses already described. He should have abundant opportunity to observe the activities of children and the procedure of schools. He should then be given the opportunity, under guidance, to teach and perform other activities of the school in preparation for his own independent service.

In the preparation for teaching and other educational services there should be no discrimination between men and women. Both should have equal opportunity to qualify themselves for educational services at all levels of education. The most economical way to do this would be to admit men and women to the same institutions. Still more important, the educational preparation of men and women in the same institution would give them the experience of living and working together which would be of great advantage in their work in the profession.

This calls attention to the general need of prospective teachers in social as well as in academic education. They should become familiar with the life of the community and should learn by experience how to participate in it.

The foregoing discussion has dealt with the preparation of teachers. Provision should also be made for the professional education of other school officials such as principals, heads of educational divisions and government officials. In the first place, each one of these functionaries should have had the basic preparation which is required of teachers and should have had some experience in teaching. Beyond this, they need a broader preparation in the foundation of science and theory of education, in the organization of the school system, in the principles of the curriculum, and in the procedures of administration. This education should be provided by the universities. For those who have not had such preparation before assuming their official duties, abbreviated in-service courses should be provided. Other means should also be taken to prepare them for the adequate discharge of their duties—such as conferences, extension courses, and literature consisting of literature and books.

Conclusions and Recommendations

1. Professional preparation should be extended to all types of teachers and to all teachers of each type.

2. All school officials should have had experience as teachers and should have professional preparation.

3. Definite responsibility for the re-education of teachers and for their further education in service should be assumed by educational officials and educational institutions.

4. Departments or faculties of education and a definite program for the professional preparation of teachers should be set up in all institutions whose graduates enter teaching.

5. The preparation for teaching should include: (1) adequate general or liberal education; (2) a special knowledge of the subject to be taught; and (3) an enriched program of professional work in education.

V. THE NORMAL SCHOOLS OF JAPAN

1. The Functions of the Normal Schools

When in 1872 Emperor Meiji proclaimed the code of education ordering that universal elementary education should be provided for Japanese children, the

Government correctly recognized that an effective program of elementary education would be impossible without qualified teachers. Accordingly, steps were immediately taken to organize a normal school for the preparation of teachers, and in May 1872 the Tokyo Normal School, the first in Japan, was opened. From the inception of this first normal school, the purposes of normal schools in Japan has been to train individuals in loyalty to the Emperor, love of country, and obedience to authority, so that they (teachers) would become models for pupils to emulate. "To lead men to righteousness is far more important than to make them learned" was accepted as a policy which has accounted in no small degree for the formal, non-creative, unintellectual program of the normal schools.

Since 1872 the number of normal schools has increased and the effort has been made to provide teachers through these normal schools for all of the primary and intermediate schools of Japan. The first normal school was established to prepare elementary school teachers, but later the need for teachers for the middle schools made it necessary that the program of the Tokyo Normal School also include the preparation of middle school teachers. Today, the normal school system includes normal schools for the preparation of elementary school teachers, higher normal schools to prepare teachers for secondary schools, and various types of special institutions to prepare teachers for youth schools, for vocational teaching, physical education, and in music and the fine arts.

There are now four higher normal schools for men, three higher normal schools for women, and fifty-six regular normal schools. Also, there are forty-six normal schools for training youth school teachers, twenty-nine of which have programs for both men and women. Also, there are seventeen vocational, agricultural and technical teacher training schools and one in physical training, one in music, and one in the fine arts.

The number of graduates from the normal schools has been insufficient to supply the public schools of Japan with teachers. In the elementary schools, for example, Ministry of Education figures show that in 1941, 56.8% of the teachers were normal school graduates, and in 1944, 49.41%. The additional teachers required have come from various sources including private institutions, graduates of middle schools, or persons having sufficient educational background to pass the examinations for a certificate, or to meet the requirements for certification without examination.

The problem of teacher education in Japan is two-fold: first, is that of an adequate supply of teachers to staff the schools; and second, and even more important, is the problem of the qualifications of these teachers to meet the needs of a nation that wishes to gain for itself a place in the family of free democratic nations of the world.

2. Evaluation of Study and Observations of Pre-service Education
in Japanese Normal Schools
a. General Pattern of Normal Schools

We believe that the normal schools have carried out rather efficiently the narrow, formal, ultra-nationalistic and militaristic purposes of Japanese education. The normal schools have been instruments to carry out the national conception of education as directed by the Ministry of Education. Normal schools have not been free to develop their own curriculums and subject matter has been prescribed by higher authority. Periodic inspections have been made by the Ministry of Education. Reports of compliance with regulations have been periodically required.

Emphasis has been placed upon rote learning. Methods have, therefore, necessarily been formal, largely on the lecture and telling basis. Little use is made of libraries since there is practically no study required beyond the prescribed textooks.

b. *Admission Procedures*

Students entering higher normal schools for men are either graduates of the regular normal schools or middle schools or of schools rated as of equal grade by the Ministry of Education. Admission to the higher normal schools for women is on much the same basis as that for the men. To be admitted to the regular normal school, the student must either be a graduate of the higher elementary school or of a middle school or girls high school or have equivalent qualifications for admission.

During normal times, as few as ten percent of those wishing to enter the higher normal schools and twenty percent of those applying for admission to the ordinary normal schools are admitted. The chief basis of admission is the entrance examination. However, the student must also be recommended by the school from which he comes and in most instances interviews with members of the normal school faculty are also required. Because of the economic status of the teacher and the narrow educational opportunities offered by the normal schools, a large percentage of the young people applying for admittance to the normal schools have done so only after having failed in admission to other higher schools.

c. *Educational Program*

In considering the educational program, we are thinking in terms—
  (a) of the course of study or regular teaching curriculum, and
  (b) of extra-class activities, including various student organizations, discussion and forum groups organized on a voluntary basis, assemblies, athletics, and other activities in which students are free to participate.

Inasmuch as the higher normal schools for men and the higher normal schools for women require graduation from a middle school or its equivalent for admission, and the curriculum of the school is four years in length, and also because the teaching for the most part is done by graduates of the universities, much of the work being taught would seem to be comparable to the higher educational level of the Japanese School system. In the regular schools, the work would seem to be of the level of the middle school, or possibly lower since much of the curriculum of the primary school is being taught to the students of the normal school.

In all of the normal schools for men much attention has been given to gymnastics and military drill, and emphasis has been placed on the teaching of morals which has been largely a program of indoctrination in the "Imperial Way." Each curriculum is prescribed and no effort is made to take into account differing backgrounds and abilities of students.

Because of the formal, prescribed, textbook nature of the curriculum, little use is made of library material. In the regular normal schools only a few students each day make any use of the library, and while in the higher normal schools there is more opportunity for library reading and study, we found no evidence that there was any broad program to encourage wide reading and the use of library books and periodicals.

d. *Observation, Participation and Practice Teaching*

Each normal school has an attached elementary or middle school for observation or student-teaching purposes. In selected Japanese schools, we saw evidences of good teaching in a number of classrooms. A cordial, friendly, pupil-teacher relationship was found in a number of the classrooms. A number of teachers were using methods which gave opportunity for participation on the part of the pupils. Some of the classrooms were home-like and the work of the pupils was displayed on work tables and on bulletin boards. A number of teachers were using various teaching aids and equipment to objectify and motivate teaching. We also saw much very formal teaching in which the teacher was lecturing or telling the pupils, formal textbook procedures were being used and the classrooms were unattractive and uninteresting.

We also found inadequate provisions in the normal school programs for observation, participation, and student teaching. As nearly as we could discover, little demonstration teaching was being done, and no opportunity for individual or group observation was being provided. In none of the many classrooms visited did we see normal school students observing the work in the classrooms or participating as assistants to the classroom teacher. All directed observations on student teaching are confined to 30 to 40 hours during a twelve-week period in the last term. The maximum amount of actual teaching during this time does not exceed 10 hours. The remainder of the time is devoted to observation and assisting the regular teacher.

e. *Student Personnel, and Student Life Services*

We found little evidence of guidance or personal assistance to the student in the development of his personality or in the solution of his personal and educational problems. The student is selected on a competitive basis and it is assumed that every individual can meet the requirements of the program for graduation and placement as a teacher. At the time of entrance, a physical examination is given. During the school term, doctors visit the school periodically to give attention to students needing medical care. Prior to the war, dormitories were maintained at all of the normal schools and students have some freedom in setting up faculty-sponsored organizations in which there is opportunity for student leadership and expression.

f. *Graduation and Placement*

In general, all students admitted to the normal schools graduate and are placed in teaching positions. In other words it is assumed that if the student is eligible for admission, then he must be eligible to teach, and, therefore, there is no further effort at selection after the student is once enrolled in the normal school. It would seem that if such a procedure is followed, the greatest of care would have to be taken in the selection of students for admission in order that the future success of the student as a teacher could be assured. We doubt if any such assurance is possible.

g. *Preparation and Selection of Faculty*

Many of the members of the faculties of the normal schools have had no advance study in colleges or universities. Also many of the faculty members, both in the regular and higher normal schools, have had little, if any, preparation in the field of education. After appointment to a staff position in a normal school, there is very little opportunity for advance study or for a leave of absence that would enable the teacher to work towards an advance degree. If the staff member wishes to go to school for an extended period, he is compelled to resign his position.

h. *Administrative Organization and Control*

The normal schools have been entirely under the domination and control of the Ministry of Education. The administrative organization is highly certralized and there has been little, if any, academic freedom on the part of the teachers.

In the past, any teacher who deviated from the prescribed curriculum or was too liberal in his ideas could be discharged or transferred to some other position. Teachers' meetings are held regularly but there is little evidence of freedom of discussion or of faculty participation in the setting up and control of educational policies.

i. *Physical Facilities, Laboratories and Libraries*

For the most part, the physical facilities at the normal schools are inadequate, even at the schools that were not damaged by bombing. Many of the buildings are old, shabby, wood structures that are fire hazards and a menace to the health and safety of the students. Some of the normal schools have fairly modern buildings, but for the most part not well kept and in a bad state of repair. A much better condition prevails in some of the practice schools. Some of the primary practice schools have good, modern buildings and are well equipped. Some of the best instructional facilities in the normal schools are the laboratories for physics, chemistry, and biological science. The libraries are very inadequate, with limited reading room space, although under present conditions little reading room space is needed as few students work in the libraries. A considerable number of books is to be found at each normal school but there has been very little recent material purchased and there are practically no periodicals and newspapers coming regularly to these libraries.

j. *Financial Support*

The condition of buildings and equipment, and the salaries being paid to the teachers would indicate a lack of adequate financial support.

3. *Recommendations*
a. *General Recommendation*

We believe that the normal school system should be retained. However, normal schools should be reorganized on a higher level so as to offer better professional preparation and broader and more adequate liberal education. In short, the normal schools should become higher schools or colleges for the preparation of teachers. Four full years beyond the middle school should be offered by all the normal schools, although it may be necessary to certificate primary teachers at the end of two years. Later opportunities should be provided for these two-year graduates to complete the four-year course.

We believe this recommendation to be sound because the normal schools offer the best means for preparing an adequate supply of qualified teachers for the primary and middle schools of Japan. However, adequate preparation for any level in teaching requires at least four years beyond the middle school.

b. *Admission Requirements*

As previously stated, a broader educational base should be laid by requiring middle school graduation for admission. Selection of students for the normal schools should begin in the middle schools and an effort should be made to encourage young people who have the personality, ability and aptitudes for teaching to seek admission to the normal schools.

c. *Educational Program*

(a) Within the limits of minimum standards (see Section II), the faculty of each normal school should be free to determine the curriculum of the normal school and make such changes from time to time as may seem necessary. Such changes should be made after a thorough study of all available resources and should be determined on a cooperative basis by all departments and staff members concerned after free and full discussion. Studies should be conducted regularly and changes made from time to time as improvements in the curriculum seem desirable. Cooperative studies should be made by representatives of all of the normal schools working through the voluntary association of normal schools as suggested in Section II.

(b) The curriculum of the normal school should be designed to educate the prospective teacher as an individual and citizen. To this end much of the curriculum should be devoted to general or liberal education, in the humanities, social studies, natural sciences and the arts. Students preparing to teach in middle schools should, of course, specialize in their major fields but this should not prevent sufficient breadth in general education.

(c) Normal schools should be free to develop the theory and practice of education without specific direction from government ministers, inspectors, or bureaus, except as may be necessary to maintain minimum standards for certification and teaching. In all courses of education, the aim of the development of the individual should be placed on an equal footing with duty to the nation.

(d) The studies of all persons preparing to teach in primary and middle grade schools should include an ample group of courses designed to give a true perspective of the nature and organization of human society or civilization beginning with the home and local community and extending to the entire family of nations and races. In these courses there should be a study of Japanese history and culture in relationship to world history and culture. Courses in the history of Japan should accurately acquaint the student with the development of Japan's culture and institutions and should lead to an understanding of the relationship of Japan to the rest of the world. In the development of the history of civilization, the relation of society to the individual among different people should be brought out. Feudal and industrial societies should be compared. The characteristics of different forms of government and different economic systems should be dealt with. Problems arising out of the conflict between classes and nations should be discussed. Course dealing with international relations should be offered for the purpose of promoting not only understanding of Japan's relationship to world problems but should include a study of methods through which peace and good-will among nations can be maintained, and differences between nations settled without recourse to war. Special attention should be given to the United Nations Organization and all means being attempted by nations to promote world peace and security.

(e) The history of education should be completely rewritten by competent scholars to give an objective and critical view of Japanese education, with some comparison of education in other countries.

(f) The study of children should be made a prominent part of all preparation for teaching.

(g) The curriculum should provide opportunity for the study home and school relationships. Teachers should be prepared to give guidance to parents in problems effecting child growth and development and should be qualified to conduct discussion groups of parents or to participate in meetings of parents. Basic preparation should also be given in the curriculum to qualify visiting teachers or specialists who will work with the home in the solution of problems affecting children.

(h) Each normal school should provide courses, demonstrations, conferences, forums and other means for the reeducation of teachers. A first purpose should be to reorient teachers in the democratic conception of education, and second to give them opportunity for continued study and growth, both in professional and general education fields.

d. *Use of Library*

Adequate library facilities should be provided and much of the work in all of the courses should be prepared through the use of library books and periodicals.

e. *Observation, Participation and Student Teaching*

More opportunity should be given for observation, participation and student-teaching. Much observation work should be done in connection with psychology and in education courses. Considerable opportunity should be provided for graded participation in the activities of the classroom and school, and extended periods of student-teaching should be provided. All of the student-teaching should probably not be in one term, but probably should be distributed through two terms of the senior year. In the preparation of teachers for the primary schools, if teachers are to be certificated at the end of two years, then student-teaching should be provided at the end of the second year.

f. *Student Personnel Services*

Students should not only be carefully selected for admission to the normal schools, but should have careful orientation and guidance throughout their career as students. This should be done for two reasons: first, in order to insure the greatest possible development of the future teacher; and second, in order that the students may learn the principles and techniques of guidance for later use with their pupils.

Good guidance is good teaching, and the reverse is also true—that good teaching represents good guidance. The teacher must know how to guide every child in order that he may make the greatest possible growth in school.

g. *Faculty Preparation*

The teachers in the normal schools should have had the preparation equivalent not only to graduation from the four-year normal school course or college, but should have one year or more of work in a university or school having a high-grade program in the field of teacher-education. Faculty members should also have the opportunity from time to time to continue their study in order to keep up to date in their knowledge and understanding.

h. *Administration and Control*

The general control of the normal school should be at the prefectural level, a prefectural committee or board of education approving budgets and general policies, but each normal school should have freedom in its organization and control. Educational policies and changes in curriculum should be made by the faculty or by faculty-councils or committees. There should also be freedom of expression of ideas, and creative thinking on the part of every member of the faculty should be encouraged.

i. *Physical Facilities*

As soon as possible, all buildings that are hazardous and inadequate should be replaced with good, modern, fire-resistant buildings and good lighting heating and plumbing facilities should be provided. Fire-proof stacks should be provided for libraries, as well as ample space for rooms.

j. *Financial Support*

Sufficient budget should be provided for the normal schools so that adequate salaries can be paid to the members of the faculties, and so that the buildings and equipment may be kept in good condition and additional equipment, books and materials be purchased as needed.

k. *Voluntary Association of Normal Schools and Schools of Education*

A voluntary association of institutions responsible for the preparation of teachers for the schools of Japan should be formed. This association would have purposes similar to the following:

(1) To encourage cooperative endeavor in the improvement of programs for the preparation of teachers.

(2) To promote the development of teacher-education in accordance with the principles set forth in the recommendations enumerated above.

(3) To develop standards in teacher education that would make unnecessary centralized control and uniform standardization of the normal schools by the Ministry of Education.

VI. THE PREPARATION OF TEACHERS AND SCHOOL OFFICIALS IN COLLEGES AND UNIVERSITIES

A large proportion of teachers receive their education in colleges in which they receive little or no professional preparation. Programs for the preparation of teachers should be set up which are similar in their essential features to those recommended for the normal schools. That is, they should provide a broad general education, a suitable concentration of courses in the subject they intend to teach, courses in education of the kind already described and supervised teaching. Graduates of these colleges should not be permitted to teach after training in the subject matter of teaching alone.

We come now to a more particular discussion of the functions of the university in education. A large number of the graduates of the universities become teachers. The greater part of these specialize in subject matter departments. A comparatively small number specialize in education. For example, in the Tokyo Imperial University in 1943 out of 1231 students in the Faculty of Letters only 78 were specializing in education. However, a very large percentage become teachers. It is obvious, therefore, that the vast majority of the graduates do not specialize in education.

Furthermore, the students who major in other sections than in education are required to take only two units of education in order to qualify for certification for teaching. The courses which they usually take are general principles of education and history. In the section on education itself, the chief emphasis is placed on history and the theory of education. There is little or no psychology of education, no treatment of the social and cultural foundations of education, no treatment at all of problems of curriculum of curriculum construction, and very little treatment of practical problems such as those of administration, supervision, and educational measurement. In general, there is neglect of the scientific foundations of education as distinguished from the theoretical foundation, of the social foundation, of the study of child growth and development and of the curriculum.

Students who major in a particular field usually take two-thirds or more of their courses in the section of their choice. They take a few prescribed courses in closely related departments and have a slight option of other courses. There is nothing to correspond to general or liberal education. The prospective teacher then makes a highly intensive study of one particular field, has no general background of liberal education, and makes little or no study of the principle of education itself.

The remedy for this narrow and highly specialized education would involve a far-reaching reorganization of education at the university level. It may also be said that it would involve a reorganization of secondary education, since this is also highly specialized. A beginning could be made in the modification of the work of the subject matter of departments by introducing courses which would be of special use to teachers, both those who specialize in the departments themselves, and those who specialize in other departments. The courses of each department appear to be highly specialized and designed mainly for students of that department. New courses might be organized which would give students a broader view of the field. These courses might at the same time so treat the subject that they would bring out the problems of teaching that are connected with them.

It would also involve a reorganization of the work of the section on education and possibly the creation of a faculty rather than a section on education.

A beginning should be made in the reorganization of education. This work should be expanded to include those courses in those fields which have already been mentioned. Work designed particularly to meet the needs of school administrators, inspectors, and other officials should be introduced. Opportunities should be provided for teachers who wish to take advanced work, and for administrative and supervisory officials to avail themselves of the opportunity of this work in the universities. To this end, it would be necessary to liberalize the entrance requirements at least to the faculty of education so that selected and well-qualified persons who have not gone through the preparatory school may be admitted. If the secondary school is expanded and if the opportunity to enter the university is liberalized in general, this condition may be met. If not, special arrangements for the admission of students of education should be made.

The university should expedite leadership in other ways. It should have on its staff specialists who will investigate problems of learning, of individual differences, of social foundations of education, of the curriculum, of methodology, and the like. The university, in other words, should become a center of research in education. It should have the personnel and facilities to investigate not only problems in history and theory, but also those of a more practical nature. It should be equipped with the laboratories, facilities for statistical work, libraries, and, particularly, the affiliated schools in which experimentation may be performed. It should provide opportunities for advanced study for students in large numbers to carry on research in the pursuit of an advanced degree. It should conduct conferences of leaders in educational positions throughout the country for the purpose of acquainting them with the advances in the study of education, as well as to consult with them concerning problems which they meet in the field. It should provide a forum at which teachers and administrators may discuss their mutual problems and receive assistance from the specialists in the university. It should stimulate research activities and the discussion of additional problems in other fields beyond the university. In these ways, the university may create a forward movement in the whole educational system of the country which will eventually extend to its outermost bounds.

The changes which have been recommended in the provisions for work in education in higher institutions, particularly in universities, will require careful study. It is recommended that a commission be appointed consisting of representatives of universities, and also of teachers and educational officials outside the universities, to consider fully the ways in which the universities may enlarge and develop faculties or schools of education so that they may exert the leadership which it is their province to exert.

Conclusions and Recommendations

1. The universities should enlarge their programs for the professional preparation of their students who enter teaching.

2. The universities should provide specific professional preparation for administrators, inspectors or supervisors and other functionaries who are not now provided for.

3. The universities should provide opportunities for broader general or liberal education for those who are preparing to teach.

4. The work of the education department of faculty in the university should be expanded to include more emphasis on learning individual differences, child

development tests and measurement, the social foundations of education and the curriculum, and administrative problems.

5. The university should provide for extensive programs of research and thus lay the scientific and theoretical foundation for instruction in the subjects within its field.

6. The university should provide a forum for the discussion of educational problems on the part of teachers and school administrators.

7. A commission should be set up to consider how these recommendations may be put into operation.

VII. SUMMARY OF RECOMMENDATIONS

1. Prescribed and stereotyped teaching methods emphasizing memorization, conformity, and a vertical system of duties and loyalties should be modified to encourage independent thinking, the development of personality, and the rights and responsibilities of democratic citizenship.

2. A program of re-education of teachers should be set up to further the adoption of democratic methods in the transitional period, which program will gradually merge interest of in-service education.

3. Morals should be taught less by precept than by instruction related to concrete situations through knowledge of community affairs, experience in group control, discussion, individual guidance, group games, and other activities.

4. The way should be open for graduates of normal schools to continue their education so far as their abilities permit.

5. Normal schools should admit students only after completion of the middle grade school, thus eliminating the normal preparatory courses and the lower normal schools as now constituted.

6. The reorganized normal schools, at the level of the present higher normal schools, should become four-year institutions continuing general education and providing adequate professional training for teachers in elementary and secondary schools. In periods of teacher shortage, a two-year temporary certification should be permitted.

7. Other institutions for preparing teachers for certification should satisfy requirements equivalent to those of the normal schools.

8. The modified program for the preparation of teachers should include:
   a. General education, particularly in the natural and social sciences, the humanities, and the arts.
   b. Psychology and sociology, including growth and development, learning, mental hygiene, and social adjustment.
   c. History and philosophy of education re-written to include western developments and applications to educational situations.
   d. Curriculum and method, as adaptations of means to the democratic objectives.
   e. Observation and practice-teaching.

9. School administrations and supervisors, and other educational officers should have the professional education equivalent to that for teachers and should have, in addition, such special professional training as will fit them for their duties.

10. Beyond basic minimum requirements, the Education Ministry should exercise no control over teacher-training institutions, but should increase the opportunities for them to develop the theory and practice of education themselves.

11. Modification of methods in the preparation of teachers should include more freedom of discussion, with greater emphasis on originality, problem solving, and critical thinking.

12. Plant and facilities, particularly libraries, should be improved and developed as rapidly as the economic situation permits.

13. Teachers in institutions for the preparation of teachers should themselves have professional preparation beyond the completion of the program in which they are teaching.

14. Universities and other higher institutions should develop facilities for advanced study for teachers and administrators, promote research, and should exert educational leadership.

15. A voluntary association of institutions responsible for the preparation of teachers for the schools of Japan should be formed.

[*Source*: Trainor Papers, Hoover Institution Archives, Stanford University]

3. Administration of Education in Japan at Elementary and Secondary Levels
Committee III, U.S. Education Mission

BASIC EDUCATIONAL PRINCIPLES

The inalienable and universal rights of human beings to life, liberty and the pursuit of happiness are realized largely through the process of education.

Schools are established to supplement and enrich the experiences of human beings. The individual is educated as he reacts to his experiences.

That education is most desirable which results in the individual's attaining progressively throughout life his own best self.

According to the democratic philosophy, the individual human being is of surpassing worth. Those responsible for school experiences should know the needs, interests, and abilities of each individual. They should make such instructional and administrative adaptations in the school program as will increasingly serve to recognize the importance of the individual both as a person and as a member of society.

While the individual human being grows as a whole person, all phases of his being, such as the mental, physical, and emotional should be afforded adequate opportunities for development.

Human culture belongs to all persons. The school should transmit the essential elements in the inherited culture, should help interpret that culture in terms of modern life, and should provide opportunity for the adaptation and expansion of human culture.

The human mind can be trusted provided the minds of all man are *set* free. Therefore, educational opportunity, commensurtate with individual ability, should be equally available for all people regardless of sex, race, creed, or color. Racial, cultural, and political minorities should be respected and valued.

Schools should be integral parts of the communities which they serve. The more formal experiences of the school which constitute its curriculum should be closely associated with and related to the out-of-school experiences of those who go to school.

All human beings should participate as widely as possible in worthwhile experiences. The school should afford to every person concerned, whether parent, pupil, teacher, or administrator, such opportunity to participate in the development of school experiences, including policies and procedures, as is consistent with individual maturity of judgment and background.

The school should help every individual to develop strong and worthy personal, family, civic, and social loyalties. It should not exert partisan influence on the individual in the development of his loyalties but should help him acquire an inquiring mind and an attitude of open-mindedness in the process of building his loyalties. Intelligent citizenship, based on freedom of thought, communication, and criticism, should be one of the important outcomes of school experience.

REORGANIZATION OF THE

JAPANESE SCHOOL SYSTEM OF THE

ELEMENTARY AND SECONDARY SCHOOL LEVELS

A. BASIC CHANGES

The responsibility assigned to USEM by SCAF is to help provide for Japan the kind of school system (1) that will promote among the people of Japan the democratic and peaceful way of life, and (2) that will be least susceptible to control, manipulation, and exploitation for militaristic or ultra-nationalistic purposes.

Viewed from the standpoint of this assignment, we believe that the schools of Japan need correction in two basic respects.

I.

Individual human beings are of surpassing worth and their interests should not be subordinated to those of the State. A denial of this democratic philosophy has exhibited itself in many ways and at many points in the Japanese school system.

Our first and foremost recommendation is that a new philosophy, new procedures, and new structure and form be adopted for the schools of Japan. This should be done in such manner as to recognize the development of human personality as of paramount importance and the State as a means to that end.

As the first step in that direction, we recommend the discontinuance of partisan political, or *sectarian* religious teaching in the *public* schools.

The ceremonial use of Imperial Rescripts and the practice of obeisance before the Imperial Portraits, have in the past been powerful instruments for regimentation of student thought and feeling. They have served the purposes of a militant nationalism. We consider these practices undesirable in the development of personality and incompatible with a proper system of public instruction in a democratic Japan. We strongly recommend that these practices be *discontinued* (prohibited in whatever manner will most likely insure their permanent discontinuance).

II.

From the standpoint of structure, form, and procedures, individual schools and school systems may be characterized by (1) centralized autocratic controls, or (2) distributed democratic controls.

If the centralized type of school system becomes autocratic, authority proceeds from one person or one institution or one agency. It is reasonable and experience certainly indicates that the centralized system is more vulnerable from the standpoint of manipulation and exploitation by powers either outside or inside the system.

Not only has the Japanese school system been highly vulnerable from the standpoint of (possible) exploitation by outside power, but also it has been vulnerable because it involved lines of control from outside agencies directly into the very structure of the system itself.

At many points from top to bottom of the system strategic positions in the hierarchy have been filled by persons without training as educators. Many educational officials have been appointed by and accountable to the Minister of Home Affairs or his representatives.

We propose that there must be provided a framework upon which the substance of the peaceful and democratic tradition may be built. The organization of education must be weighted on the side of the development of a peaceful and democratic atmosphere in Japan. It must be made more difficult, if not impossible, to manipulate or control both the system and those whom it is designed to serve.

Therefore, we propose that two fundamental changes be made in the Japanese educational scheme, both as a whole and in its parts.

1.

All personnel dealing with the schools in relation to instruction or the administration or supervision of instruction should be trained as educators and should be appointed to their positions by authority vested in persons or agencies established as a part of the educational structure.

2.

The control of the instructional program should be dispersed rather than centralized and vertical lines of authority and responsibility should be definitely broken at certain levels of the system.

B. NECESSARY ADJUSTMENTS

I. Form and Structure

The form and structure of the school system of Japan should be changed so as to promote democratic tendencies.

The elementary school is too formal. Too much of the children's time is used in committing to memory and giving back verbatim to their masters—the teachers— much material and information not vitally connected with the lives the children live. Entirely too much time is given to partially learning a cumbersome Japanese written language. This language should be drastically changed, simplified and made into a tool to help the people rather than to handicap them.

Entirely too much time and energy is given to preparing for examinations intended to screen but all children not endowed with academic brilliance and thus deny to a great majority of children any chance for further schooling. The system involving the strict and inflexible use of rigid, extremely difficult and highly competitive examinations to determine who shall have the privilege of continuing with each succeeding higher level of education after the elementary school should be abolished. Such a system tends to develop ideas of personal superiority or inferiority and to produce a society that is stratified on the basis of artificial measures of intellectual competency. It tends to intensify the placing of political, economic and social controls in the hands of an intellectual oligarchy which cannot be expected to give major attention to the welfare of the people. Such intellectual competition should give way to a program of intellectual cooperation which looks toward the extension of educational opportunities at higher levels to all who can and will continue to improve by study.

The six-year elementary school should be entirely free and attendance compulsory. No form of tuition should be charged. The program of instruction should be such as to prepare children to become healthy, active, thinking citizens eager to develop all of their innate abilities and to be prepared to take their places in a society that is becoming more and more free.

We are convinced that girls are the equal of boys mentally. We therefore recommend that schools be conducted on a co-educational basis. We recommend that the five-year middle schools be made easily available to all the girls and boys on a coeducational basis and that they be free from all tuition costs to children. We recommend that attendance of all children be compulsory during the first three years.

These middle schools should be adapted to the personal needs of all the children giving opportunity for the development of all talents and preparing all children to live useful and happy democratic lives participating skillfully in all lines of endeavor in Japan.

Counselling help should be made available in order that each child may be helped to prepare for the work which he will do well and enjoy.

Higher schools should be free and open to all. They should be co-educational and expanded to include sufficient course offerings to serve the needs of all who wish to attend in order that they may develop personally and be better prepared to participate in the varied activities of their country.

Youth schools are inadequately housed, poorly programmed and lacking in facilities and leadership. We suggest that they be developed into full scale vocational schools. Vocational schools should provide full opportunity for the development of skill and proficiency on the part of these who desire to prepare for specific occupations.

Courses in industrial, commercial, business, agricultural, home-making and vocational education, for all who desire them, should be available in the middle and higher schools.

Evening schools, continuation and refresher courses should be provided for in the public schools.

Courses and special work should be provided in the regular elementary, middle and higher schools for physically and mentally handicapped children. Their attendance at these schools should be governed by the regular compulsory attendance laws. Special schools should be provided for the blind and the deaf.

Provision should be made for easy transfer of pupils from one course to another or from one type of school to another with the minimum loss or inconvenience to the pupils.

The ultimate success of the effort to build a democratic educational system in Japan depends on the understanding and acceptance of the program by the masses of the people. High resolves will collapse if beneath them there is no foundation of public support. Consequently, we recommend the development of a program of public adult education which will insure an understanding by all the people, old as well as young.

The teacher of Japan in all areas of education should support a voluntary unified professional organization. This national organization of teachers must be free to act on all professional and welfare matters with initiative and vigor. Although cooperating closely with all other organizations and institutions which have concern for the betterment of the condition of the people through education, the national professional organization of teachers should maintain its independence. Teachers, like all other citizens, should have freedom of thought and speech.

As needed changes are made and adequately financed in the regular public school system, we recommend that the expansion of nursery schools and kindergartens be encouraged.

Private schools which meet the regular standards set up for the public schools should be accredited. The transfer of students from *public* to *private* schools should be possible without loss or inconvenience to the pupils.

II. Administrative Organization

In order to provide the degree and type of decentralization of the Japanese school system which we believe will prevent or at least reduce materially the danger of manipulation and exploitation which has characterized the highly centralized school system of the past, we propose that school codes be adopted by the chosen representatives of the people at the State and prefectural levels to give effect to the following recommendations:

1.

At the National Level

The Ministry of Education has been the seat of power for those who control the minds of Japan. In the past, regimentation has been compelled by a system of inspectors. This system of inspectors should be abolished. In its place should be established a system of competent technical advisers and consultants who will provide inspiration and guidance but who shall have no policing or administrative powers.

The Minister of Education should be a qualified professional educator. He should be a member of the Cabinet. He and his staff should be completely free from control or domination by the Ministry of Home Affairs or by any other governmental executive officer or agency. He should be the head of the Ministry of Education. The members of the staff of the Ministry should be professional educators through whom the Minister of Education may perform his duties and responsibilities.

His powers and duties should be to:

a) Represent the government in all educational functions affecting relationships with other countries.

b) Advise other departments of the State and the Diet on educational problems.

c) Submit to the Prime Minister and the Diet his recommendations for legislation concerning educational matters throughout the nation.

d) Exercise broad professional leadership through research, surveys, publications, and reports.

e) Provide expert technical consultative services in the various fields of education such as curriculum, methods of teaching, materials of instruction, school building construction, maintenance and operation, textbooks, financial records, accounting and reporting.

f) Exercise certain specified powers of negation concerning prevention of militaristic or ultranationalistic activities in the schools, such powers to be specifically stated in law and limited to the purposes mentioned above.

g) Represent the highest educational ideal of the people of Japan and demonstrate personal and professional qualifications to uphold high educational principles.

h) Certificate teachers on the basis of objective standards.

i) Submit to the Diet the national educational financial needs.

j) Distribute all educational funds provided by the national government, such distribution to be on the basis of on objective formula written into law.

k) Perform at the national level only these educational functions which cannot be properly and adequately performed at the prefectural level by the duly constituted educational agency of the Prefecture.

Recommend [1] Establish objective standards for the recognition or accreditation of schools and educational institutions of all types at elementary and secondary levels. Recognition or accreditation shall be the responsibility of prefectural educational authorities.] [later deleted]

2.

At the Prefectural Level

Primary responsibility for the actual administration of public schools and other public educational institutions should rest with the Prefecture and with any local sub-divisions as may be determined by the Prefectural Assembly.

We recommend that in each Prefecture there be established an educational committee or agency, which shall be politically independent and composed of representative citizens elected by popular vote without political party designation. This committee shall have general charge of all public schools within the

Prefecture in accordance with laws passed by the Prefectural Assembly. It shall appoint a prefectural educational leader who shall correspond on the prefectural level to the Minister of Education on the National Level. His training and experiences should be in the field of education. His powers and duties shall be to:

    a) Represent the prefecture on all educational matters affecting relationships with the Minister of Education and with other prefectures.

    b) Advise other departments of the prefectural government and the prefectural legislative assembly on educational problems.

    c) Submit to the Governor and the Legislative Assembly his recommendations for legislation concerning educational matters throughout the prefecture.

    d) Exercise broad professional leadership and general supervision of the schools.

    e) Uphold and maintain minimum standards for the public schools of the prefecture.

    f) Appoint the teachers who shall be nominated in writing by the local school authorities.

    g) Apportion financial support voted by the profectural assembly according to an objective formula established by the assembly.

    h) Equalize educational opportunities within the prefecture insofar as possible.

    i) Approve adoption and purchase of textbooks recommended by the local school authorities. Teacher committees should be given large responsibility in the selection of textbooks.

    j) Provide In-Service Training for teachers and such other professional meetings as will tend to improve teaching techniques.

    k) Recognize (or accredit) schools and educational institutions at the elementary and secondary level in accordance with standards established by the Ministry of Education.

3.

At the Local Level

If the schools are to become effective instruments of a strong and virile democracy, they must be kept close to the people. The citizens of each locality must look upon the local schools as their schools. Administrative organization must be such as to promote the active, intelligent interest of local citizens in education. Also it should cause them progressively to assume increasing responsibility for the maintenance and success of their schools as free institutions.

It is essential that teachers, school principals and local heads of school systems be free from domination and centralized control from higher ranking school officials. It is likewise essential that these educators directly in charge of school administration at every level be held accountable to the people whom they serve.

This very process of participation in the management of their own schools offers one of the meet effective opportunities for growth in citizenship. The people will learn to live democratically as they practice its processes in meaningful civic situations.

We recommend that in each city, or other prefectural subdivision, with an elementary school population of 5,000 or more, there shall be established a lay educational agency elected by the people, which agency shall be in charge of all public, elementary and secondary schools in the respective localities in accordance with laws enacted by the Prefectural Assembly.

This agency shall nominate in writing to the head of the Prefectural Bureau of Education a professionally qualified educator to be appointed as the head of the school system for the city, town, or village, as the case may be. The duties of the head of the local school system shall be to:

a) Serve as executive officer of the lay educational agency.

b) Administer or direct the educational program of the city *town or village* in accordance with prefectural law and under the general policies adopted by the local lay educational agency. He shall recommend the teachers to be nominated and appointed for the schools under his supervision.

c) Represent the city government in all educational matters affecting relationship with other cities or towns or with the Prefectural Bureau of Education.

d) Submit to the local governing body his recommendations concerning local financial support for the schools.

e) Supervise the instruction in the schools and aid principals and teachers in the development of courses of study and the selection of teaching materials and textbooks to be recommended for adoption.

f) Survey the educational needs of his area and determine the location of school buildings and supervise their construction.

g) Encourage the organization of parents and teachers to promote child welfare, to study home, school, and community relationships for effective cooperation and to improve the educational program.

FINANCIAL SUPPORT

It is realized that the financial support of schools depends potentially on the general economic level of the society of which the schools are a part. However, the people of Japan have already demonstrated their willingness to support their schools and other cultural institutions on a relatively extensive scale. We believe they can and will, even at the cost of enormous personal sacrifice, find a way to provide more adequate and effective educational opportunities.

As we see the financial problem confronting Japan in the reorganization of its school system, it focuses in several major areas:

1. Teachers Salaries

At all levels, the salaries of both teachers and other school officials have been and are decidedly below a level commensurate with the importance of their work. Without supplements to these salaries in the form of additional service outside their schoolwork or through family subsidy in one form or another, they cannot maintain standards of living that should be possible for persons in this type of service. We recommend that the Minister of Education and the corresponding educational leaders in the prefectures develop reasonable minimum salary schedules for all school personnel and that the proper legislation be enacted to establish such schedules.

2. Class Size

As we have visited the Japanese schools, and from statistics that have been made available to us, we have found that classes are excessively large at all levels. The classes may have been smaller before the war but it is very likely they have always been too large. It may be possible to carry on a highly centralized type of instructional procedure of the memory-recitation or teacher-lecture type with large classes but these instructional procedures designed to promote democratic objectives cannot be realized efficiently with large classes. Pupil discussion, the expression of critical judgment, the development of individual initiative and desirable attitudes, appreciations, and ideals, worthy habits of conduct based on intelligent choice, cannot be realized if each teacher is responsible for too many students.

While there is still much research needed to determine the question of class size because it undoubtedly varies according to different instructional situations, it seems to us that a desirable next step for Japan would be to provide at elementary and secondary school levels for an average pupil-classroom-teacher situation a ratio of approximately 30 to 1 on an average daily attendance basis. As economic conditions warrant, it may be possible through the years to lower this number and the more favored communities should be encouraged to lower it as soon as conditions permit.

3. Supplies and Equipment

In addition to the payment of adequate salaries and the provision of a sufficient number of teachers and other school personnel to make possible a democratic school system, there should be provided an adequate supply of text and reference books, library books, and other instructional equipment. Visual and aural aids to instruction should be available for use more extensively than has been true heretofore.

4. School Buildings

It is very evident that the condition of the school plant in Japan constitutes one of the major financial problems confronting the nation. Not only have a large percentage of the buildings been destroyed but also the conditions of the last few years have caused a neglect in the program of upkeep.

We believe that new buildings, as they are provided, should include many of the developments that have taken place in school construction in the last few years. We have in mind particularly developments in fields of lighting, heating, ventilation, and the use of electrical equipment related to an expanded visual and aural instructional program. Also the buildings should be so constructed as to lend themselves to the maintenance of the proper standards of cleanliness.

5. Fees and Scholarships

We recommend that the payment of fees by the students at both the elementary and secondary school levels be discontinued. Free public education throughout the compulsory school period or through secondary school is essential if schooling is to be regarded on a democratic basis. Scholarships at public expense might be necessary and desirable to provide education to meet individual needs at the secondary school level, especially if desired school facilities are not locally available. As far as possible, no boy or girl should be denied at least a secondary school education if he desires to have such schooling and this should be true regardless of the individual's ability.

6. *General Support*

Some plan should be worked out, as a result of most careful and comprehensive study by educational and taxation authorities, for the adequate financial support of the schools. It is clear to us that this plan should define the relative contributions to be made by the State, Prefectural and local governmental units.

The basis upon which the national government should participate in the program of support should be determined on some fair and equitable equalization principle. It is in the interests of the national welfare that the national government guarantee to every child, youth, or adult in Japan a reasonable educational opportunity consistent with the national welfare. The plan of equalization should be worked out in such a manner as to give effect to this principle.

From what we have seen, there is evidently great disparity in the ability of local communities and prefectures to support an adequate educational program. At the prefectural level, the principle of equalization should again be applied in the distribution of school support. However, a large percentage of the cost of the schools should be provided at the local level to make the people feel justifiably that the schools do belong to them. What this proportion is will vary with the communities and with the conditions as they develop through the years, and this whole program should be a matter of continuous study and research.

CONCLUSION

The essence of a great school system is in its spirit and substance rather than in its form and structure. However, it has been the experience of mankind that the plan under which aspirations are to be achieved does determine direction and possible success in the attainment of ideals.

We have tried in this report to point out a few changes that we regard as fundamental next steps in the establishment of a democratic school system in Japan that may be free from political domination. We trust to the evident genius of the Japanese people to take the succeeding steps if these first steps are made possible for them.

We have found little to criticize in the hopes and aspirations of the Japanese people for the establishment of a democratic society, especially as it has been expressed to us by the Japanese people in all walks of life, who see beyond the war days and are able to look into a more glorious future for their country. But we believe there is little hope of building the kind of Japan that now resides in the minds and hearts of a large part of the Japanese people unless fundamental changes can be made in the Japanese educational scheme that will give an opportunity for the seeds of democracy to grow and flourish.

[*Source*: Wanamaker Papers, Henry Suzzallo Library, University of Washington]

4. Special Report by Shigeru Nambara, President, Tokyo Imperial University, and Chairman of Japanese Committee, to George D. Stoddard, March 21, 1946

The report below is essentially verbatim. It was given orally by Dr. Nambara as "information for the United States Committee."

FUNDAMENTAL PRINCIPLES IN THE REFORM OF JAPANESE EDUCATION

  I. *Basic Defects in Japanese Education with Suggestions for Reform.*
    A. General Observations:
      1. Overemphasis on the oriental or Japanese spirit—it is irrational, mystic and pantheistic.
         Q. How overcome this?
         A. By a cultivation of the critical attitude, by objectivity and rational thinking.
      2. There is an overemphasis on <u>rational</u> education.
         Q. How reform this?
         A. By full recognition of the worth of the individual, by self-dependence; to develop the human aspects of living, self-reliance and humanism should be the chief goal. We are in need of a true Renaissance, which was missed by Japan. Now is the time for humanism. It must penetrate into the hearts of all the people, replacing a cold nationalism.
      3. The Imperial household and the Emperor are too much of an absolute concept.
         Q. How shall we change this?
         A. By humanizing the household and the Emperor.
            The relations of the Emperor to the people should be based on mutual respect as human beings.
            <u>The SCAP directive abolishing State Shintoism was very effective</u>— the most valuable of all the directives. Of like effect was the Imperial Rescript of January 1, renunciating the divine character of the Emperor. But the decisive objectives are not achieved by this directive and the Rescript. The problem of a religious reformation has not been attacked. What religious philosophy and practice should replace national Shintoism? We need a reformation—a new kind of Luther. Confucianism and Buddhism do not meet the new spiritual needs of the people. The new role should be played by Christianity which should be given full freedom and an opportunity to show what it can mean for the Japanese people.
            While the old Constitution granted religious freedom, it was a superficial act; Christianity was truly limited in scope.

4. There has been too much ultra-nationalism and imperialism—Japan *über-alles*.
   Q. How change this?
   A. Japan must be taught to respect the individual culture of each nation and to cultivate an international spirit. The world culture of mankind should be the new Japanese ideal. That item is two-fold:
   (1) This universal world-wide culture in which Japan partakes, and
   (2) an indigenous Japanese culture.
   The two must be merged in such fashion as to create a new Japanese culture.

II. *Moral Education*

There must be an emphasis on the individual liberty and the value of personality. This is to be the ideal of education and the core of all democratic education in Japan. At the same time, we must be aware of the defects of democracy. Liberty when abused becomes caprice and irresponsibility. Therefore, the concepts of responsibility and duty must accompany the new ideas of liberty. This is especially important for the Japanese at present, for they tend to go to extremes. Since there are limits to individualism, this concept cannot be the only main principle of ethics. Also basic are social ethics, community ethics, and national ethics. In these respects there is great strength in Japanese traditions, for feudalistic ethics is not wholly bad; it is a question of redirection, of new balance and harmony.

III. *Intellectual Education*

We must emphasize the importance of the rational approach. We must turn toward the Greek type of learning, cultivating the power of critical judgment through—

(1) Free Discussion

Thus the initiative of the Japanese may be better developed than it is at present.

(2) We must advocate science education, which consists of a recognition and analysis of objective fact. This is of the highest importance. Also, the application of scientific knowledge to practical life is demanded, it is now largely lacking. We can learn much from American pragmaticism and British utilitarianism.

(3) We should also develop an interest in philosophy and metaphysics, thus unifying, organizing and synthesizing knowledge. Perhaps this is a crisis in universities, not only in Japan, but everywhere. Science alone is not enough; pragmaticism is not enough, and it becomes relativism.

(4) The right path in intellectual education includes religion, devoted to the highest values and pruposes. It carries beyond science. This does not mean that religion should be taught in the schools. Students should acquire religious insights by their own private activities in school or out. The purpose of religion is to get beyond scientism and modern philosophy.

IV. *Education for Emotional [and] Physical Life*
   1. On the emotional side, there should be an emphasis on music—especially music available to the whole world; e.g., German, French, English, Italian, Russian and American. Students in colleges are now much interested in such music; it needs strong encouragement to spread to all levels. Perhaps there are a few Japanese composers who can contribute to this world interest. During the war no orchestral instruments were prohibited; however, French, English, American and Russian music was stopped. Encouragement should come through the schools and through the theater, concerts, music societies and associations. The Government should help sponsor such enterprises.
   2. With respect to physical education, the wartime type of training should be abolished; for example, military training of the type demonstrated to the committees here. More important than the particular kind of training is the artificiality and unnaturalness that penetrates all physical training from the elementary schools up.

      Q. How reform this?

      A. Replace such stiff, mechanical uniformity with serene and gay activities which improve the body, introduce the idea of fair play and competition, and respect for others, stress freedom and spontaneity—the natural forces within children and youth rather than a rigid conformance. The other half of the problem in improving the inferior condition of Japanese physique is to carry on improvements in the Japanese diet through knowledge and habit. For example, a more scientific diet would reduce the dependence on rice.

V. *A Practical Scheme of Educational Reform*

   There should be a remodeling of the school ordinances or statutes from the elementary levels upward, fundamentally changing the objects of education in Japan. Thus far the object has been (a) to follow in the way of the Imperial Japanese and (b) the training of students as nationals. These two objectives characterized the elementary and middle schools. Even at the university, the object of study was learning considered indispensable for the state.

   Q. How reform this?

   A. (1) In the lower levels the object should be the development of humanity in the individual. At all levels we must combine humanity, objectivity, and the liberal spirit. At the university levels study must be for its own sake.

      (2) The idea of national textbooks should be abolished.

   Q. Who should choose the textbooks?

   A. The choice should be left to the schools, to the teacher or the principal, who should also be allowed to compose textbooks and teaching materials. However, at the elementary and secondary levels, the prefectural government should approve the textbooks, not capriciously, but through a qualified educational committee. Above the level of the Semmon Gakko, textbooks should be chosen by teachers or professors.

(3) There must be a freedom of study—a freedom in teaching or instruction, and in learning. There are too many regulations from the Mombusho; for example, regulations covering the contents of courses. Such matters are minutely decided, and teachers have little freedom of choice. Academic freedom must be established. During the war the Imperial universities have done fairly well on this, with certain subject matter exceptions. Private universities have suffered more in this respect, for they did not force the issue—they gave in. All universities are enjoying freedom now except as noted below: (This point is regarded as particularly confidential. It is not to be ascribed to any member of the Japanese Committee. GDS):

Through SCAP we have too much restriction on educational freedom and on freedom of speech. Not only teachers and professors but people in general are restricted. It is not my idea to contravert the principle of the occupation, but to suggest that constructive criticism might be offered on various issues. Such freedom is supposed to exist, but actually those exercising it are censored. SCAP does this in some ways more strongly than the Japanese war leaders. I do not refer to the expunging of militaristic matters or materials in textbooks but to the censorship of writings on social, economic, political and philosophic matters—in short, the work of scholars. All books are reviewed by the military, and they are censored, in advance, at times in accordance with poor standards. During the war there was no pre-censorship. Now publication cannot be achieved until the approving of the contents has been obtained. Hence, the people do not know what was taken from the books, while during the war they did. If possible, this should be changed, and at least the <u>standards</u> of censorship should be raised.

(4) The relation between public and private schools should be improved. Generally, the private schools need emphasizing in order to preserve their individual characteristics. There should be less attempted unification here by the Mombusho, for it leaves little room for deviation, originality and experiment. Even if Mombusho allows deviation, there are penalties in terms of administration standards. It may be the schools will remain small-scale for financial reasons, but they are worth encouraging. Gifts and endowments should help, along with tuition and the students should be granted equal privileges with those from other schools.

(5) <u>Private Universities</u>—The number of private universities should be reduced, for too many of them are merely money-making business enterprises—proprietary schools. On the other hand, private universities of good standing should be brought to the level of the Imperial universities. For example, Waseda. Hence, they should be given autonomy; they do not have it now. The faculties are too dependent upon the Boards of Overseers.

Hence, for both public and private universities, we should (1) encourage professors' associations; (2) arrange for the exchange of professors to some extent. However, I do not believe that a free exchange of students among the public and private universities is possible. There is a lack of facilities in the government universities and a great student demand. Under present conditions, the flow would be only from private to Imperial universities.

(6) I believe that education in special fields is well done, but that general or liberal education is weak. We can improve this by better general teaching, by more synthetic study for both teachers and students. In this way we could achieve a harmony between the cultural courses and the scientific courses. Professors could be employed on a less compartmentalized basis.

VI. *The Reconstruction of the School System*
(There was not time for expansion of these ideas, and they are presented in outline form, as given by Dr. Nambara. GDS)

1. Revise the Koto Gakko, the junior college system.
2. Model the whole scheme after the American plan, building up elementary schools, high schools, colleges, and universities in a natural sequence with wide opportunities at all levels.
3. The Semmon Gakko should become a real college system for both boys and girls—not separate for each.

    The reforms above are being planned, but Mombusho is hesitating on this. I regard these reforms as crucial, otherwise a revision of the clique system is impossible.

4. A decentralization of the educational system is highly important. There should be less authority for Mombusho; more for local committees, more at the town and prefectural level.
5. There should be better conditions and payments for teachers. There should be established a strong association of teachers, but the Japanese Educational Association does not serve as a model for this.

[*Source*: Wanamaker Papers, Henry Suzzallo Library, University of Washington]

5. Report of Committee No. 3 (Japanese Education Committee) Concerning Youth Schools et al.

A. The improvement and expansion of youth schools is of the utmost importance as they are the educational institutions of the people at large.

1. The present educational system will be completely changed as follows: the elementary school course will cover six years and the secondary school course will

last for six years, which will be divided into two stages, three years for each of them and all schools of the same level such as middle schools, girls' highschools, vocational schools will be included in this category, and youth schools will also come under this category. At present youth schools are excluded from the system of schools in general and receive special treatment in many respects. This is a great disadvantage to encouraging the pupils' study and inviting good teachers, and has a very bad effect on their improvement.

2. With regard to the question whether or not the higher course of the elementary school which admits the entrance of about 70 percent of the graduates of the lower course of the elementary school will remain, we think it suitable that it will be merged in the youth school of the lower stage lasting for three years, and that by changing the names of both of them we shall establish a new school.

3. Practically there is no difference between elementary schools and youth schools in the fact that part of the salary of their teachers is defrayed by the national treasury, but there is a legal distinction. To put an end to this distinction by unifying these laws under the name of the law regarding the defrayment of expenses for compulsory education by the national treasury will serve to attach much more importance to youth schools.

4. The execution of the compulsory education for women on this level, which is now being postponed, will be put into practice at once.

5. The plan will be made for the improvement of the school facilities which have been neglected so far.

6. There is a considerable difference between the training school for teachers of youth schools (i.e. the normal school for youth schools) and the training school for teachers of elementary schools (i.e. the normal school) regarding the treatment of their teaching staff and school buildings and other facilities. An improvement is necessary in this respect, too.

B. Matters concerning the private schools on and under the level of secondary schools.

1. The Elementary School Ordinance which denies the establishment of private elementary schools will be amended.

2. Of 3600 secondary schools one-third are private schools. Many of them are situated in Tokyo, the number of which is one-third of the total number of private schools. This peculiar phenomenon is related to such questions as how to prevent the congestion of population, but at present there is the question of the number of pupils which does not enable us to consider only the quality. But we believe it is necessary to consider how to improve them.

3. Generally speaking, the improvement of the quality of the teachers is required, and at present when it is very difficult to ask for a large amount of contribution for that purpose, there is nothing for it but to rely upon the subsidies of the state or the local associations.

4. There are some small foundations for private secondary schools, and it is necessary to expand and strengthen them. I also believe that it is a means of improving the position of private schools to establish powerful organizations of supporters and associations of schools. Usually these organizations of supporters will be composed of those who have some relationship with schools, but we can

also take it into consideration that those influential persons who are interested in education and have leisure time or can afford it may be persuaded to become members.

C. The ordinace clearly indicates that no tuition fees shall be charged in the lower course of the elementary school where the education is compulsory. But it also acknowledges the exception that according to the financial condition of the locality they can charge a very samll amount. Before the World War II the schools which charged tuition fees were 685 in number, most of which were city schools. The principle of no tuition fees for compulsory education will be strictly adhered to. Rather we are to make efforts with a view to abolishing the exceptions. But in my private opinion, it is proper to make the protectors of pupils pay the local tax equivalent to tuition fees in order to make them share the burden. The expenses for textbooks are very small compared with the prices of other commodities at present, and so apart from the ideal, I do not think it is an important question.

As for the secondary schools, our hope is, needless to say, no tuition fees for the three years' course in the lower stage in the above mentioned new system, but in present circumstances it will be difficult.

The encouragement of education has been expounded again and again by the successive authorities and influential persons in general, but the increase of the budget for education has been refused by Finance Ministry in the center and local governments in provincial districts and has not been realized, to our great regret. Therefore those who understand education will be members of the financial authorities and also people should awaken to the importance of education. At the same in various districts the independence of school districts with the right to impose tax and the making of the law which will safeguard the self-independence of the budget for education will be considered.

The Organization of Teachers
The organization of teachers' unions based on the law of labor unions is necessary. But at present when the chief purposes of these labor unions are the improvement of their labor conditions and making their positions secure, and chief measures resorted to are strikes, it is absolutely necessary to establish [ ] independent teachers' unions. That is to say, in order to facilitate for the teachers to cultivate themselves and study freely and at the same time to promote their walfare, powerful teachers' unions will be organized. I believe that local teachers' unions will gradually lead to the formation of a larger association. As for the question whether these local teachers' unions and their central association correspond to or can be adapted to the existing local educational associations and Japan Education Association, I find it impossible to express my opinion now.

Examination System
There is no fundamental solution of the examination problems except the enlargement of the present capacity of higher grade schools so that they may admit [ ] the applicants, and the standardization of the levels of the secondary schools in the higher stage. But this solution can not be realized soon and easily. Accordingly, we cannot but admit the examination system at present, and [ ] had better concentrate

our effort on how to lesson the burden caused by this "devilish examination" as it is called in Japan.

1. To bring all schools under the category of secondary schools with the same designation in form as has been stated in regard to youth schools, will be one means of solution.

2. In public schools the distribution and exchange of teachers and the equitable improvement of facilities will be taken into consideration as a means of realizing this object. With regard to the private schools which are poor in their contents, a measure will be taken to organize specially powerful organization of supporters.

3. The method of examinations has been reformed again and again with no great good result, and the report sent by the elementary school concerning their graduates are not very trustworthy. But constant attention will be paid to the improvement of the method of examinations so that people in general, especially the parents or other protectors of the pupils may be convinced of its appropriateness. It may be a good plan to organize a committee with educators, educationalists and laymen as its members, in the town where it is necessary, and make them invent a good plan, because the crux of the examination problem lies in the parents of pupils. The fact that since the air-raid of Japan proper commenced this problem has ceased to be regarded as a serious problem is an evidence for the above statement.

4. Strict superintendence will be carried out so that the examination might not be an obstacle to the regular education of the schools where the applicants come from. At present there is a bad habit of overlooking it. Without resolution and strict measures, this bad habit cannot be mended.

[*Source*: Wanamaker Papers, Henry Suzzallo Library, University of Washington]

6. Statement of Japanese Committee No. 3 (Japanese Education Committee) Concerning the Imperial Rescript [on] Education

1. In view of the present situation of Japan in Strum and Drang the history has never seen before, we, the Japanese members of the Committee No. 3 all agree to see a new Imperial Rescript promulgated, along with a new Constitution to be proclaimed in near future.

2. It is an affair of a bygone year of 1890 that the present Imperial Rescript [on] Education was promulgated, when we saw a chaotic turmoil in the field of thought and idea. The Rescript worked, it is generally perceived, as the only and sole factor, to stabilize this chaotic condition after the Restoration of Meiji. It has also worked over these fifty years as the fundamental and universal law of morality, keeping and developing the ethical base of the thoughts of Japanese people. This has been resulted not only from the fact that the Rescript is, in its character and contents, a statement setting and cultivating the moral standard of human beings, but also from the fact that it is, in its form and style, the words of the Emperor

toward whom every Japanese people entertains affection and respect just the children do toward his father.

3. There are some opinions that the basic law concerning the ethics of Japanese people is to be proclaimed by the Government, because, in new Japan, the political authority lies in, and is to be exercised by, the representatives of the people. But we deem it rather proper that it is to be expressed by the words of the Emperor who is the symbol of the state and the unity of the Japanese people, because the principle of morality is independent of time, place and person and must not be affected by any specific politics. It is the principle constant and everlasting.

It goes without saying that a Rescript is not Emperor's personal promulgation, but is promulgation to be made by advice and approval of the Cabinet which is, in new Japan, the only representatives of the people.

4. Some may again think that the Imperial Rescript may exercise oppressive influence upon the people solely because it is uttered by the Emperor, but in new Japan where the political power is in the hands of the people, we believe there will be nothing of the kind. Too much ceremonious reverence paid to the Rescript is the outcome of ultra-nationalism which has risen in recent years. In the Meiji and Taisho periods there has been no such extremities. Especially the Emperor's message issued on the New Year's Day denying his divinity will certainly work to change such attitude on the part of the people. Freedom of opinion and publication will moreover allow the free criticism of new Imperial Rescript. We may rest assured that Rescript will never hinder the establishment of democratic education of Japan because of its being the Emperor's Rescript.

Mention must be made in this connection that an Imperial Rescript [on] Education does not stipulate any contents and forms of education, but only expresses the Emperor's opinion how to establish, from the viewpoint of education, new Japan on a sound basis. It is therefore an instrument stimulating and encouraging the initiative of educators.

As a conclusion, it is our firm convication that a New Imperial Rescript will be the most useful instrument that encourages initiative of Japanese educators and realizes the democratization of Japan, thus resulting in the establishment of peaceful Japan.

[*Source*: Wanamaker Papers, Henry Suzzallo Library, University of Washington]

7. The Aims and Freedoms of Higher Learning
Committee IV, U.S. Education Mission

[I]
The Place of Higher Learning in a Free Society

The university is the crown of every modern educational system. In a free society it discharges with equal concern three great functions. First, it guards as a treasure beyond price the tradition of intellectual liberty, stimulates freedom of thought, perfects methods of inquiry, promotes the advancement of knowledge, cultivates science and scholarship, nurtures love of truth, and serves as a source of perpetual enlightment to society. Second, it prepares young men and women of talent, industry, and devotion through acquaintance with the best thought and finest aspirations of all ages and peoples, for positions of leadership in the improvement of family and community life, in the more efficient and humane conduct of industry and government, and in the fostering of understanding and good will among the nations. Third, it trains selected young men and women for technical competence and proficiency in both old and new professions, being ever sensitive to the changing and emerging needs of society. All of these things the university does in the spirit of service to all the people.

Under such a charter the colleges and universities of every country can steadily realize those aims of higher education suited to its social and economic needs. Every country through their strength can reach other countries through the freedom of mind and spirit generated in institutions of higher learning. Any nation can make its influence on mankind beneficent. The process of change in higher education of Japan must begin under difficulties. Traditionally higher education here has been both insular and insulated. In spite of the traditional burden put upon student and teacher and in spite of the restraints of war, the elements of growth have persisted. Her own scholars and scientists have the power to bring the values of higher learning to the unidentified millions of Japan—not today or perhaps tomorrow, but by following the universal patterns of intellectual progress.

In the world of science it is said that Japan's participation has been too imitative and absorptive. It is said further that science has been hampered by the language and continuing failure to meet on equal terms the scientists of other countries. Nevertheless, Japan has clearly a latent genius for independent research, as appears in the fine contributions of scientists who have been freed for exploration of many areas of human knowledge.

Clearly, the university system in Japan must rest upon the usual elements in any national program for higher education. The country must have the proportion of young talent continuously and amply provided by colleges, and there must be four faculties in the universities' standards of defined character. Recognition of the right of access to higher learning can be made clearer to the people and to the administrative powers controlling higher education as prerogatives and special advantages of the few are relaxed and redefined for the many.

Graduation from an Imperial university is given a special preference. That fact is not to be over-emphasized by those who want freer access of graduates to all positions of importance. The leadership of the Imperial universities should be maintained and fortified by emphasis on excellence in all processes of selection and achievement. All will agree that the spirit of free thought and action must dominate the processes of higher education here as in every country.

Institutionally the aims and freedoms of higher education in Japan will be realized by giving all possible recognition to the private colleges and universities of the country. Many have broad cultural objectives, others an essentially religious purpose. Both forms of institution contribute to the variety and strength of

Japanese culture. Those institutions that seem unworthy of Japan in educational standards or in their impartial concern over higher learning, surely should be discouraged or improved by new standards and new safeguards. In negative ways as well as in positive action the leaders of higher education will elevate the social values of their institutions.

The opportunity for free study and free expression must be restored to all worthy institutions in order to give Japan a normal development of public interest in new ideas. In some measure the Allied Powers have placed restrictions upon the educational processes of the country, yet such directives are not presumably to restrain minds and spirits of individual men and women from their desires "to strive, to seek, to find". Such desire is latent in the human mind and will rise above traditional or temporary repression.

The conservatism of Japan in higher education can be broken. We think, in the interest of world welfare and the welfare of Japan, that it should be. But the allied Powers can do no more than to give the people of Japan, free of political interference, the opportunity to do this for themselves. If Japan needs spiritual leadership—which gradually may be reflected in its own economic, political and cultural life—its greatest single resource will be the men and women educated and trained in its own colleges and universities. This leadership must be <u>of its own making</u>. Even with the best of intent no other nation can do this for Japan. The United States and other Allied Powers in many ways may give advice and encouragement, and over the years they may share with the Japanese the mutual benefits of international intercourse. But to convert these into an uplifting of the life of the Japanese people is a task for them alone. For the discharge of this duty the colleges and universities of Japan, the principal sources of educated trained men and women capable of leadership, have an inescapable obligation and an unprecedented opportunity.

[III]

Freedom for the Individual

From the charter for higher education that has been put at the opening of this section, some practical conclusions are to be drawn with regard to the institutions of Japan. The country lacks much more than financial support for both private and public universities. It lacks a full sense of its duties to the individual teacher who strives to serve in such ways as are described here. First in order is academic freedom and second is economic security. Each deserves full emphasis in all studies of university reform in the interests of a democratic society.

Academic freedom exists when the faculties of any university or college, public or private, are allowed to experiment with ideas as well as with apparatus in the search for new knowledge. Knowledge, in the social sense, may be hard to accept in the very society that produces the data for proof. Worse still, that society may use its power to prevent the collection of the data itself. The barrier of restraint on faculties is easy to set up in any nation, most harmful during a period of war. Recovery of spirit, therefore, is the first and greatest need today in Japan's higher institutions of teaching and research.

One sure way to make progress here is to give authority to the faculties in academic affairs, whether the institution be controlled by government charter in a formal sense or even dependent upon government for its support. Standards in the family are set by the spirit of all, and so in each human relationship within every community. The community of scholars is no exception. They will gain individually by every step toward a national association of professors and another of universities, both of these being governed by the spirit of a social responsibility to share the rights of scholar and scientist for the good of all. High standards of teaching and research are set by men and women in active service, not by statute. They themselves must participate in all efforts to raise the standard of performance and must resist all attempts to prevent any one of them from showing the truth as he understands it.

On the side of economic security, the governing powers or the individuals supplying yearly support to a university must be both responsible and conscientious. If the institution is worthy of freedom to serve society, it is worthy of freedom from intellectual surveillance. Caution is therefore necessary whenever an issue arises that puts financial pressure upon academic freedom. The aims of trade and higher learning are as distinct as those of church and state, and they must be kept so.

To be sure, the scholar or scientist has deep obligations as an individual—to his students, to his institution, and to society at large. The saying on this issue by Carl L. Becker, in his book *Freedom and Responsibility in the American Way of Life* sums up these obligations. He wrote (p. 56): "The education of college students for leadership in the community, if it be not constantly based on the results of current critical research, tends to become conventional and dogmatic and to leave the student with a body of information learned by rote and housed in a closed and incurious mind; while research, carried on by professors secure in their tenure under no obligation to concern themselves with the social significance of learning to teaching, tends to run into barren antiquarianism, as harmless and diverting and about as socially useful, as cross-word puzzles or contract bridge." These sentences were written to American readers, but they are timeless and universal.

These are words, therefore, useful to Japan today. But where shall beginnings be made with forwarding the use of higher education in Japan through higher regard for the value of the individual? How shall the minds of men and the policies of institutions be turned toward freeing mind and spirit to the highest forms of service to others?

One clear change touching the inner life was made by the SCAP directive to abolish state Shintoism. The individual has now an unprecedented opportunity to bring spiritual freedom and the new spiritual needs of the people into relationship. Not simply through an act separating one element from another, but by making both free to live individually this act has defined the future place of the spirit in Japanese life.

Another change through individual leadership will be a cultural renaissance in which man today brings new interpretations into the arts and letters of Japan. Here, as in spiritual matters, the movement through forms of indigenous Japanese culture into universal values depends upon individuals.

Third, in the fields where objective use of facts is fundamental, Japan now has another opportunity to serve mankind and herself as well. The rewriting of history and the scholarly exposition of Japan's cultural literature are tasks for highly trained, objective scholars and scientists. The world will welcome results that put Japan into accord with other countries through exchange of research findings in the fields of mythology, archeology, anthropology, language, and fine arts.

In all these directions the universities must be leaders of the way. They can become so by making every student and teacher a full member in the community of scholars according to his developed powers, and from the first a fellow member with the rights of free inquiry and of free expression. The test of any university is in its power to combine generosity of opportunity with intensity of objective criticism toward the members of its community.

The tools of his trade, briefly noted, are laboratories and library resources. The scientist wants apparatus and journals; the scholar needs the book or scholarly monograph in his hand. Therefore, as a minimum for high endeavor, these inquirers after their own forms of truth must be given better facilities here. This calls for a slow, undramatic process of building up libraries covering the primary categories of knowledge, of developing the laboratories needed by generalists and specialists: the two requirements are first an inventory and then a national program. From the present devastation may come the chance of fundamental reorganization.

Other tools of the specialists eventually will be made ready in Japan. These are the needs of the humanist plus libraries, museums, galleries of art and archeology, bibliographies and journals covering special areas. For the social scientist, in addition to the resources to be found in print, are such well-recognized needs as statistical laboratories, mechanisms and centers for gathering data on social change, access to the records of governments and institutions at home and abroad. To arouse interest in comparative studies within the fields of science, every country that has developed historical museums of science and industry has benefited; to encourage growth in creative arts, there must be places that become the sources of national expression in design, in all the recognized mediums of artistic expression, and in music.

Such measures for freeing the individual mind in a university setting will depend for success upon the quality of mind received from the Semmon Gakko and Koto Gakko. Japan has at this point the problem of every country in devising terminal education for its more general needs of society, at the same time developing under encouragement the powers in individuals who will be ready for the freer growth processes of university life. Specialization in the university should be less consuming of time and less compelling in its drive than today is true in typical universities of the country. The well-developed product of the Semmon Gakko and Koto Gakko centers for both men and women must still have freedom in the university to develop individual qualities of mind and spirit. It is entirely clear that the educational planning of Japanese universities is to include reforms that will give to the individual these chances for a greater fulfillment of personal powers. That fulfillment is to come by a use of freedom with responsibility, by a wider contact with the work of other scholars and scientists as a means to his own interpretations of humanity and his own discoveries through nature.

(*Note on the draft report of the subcommittee on higher education in Japan*)
This is decidedly a Univ. of Chicago product, reflecting ideas generated there by George Counts and David Stevens before leaving for duties elsewhere. It deserves a note.

Teams of four were set going after two weeks of survey and conference with Japanese specialists—each team to develop a statement for discussion with a view to its approval by the 24 ahead of final draft for the Japanese government and its educators on the future steps at all levels, for the revitalized and modernized programs.

This committee on higher education and research had as members Compton, then a president of a Washington state university and by profession a lobbyist for lumber interests in Washington—excellent personality, quite lacking experience but made chairman; Miss Gildersleeve, of Barnard, who with DHS drafted a few sectors before work with Counts; Miss McAfee, then president of Wellesley and head of the Waves, who sat in only one brief session before an early departure on a chartered Navy plane; Counts, the strongest generalist in the entire commission, with balance and depth in judgment.

At the critical time Compton went to visit an institution saying he would work on a draft. Counts and I in Tokio did a considerable review with Japanese of findings, and wrote a statement. That and the one brought by Compton were read, as were all, to the full committee. Stoddard's comment was to give him ours, as he really could do something with it. This is the rough draft given over as asked.

In the final of four weeks, evening sessions covered all the sub-committee reports. Noteworthy is that on teacher training and what came of the discussion. All members had come out of Teachers College, Columbia. As it was read and ended, Charles Johnson, president of Fisk University, spoke after the long silence: "That could have been written as well on Morning-side Heights as in Japan." The report was returned to be done over. At the final dinner before we left, this committee—under Stoddard of California—asked to give a song. They stood before the dinner group of 25 Army officers and the committee, to sing "I'll go where you want me to go, dear Lord," etc. through the significant third line "I'll say what you want me to say, dear Lord."

Eby, a Chicago specialist in Labor, left the group on landing to spend all his time with Japanese labor organizations and so to create a remarkable, objective statement on such values.

[*Source*: Stevens Papers, Joseph Regenstein Library, University of Chicago]

8. Recommendations of the Japanese Education Committee

I. IMPERIAL RESCRIPT ON EDUCATION

1. Although the former Imperial Rescript on Education unmistakably manifests universal ethics, it is inadequate for the future spiritual life of the people. It is desirable that an new Imperial Rescript on Education make clear a new national educational plan and also show a new path for the spiritual life of the people. This

will be the foundation of a peaceful Japan. The Imperial Rescript should apply not only to teachers and students but to the entire nation.

    2. The following points are desirable in the Rescript:

        a. Humanity (Full development of the individual and mutual respect, generosity and harmony, religious sentiments, etc.)

        b. Spirit of self-government (Spontaneous and creative life, etc.)

        c. Logical spirit (Ability to criticize, contemplate, etc.)

        d. Social life (Freedom and responsibility, self-government and law-abiding spirit, social justice, etc.)

        e. Family and neighborhood life.

        f. National life, (Community of Japanese People).

        g. International spirit.

        h. Peace and culture.

Such various sentiments as the above should be stressed. It is desirable that these points just mentioned not be merely listed and that the Emperor avoid making the Rescript in the form of a command. The Emperor should manifest to the people that he, more than anyone else, is concerned for the nation's future and has a great respect for education.

3. In the former Imperial Rescript family morals, social morals and national morals were clearly indicated but Universal Morality, which is the essence of humanity, is more fundamental than these.

Those sentiments which were mentioned in "2" are, in general, this Universal Morality and they are missing from the former Imperial Rescript. It made national and Imperial prosperity the first and the last object of education. It appears as if the values of the individual and the human race were disregarded. It is requested that a revision be made on these points. Such phraseology as "Ye, royal subjects ... must" should be avoided.

4. The Imperial Rescript should be simple and friendly and if possible should be written in the grammar of the spoken language. As a whole it is desirable that it follow a form similar to that of the New Year's Day Rescript.

II. ESTABLISHMENT OF EDUCATIONAL AUTHORITY

Basic Recommendations

5. Although there are various methods of considering the establishment of educational authority, this Committee has decided to follow the "Board of Education" system suggested by the U.S. Mission.

The U.S. Mission's recommendations cannot be realized in Japan as presented. National conditions and the history are different. However, it is worthwhile to consider fully the recommendations for the establishment of the national (elementary) and secondary school educational authority.

6. In general we are agreed on the following points as a practical plan:

    a. Limitation of supervisional authority of the Mombusho and local governmental offices over school affairs should be general.

    b. A District Educational Association (hereafter to be called "Board") should be established in the prefectures and the educational committee system should be discontinued.

The Board of Education

7. The following provisions are recommended for the establishing and functioning of the Board of Education:

a. The Board should be established by law.

b. Although the Board is under the supervision of local government it should be a legislative organ.

c. Ten board members should be the standard and they should be selected from among active teachers, district educational officers and laymen. The educators who are to be board members should be selected by the teachers and the laymen representatives should be selected by general election.
They should meet certain qualifications and the number of representatives from each group must be decided after study; but the number of governmental officials should not exceed two in a Board of ten.

d. Prefectures should be divided into several districts and a Board should be organized in each district; the number of the members will have to be determined. If the supervised area is too large, the committee will be out of touch with local conditions. However, if the number of committees is too many the members will become influenced by personnel considerations.

e. The Board will naturally carry on the duties connected with the national (elementary) schools and the secondary schools of its area. It must first realize a system which will correct the feelings of superiority and inferiority between the teachers of these two school groups. Accordingly, the educators' qualifications, the training organization and treatment of these two groups must be unified.
The revision of the salary law and government official system which was effected April 1 agrees with this plan but greater effort must be made to do away with the discrimination between these two groups.

f. The committee can advise the government on these matters: appointment of teachers, the selection of textbooks, (abolition of national textbooks) and standard curriculum. The school supervisor should give advice and instructions only on matters which concern school management and should discontinue participation in matters of personnel. He can submit to the governor and the Committee a report giving his opinions on matters pertaining to personnel.

g. The salaries of the teachers of the national and youth schools are determined by law to be paid by the government and prefectures. So in regard to this point the establishment of educational authority cannot be disturbed. In order to lighten the problems of asking for assistance from parents' associations and municipalities in meeting school expenses and also to establish educational authority, it is necessary to fix the amount per student. But this amount should be the minimum expense to maintain the school; and if school and municipal authorities cooperate, educational authority can be sufficiently established. The minimum amount will depend upon local conditions and the type of school. This will be determined by the Committee. The government and the prefecture should, moreover, pay the school expense.

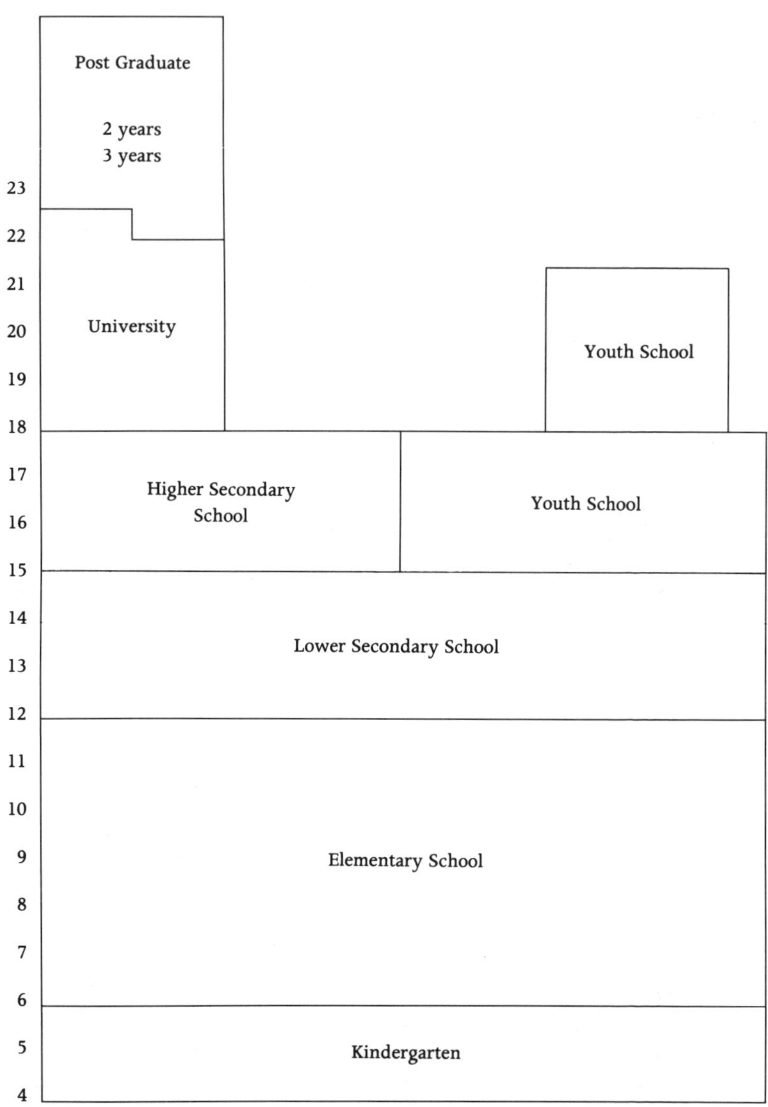

Chart A: The First Plan

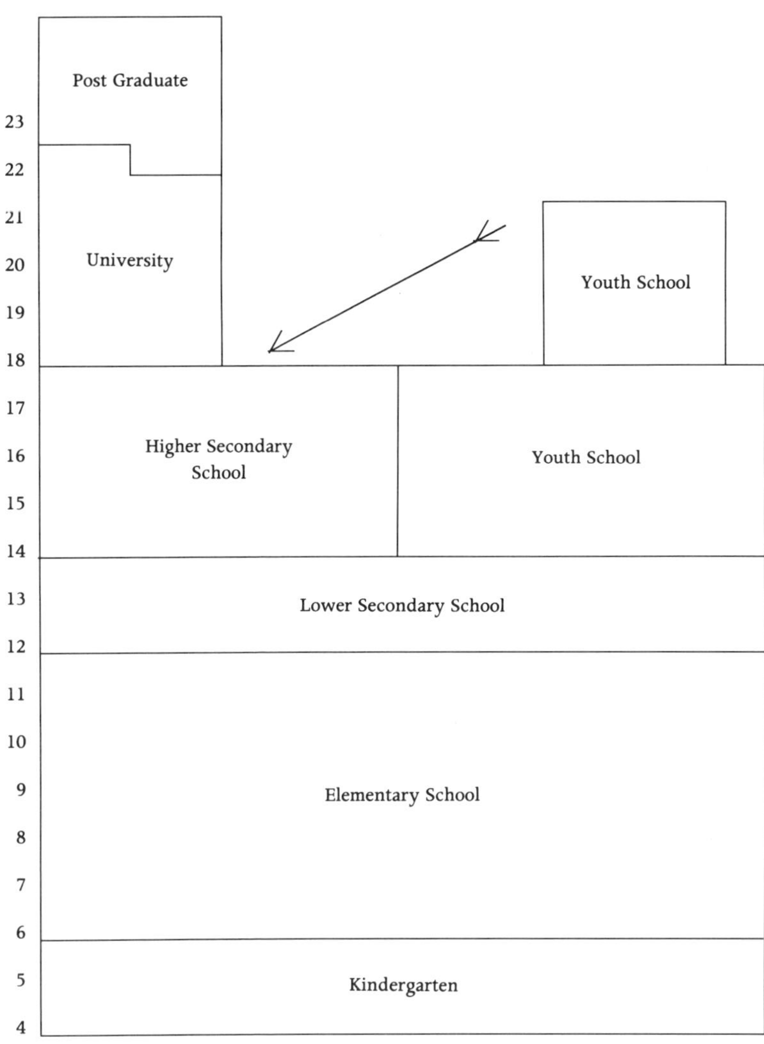

Chart B: The Second Plan

III. THE SCHOOL SYSTEM

Present System

8. Following are the three school systems through which at present all graduates of the national school must pass.

1. Secondary, College Preparatory, and University.
2. Secondary, College.
3. National School Higher Elementary, and Youth School.

The first is the best and the second and third systems are the second and third best.

There is no connection between these school systems. These systems have contributed to the establishment of class distinctions among the people and are inadequate in giving equal opportunities for the betterment of the peoples' lives and encouragement to learn in accordance with their abilities. Those who pass through the first system enjoy the best situation in having more numerous opportunities to obtain higher positions than those who graduate from the second and the third systems. Regardless of superior abilities and characters displayed in their secondary school period, those who enter the College are handicapped in continuing their education in universities and are placed in an inferior position compared with graduates of the first system. Furthermore those who pass through the third system are not allowed to shape their courses and it is practically impossible for them to enter higher schools.

To have distinction in society may be more or less unavoidable but in this democratic era should not an educational system that tends to foster class distinctions be changed?

9. As to the reformation of our school system, there was proposed more than thirty years ago by educators of vocational schools a plan which advocated two levels rather than the three: (secondary, vocational, higher vocational, and engineering dept. of the university.)

Mr. Tairoku Kikuchi also gave an opinion and later in 1937 the Education Fraternity proposed a plan. They all agreed upon the unification of the first and second of the present systems. The plan of the Education Fraternity was discussed by the Educational Investigation Committee in 1937. It was supported by many educational leaders but its adoption was defeated by one vote.

Recommendations

10. Present national conditions however, are different from those of 1937. After much discussion the "Japanese Committee to cooperate with the U.S. Mission" has now drawn up two plans with which we hope to promote the democratization of our educational system as well as raise the cultural standard of our people. These plans are to be regarded as references and not as decisions. These two plans are shown graphically in Charts A and B.

11. The first plan sets up the following system:

a. A kindergarten period of two years from the age of four to six. One year, from five to six, to be compulsory if possible.

b. Compulsory entrance to a 6-year system Elementary School at the age of six.

c. Three years of Lower Secondary School (or Secondary School) to be compulsory. A general education and not vocational.

d. A three-year Higher Secondary School and a three-year Youth School, either of which may be entered after the Lower Secondary School. The Youth School will provide vocational training.

e. After three years of Higher Secondary School a four or five year University, and all graduates of the Higher Secondary School regardless of the type are to be admitted to the University.

f. Three years of Experimental Course for those who finish the three-year Youth School. Those who complete the Experimental Course will have the same qualifications to enter the University as the graduates of the Higher Secondary School.

g. The University is the highest form of educational institution, but for those who wish to continue their studies of theories and their applications, a post-graduate course is to be provided within the university. Qualifications to take the post-graduate course should be equal for all those who graduate from any University.

h. The present Normal School should be reformed and changed to Teachers' College and the qualifications to enter the Teachers' College should be the same as those for any other Universities. While graduates of the Teachers' Colleges can become teachers of either the Elementary or Secondary Schools, those who graduate from other Universities can also become teachers after a certain probationary period. The certification for teaching in Higher Secondary School is to be granted to those who specialize for a certain period and who can pass a State examination in their special fields.

12. The second plan differs from the first as follows:

a. Lower Secondary .... 2 years
b. Higher Secondary School .... 4 years
c. Youth School .... 4 years.

Explanations of these plans:

13. The people as a whole feel that:

a. It is desirable to extend the period of compulsory education. The present system calls for eight years and it is desirable to extend that to nine years. (The reason for this is that under the present system, it is not possible for one to obtain an adquate knowledge of economics, politics and culture. At present it is even difficult to understand fully the important news articles of the daily papers. Although this may be due partly to faults in educational methodology, the period of education is too brief.)

b. In establishing a nine year compulsory school system it is desirable to have a two level system . . . a six year elementary and a three year lower Secondary School. The reason for this is that physically and psychologically a student will change greatly during this period and to retain a student in a one level system for this period of time will result in difficulties. After graduating from the elementary school, a student will receive a new stimulus by entering the Lower Secondary School.

c. In the 2nd plan it is possible to change the present Higher Elementary School to the Lower Secondary School. This is a special advantage of this plan. However, in a two year school system there are also disadvantages. If it is impossible to extend the period of compulsory education to nine years, then the 2nd plan should be used.

d. The present school system divides the students who go to the Secondary schools and those who enter the Higher Elementary Schools at the termination of the lower elementary period. This has a tendency to indicate class distinctions while the students are still in the elementary schools. It is desirable that the separation of those who are to continue their education and those who are not to continue be made after the termination of the period of compulsory education. Since the student has received a general education in the Lower Secondary School, he can continue such studies in the Higher Secondary Schools; and he can also obtain a vocational education. Therefore it will be possible to give the middle class of people an adequate education. The reason for a four-year Secondary School system in the 2nd plan is that it follows an eight-year system. Also in these four years the aim is to give the student an education comparable to that received in the second year of a Higher School or a College.

e. The greatest difference between the present system and the systems proposed in plans I and II is the elimination of the College. The Governmental Colleges of today constitute industrial, agricultural, commercial and other such schools. But these are similar to the industrial, engineering and economic department of universities. It is difficult to give any particular reason for the existence of these Colleges. There is also this opinion. Even from the standpoint of technology, if there is a technician of the level of a higher secondary school graduate to work under the supervision of a university graduate technician there is no special reason for the necessity of a technician who is a graduate of a College. The College graduate is the average of these other two. It seems that there is an undesirable competition between the graduates of a university and those of a college. There is also this current belief that the college graduate becomes discouraged because he is regarded in an inferior light. Thus it is preferable that the present so-called "Colleges" and other such schools either be abolished or if possible, become real colleges.

f. By the proposed plan there is to be a 4 or 5 year university ... which will mean the shortening of the period between Higher Secondary School and graduation from college. This may result in the lowering of the caliber of a college graduate. However, if the Higher Secondary School should give the student an education that is comparable to the two years of the present Higher School and if in the first year of college a general course is given, this danger can be eliminated. However, even if the caliber should drop slightly, it will be a greater benefit for the advancement of the people's culture to have four university graduates rather than to have one university graduate and three College graduates as under the present system. Furthermore, if the post-graduate teaching methodology is improved, it will be possible to turn out into society a greater number of talented citizens.

g. The Higher School has an advantage in that it is possible to turn out men of talent. This feature is missing in our proposed plans. The merit of the

Higher School is said to have been that it gives the student a broad outlook on life. However, is this obtainable only in a Higher School? There appears to be a difference in the fostering of this sentiment in the Higher School of 1918–19 and that of today. The question of considering whether after graduation there is another school is said to have a relationship with the fostering of this sentiment. If this is so, then this same attitude can be sufficiently fostered in the Secondary School. The main point is the establishing of confidence of a higher level school in a lower level school.

If the special feature of the Higher School is the developing of a man of talent, then only the students of approximately thirty (30) Higher Schools will enter the universities and only they will receive the privilege of becoming the future national and social leaders. Another special feature of the Higher Schools is the study of foreign languages for the purpose of continuing college education; this is an error in the teaching of foreign languages. It is preferable that this training be given in a previous school.

h. All conventionalities concerning the Normal Schools should be done away with and for training those who wish to engage in the field of compulsory education, a Teacher's College should be established in every prefecture. It is extremely convenient to have such an institution to fill the vacancies in the teaching staff. The Teachers' College, however, should be entirely on the same level as that of any other university. The students should have no special privileges and although they can work as elementary and primary secondary school teachers, they should not be placed under any special obligations. If the Higher Secondary School is to be comparable to the second year of the present Higher School, the teachers in these schools should be equipped with considerable specialized knowledge. Consequently they should study two years or more in Post Graduate work and should pass an authorized examination.

IV. TEACHERS' ASSOCIATIONS AND LEAGUE OF TEACHERS

Main Points

14. The teachers' organization and the league of teachers based on the guarantee of the Constitution of freedom of associations and with the spirit of mutual aid and cooperation, were composed of educators as self-governing voluntary organizations. Therefore, governmental educational authorities and school directors cannot suppress the establishment of the organizations. Rather they should encourage the movement and moreover should aid in the continued healthy development.

Purposes

15. The teachers' associations and the league of educators should autonomously and systematically endeavor for the attainment of the following objectives:

a. Improvement of living conditions and security of position.
b. Refinement of intellect, fostering of morality, advancement of social service.
c. Reform of educational system, perfection of educational content, democratization of school adminstration.
d. Advancement of welfare, mutual aid.

Organization

16. The organization, management, etc., of these teachers' associations and league of educators may be considered as follows:

    a. The unit of organization is composed of teachers, (including directors) of the same level of schools in a certain district (for example, city, ward and county). The committee is to be selected by members.

    b. The above-mentioned units of organization should compose a still larger unit of organization (for example, prefecture) and these units should cooperate with units of the same type and level to form a national incorporation. (Horizontal incorporation).

    c. The above mentioned district and national incorporation of certain levels should incorporate and cooperate with other horizontal incorporations of other levels and build district and national incorporations. (Vertical incorporation).

    d. The above mentioned vertical organizations are to cooperate with other vertical organizations to form an all-inclusive incorporation.

    e. Upon the establishment of the above mentioned all-nation organization, it should absorb the system and the activities of the present Greater Japan Education Association and the Greater Japan Education Assistance Association.

Relationship to Labor Unions

17. Since the teachers' associations and the leagues of educators' chief objective is the betterment of living conditions their character is very similar to that of the labor unions.

V. EDUCATIONAL METHODS

Introduction

18. The result of education is realized by the method of education; and the result will vary according to the methods. At this time when the entire education of our country is undergoing a reform, the problems of teaching methods, along with the problems of school system and educational system, are extremely important. Especially important is the study of the student's individuality and sociability in order to develop the students' spontaneous active character.

19. The U.S. Education Mission along with other important problems undertook the problems of educational methods and the fact that it has pointed out the weaknesses of our past educational methods indicates to us that they had this point in mind. However, these weak points have been recognized by our progressive educators and this committee, taking this opportunity, urgently desires the realization of this renovation.

20. The teaching methods must not swing too radically to one side just as the aims also must not be one-sided. Morality, intelligence, health, knowledge and other factors which have important bearing must be considered. Again the teaching methods must not be all technical methods and the personality of the instructor and the spirit of education must have deep connections. The reform of educational methods must be rapid and the changes must be broad, deep and wide.

Basic Ideas for the Reform of Educational Methods

21. Educational methods must be manipulated minutely and precisely, and they must be at all times practical. However, the direction of education can be directed by ideas concerning educational activities.

22. The major basic ideas are discussed as follows:

a. Student and subject-matter are the main points on which the actions of the teachers are based. Neither student nor subject-matter can be slighted but heretofore there has been a tendency to place greater emphasis on subject-matter. We can go so far as to say that there was a tendency to have education for subject-matter. In this case the methodical contrivances and the educational interest of the teacher swung to the educational method of <u>teaching subject-matter to students</u>. Even though it may not have been cramming-ism and memory-ism, the methods terminated in the agony of making the students absorb. Therefore there was no opportunity for the development of the students' spontaneous activities. Contrary to this, in case the main points of education are centered on the student life activities, the interest and the methodical contrivances of the instructors will be directed toward the student and be studied on the basis of principles of educational psychology. The curriculum will thus be the tool for the attaining of this objective. The student is not for the curriculum but the curriculum is for the student. Naturally, curriculum must be respected for its cultural value and its various psychological characteristics. And the concern of the teacher should be centered heavily on this point. However, the student must not be made a receptacle for the curriculum. This is most important. Thus there is the distinction of education centered on subject-matter and education centered on the student.

b. School is the place for educational activity.... Is it merely a place of education?—or a place of educational activities? One of the factors which direct the educational activity of the instructor is his outlook on schools. Although the school is the place where the instructor teaches, does this mean that he is merely teaching in schools or teaching with schools?.... These two thoughts exist. If it is to be the former outlook, the direct activities of the teacher must consist of such teaching methods as lectures, explanations and such. Therefore, here the educational methods will be planned and developed in the narrow sense of ped[o]gogics. When the child is directly led by the activities of the instructor as an adult, the life of the child himself might not fully develop. However skillful the ped[o]gogics, the positive and the spontaneous development of the child will nevertheless be hindered. If the school is to be a place for the platform of the teacher and a place for the little desk of the pupil, then this is an unavoidable result. In the second outlook, the school does not exist as merely a place, but as an establishment where the student's activities of self-learning are drawn out vividly, abundantly, systematically and completely. The school itself must be the educational method. Child psychology proves that the child possesses lively spontaneity, interest, originality, and creativeness. These traits, in order to be transformed into real life activities, are dependent upon environmental opportunities. If we are to rely on merely an empty, walled classroom, much cannot be expected. The real character of school education can be attained only when environmental opportunities are provided. In such a school the educational method whereby a child himself educates his own life by action can be realized. In short, the latter can be said to be an educational method based upon life instead of the teacher. The educational enrichment of environment and the guidance of life can be fulfilled only by the teaching methods of the educator. Therefore, it is actually not a neglect of the teacher. However, it may result in much effort and labor on the part of the educator. Furthermore in regard to this point, our schools are extremely poor, not only because of economic reasons but also could it not be that our concepts regarding the school are too conventional? Unless these school concepts and the important points concerning school adminstration are corrected, new results in educational methods cannot be realized. Various past educational studies clearly reveal this fact.

  c. Textbooks are tools of educational methods. The textbook is representative of the curriculum. Therefore, factors which are considered in the establishment of the curriculum indicate the position of textbooks in teaching. However, under the old Japanese concept of education which placed too great an emphasis on respect for books and letters, the textook held a peculiar position; it had a tremendous influence upon educational methodology. If the textbook is to be the nucleus of education, the life activities of the child become passive. At the least it becomes merely a stimulant of reading interest and in reality terminates in the tendency to absorb knowledge. If this be true then what type of book can be called a real textbook? This cannot be easily answered. A school, as a place of self-learning, should have two types of textbooks ... the many books which the student may use for his own reading, recitation and reference as real materials for learning, and the others which are the guide books which will stimulate his advancement of self-study and self-learning. The current textbooks belong to neither of these two classes and in attempting to serve both purposes they bring about tremendous difficulties. The proper thinking on textbooks is that they should constitute both the result and the starting point of teaching methods.

23. For the realization of better educational methods based upon the basic ideas previously described, we can make the following statement of facts necessary for their realization:

  a. The study of educational psychology both before and after becoming teachers is important. It goes without saying that this study is currently considered as an essential feature of the science of education. But it is unfortunate that in our country this is so extremely deficient. In other words, knowledge of educational psychology has not permeated into the real educational method and also there is a lack of actual study of educational psychology which is applied psychology. A plan for solution of this difficulty is not to rely upon individual experiments for our educational psychology but to establish a single large experimental institution for this purpose. Although study of our entire education is necessary, educational psychology must not be neglected. Since the study of educational psychology should be based upon actual educational experiences in order to conduct accurate experiments, greatest emphasis in this study should be placed on re-education after the individual becomes a teacher.

b. School management for the completion of various provisions as aids in teaching methods is important. This point concerns school management. Considering the present conditions within our country we cannot hope for too much. However we urgently desire that there be understanding and efforts on the part of the principals and teachers as well as the school supervisors. Student libraries, specimens, experimental apparatus for various courses, magic lanterns, moving pictures, radio and school work-shops are essential items of a school. Before the student actually steps out into real life and before he enters into a professional vocational life, he should be given an overall vocational training. Thus equipment for various vocational activitives must be prepared.

c. Liaison between various social education establishments outside the school and their systematic use are necessary. It is extremely advantageous for the schools themselves to have various establishments as a part of educational method and also to make broad application of social education institutions. The teacher must endeavor to make these applications and should have an active interest in these institutions. For example, libraries, museums, zoos, botanical gardens, fine arts museums, theaters and the like constitute an extension of school education. Up to now these institutions were simply places to visit but their application must not stop here. If they be utilized systematically, freely, and fully as a part of the classroom, they will then constitute an advantageous self-study of any particular subject and moreover will be a special method of public training. Another thing which must be considered as a part of this problem is the value of the use of the radio in education. Although these things have been discussed previously, the actual application is far from satisfactory. We cannot help but hope for understanding and enthusiasm between the radio officials and educators.

d. Application of various methods to guide the learning attitude of the student is important. The problem of educational methods is the problem of the student's learning attitude. Previous statements were made with the view of developing learning attitude. The instructor must not be negligent in application of various educational methods. Although there may be numerous methods, teaching is not an educational formality of teacher-pupil. The pupil must himself work, experiment and the pupils themselves must question, negotiate, help and be helped; and thus in this manner individually and socially, spontaneously and actively the development of character can be fostered. For this purpose work, especially cooperative work, group study, mutual study based upon discussion, self-governing group activities and the like are very effective teaching methods. These should not be adopted merely as new types of educational methods. Only if they arise as the result or true spontaneity on the part of the child, can the true educational significance be manifested. Play best displays the true spontaneity of a child. With the understanding of the value of play, a study can be made on the processes of evolution of play to work. The results of this study can be used to establish a principle for the guiding of the child's self-learning attitude. In kindergarten play guidance is the most important, and in this meaning kindergarten education can be thought of as the basis for the formation of learning attitude in the elementary school.

Abolition of obstacles in the realizing of correct teaching methods.

24. Educational methods is at all times a practical problem. Even though there be such things as theoretical studies and practical techniques, if there exist obstacles in the real condition of the school and teacher the realization of these theories and techniques will be difficult. These obstacles are to be found in these places: educational system, school system, teacher's problems and the like. Unless the problems be solved from various directions, there is nothing that can be done. The present condition of education in our country is truly deplorable.

25. The major problems are discussed as follows:

a. Too many students and classes.

    It can be said that all new educational methods place great emphasis on the individuality of the student and also are based upon individual activity. However, in a situation where the number of pupils exceed sixty, free and orderly action becomes practically impossible. Therefore it is a choice of either confusion or strict discipline. To increase the number of teachers and to divide the classroom into numerous parts do not solve the problem. The number of pupils must be lessened. From the standpoint of educational methods this problem must be solved quickly.

b. Unification of curriculum.

    If the development of the life of the child is to be the chief objective, then a curriculum must not disregard type of school, year, the individual child, the child's ability to advance and his character. It is apparent that because a unified fixed subject-matter was sought the manipulation of teaching methods was obstructed. There exists a misconception concerning subject-matter in both family and society which must be immediately corrected.

c. Abolition of system of ranking students in accordance with examination grades and entrance qualification examination.

    The above is a typical example of the type of standerdization that is prevalent in our current school system. There is no greater obstacle in true educational method toward developing the life of the child. Because of this both teachers and students were shackled by curriculum-ism and memory-ism. If examinations are to be used, they should be simply a method of teaching and should be based on well-selected problems. The examination should not be a law of judgment of the student's standing.

d. Dismissal of teachers who are not trained in educational methods.

    The qualifications of the instructor are naturally his personality and his knowledge of the subject matter. However, insofar as the main object of education is the life action of the child, a teacher who is not trained in scientific educational methods does not possess the proper qualification. During the war assistant teachers who were untrained in educational methods were used in the Elementary School and this had a negative effect on the children. In the secondary schools the teachers had a tendency to place greater emphasis on the student's absorbing knowledge than on teaching methods.

e. Overworking of teachers.

The teaching methods, especially the method of making the life activities of the student the main objective, cannot be realized unless the teacher himself is full of life. The current social respect for the teacher, the understanding of his daily obligations and security of status and also that of living cannot be said to be proper. Unless there be a solution for this shortcoming the biggest problems of educational methods cannot be solved. This is a very unfortunate thing for education.

VI. NATIONAL LANGUAGE QUESTION

Simplification of the National Language

26. The present-day national language contains an overabundance of incomprehensible Chinese words and difficult-to-read Chinese characters. Even in expressions there are intermingled many difficult Chinese and European meanings. Because of this situation, the language life of the people is hindered and the education of the nation is incomplete. These are well-known facts.

Although movements to eradicate these difficulties have been made repeatedly since the Meiji era the results are still unsatisfactory. Today when it is the time to reform all things there is a growing interest among the people concerning a new movement for the simplification of the national language. The Ministry of Education should recognize naturally this tendency, renew former efforts, and in order to develop national culture make all positive efforts in this direction as soon as possible. The day of debate has already passed.

27. The field of simplification of the national language is extremely broad. However, we must first emphasize the following points:

a. Unification of Style.

There are many styles at present. There is the spoken style (vernacular), the regular literary style, and the epistolary style. Instead of adhering to the old ways of writing, all writing should follow the spoken style. National laws, instructions and their applications, correspondence of the government and of private firms should conform to this style. "Kana" (Japanese syllabic alphabet) used in the laws should be "hiragana" and furthermore sonant signs, symbols for semi-voiced sounds, and punctuation marks should be used.

b. Limitation of Chinese Words.

Difficult Chinese words and those which cannot be understood by sound alone should be eliminated. Use of phonetic equivalents must be discontinued. Care should be exercised in using technical terms to make the words as simple as possible, both from the standpoint of charaters and of wording.

c. Limitation of Chinese Characters (Kanji).

Difficult "kanji" should not be used. Even the use of simple "kanji" which are difficult in usage should be avoided. There should be a limitation not only of the number of characters but also of the usage. There should be a limitation of the varied readings of the "kanji" ("on"—Chinese sound; "Kun—Japanese sound). It is also necessary to limit the forms of characters.

d. Solution of the problem of "kana" usage.

As a result of the limitation of "kanji" there will be a greater necessity for using "kana" instead of "kanji" (Chinese charaters). Consequently the problem of "kana" usage becomes important. There is very little question regarding the use of "kana" to express a Chinese sound. However in the use of "kana" to express Japanese words there is still a great tendency to use the historical method. Consequently it is perhaps better to use "kana" phonetically for the present.

e. Solution of the question of horizontal writing.

In horizontal writing, the writing should be from left to right as a general rule.

Standardization of the National Language

28. The simplification of the national language will not result in the lowering of the level of national language culture. On the contrary, it may be expected that the beauty of simplicity in the national language will be manifested. At any rate this language has been transmitted to us from our ancestors and we have as our duty its improvement and also its transmission to our descendents. It is needless to say that the standardization of the language must not be hindered. In order to maintain that standardization and also to improve the language we must always take loving care of our national language. There are numerous items of investigation and study concerning the national language. Among them are the problems of the establishment of a standard language, the study of standardized pronunciation, the selection of a standardized vocabulary, the arrangement of standardized diction, and adopted foreign words. These problems should not be left to scholars alone; the governmental education authorities should not be indifferent to the language policy.

The Problem of Romanization

29. It is all right for elementary school students to study "romaji" (western alphabet); but we cannot agree to the system of mixing "romaji" with "kanji" and "kana" in horizontal style in elementary school textbooks, with the view of eventually replacing all characters and "kana" with "romaji". It is still too early for this move.

Even with the study of "romaji" it is difficult as well as undesirable to conduct it nationally in a uniform manner. There are differences between cities and villages. Whatever the case may be, it is probably more suitable to let the school principal decide according to local conditions.

Need for Study and Research on the Present Language.

30. From the standpoint of both the simplification and the standardization of the national language, research and study of the present-day language are essential. Even in the compilation of the elementary school language textbooks there must be a basic investigation of just what vocabulary is essential to the students. However, up to now, there has been very little thought given to this study. What studies have been done were conducted only on a very small scale. It is re-

quested that the governmental education authorities give special consideration to this point.

Compilation of Dictionary of Present Japanese Words.

31. It is a very regrettable fact that up until now there has been no work done on the compilation of a large dictionary of Japanese words. We, as a link in the chain of compiling a great Japanese dictionary, must cooperate in the task of research study of present-day Japanese and must coordinate the work. We believe that this is a very significant factor in the development of a new Japan.

[*Source*: Trainor Papers, Hoover Institution Archives, Stanford University]

APPENDIX D: REMINISCENCES AND RECORDS

1. Memorandum: U.S. Education Mission to Japan, March 1946
Gordon T. Bowles

The cable sent by SCAP to the War Department on January 4, 1946 requesting that 30 named individuals be sent to Japan to make recommendations applicable to educational reforms was directed to the Civil Affairs Division but the contents were apparently made available simultaneously to the New York Times. Unfortunately, I do not have a copy of the article, but I well remember seeing my name listed as one of the "educators" during my usual scanning of the daily news. Later I was shown a copy of the cable by the Chief of the Civilian Affairs Section of the War Department, but I recall very clearly in subsequent conversations with the General in charge that the first inkling he had had of the proposed Mission was also the Times article and not the cable. It seemed apparent from the wording of the cable that, by implication, the Commissioner of Education, Mr. Studebaker, would probably be the officer in charge of the Mission.

As I had been trained professionally in Anthropology and not Education it was obvious that my name had been included not because of my training but because I was at the "Education Desk" in the Department of State under Assistant Secretary William Benton. The rationale for occupying this post was because of my background familiarity with Japan which included two years of college preparatory level teaching and I had served as drafting officer for the SWNCC (State–War–Navy Coordinating Committee) policy paper on Educational Reforms for Japan. Clearly an effort was being made to include the Department of State.

Sometime during the day the New York Times article appeared I received a call from Assistant Secretary Benton. After I had assured him I knew nothing about the proposed Mission, he assigned me the task of finding out whether or not it was a bonafide request and, if genuine, to ascertain what significance was attached to it by the Occupation Command and to make suggestions concerning the extent to which the Department of State might logically be involved.

The above reaction of Assistant Secretary Benton must be understood in the light of existing cabinet level decisions concerning roles of the respective departments as these related to occupied areas—in this case Japan. Acting for the Allied Powers (16 co-belligerents) SCAP had the authority to request such a Mission, but normal protocol in non-military affairs and especially to those concerned with socio-economic, religious and educational reform (democratization etc.) would be expected to receive the approval of the Council for the Allied Powers. In this instance, it appeared that SCAP recognized the urgency to provide operational guidance to the C.I. and E. section (Civil Information and Education Section) and military government teams concerned with the supervision and enforcement of directives at a time when schools were beginning to open and the Ministry of Education was faced with the difficult task of providing guidelines to the prefectural offices concerning the philosophy and content of educational materials and the role of the central government in their dissemination.

The initial SWNCC policy paper provided merely broad philosophical directives and not operational guidance. Certain C.I. and E. and related military government personnel, especially those trained by or associated with the Military Government training programs prior to surrender had already begun the task of changing the direction of educational goals, but responsible officers in the occupation command soon recognized that they lacked the necessary authoritative reassurance possessed by life-long specialists in different aspects of the educational process: philosophical, administrative, character building and content. They lacked the professional status for achieving an effective operating relationship with the Japanese Government, the recognized instrument for carrying out Occupation directives. As ex-Minister of Education Tamon Maeda later explained to me sometime after his removal from office, "it was extremely difficult and embarrassing for high government officials to accept and enforce or even to interpret adequately to subordinates or Diet committees and branches of government or the public at large just why the government was obliged to carry out directives signed by military colonels and not infrequently even by sergeants which were aimed at altering the course of government in matters affecting educational training or the rights and privileges of individuals—what he is expected to learn, his place within the family and society, and his freedom of choice in religious matters." Officers in C.I. & E. were aware of the problem and were the initiators of the request for help.

It would be difficult to single out any one individual as the responsible officer, but this was of little moment after the request had been made public. The problem was to decide who would undertake to organize such a group and how powerful a document was expected as a result of the group's survey.

Following the initial inquiries Benton called Studebaker. The latter's view was that as SCAP had already named a panel it would be inappropriate for his office to take over the task of organization, the more so as the list contained names of persons, however competent, he personally could not endorse as members of such a proposed Mission. He added further that in view of these considerations he would be requesting withdrawal of his name, but as a demonstration of good faith and his interest in the project he would recommend Assistant Commissioner Harold Benjamin as his alternate.

Thus it was left to the State and War Departments to settle the matter. In subsequent phone conversations, the Civil Affairs Section of the War Department took the position that, since the purpose of the Mission was to make recommendations concerning the direction of goals and changes to be initiated and hence more an elaboration of articles incorporated within previously issued policy papers, and was not primarily operational, it would follow logically, therefore, that the Department of State should be the agency to assume the organizational responsibility of the group and for the War Department to take care of operational details to and in the field. Expenses would be charged to SCAP. Benton concurred and assigned the task of organization of the group to me, with the injunction that I was to confer with both the Office of Education and the Civil Affairs Division of the War Department and finally with the divisional chief in State on all major issues such as completion of the panel and determination of leadership of the group. The timing of departure and return and items to be included in the schedule of activities in the field were to be SCAP's responsibility.

I discussed procedural matters first with Studebaker and Benjamin and subsequently with Civil Affairs. During the initial discussions it was decided that I should first phone all of the persons listed by SCAP, bearing in mind that if there was anyone on the list judged to be qualified to assume the role of chairman of the group he or she should be called into consultation both for completion of the panel's members and for all related procedural matters relating to formation of the Mission. The plan was approved by both State and Civil Affairs and, as I recall it, after telephoning everyone on the original list of thirty, the number was reduced to something like fourteen or fifteen available candidates. Several on the original list could not adjust their schedules to the specified period abroad and at least three were dead.

During the discussion with each listed individual it was made clear that his or her name had been suggested by SCAP but that, inasmuch as it was the intent of the Department to create as nationally and substantively representative a Mission as possible, the purpose of the call was primarily to ascertain interest in the proposal, ability to accomodate to a specified period abroad and willingness to be a member of such a group, and that the call was not necessarily to be construed as an invitation. It was explained also that "education" was being defined in the broadest sense to cover a wide variety of fields including textbooks, library resources, counseling, education in labor, the adult sector, and political, social and religious affairs. Each person was advised that in the interest of achieving a balanced Mission, invitations might not necessarily be issued to some named individuals no matter how highly qualified. To my knowledge, this interpretation was unanimously acceptable and the only subsequent complaints raised were directed primarily to lack of specific regional, substantive, sectional or sectarian representation and not to the participation of any particular member of the Mission.

Concerning selection of the chairman, I do not believe that George Stoddard's name appeared on the list of initially suggested names but both Studebaker and Benjamin pointed out that his experience on the Board of Commissioners of New York, his broad familiarity with a variety of educational spheres and his demonstrated ability to organize and proceed effectively were well known. It was Benton who called Stoddard and asked him to serve as Chairman of the Mission and who signed the letters of invitation when they were sent.

Five general criteria served as the basis for the next round of name selections although they served mainly as general guidelines and were never spelled out in detail. They were:

1) demonstrated knowledge of and practical experience in a given field of specialization;

2) breadth or significance of regional or sectional representation and awareness of culturally and politically conditioned differences in educational policies and practices;

3) willingness to participate in view of the Mission's breadth of representational scope and recommendational limitations of its authority;

4) known ability to participate as a member of a team and to compromise constructively in joint decisions;

5) physical fitness to travel and live under military orders without serious medical consequences to the individual or impositions on the military command.

Thousands had seen the Times article and therefore a number of considerations determined completion of the roster. Hundreds of letters, phone calls, and personal inquiries were received from the public at large or from within the Federal Government nominating specific individuals or offering their services and listing qualifications. Many were addressed to Assistant Secretary Benton, the Office of Education or the Civil Affairs Division of the War Department. I must have received at least fifty addressed to me and many more were referred to me from responsible officials with comments varying from polite rejection to strong endorsement.

Inasmuch as SCAP represented all of the Allied Powers it was my personal opinion that at least five or six non-Americans should be included, but this was not approved for a number of reasons:

1) such inclusion might set a precedent which could interfere with plans for the panel of judges participating in the military trials or other panel activities;

2) nations not represented might raise questions;

3) the non-Americans might well be unintentionally slighted or feel out of place;

4) much time would have to be spent and effort expended to make special arrangements and interviews during the tour of Japan;

5) objections were certain to be made because of the biased appointment of a specialist in this, that, or the other field by specialists who had been ignored.

The inclusion ultimately of one Canadian (Isaac Kandel) was approved but mainly because he was directly associated with Columbia University and not because of his nationality.

In completing the roster specific attention was paid to representation of minority populations, administration at the national, state and local levels (School

Boards, PTA, etc.) public, private and religious oriented sectors, education for the labor, adult, and handicapped groups, and the broader fields of libraries, museums, recreation and the Foundations.

It should be added that Stoddard insisted on a strong secretarial staff—six were ultimately included—which cut the panel of specialists to twenty-three, not including myself as Far Eastern Adviser to the Mission and as liaison officer representing the Department of State. Col. Andrews was attached to the Mission not as a member but as liaison representing Civil Affairs of the War Department.

Upon arrival in Japan the group was cordially received by General MacArthur who stressed that members of the Mission were expected to express their views freely, both individually and collectively, and that insofar as possible, efforts would be made to ensure that they met with those whom they wished to see or who wished to see them.

During the initial briefing sessions members were advised that they were not to be hindered by the "non-fraternization" directive which applied to military and civilian personnel in the Occupation only, but when they embarked on the arranged schedule a number of problems arose. All Mission personnel, including secretaries, were given the assumed rank of one-star generals in order to comply with flight, ground transport and billeting requirements. In arranging the schedule, however, the officers in charge had to bear in mind the timing of military trains and availability of accomodations which presented logistic problems in coping with a group of thirty people. There were frustrations for Mission members in trying to meet with previously known friends or newly met Japanese colleagues. Travel with Japanese was restricted since Japanese were not allowed to travel on military trains and private transportation was virtually non-existent. The group also developed a sense of being herded as if on a tour.

It had been expected that the Mission would spend the entire time on tour or in conference on a scheduled basis and that a report would be prepared after return to the U.S. Stoddard insisted, however, on reserving the last week for completion of the report as a group before departure for the U.S. The result was that a complete re-scheduling was necessary after arrival in Japan, but there was unanimous agreement that Stoddard was right in his insistence.

The selection of the Japanese group of educators who served as "opposites" for the Mission group was mainly limited to those whose English was adequate at the conversation level. This tended to limit representation in many fields of specialization and to bias the Japanese group in the direction of those already familiar with and attuned to western and especially American education and goals in the broadest sense.

At the suggestion of the Japanese educators and in keeping with Japan's traditional red carpet treatment of visiting guests as well as a gesture of appreciation on the part of SCAP for the Mission's services and advice, a rather elaborate schedule of tourist sites and events had been arranged—temple tours, garden parties, receptions and finally an audience with the Emperor. All of this was probably necessary, but it tended to limit time available to meet with Japanese friends, groups and colleagues.

Finally, the drafting and approval of the report was extremely difficult. While Kawai Kazuo's opinion that the Mission's report merely rubber-stamped the views of C.I.&E. is too sweeping, it must be said that there was a considerable amount of lobbying by officers within that section on MacArthur's staff to make sure that their views and personal experiences were adequately and, in some instances, persuasively presented to members of the Mission either individually or in small groups. In many cases MacArthur's staff officers, especially in C.I. & E., had been students of various of the Mission members so there may have been some undue pressure, but there was also some fear that the Mission members might not have been adequately exposed to all of the existing problems facing the Japanese Government and the nation to be able to make appropriate recommendations.

Another factor also was the existence of pressure groups and suggestions of "cliquiness" and directional bias which had developed within the Mission— reflections sometimes of incidents or conditions which translated their own experiences at home or those of their Japanese colleagues which had been relayed to them. There was always the realization, however, that the Mission was not altering policies but merely making recommendations—a limitation of authority which permitted considerable latitude in expressing opinions. It was necessary however to have advisors from SCAP constantly available to provide information on what was either logistically feasible or under Occupation policies possible and to provide statistics when necessary.

Shortages in Japan of materials such as paper or lack of facilities or adequately trained personnel were ever present considerations for Mission members.

Under the above circumstances and in the dual role of regional or what I preferred to view as "cross-cultural" advisor and of representing what I believed would be the collective views of the Department of State, I sometimes found it necessary to propose changes in the intensity or direction of a given recommendation or to introduce items which were not included.

One of the major points at issue was the question of the Japanese script. The majority of the Mission members thought that pressure should be brought to bear to change the system of writing and to make use of either the Latin or Roman alphabet compulsory. They had been informed during the course of required orientation sessions that the equivalent of two years of schooling time were required simply to become sufficiently familiar with the stipulated number of Chinese ideographs to meet the existing literacy tests. Members were also aware that the existence of a phonetic "kana" syllabary meant that a total shift would not be an impossibility. I took the position that such a drastic recommendation would go far beyond the limits of reasonable action on the part of Mission members and might well jeopardize the net benefits which were likely to be achieved by the report as a whole. My point was that the type of writing used by a literate people was inherently a part of their cultural heritage and such fundamental changes as those being recommended by rank outsiders, no matter how good their intentions, would result in an unfortunate backlash which could undo much of value in Occupational policies as a whole. I took a strong stand in asserting that the draft form of the Report would certainly run counter to the stated position of the U.S. Government that the purpose of the Occupation was demilitarization and greater freedom for the individual and not a broadside attack upon such a fundametally neutral cultural institution as the system of writing. My position was subsequently endorsed by the Policy Committee of the Department of State and the Asst. Secretary himself in a response memo to my request for clarification, but some form of simplification was insisted upon in fairness to the educational development of the individual.

The only other major objection I had to the initial draft was to strong wording of the shift to the 6–3–3 system. Here again, as in the case of the script argument, the wording as initially proposed was so strong and without adequate educational rationale included in the draft that it would certainly have been construed as an overstepping of the Mission's purpose and contrary to the Occupation intent. It appeared obvious that those within the Mission who were aware of the value of the 6–3–3 system as a structural feature of the educational process, as well as the Japanese and American pressure groups who were influencing them, were trying to retain wording which would have to be labelled as compulsory in tone rather than recommendational. It would have been challenged immediately by critics as a further effort to Americanize rather than educate. In the final report the recommendation was included, but the wording was considerably modified to the point where I did not think that a memo of support from the Department of State was necessary.

Dr. Stoddard and I spent virtually the whole of the last two days going over the draft reports which had been prepared sectionally by different groups of Mission members appointed by Dr. Stoddard. Following this was a meeting of the entire Mission which considered the report as a whole. At this time, George Counts and I believe one or two others did present differing views on a few points. These were submitted with the final report which Dr. Stoddard and I had prepared after going over all points and wording in detail. I do not recall the contents of the "minority report". The evening before the Mission departed Dr. Stoddard and I had a fairly long interview with General MacArthur to whom Dr. Stoddard submitted the report.

An assessment of the gaps between intent of the report and the realization of its goals would mean the drafting of another and far lengthier memorandum.

I think it is only fair to add as a postcript that I had previously taken exception personally to the wording of the original SWNCC Policy which had used the word "morals" or "moral principles" as the English equivalent of "shushin". I had taken the position that the longer phrase "indoctrination of moral principles" was not the semantic or culturally conditioned equivalent of the English phrase "education in the principles of morality". I did not gain my point and the final wording of the policy paper meant to me that all teaching of morals in the substantive content of the school curriculum was to be eliminated. I still believe the wording was poor and can only add that any policy paper is a positional paper and does not express the views of any single individual. Every policy paper characterized as "re-orientational" is necessarily screened through a series of reviewing committees.

2. Reflections on the March 1946 U.S. Education Mission to Japan
Gordon T. Bowles

Many times during the past few years I have thought about the United States Education Mission, and invariably my thoughts have focused on the answers to two questions. First, did the Mission accomplish its intended purpose? Second, what, if any, have been its lasting effects, most especially the impact of the recommendations contained in the Final Report?

The Mission's stated purpose was to advise General MacArthur, the Supreme Commander for the Allied Powers, and his staff (both commonly referred to as SCAP), in carrying out overall policy directives with respect to revision of the entire educational system and process so as to conform to the spirit and objectives of the Potsdam Agreement—the declaration adopted by the Allied Powers as the basic pattern for democratization and re-orientation of the peoples of both Germany and Japan. General MacArthur made it specifically clear to the Mission upon their arrival in Japan that any and all recommendations submitted in their Report were to be couched in terms of the future, and that existing economic and related problems were to be ignored.

Long before the termination of hostilities, it was realized jointly by the Allies that, unlike the situation in Germany, the greatest problem in the occupation of Japan would be communication. In order to overcome the language barrier, it would be necessary to retain the Japanese Government in as intact a condition as possible and, to avoid chaos, there would have to be a unified command under a single authority. It is a matter of history that General MacArthur made use of this authority on more than one occasion. Fortunately, an early suggestion to place the northern half of Japan under Soviet control was quickly abandoned.

Once SCAP was in control, it was soon realized that coping with entrenched bureaucracies such as the Ministry of Education and other departments of government would not be easy. Apart from mutual uncertainties and suspicions in the educational field, for example, it was often exceedingly difficult to communicate procedural directives successfully at a time when there was a shortage of both teachers and supplies and many of the schools had either been destroyed or were being used by the Occupation forces.

Even in contacts between Japanese Government officials and officers of the Civil Information and Education Section of SCAP (C.I. & E.) there were frequently problems of interpretation. During the Mission's stay I was privileged to have an interview with an old acquaintance, Mr. Tamon Maeda, the first post-surrender Minister of Education, who was then in retirement. He described how awkward and embarrassing it was to try to explain to some relatively uninformed and frequently junior C.I. & E. officer that such matters as changes in government priorities or conflicts due to recent Cabinet decisions or to newly enacted regulations would make it impossible to carry out the terms of a specific directive or program within a specified time frame.

The overall policy directives issued to SCAP by the U.S. Government and ap-

proved by the Allies were stated in general terms as guidelines and not as procedures, and it was left to SCAP's discretion to determine what and when specific
changes should be initiated. It was in relation to these details that both the Mission
and their Final Report were so important. The recommendations contained in the
Report not only helped to clarify SCAP's goals, but were generally sufficiently
explicit to indicate the sequence in which changes might be undertaken. The
Mission, furthermore, had sufficient standing both academically and administra-
tively to command the respect and attention of both SCAP personnel and Japanese
Government officials at all levels. The most important point, however, was that
although the Report was drafted by the Mission, most of its provisions were the
result of careful discussions with the Japan Education Committee and various
SCAP personnel which resulted in much needed stimulus toward the formation of
both separate and joint working committees. On the Japanese side some of these
committees, moreover, or their successors designated liaison persons at both national and prefectural levels who were able on several occasions to encourage
enactment of appropriate new legislation in the Diet.

Whether or not the Mission met the expectations of the Japanese is another
matter. It undoubtedly assisted the more liberal and progressive-minded, who
welcomed the Mission's presence and cooperated in its activities. Among the
most prominent leaders were such people as the Minister of Education Yoshishige
Abe, Shigeru Nambara, President of Tokyo University and Chairman of the Japan
Education Committee, and all of the Committee members. In addition, there were
hundreds if not thousands of liberal-minded Japanese in all walks of life who were
anticipating changes not only in the educational system, but in all aspects of life
affecting the public domain.

When the Mission arrived in Japan there was a great deal of speculation among
well-informed Japanese concerning its constituency. "Why wasn't so-and-so included? Why didn't the Mission plan to stay longer? Why select people with little
or no prior knowledge of Japan and the Japanese people? etc. etc." There was
little awareness of the nation-wide interest in the Mission among leading American
educators at the time of its formation, and of the impossibility for most of them to
abandon their responsibilities on short notice. They did not realize, moreover,
that a number of American educators were already involved in plans for a similar
Mission to Germany, and that more than a hundred other prominent educators
were suggested or had been directly solicited and many more were recommended
or personally volunteered but could not be accommodated. They did not know,
also, that under the heading of education would be included a wide range of subjects such as adult education, education in labor, libraries, museums, philanthropic
organizations and foundations, as well as private versus public institutions, government representation at both national and local levels, teachers' organizations,
etc. and that regional American representation would be expected. The anxiety of
concerned Japanese was allayed, it is true, when it became understood that in the
future, and as circumstances justified, the assistance of specialists in different
fields would be made available.

To say that the Mission and its report had fully met the needs of SCAP personnel or the expectations of liberal-minded Japanese educators would be an exagger-

ation, but I believe it can be said that, given the circumstances—the shortness of notice and the necessity to accomplish its mission and prepare a final report within the space of one month—the Mission deserves high marks. Much of the credit must certainly be given to George Stoddard, who insisted on having a secretarial staff large enough to meet the needs of four sub-committees and on reserving the last week of the Mission's stay in Japan for writing the Final Report. As a result of several years' experience as Commissioner of Education for the State of New York, Dr. Stoddard knew how frustrating it could be to try to re-assemble a group of busy educators once they had disbanded. His insistence, also, that only majority opinions should be expressed was crucial. He knew that ambivalence or incorporation of differing views would only lead to further debate and confusion.

There is no doubt that a differently worded report would have been forthcoming had it been prepared by a "perfect" Mission with the advice of a "perfect" Japanese Committee, and had the collective time at their disposal been extended. It is doubtful, however, if the general content would have differed substantially from the prepared document. There are a few recommendations, in my opinion, which may have been unduly emphasized. Decentralization is one that comes clearly to mind.

Several members of the Mission felt that democratization could be realized only if school texts beyond the elementary level could be de-standardized. They advocated that encouragement should be given to emphasis on differences in localized subcultures and environments within Japan—to variety rather than commonality. Personal freedom and individualism could only be realized by emphasizing local differences. These were the only true safeguards against centralized autocratic domination.

Even though I was not professionally trained in education, I was voted to full membership in the Mission at Dr. Stoddard's suggestion. My official status was as Department of State representative and adviser to the Mission on Japanese culture generally and Japanese education in particular. I chose not to be attached to any of the four sub-committees, but to be permitted to attend any of them as time and circumstance permitted. I was, in fact, so busy arranging interviews, discussing matters with SCAP officials or the Political Adviser, or with Japanese officials and educators, that I would not have been a good member of any of the subcommittees. I did make it a point to be present whenever proposals relative to changes in the written language or the 6–3–3 issue were under debate.

I openly challenged the justification for demanding a change in the method of writing. Japan's method of writing had nothing to do with a militaristic past, but had its roots deep in Japan's cultural heritage, and was profoundly a part of Japanese art and classical literature and of the nation's historical ties to both China and Korea. During the orientation sessions before leaving Washington, I had tried to make clear the differentiation between a phonetic or sound-based method of writing and an idea, concept or thought-grouping method in which a fair share of the reading and writing battle was won when roughly two hundred radicals had been mastered. Furthermore, if a full year or more of compulsory educational experience at the elementary school level had to be devoted to the study of "kanji" in order to be considered literate, this would probably not be much more of a burden to a child than the mastering of English spelling.

It was also difficult for most of the Mission members to comprehend that the use of the phonetic "furigana" (either "katakana" or "hiragana") could be increased and the number of required "kanji" could be decreased if necessary, but that there would have to be substantial changes in the spoken language as well if a phonetic script alone were to be made mandatory. It was clear to me that no matter how much I emphasized these points, the majority of the Mission members and especially George Stoddard, Chairman of the Mission, as well as my superior, Assistant Secretary of State William Benton, sincerely believed that forcing a child to master between one and two thousand characters would definitely have a crippling effect on the child's education and impose an unwarranted burden on the whole educational process. I can at least take satisfaction in knowing that the results of my last minute efforts did produce a tempering effect on the wording of the Report and that, instead of recommending that all elementary textbooks be written in Romaji, or Latin script, it was simply urged that some form of Romaji should be learned and that the use of Romaji as an alternate form of writing be given careful consideration. I felt at the time that recommending a committee or commission to study the matter of simplification of writing was a major victory.

On the 6–3–3 issue, when I became aware of the factionalism that existed among members of the Japanese Education Committee concerning the 6–3–3–4 versus the existing 6–5–3–3 system, and that President Nambara was himself in favor of the change, it seemed to me that there should not be undue pressure from the outside and that the matter should be left to the Japanese themselves to decide. Having been educated myself under the old American 8–4–4 system, I knew something of the problem my own country had faced in shifting to the 6–3–3 system. Furthermore, I had not been aware until then that the proposed change was designed to group children by class years to conform more closely to the physiological and psychological stages in the child's growth, and that the 6–3 portion, at least, was the prevailing system in most of Europe.

I certainly cannot support the recent cries from various quarters that the 6–3–3 system was forced on the Japanese people. The matter was thoroughly debated and decided by the Japanese educators themselves and their decision coincided with the majority opinion expressed by the Mission members. The change has brought the Japanese system in line with the general practice adhered to in most of the literate world.

After reading and re-reading the numerous books, letters, reports and critical analyses of the Occupation and, in particular, the role and effectiveness of the Education Mission, it seems to me that the greatest service rendered by the Mission was unquestionably to provide an opportunity for a sizeable number of Japanese educators to meet and converse at length, on a person to person basis, with their American counterparts. Conversely, it was a unique opportunity for the Americans to see and hear at first hand the problems faced by their Japanese colleagues, and to ascertain personal and professional views concerning changes that would be beneficial to the Japanese people in the development of a more democratic and egalitarian society.

So far as the long term impact is concerned, it seems to me that in no small part the remarkable changes which have taken place in the Japanese educational system can be traced to the recommendations incorporated in the Mission Report. The Report emphasized equal opportunities for all regardless of sex or economic circumstances throughout the period of compulsory education. It recommended also de-emphasis on elitism by greatly expanding the number of higher educational institutions and increasing the range and volume of library and other resources. The Report also strongly urged the collective participation and debate of local and national educational issues by parents and teachers alike within their respective local communities.

In fairness to those concerned, it bears repeating that such changes as have occurred are due primarily to the efforts of the Japanese Education Committee, strengthened by a wide range of many other liberal-minded Japanese over the past few decades. Only to the extent that the Mission provided opportunity to Japanese educators to express themselves and to utilize the Report as a foundation for realizing their hopes and convictions and strengthening their positions does the Mission itself deserve credit for any lasting results. Without the Mission, transformations would undoubtedly have occurred, but progress might have been slower and possibly not as far-reaching.

(April 1987)

3. Tokyo and Return
Willard E. Givens

On Tuesday, February 26, the United States Education Mission, which was originally proposed by the Supreme Commander of the Allied Powers in the Pacific, General Douglas MacArthur, left Washington for Japan. We went because our country, through its State and War Departments, had asked us to render this service to a defeated country. We did not go in the spirit of conquerors but as experienced educators. We believed that there is an unmeasured potential for freedom and for individual and social growth in every child, youth, and adult. Our hope was in the children. Sustaining as they do the weight of the future, they should not be pressed down by the heritage of a heavy past. We sought through every means at our command to equalize their opportunities. It was clear to every member of the Mission that any residual dislike or distrust had no place in our report. Our concern was, as Lincoln said, "too great for malice." We believe that in the long run a nation must free itself and that freedom comes through the practice of freedom.

We traveled to Tokyo and return on a C-54 plane, a four-motored aircraft with space for forty passengers. We flew from Washington to Topeka, Kansas, on "The Ambassador" in seven hours. After refueling and oiling the plane and having a fine dinner at the Officers' Club at a table reserved for "American statesmen", we left for Hamilton Field, San Francisco. We arrived at Hamilton Field, after eight hours and fifteen minutes' flying, in the early morning of Wednesday, February 27. We were taken to an Army hotel on the Field. At breakfast we met the West Coast members of the Mission, after which we went to the Administration Building for bubonic plague shots. At 2:00 P.M. that afternoon seventeen of our group left for Honolulu. Eleven were held over for the next day. After lunch eight of us went to San Francisco in a State Department station wagon. The fog between Hamilton and San Francisco was so thick that we could not even see the sides of the Golden Gate Bridge as we crossed it. I went to Oakland where I spent the night. The rest of the party returned to Hamilton Field that night through the fog. I returned the next morning when it was beautifully clear, the fog having entirely disappeared during the night. We left Hamilton Field Thursday afternoon, February 28. As we left the Field we circled back twenty-five miles over San Francisco Bay and flew out over the Golden Gate Bridge and were on our way to Hawaii. My friends had the opportunity then to see the beautiful Bay region which I had described to them as we flew across the United States and which they had been denied the privilege of seeing the day before because of the fog.

After twelve hours and fifteen minutes of flying we arrived on Hickam Field at Pearl Harbor near Honolulu on Friday morning, March 1. We were met here by Superintendent and Mrs. O. E. Long and Harold Loper. Harold Benjamin and I went home with the Longs and George Counts with Harold Loper. The rest of our party stayed at Hickam Field.

After a very pleasant day in Honolulu in which we were privileged to have a conference with several people well acquainted with the educational problems of Japan, and to have a delightful luncheon in the Moano Hotel on Waikiki Beach to see the city, and to visit some schools, we returned to the airport, and at 6:15 left for Johnston Island. After four hours and ten minutes we arrived at this tiny speck of land in a great and quiet ocean. After a brief stop for refueling we left for Kwajalein Island. Between Johnston Island and Kwajalein we crossed the international date line and therefore jumped entirely Saturday, March 2, going directly from Friday night, March 1, to Sunday morning, March 3. We arrived at Kwajalein Island, a small coral reef, at 8:00 o'clock, after eight hours of flying. After refueling and having breakfast we left for Guam where we landed after seven hours and twenty-five minutes. Here we caught up with the other members of the United States Education Mission who had been held up on Guam because of a blizzard in Tokyo, making weather conditions undesirable for landing on Atsuge Airfield. Our party arrived at Guam on Sunday evening, March 3, and did not leave until Thursday morning, March 7, spending three days and four nights on this island which had figured prominently in World War II—first when the Japanese captured it, and, second, when we recaptured it from the Japanese. If anyone doubts that the Army was prepared to make a landing on the coast of Japan, he should spend a day or two on the Island of Guam, surveying the tremendous stockpiles of all kinds of equipment, munitions, and supplies that were stored there ready for the attack on Japan.

Most of the men of the United States Education Mission to Japan will remember quonset hut #30 for a long time to come. A few of the men and all of the lady members of the Mission were privileged to stay in the home of General Parker, Commanding Officer of Guam. We had one all-day meeting of the United States Education Mission in General Parker's beautiful home on Guam. Later during our stay in Japan we were all saddened to learn of the untimely death of General Parker and his fine staff, most of whom we had met on Guam. Unfortunately, the bomber in which they were traveling crashed into the side of a mountain during a storm.

On Thursday morning, March 7, our contingent of the Mission left Guam for Tokyo where we arrived that evening after eight hours and thirty-five minutes of flying. On our way to Tokyo we flew over a volcanic island being formed in the ocean. We could see the volcano in action and see the island being formed in the water. When we arrived at Atsuge [Atsugi] Airfield, just out of Yokohama, we had our first view of Japan's famous mountain, Fujiyama. We arrived at Atsuge Airfield ten days after we left Washington and after fifty-five hours and forty minutes of actual flying time. We drove twenty-nine miles through Yokohama and Tokyo to the Imperial Hotel which was to be our home for one month. Throughout this distance we saw nothing but rubble, rubble, rubble,—occasionally a smoke stack or a chimney standing amid square miles upon square miles of fallen stones and burnt metal. We were passing through what had been two of Japan's great cities and one of the three largest cities in the world. Of Japan's sixty largest cities only Kyoto, the ancient capital, now stands.

On Friday morning, March 8, we had our first meeting with the Japanese committee appointed by General MacArthur to cooperate with us. We met that morning also with the Civil Information and Education Section of General MacArthur's Headquarters Staff, consisting of about twenty-five officers headed by General Ken Dyke who, unfortunately, was in the United States during our stay in Japan. At this first meeting with the education committee of Japan we were addressed by the present Minister of Education. Mr. Abe, who had recently been appointed by General MacArthur. Mr. Abe is the first educator to serve as Minister of Education during the entire history of Japan. During his address he stated that ''while war is the most deplorable and abominable happening for the human race, we cannot overlook the fact that through war peoples are brought into closer contact with each other. Actually as a result of our defeat a great number of your countrymen, such as was never seen before, have come to our land. We are to be under the control of your countrymen in everything—in our politics, economy, culture, and education. Although we cannot call it an honor for us, it is yet undeniable that it serves to make our contact with your people more frequent and more profound than ever. In fact, our daily life—mentally and spiritually—has come to be un-thinkable without taking into account the influence which your country and your people is exercising upon it.... We believe that your country is not going to violate truth and justice on the strength of her being a victor. And we pray that the pressure brought upon us by this victory—for we cannot help feeling it as pressure—will help to make truth and justice permeate all our country, and serve as a chance for us to eliminate quickly and vigorously all the injustices and defects existing in our society and all the weaknesses and evils underlying our national character and customs.... In a word, we wish to render as significantly as possible this opportunity to come in contact with your country and your people—an opportunity that was brought to us through the war—and we shall be happy if we could do this not only through our own efforts but also through the good will and assistance that may still be granted to us by your country, victor as it is. As you may guess, it is a severe trial and a hard task to be a defeated country and a defeated people, but if I may say so, it must also be a very difficult thing to be a good victor.''

At 1:00 P.M. the last twelve of the Mission to arrive in Japan were entertained at lunch in the American Embassy by General and Mrs. MacArthur. During the lunch we asked the General many questions. He was well informed and an interesting, effective, and dramatic speaker. He paid high tribute to the work of public education in the Philippines. He expressed deep appreciation for the part which the Philippine people had taken in the war. He answered all of our questions with sincerity, frankness, and candor. He made it clear that he wanted us to study the Japanese educational system, to report what we found, and to make recommendations for both the immediate and the long future of Japan. He assured us that our report would be published in Japanese and widely circulated throughout Japan. He asked that the report be submitted to him as a confidential report before we left Japan. He said that such parts of it as were immediately applicable would be put into effect during the new school year which would open in Japan soon.

We met in the afternoon with the Japanese committee and with the Education Section of General MacArthur's Staff and listened to a presentation by staff members of some of the educational problems in Japan.

On Saturday morning, March 9, we had our first meeting of Committee #3 which was the Committee on the Organization and Administration of Education. We met first with the Japanese members designated to work with us. The Japanese members of our Committee were: Sadasuke Omano [Teiyu Amano], Director of the First Higher School of Tokyo; Shunsaku Kawahara, Privy Councillor; Suteji Kumaki, Director of the First Tokyo Normal School; Masanori Oshima, Retired Professor from Tokyo Imperial University; and Tsuraki Yano, Director of the Meijigakuin College.

After we had met with the Japanese members we had a meeting of our own members. Our Committee consisted of: Kermit Eby, Director of Research and Education of the C.I.O.; Willard E. Givens, Executive Secretary, National Education Association (Secretary of Committee #3); Frederick G. Hochwalt, Secretary, National Catholic Education Association; E. B. Norton, State Superintendent of Education, Alabama; A. J. Stoddard, Superintendent of Schools, Philadelphia (Chairman of Committee #3); and Pearl A. Wanamaker, State Superintendent of Public Instruction, State of Washington.

In the afternoon we met with the whole United States Education Mission, the Japanese committee, and the Education Section of General MacArthur's Staff. The organization and the educational program of the primary school and the middle school were discussed.

On Sunday morning, March 10, a party consisting of A. J. Stoddard, Harold Benjamin, George Diemer, E. B. Norton and myself left by automobile for the resort city of Atami. We drove through some of Japan's best farming country. Every inch is being cultivated. People are better fed, better clothed, and seemed much happier in the country than they do in the cities where they have lost practically everything on account of the bombing. We drove through many small villages but only one that had been bombed—this one on account of industry being located there. After driving through agriculture country for many miles we came to the mountains and drove through some beautiful country to Atami, located in the mountains but also at the edge of the ocean. We passed many orange trees; lots of plum trees in bloom; some peach and japonica trees in bloom; but no cherry trees in bloom, as it was too early for them.

When we arrived at Atami we went to the Onoya Hotel where we took off our shoes according to Japanese custom, put on sandals, and were taken to our room. There was a low table in the middle of the room and cushions on the floor. Plans for the luncheon had been arranged for us by the Assistant Manager of the Imperial Hotel in Tokyo. While the Japanese cooks were preparing the luncheon A. J. Stoddard, E. B. Norton and I took the famous Atami hot baths. The temperature of the water was 130°. Some of the smaller baths were much hotter. Our luncheon was served in real Japanese fashion. After lunch we went down to the village of Atami and Jerry took some pictures along one of Atami's most noted streets. After this we drove home through a snowstorm.

Monday morning, March 11, we had a general meeting with the Japanese committee of the Education Section of General MacArthur's Staff in which we discussed the problems of elementary, secondary, and higher education. In the afternoon Jerry got a movie of General MacArthur leaving his office to go home for lunch. Several hundred people were there as usual to see him leave. Most of them were Japanese—all of them dressed in their best clothes. As General MacArthur came out of the door of the office building, the Japanese people all made their lowest and most reverent bow. General MacArthur saluted them, came directly to his car, and got in. The crowd moved back from the front of the car as one man. The car moved slowly away. When it was gone the crowd quietly dispersed. A crowd like this gathers every day to see the General leave for lunch.

In the afternoon Committee #3 on the Organization and Administration of Education met with the Japanese members. Chairman Stoddard explained to them how our system of schools is organized so that the control is in the hands of the people whose children are being educated. The Japanese members were very much interested in this and asked many questions. It was during this committee meeting that Chairman Stoddard made his famous "phooey speech." He explained that he was Superintendent of Schools in Philadelphia and that Philadelphia determined what kind of schools they had; that if anybody in Washington tried to tell Philadelphia what to do in their schools, he would tell them "phooey." The

Chairman then turned to Mr. Maeda, our Japanese interpreter and son of a former Minister of Education in Japan, and asked him to explain that to the Japanese members.

Tuesday morning, March 12, we met at 9:00 A.M. in a little theater to see motion pictures of the Japanese schools. These pictures were taken previous to the war. The temperature of the room was 45°. Like practically every place in Tokyo, there was no heat. The pictures were idealistic and showed only the best in Japanese education but were quite artistic and well done.

In the afternoon Committee #3 met with the Japanese committee and discussed the administrative organization of the schools of Japan. That evening we had a meeting of the whole United States Education Mission to discuss our trip to Kyoto and other subjects dealing with the work of the Mission.

On Wednesday morning, March 13, at 9:00 A.M., we met as usual in the Peers Theater where Commander Hall of the Education Section of the Headquarters Staff discussed the Japanese language. A noted Japanese authority talked upon the subject also. The Japanese language is one of the real handicaps to education of the masses in Japan. This discussion was followed by Captain Griffith who presented the problems of teacher education. Several Japanese people helped him with this program—each one presenting a different phase of the education of teachers. One of these was a teacher of the sixth grade from Kyoto—a married man with a wife and two children. He gets 3,000 yen per year—equivalent to $200 American money. He teaches sixty-seven children. He needs 9,000 yen or $600 per year American money to exist in any degree of decency. Resources in addition to his meager salary come out of former savings or from the black market or from food provided by relatives on farms or he goes with practically nothing to eat, as many teachers in Japan are doing now. This is typical of all the Japanese teachers with whom I talked.

At 1:30 we had a meeting of the United States Education Mission as a whole. At 3:00 o'clock we attended a tea at the home of the Premier of Japan, Mr. Shidehara. The tea was very informal and interesting. Premier Shidehara made a short talk to us. The speech was very appropriate and quite oratorical. Dr. George Stoddard, Chairman of the Mission, replied. We were entertained by artists, some of whom worked in sand and others made beautiful flower arrangements. When the food and tea were served it was evident that many of the Japanese people were very hungry.

On Thursday morning, March 14, we met at the Peers Theater for a presentation and discussion of the health and physical education program in the Japanese schools. This was given by Major Norviel from Glendale, California. This presentation was followed by discussion of the education of women in Japan by Captain Donovan, a lady member of the NEA from the Boston schools. She was assisted by Miss Ai Hoshino, President of Tsuda College, and Miss Michi Kawai, Director of Keisen Jogakuin. They were frank and well informed. Only four-tenths of one percent of the women of Japan are privileged to attend universities.

That night we were dinner guests of Shigeru Yoshida, then Minister of Foreign Affairs, former Ambassador to Great Britain, and since our return elected Prime Minister of Japan. We were seated on the floor around typical Japanese tables. The main part of the meal—sukiyaki—was cooked on the tables where we ate.

This well-known Japanese dish consists of beef cooked with several different kinds of Japanese vegetables and served piping hot. The dishes are filled as many times as the visitors will permit. Foreign Minister Yoshida read a two-page speech in which he asked that in our recommendations we consider the fact that Japan has its own culture and may want to be democratic in a way different from America. He stated that the Japanese faced the future with confidence and hope.

Friday, March 15—We visited Japanese schools all day—three elementary schools, one boys' Middle School, one girls' Higher School, and the First Higher School of Tokyo. Several buildings had been partly destroyed by bombing. Classes were crowded. None of the buildings were heated although there was snow on the ground outside.

That evening we left by Pullman for Kyoto to spend four days—March 16 to 19. At Kyoto we were met by a caravan of Army cars and taken directly to the Biwako Hotel on Lake Biwa where we had breakfast in a dining room overlooking Japan's largest lake. We made our headquarters here during the four days that we worked in Kyoto.

Saturday, March 16—The United States Education Mission and several of the members of the Civil Information and Education Section of the Headquarters Staff, accompanied by some military people from Kyoto and several Japanese people from Kyoto, went by military caravan of seventeen Army cars to Nishi Honganji Temple, one of the most famous Buddhist temples in Japan. It is the head of the Jodo Shinshu Sect of the Buddhists and occupies the same relative position in Buddhism that Saint Peter's Church does in Catholicism. This Temple is noted for its huge size and fine decorations.

We went next to Chio-In Monastery, noted for its size, beauty, and great bell. From here we went to the Miyako Hotel for lunch. We ate in a beautiful dining room overlooking the valleys and mountains. After lunch we went to see the Kinkakuji Temple where the landscaping was especially beautiful. Then we went to Ryuanji, a garden dedicated to Japanese fine art and culture. Leaving there we drove through Arashiyama which is filled with much beautiful natural scenery.

We returned to the Biwako Hotel where we had a sukiyaki dinner and were entertained by Japanese artists.

Sunday, March 17—At 8:30 A.M. we left for the ancient city of Nara, about fifty miles away. The roads were covered with melting snow and driving was slow. Due to the snow and bad roads it took us two and a half hours to drive to Nara. The countryside was beautiful. We saw intensive but primitive farming along the entire road. Crops raised here, as in all other parts of Japan which we visited, are rice, wheat, tea, grapes, onions, peas, and various other kinds of vegetables.

Upon arrival we went directly to the Nara Hotel, a Rest-Recreation Center for American Soldiers. Later we went to the Nara Museum, returning to the Nara Hotel where we ate the best dinner that we had while we were in Japan. All of the meals served to us in hotels in Japan consisted always of American food. No American is allowed to eat any of Japan's food. Japan needs more than she has to take care of her starving millions.

During the afternoon we visited the Nara Women's Normal School, a teacher-training institution for preparing teachers for girls' high schools. This was one of the best schools I visited in Japan. I visited one class in electricity, one in penman-ship, and went through one of their modern dormitories. This dormitory, like many others in Japan, consists of units to accommodate fourteen girls living to-gether, using a common kitchen and dining room. Four or five girls live in a single room twelve by fourteen feet in size. Each girl has a small table and a pillow on which she sits on the floor to work at her low table. Each has a bedroll made up of a small mattress, a wooden pillow, and a couple of blankets. This bed is rolled up and put in a little locker at the end of the room. There are five of these lockers. Each girl keeps everything she has in this small locker, including her bed in the daytime, clothes, books, etc. Each girl cooks all the meals for her unit of fourteen for one day out of each fourteen days. The room costs each girl three and a half yen per month. Food costs are shared, amounting to about forty yen per month per girl.

Some girls pay no tuition but have to teach from two to five years after they graduate as a part payment to Japan for their public schooling. The principal of this school made a very fine talk and the faculty served us the usual tea and cookies.

From the Normal School we went to the Kasuga Shrine. This is one of the most famous Shinto shrines in Japan—founded in 770 AD. Here we saw a religious ceremony. It was at this Shrine that we saw hundreds of stone lanterns and dozens of metal ones. The landscaping of the grounds was beautiful beyond words. I was more impressed with the beauty of this Shrine than any of the many shrines which I saw in Japan.

We next visited a Buddhist Temple where we saw the Great Buddha, huge and costly in material and labor. Following this visit we drove from Nara back over the fifty-mile route to the Biwako Hotel where after dinner we were entertained by two professional Japanese men dancers, performing Japanese dances identically as they had been performed for generations.

Monday, March 18—After breakfast we went to the Miyako Hotel in the edge of Kyoto. Here we had a general meeting of the United States Education Mission for one hour. We then divided up into our committee groups and met for two hours with groups of Japanese who had been appointed to work with us in Kyoto. In our group on The Organization and Administration of Education we had twelve Japanese men and one Japanese woman. At our request the Superintendent of Schools in Kyoto was finally located and urged to attend the meeting. The Japa-nese, apparently, had never thought of inviting a superintendent of schools to sit in an educational meeting.

After lunch we visited the Kyoto Imperial University. After dinner we went to see a Noh performance on the Kongo stage of Noh—the play being "A Robe of Feathers", written by Seami Motokiyo in about 1400. The play was one of Japan's most honored plays. It was beautiful and interesting. It lasted about one and one-quarter hours. After the men actors had changed clothes they returned and showed us many ancient and costly kimonos and a great variety of Japanese masks—all of which were used in various Japanese plays. Some of these kimonos and masks were more than 500 years old. Most of the ancient masks were made out of wood.

Tuesday, March 19—After breakfast we left to visit schools in Kyoto. We went directly to the First Middle School in Kyoto where there were 1400 boys who entered this school after very severe examinations following the six-year primary schools. The building was about seventy-five years old. As usual there was no heat. Classes were fifty to sixty in number. I talked to one teacher of geography, now teaching English, since geography, history, and morals had been ruled out by military directives on account of their Shinto indoctrination. This teacher had been in this particular school for five years. He has a wife and two children—one ten and one six. He was getting 135 yen per month—a little less than $10.00 American money. Using the Encyclopedia Britannica and three other books which he was able to find, he had written "The Life of Abraham Lincoln" which is being printed in Japanese and which he hopes will be used in Japanese schools.

From here we went to the Third Higher School. Here I met and talked to a teacher of English who had been in that particular school for thirty years and was retiring in about two weeks. The following year his thirty-one-year-old son, who had been teaching for several years in a commercial high school, was going to take his place. The retiring teacher was getting 175 yen per month basic pay, plus a war bonus called "emergency allotment", making a total of about 400 yen per month. When he retires he will get 6,000 yen in a lump sum from the Japanese Government and then get 2,000 yen per year as pension for the rest of his life. Two thousand yen does not mean very much in Japan today when a carton of American cigarettes sells for between 200 and 300 yen.

Next we went to the Kyoto Fine Arts School. This school had admitted girls for the first time. There were twenty-eight girls attending this art school. The school was doing some fine work. However, the building itself was far from artistic.

After lunch at the Kyoto Hotel we went through the Imperial Palace. Here all Emperors of Japan had been crowned. Here the early rulers of Japan lived. The grounds are extensive and beautiful, filled with costly buildings and artistic landscaping. During recent years all Emperors, after their coronation ceremonies in Kyoto, go immediately to the Imperial Palace in Tokyo to live.

Leaving the Imperial Palace we went through the Shogun's Palace and grounds. These also are very beautiful. We went through some other temples and then returned to the Biwako Hotel. We left Kyoto in the evening and arrived in Tokyo next morning.

Wednesday, March 20—We spent the day working on our report—each one in his own room pushing a lead pencil. We made good headway. At night our committee met and discussed the report at considerable length.

Thursday, March 21—We continued pushing lead pencils with vigor. About noon we met again, and I took the committee report, as agreed upon by the committee, and dictated it. In the late afternoon our committee drove out to Sugamo Prison where Tojo and many other war criminals are incarcerated. Tokyo Rose is there. She is an American citizen, reared in California. The German Ambassador and sixteen other Germans associated with the Ambassador are in prison there. The judges from eight countries are in Tokyo at the Imperial Hotel, preparing for the war criminal trials which are to open soon.

That evening I went to the home of Mr. Bishop of the State Department, along with six other members from the United States Education Mission, where we enjoyed an excellent dinner and a delightful evening.

Friday, March 22—We spent the day working upon our committee's report. In the late evening for recreational purposes our committee took a drive through Tokyo. Later that evening we visited two of the large Japanese dancehalls, supervised by M.P. 's. These are open from 1:00 to 9:30 P.M. The Japanese girls come in their street clothes, carrying a small wicker basket in which they have an evening gown. The dancehalls were well supervised. No liquor was sold in them and the M.P.'s searched each individual coming in to make sure that he took no liquor in with him.

During the afternoon while driving through one of the few sections of Tokyo where the houses were not destroyed by fire, we ran into a huge black market in whale meat. We were driving through a very narrow alley in this section of the city when we came upon tons of whale meat piled across the alley in the dirt. Japanese carts were coming in. Several hundred pounds of whale meat were being loaded on each cart and taken into various sections of the city. When the manipulators of the black market saw our Army car approaching they were frightened and excited. When we backed out of the alley and departed, the head black marketeer gave us many a gracious Japanese bow.

We went back to the hotel and spent the evening going carefully over our committee report. We re-worded parts of it.

Saturday, March 23—Plans had been made for some time for nine members of the Mission to fly to Hiroshima but when we arose it was raining and the weather conditions were such that the flight was postponed by the Army until the following Thursday. We took advantage of this time to do more work in re-editing and refining our report. I dictated the report in revised form, and that evening we had thirty mimeographed copies of twenty-five pages each for the criticism of the entire Mission.

At 7:30 P.M. we made our report. Our committee report was the only one which had sufficient copies for each member to have a copy in his hands as we discussed it. The hardest battle we had was upon our recommendation concerning the Imperial Rescript on Education. Some of our members opposed it because they thought that this might be considered an attempt upon our part to destroy Japanese culture. We also had a considerable battle on the recommendation to markedly curtail the centralized control of the Ministry of Education. Those of us especially interested in public school education on elementary and secondary levels were determined to make recommendations that would guarantee to the great masses of Japanese people some opportunity for a reasonable education. Our report was discussed, sometimes with considerable vigor, until 11:30 P.M. when it was approved with certain suggestions for re-writing, deleting, and expanding, after which it was to go to the Editing Committee to be made a part of the entire report.

Sunday, March 24—The Committee on Teacher Education had co-chairmen—Dr. Freeman and Dr. Diemer. Dr. Freeman made opening remarks concerning the report and then called upon various members of the Committee to make additional reports. After listening to this interesting report several suggestions were made for its improvement. The next committee to report was the one on curriculum, of which Dr. Kandel was the chairman. He read a rather long report which was criticized by some as being too academic.

At 1:00 P.M. we adjourned for lunch, after which the United States Education Mission visited Tokyo Imperial University. We were transported to several buildings—Medical Building, Naval Architecture, Electrical Engineering, and finally to the Rockefeller Library, donated by John D. Rockefeller following the 1923 earthquake.

President Nambara and his faculty had the most elaborate tea that I have ever attended in any place at any time. He made a short but excellent speech to our group. President Nambara had just been named as a Peer. He served as chairman of the Japanese education committee which met with the United States Education Mission. I talked to one of the faculty members whom I had known for a good many years. He told me with some pathos that the future looked black for Japan. Each Japanese family was rationed one pound of sugar per week when the war started. After some time each family was reduced to one-quarter of a pound per week, and for the past year and a half they have had no sugar.

Mr. Stevens of our Mission told me a story which indicates the situation so far as inflation is concerned in Japan. He had spent the night with a Japanese friend just outside Tokyo who brought him back the next morning in a little Datsun Sedan—the size of our Crosley or Fiat. The man had bought this miniature Sedan eight years before for 2,500 yen. He was recently offered 35,000 yen for it.

After dinner we met to consider the committee's report on higher education. We also discussed further the report on curriculum and T. V. Smith's report on ethics. We considered also the report on language by Dr. Counts. During the report on higher education when criticism and suggestions were being made, Dr. Compton remarked that "It is very difficult to get hold of a handful of rain water."

Another amusing incident occurred when I was in the dining room with Dr. Kandel and a Second Lieutenant came to the door and sent in word that he wanted to speak with Colonel Andrews. The main dining room in the Imperial Hotel was reserved for officers who are full Colonels or above. As this Second Lieutenant stood outside the door and sent in word asking if Colonel Andrews could come out and speak to him about some business matters, Dr. Kandel remarked that this Lieutenant was one of the men who had just been appointed to serve on the committee to investigate the Japanese caste system.

Monday, March 25—At 9:00 A.M. the United States Education Mission met with the Japanese committee to give them a final opportunity to present any additional problems which they thought should be considered. Mr. Yamagawa [Yamagiwa] gave an interesting talk on elementary education. He stated that fifty percent of the primary school buildings in Tokyo and the other large cities had been destroyed. Mr. Ariga [Aruga] discussed the Youth Schools. Reverend Kozaka [Kazaki] of the Tokyo Congregational Church spoke on Religious Education. Mr. Yanaki [Yanagi] discussed the handcraft work in Japan. Among other things he explained that Japanese textiles are dried in the sun for forty days. This process prevents any fading of colors. Mr. Youeno [Ueno] spoke on fine arts and showed several slides.

In the afternoon our committee met at 2:00 P.M. with representatives of teachers' organizations. At 3:00 P.M. a Middle School teacher met with us. He had a wife and three children and got 100 yen per month basic pay and about 200 yen emergency allowance, or war bonus, making a total of 300 yen per month. It cost him 1,000 yen per month to live. He had 7,000 yen in the bank originally and was drawing upon it to add to his meager salary. When his bank savings were gone, he didn't know what he would do.

Tuesday, March 26—At 9:00 A.M. we went to the Nippon Times to see recent motion pictures taken by the Japanese of their elementary schools. At 2:00 P.M. I showed the NEA motion picture, "Assignment: Tomorrow", to about sixty Japanese educators from all areas of education—President Nambara of Tokyo Imperial University and the Vice-Minister of Education, along with some teachers who had been incarcerated as political prisoners during the war, and many in between these two extremes including several women. I showed it once without any comments. Then we ran it through a second time, and I explained through a Japanese interpreter the significance of each scene. I then answered questions for one and one-half hours—questions which were intelligent and pointed and showed a keen desire to find out how they might develop their schools along democratic lines similar to the ones they had just seen in the picture. Later the film, "Assignment: Tomorrow", was presented to the International Cultural Association with the compliments of the National Education Association.

Wednesday, March 27—Our committee met in the Imperial Hotel with two educators from Korea to talk over their educational problems. At 11:00 o'clock I met with three Japanese men who wished permission to translate our Educational Policies Commission's publication, "Learning the Ways of Democracy." Permission was given to them and this book is now being printed in Japanese for use in the schools of Japan.

At 1:30 we left the Hotel to visit the Emperor of Japan. We were taken by Army convoy to the Foreign Relations Building in the Palace grounds. We walked up four flights to a large room with beautiful tapestries on the walls and were greeted there by Mr. Goto, Chief of the Protocol Division of the Foreign Office. After some time we went single file to another room to meet the Emperor. This room was a very simple, plain room with no furniture and no pictures—only a red rug on the floor. The Emperor and his interpreter came into the room, went directly to Chairman George Stoddard, shook hands with him, and welcomed the Mission to Japan. He then shook hands with Gordon Bowles and told him how glad he was to have him back in Japan again. The Emperor then came around the semi-circle, shaking hands with each one. When he had finished he went back to where Chairman George Stoddard stood and spoke to the Mission briefly. Among other things, he said that he hoped that we liked Japan and that we would make an understanding and helpful report—one that would be useful to Japan in improving her school system. After he had finished talking to us Chairman Stoddard responded for the Mission. Before the Emperor left the room he asked Chairman Stoddard to recommend a teacher from America for his fourteen-year-old son. After this he shook hands with each member of the Mission and left.

We went in our convoy of cars to another building in the Palace grounds where we met the Emperor's brother, Prince Takamatsu, and his wife. Prince Kuni, brother to the Empress, was present also. They entertained us in the Emperor's

Court with two ancient court dances—first, the Polo Dance, and, second, the Snake Dance. The courtroom in which the plays were given was large, dignified, and highly decorated. The members of the orchestra and the actors were dressed in costly rich golden attire. After the Court entertainment Prince Takamatsu and the Princess, along with Prince Kuni, had a very simple, informal tea for us—the simplest and most informal tea which I attended while in Japan.

We returned from the Emperor's Palace with many questions in our minds and all of us filled with pride for our good old U.S.A. where every man is a king and nobody an emperor.

That evening I was picked up at the Imperial Hotel by three men from the State Department and went in company with Mr. Leebrick, Mr. Bishop, and Mr. Seabald to an elaborate Japanese dinner given by former Ambassador Kuwashima at the Rinsinso—a man's club—the English interpretation of which is "tavern by the river." This Japanese meal started by each of us being served a hot face towel on a bamboo wicker basket. The towels were steaming hot. Each member of the party soaked his face with this hot towel; then wiped both his face and his hands with it before proceeding to eat a fifteen-course dinner. We had three soup courses and three fish courses, and the usual Japanese sukiyaki, deliciously cooked on the low table from which we were eating. One course consisted of hot, freshly roasted peanuts. The dinner was ended with fresh grapefruit and tea for dessert. It was the most elaborate and enjoyable dinner which I ate in Japan.

Thursday, March 28—A trip was planned for last Sunday, at which time nine of us were supposed to fly to Hiroshima but due to weather conditions, the trip was postponed until today. The trip was cancelled again today on account of weather conditions. After this trip was cancelled a few of us decided to take a drive into the country. We drove for two and a half hours over a reasonably good Japanese road and arrived at Lake Hakone. We looked at the Lake, a beautiful one, in which on a clear day the famous Japanese mountain, Fujiyama, is reflected, and then drove back for about thirty minutes to the little town of Miyanoshita and had lunch at the Fujiya Hotel. This is said to be Japan's finest hotel.

We ate lunch in a unique dining room where we enjoyed some of Japan's finest mountain scenery. After lunch we drove back through the country to Tokyo. We had a dinner at the Imperial Hotel in a private dining room for all of the members of the Civil Information and Education Section of General MacArthur's Headquarters Staff. The dinner was a very fine affair. T. V. Smith was toastmaster. George Stoddard gave a good talk. Colonel Nugent discussed some of the educational problems in Japan.

Friday, March 29—After breakfast we drove to the Diet which houses the lawmakers of Japan. We visited the meeting place of the House of Peers. This is a beautiful room which seats 410 members. It also has seats for the Emperor and Empress and a speaking place for the Emperor. The upholstery is a beautiful light blue; the wood is golden oak with exquisite carving. This Diet building was finished in 1936. The other meeting room for the House of Commons is very similar to the House of Peers but is larger, accommodating 485 members.

After we left the Diet building we drove to the War Ministry Building to see the lay-out for the trials for the war criminals. We were taken through this Building on an especially conducted tour by Judge McDougall of Canada. He showed us Tojo's former office. Tojo's office is now being used by one of the judges who will pass upon the charges against him as a war criminal. We also visited the Court Room where the trials are to be held. The war criminals are being held in Sugamo Prison which is located in the City of Tokyo. We visited all of the rooms prepared for the judges. Judge Higgins from Boston is the American judge who is to sit in the war criminal trials. Sir William Webb of Australia is president of the panel of judges who will conduct the hearings. The judges from Russia, France, and China had not yet arrived when we were in Tokyo.

In the afternoon we drove about Tokyo and got a beautiful view of Mount Fujiyama and the sunset over the Mountain.

At night the Mission attended a dinner at Yeno [Ueno] Seiyoken, a large restaurant in Tokyo. The dinner was given by the Minister of Education, Mr. Abe, and attended by leading Japanese educators. It was quite an elaborate dinner at which Mr. Abe read a short paper in English.

Saturday, March 30—At 9:00 A.M. we started to drive to the Mingeikan Museum of which Mr. M. Yanagi is the Director. We had considerable difficulty in finding the Museum but finally did. Mr. Yanagi showed us through with eagerness. The Museum displays the handcraft of Japan. We saw many interesting pieces—the most interesting, from the standpoint of fine workmanship, being the various pieces made out of wild cherry trees. After we had looked through the Museum we went across the street to Mr. Yanagi's home and had tea with his family. His house is a typical Japanese farmer's house.

In the afternoon we packed and took our large pieces over to the Air Transport Command Station and checked them.

At 4:00 P.M. we had the final meeting of the United States Education Mission. We agreed to make a gift from the Mission to the children and teachers of Japan of approximately 1000 yen each for the purchase of books to be sent to Japan as soon as we had made a collection after we returned. A committee of three people was appointed for this purpose, consisting of Dr. Carnovsky, Dean Virginia Gildersleeve, and T. V. Smith.

Sunday, March 31—We were to be ready to leave Japan at 7:00 A.M. At 7:00 o'clock we got a weather report which stated that a typhoon was playing around between Guam and Manila. We were told to be ready to depart at 5:00 P.M. that afternoon. After having the word that we would not go until 5:00 P.M., a few of us left in an Army car to drive through the country toward Necco [Nikko]. We drove out Route 1 for about 60 miles. We got to within 30 miles of Necco but had to turn back in order to be in Tokyo by 5:00 o'clock. We passed through the best farming country that I saw in Japan. The land was quite fertile. The houses were small but nice-looking. The people seemed much better fed than in the cities. They also seemed happier.

We returned to Tokyo and were told to be ready to depart the next morning at 8:00 A.M.

Monday, April 1—We reported at 8:00 A.M. and were told to report again at 12:00 o'clock noon. In the meantime we drove out to see Yokohama Bay. As we drove onto the pier in Yokohama Bay we saw two boats loaded with soldiers. On one side of the pier was the Milford Victory, built in Baltimore, Maryland, loaded with gay, happy, noisy soldiers starting home. Directly across on the other side of the pier was the Cape Perpetua loaded with soldiers just tying up, ready to get off to serve in Japan. They were silent, tensive and not talking, but they were there unloading, ready to do the work assigned to them. We walked to the end of the pier and saw one big English ship, the Duke of York, lying in the harbor. We also saw General Eichelberger's house. His house overlooks Yokohama Bay. We went down in Yokohama later to where there are acres of American planes, tanks, ambulances and other war materials stored.

We returned to the Imperial Hotel for lunch and were told that weather conditions were good and that we would leave the Hotel at 7:00 P.M. that evening for Atsuge Airfield and would take off at 9:25 P.M. Shortly after 7:00 P.M. we started for Atsuge Airfield. After arriving we signed a couple of papers which were part of the routine of leaving, and boarded a C-54 Army Transport Plane bound for Hickam Field.

Tuesday, April 2—We landed at Guam at 4:40 A.M., and took off at 7:40 A.M., Guam time. We had a delightful ride from Tokyo to Guam, taking seven hours and fifteen minutes. It was a beautiful pacific day as we flew on from Guam to Kwajalein, landing at Kwajalein at 5:35, Kwajalein time. We were met at the plane in the rain by a bus and taken to the officers' mess hall where we had a typical Army meal. This particular one consisted of tomato soup, crackers, boiled beef, potatoes, string beans, apple sauce, lemonade, coffee, bread and butter, and apple pie. The cost to each of us, flying as guests of the United States Army, was $.20.

The island is only seven feet above sea level. The people there were worried over a reported tidal wave which was approaching. We remained at Kwajalein exactly two hours and then left for Johnston Island. We were in the air for seven hours and fifty-five minutes flying from Guam to Kwajalein. We left Kwajalein at 7:30 P.M., Kwajalein time, Tuesday, April 2. After flying east of Kwajalein for about two hours we passed the international dateline and then turned our time back one day to Tuesday morning, April 2, although it was then almost midnight of April 2 on the Guam side of the international dateline.

We arrived at Johnston Island at 3:05 A.M., Tuesday, April 2—the flying time from Kwajalein being seven hours and thirty-five minutes. We had breakfast at Johnston Island and left there at 4:20 A.M. for Honolulu.

The flight during the night was unusually smooth. Most of us slept on the floor of the C-54. The only disturbance was a slight vibration from the engine. We arrived at Hickam Field, Honolulu, at 8:30 A.M., Tuesday, April 2, Johnston Island time, and 10:00 A.M., Honolulu time. Our flying time from Johnston Island to Honolulu was four hours and ten minutes. There being no place to clean up properly at Johnston Island, we were rather unkempt when we arrived in Honolulu. We all went through customs there, after which we shaved, had showers, and cleaned up at the officers' quarters. The customs officer was a former McKinley High School boy whom I had known when I was principal there twenty-five years before. Superintendent Oren E. Long came out to the airport and had lunch with us.

At 1:30 all of the Mission members took off for Hamilton Field in San Francisco except me. I had made plans to stop off in Honolulu for one week. Superintendent Long and I drove over to Honolulu. The other members of the Mission flew to San Francisco in about twelve hours. After a brief stop at Hamilton Field they flew on to Topeka, Kansas, and after one hour there on to Washington, D. C.—that is, those who did not stop at Hamilton Field. The ones from the West Coast left the party at Hamilton Field. Members of the Mission who came on through to Washington arrived in Washington shortly after midnight on Wednesday night, April 3, having left Tokyo on Monday night, April 1, at 9:25 P.M. They were in the air fifty-one hours and on the ground eleven hours—sixty-two hours elapsed time between Tokyo and Washington, D. C.

Oren E. Long, Superintendent of Public Instruction, took me in his automobile into the City of Honolulu. We stopped at his office which I had occupied twenty-one years before. After meeting some of the office people we then went to his delightful home.

Wednesday, April 3—I went to the office with Superintendent Long. The police Department sent me over a duplicate of my 1922 driver's license with their compliments. I then drove out to Palolo Hill where the Givens family lived during most of the time that they were in Honolulu. Our house at that time was in the edge of the country. Today the hillside is covered with beautiful houses. I visited Lilioukalane School which is made up entirely of seventh-grade pupils. Excellent work is being done in this School. After visiting each teacher in Lilioukalane School I went to McKinley High School where I had been principal twenty-five years ago and had lunch with the student body officers. I visited McKinley until 4:00 P.M. I did not see all of it because it is a high school which will accommodate 4000 students, but I saw much of it. It was my privilege as Superintendent of Public Instruction to help secure the site—fifty-one and one-half acres—upon which McKinley now stands, and to secure appropriations from the Territorial Legislature for the first building. Miles E. Cary, who came to McKinley as a teacher, has done a m[a]gnificent piece of work during the last twenty years as principal in developing this school into one of the great high schools of America. The student body is made up almost entirely of Americans of oriental and Hawaiian descent—a great body, carrying forward a sanely progressive and practical program of education.

Thursday, April 4—Deputy Superintendent Robinson took me in Mr. Long's car to the airport at Hickam Field where I made my reservation to return to the Mainland on Tuesday, April 9. We returned to Honolulu, and I spent an hour with Mr. McDonough, Secretary of the Hawaii Education Association. This Territorial Association is carrying forward a fine piece of work. It was my privilege to help organize this Association and to serve as its first president in 1920.

I had lunch at McKinley High School with officers of the Territorial Parent-Teacher Association. I then visited the Lincoln Intermediate School. I visited several teachers in this building and then drove out to Kalakau School on the ewa side of Honolulu where I sat in conference for an hour with Paul Sanborne, Principal of the School, and several experts in the field of agricultural education. I then drove over to the old Kamehameha Boys' School site, now occupied by the Kamehameha Preparatory School. The campus is entirely different from what it was when I served as principal of this school twenty-four years ago. A large part of the former campus is now occupied by the Wallace R. Farrington High School, one of the fine public high schools of Honolulu. Much of the rest of the campus is covered now with temporary military buildings of all kinds.

I had dinner in the evening at the Moano Hotel as guest of Mr. and Mrs. Miles E. Cary. I was privileged at this dinner to be in the company of several of McKinley's former graduates of both Japanese and Chinese descent, who are now holding important positions in the Hawaiian Islands. They are serving the Territory of Hawaii with distinction to McKinley High School and great credit to themselves.

Friday, April 5—Mr. Gus Webling, Supervising Principal of rural Oahu, took me to the Pali where we stopped and were almost blown away by the wind. We then went down the Pali to Kailua. We visited most of the schools around the Island and saw the damage done by the tidal wave of Monday, April 1. We saw the refugees from the tidal wave area residing at that time in "Green Valley", a place formerly used for training soldiers for jungle fighting. We drove by the beautiful Mormon Temple again and around the Island, visiting schools until we arrived at Wahiawa where I spent the night with Mr. and Mrs. Cosmo Wise.

Saturday, April 6—This was Army Day; therefore, Schofield Barracks was open to the public. Mr. Wise, after driving me all around Wahiawa, took me through Schofield Barracks, up to Kole Kole Pass. As we stood in Kole Kole Pass we looked down toward the ocean at a great naval station; inland we looked upon Schofield Barracks, one of the largest Army military posts under the American flag. This post has been very much expanded and developed during World War II. I saw many interesting things inside the military reservation. However, the most artistic sight that I saw was a large Tulip tree, fiery red with blossoms, standing side by side with a Jackaranda tree covered with beautiful blue blossoms.

After covering the Schofield Barracks area thoroughly in an automobile, Mr. Wise took me to Honolulu. We arrived at about 11:00 o'clock. It was my privilege to have lunch as the guest of Superintendent Oren E. Long and twenty-three members of his staff at Halekulani Hotel. This is one of the old hotels in Honolulu with a beautiful tropical setting on Waikiki Beach. I later drove over to see my friend, Harry Metcalf, who worked with me in Hawaii immediately after World War I, helping in the educational program for the military forces.

I had dinner that evening as the guest of Mr. and Mrs. James Chun, fine Americans of Chinese ancestry. Mr. Chun graduated from McKinley High School when I was principal. He owns a store in Honolulu. We had dinner at one of the large Chinese eating places downtown. They invited to this dinner fifteen former McKinley students—about half of them of Chinese ancestry and half of Japanese ancestry. The rest of the United States has much to learn, as indeed has the world, from the way Hawaii has handled and is handling the race problem.

Sunday, April 7—Oren E. Long and I went to his office where he caught up with some of his back work and where I worked on two rather important speeches which I was to give the next day—one at 8:30 in the morning to the McKinley High School body, and one in the afternoon to the teachers of the Island of Oahu.

General MacArthur having released our confidential report on Saturday, April

6, I was at liberty now to discuss this report with the Honolulu newspapers which I did at considerable length Sunday afternoon in the Long home. The papers carried fine stories concerning the report of the United States Education Mission to Japan. Mr. Long and I then went to Kamehameha Girls' School and heard a very fine program of music. After dinner we drove out to see Mr. and Mrs. Harry Wong on Mikihala Way. Harry Wong was one of the first Americans of Chinese descent I met when I first went to the Islands in 1919.

Monday, April 8—At 8:30 A.M. I spoke to the student body at McKinley High School where a large packed auditorium sang several songs, including "The Star Spangled Banner" and "Hawaii Ponoi." "The Star Spangled Banner" was sung in four parts. It was done in an artistic manner, surpassing any singing of "The Star Spangled Banner" that I have ever been privileged to hear.

As I spoke to the McKinley student body I looked on one side of the packed auditorium where there hung a flag with more than 1100 stars upon it. On the other side of the auditorium hung a flag with 113 gold stars. Most of these stars on both sides of the auditorium were in honor of Americans of Japanese descent who defended their country against attack made by the country of their fathers and mothers. No easy task, this, but anyone who doubts what the public schools and churches are doing in handling the race problem wisely and fairly should take time to read the brilliant military records of the Americans of Japanese ancestry during World War II.

When I had finished speaking to the McKinley High School student body I was met by Mr. John Mason Young, a long-time personal friend, who took me to see the Scottish Rite Cathedral and then on to the University of Hawaii. There I met President Sinclair and was taken through the excellent plant of the University which now accommodates more than 2000 students. All about the institution we saw American students of oriental and Hawaiian ancestry.

On the way back from the University of Hawaii we stopped at the Shriners' Hospital for Crippled Children. More than twenty-five years ago I helped to make the survey which demonstrated the need for this hospital in Hawaii. The Scottish Rite Fraternity now has sixteen hospitals for crippled children. The first one was built at Shreveport, Louisiana; the second one at Honolulu; and the sixteenth one has just been finished in Mexico City. I am proud to have had a part in starting this hospital because it is one of the great institutions of our present-day America —an institution that takes any crippled child who needs help, regardless of race, color, religion or economic condition, and does for him everything that medical science can do. This is democracy in practice.

I returned at noon-time and met with the Trustees of the Bishop Estate to discuss with them the qualifications of several candidates for the Presidency of the Kamehameha Schools. I then had lunch with the Education Committee of the Honolulu Chamber of Commerce—a very fine committee made up of businessmen and educators. We met to discuss the educational problems of the Islands.

I then went to McKinley High School where it was my privilege to speak to the teachers of the Island of Oahu. Following this meeting I met informally in the library of McKinley High School with people who attended the classes of 1920 and 1921 while I was principal of McKinley High School.

That evening it was my privilege to have dinner in the home of Mr. and Mrs. Stanley Miomoto. Mr. Miomoto is now principal of one of the high schools in Honolulu—another fine American of Japanese descent and a graduate of McKinley High School. I was pleased to be a dinner guest with several Americans of Japanese descent.

Tuesday, April 9—I packed and got ready to leave Hawaii Nei. I stopped at the offices of the *Honolulu Advertiser* and talked to Lorrin Thurston, owner and publisher. The *Advertiser* is located in a beautiful new building that is tropical in its setting and architecture.

From here I went to the offices of the *Honolulu Star Bulletin* and had a profitable conference with my friend of long standing, Mr. Riley Allen. He has been doing outstanding work for the people of Hawaii for many years. I discussed with him the question of statehood for Hawaii. I then returned to Mr. Long's office and dictated letters to several friends whom I had not had the opportunity to see.

I attended the Rotary Club at the Moano Hotel at noon. There I saw twenty Rotarians whom I had known twenty-one years before when I served as President of the Honolulu Rotary Club. There are still thirty in the Club of one hundred and sixty who were members when I was President of the Club. I spoke briefly to the Rotarians and received a lei from the Club presented by Duke Kahanamoku, a former Hawaiian swimming champion of world renown.

I returned to Superintendent Long's office. He took me to Hickam Field. After an active, interesting and enjoyable week, I left Honolulu at 4:30 P.M.

Wednesday, April 10—There were twenty-nine passengers and six crew members, making thirty-five on the C-54 as we flew from Hickam Field, Honolulu, to Hamilton Field, San Francisco. The personnel was all military with the single exception of me, and I was traveling as a member of the United States Education Mission with the privileges and perquisites of a brigadier general.

As we came into San Francisco I saw one of the most beautiful ocean sunrises that I have ever seen. As we approached the Mainland there was a visibility of twelve miles. We flew straight in through the Golden Gate over the San Francisco Bay and circled out past San Rafael some twenty-five miles to Hamilton Field. I checked my baggage on through to Washington; then took a Greyhound Bus to San Francisco; and went on to Oakland.

Thursday, April 11—I talked to Superintendent Odell and Assistant Superintendent Briscoe. At 4:00 o'clock I spoke to a fine group of teachers from the Oakland Public Schools and had dinner with the Oakland Principals' Club at the Oakland High School. It was a pleasure to meet and mingle again with the many excellent school people in Oakland.

Friday, April 12—I spent the day visiting schools in Oakland. I met many friends and saw much fine work being done.

Saturday, April 13—My hosts, Mr. and Mrs. Edward W. Long, drove me to Hamilton Field. I checked in, was called for "The Statesman", and at 9:40 I boarded a C-54. We took off from Hamilton Field and flew over the Bay area and started for Washington. We could see the whole country. As we left the Bay country we flew over the Sacramento Valley and then over the mountains at about 13,000 feet elevation. The mountains were covered with snow. We arrived at

Topeka where we had a fine roast beef dinner at the Officers' Club and left for Washington. We arrived in Washington at 1:55 A.M., Eastern Standard Time. We had flown from San Francisco to Topeka in seven hours and ten minutes, and from Topeka to Washington in four hours and fifty-five minutes—the flight across the continent being made in twelve hours and five minutes flying time.

The flight of the United States Education Mission to Japan and return was made in one hundred and six hours flying time—fifty-five going and fifty-one returning. The United States Education Mission to Japan returned after a strenuous month. The members of the Mission had been requested by their country to study the educational program of a defeated nation and to make recommendations that would help that country to become eventually a member of the family of United Nations. We made recommendations to General MacArthur which we hope will help a confused people, bewildered by the turn of events, to develop a more democratic society.

[*Source*: Givens Papers, National Education Association Archives]

4. George D. Stoddard and the U.S. Education Mission to Japan: A Brief Appreciation
Philip H. Stoddard

> *We are free in all respects but one; we are not free to tolerate the destruction of our freedom.*

My father's professional career spanned 50 years. It encompassed 17 books, over 200 scholarly papers and articles and many hundreds of speeches in three areas he regarded as intimately related: child development and intelligence (University of Iowa); educational administration (University of Illinois, New York University, Long Island University, University of the State of New York), and assorted other national and international activities (UNESCO, educational television, and education missions to Japan, Korea, Iran, and Africa).

George D. Stoddard's philosophy, as applied to education, reflected: impatience with dogma, pendantry and the phoney; adversion to reductionism; profound concern with matters of significance in human affairs; and a strong belief in integrity and, most important, in freedom and democracy and in the linkage between thought and action. ("The golden rule in thinking is to think straight. Thought, if it is to be effective, must be at once free and informed. . . . Freedom as modified by a liberal education leads to more freedom; through education new levels of human endeavor can be reached.")

These deeply held convictions led my father to articulate six principles—an education "matrix"—that could lead to meaning in life:[1]

1) Through science, a further penetration into the structure of matter, life, and the universe.
2) The foreshortened past as a prologue to an undefined future.
3) Nothing from fear, superstition, or magic.
4) Life fulfillment, not as an end point but as a series of actions interspersed with thought. It can be reached only through learning and the creative process.
5) An approach to philosophy that embraces all science, social structure, and human aspiration.
6) The resolution of the mind-body-soul problem through the acceptance of man as a uniquely evolved species—the one animal that conceives of a past and a future; that speaks, hopes, and despairs; that explores the universe; that cannot bear to die like other animals and, seeking gods, finds them at last in the power and beauty of his own creations.

Life thus finds meaning by transmitting:[2]

On an ever-ascending scale of wisdom, beauty, and love the unique biological resources of which we are capable. Morality and justice, no absolutes, are functional derivatives of experience and good will. Our highest involvement in this enterprise, all within the realm of the natural, rise to the rank of the *spiritual* as a figure of speech. We are moved and mystified as science pushes outward the study of natural phenomena. Beyond science it is a rewarding experience to embrace humanism. This line of thought and action runs clearly through American history—through the strong, new world of Jefferson, Emerson, Horace Mann, Abraham Lincoln, and John Dewey. It is not enought to *return* to such a world; rather, in the midst of much confusion and clamor, we should get on with it. And that is where education comes in.

This liberal, humanist outlook, with its emphasis on choice and freedom of thought, provided the backdrop for my father's participation in the U.S. Education Mission to Japan in 1946. For him the chairmanship of this diverse and distinguished group was a challenge to be approached with humility, dedication, and a willingness to work hard no matter how onerous or difficult the job might be. Most of all, he wrote, the mission was an opportunity "to bring home to Americans the magnitude of the task of assisting Japan to rejoin the circle of responsible nations."[3]

The invitation to join the mission to Japan arrived in early 1946 at a propitious transition point in my father's career. After nearly four years of Commissioner of Education (the Commissioner "pronounced on everything but was in charge of nothing") and president of the University of the State of New York (not to be confused with the State University of New York, which was established in 1948), he had accepted the presidency of the University of Illinois several months before. He was eagerly looking forward to begin dealing "hands on" with the enormous challenges of a large university widely described at the time as a "sleeping giant."

The trip to Japan also came up only a few months after the London Conference for the establishment of the United Nation[s] Educational, Scientific, and Cultural

Organization (UNESCO). My father had been one of the five members of the U.S. delegation, which was headed by his friend William Benton, Assistant Secretary of State. My father surmised that Benton had been influential in the choice of my father as chairman of this team. Its members, in New York political parlance would have been termed a "sweetheart ticket" (i.e., an electoral slate that would appeal to a broad spectrum of interest groups.) It thus contained a little of everything: college presidents, professors, school executives, women, religious leaders, a labor representative, one from the military, and one black. It was an experienced, highly motivated group that approached its difficult task with great enthusiasm. As he wrote 30 years later, "we were ignorant enough (of Japan) but we were not adrift."

One amusing event occurred before the group left for Japan. At a meeting with President Truman a problem arose: how could members of the mission stay at the Imperial Hotel in Tokyo which was restricted to U.S. military officers of the rank of colonel or above? Truman, with characteristic decisiveness, proposed to solve the problem by making members of the team temporary colonels. My father, as chairman, would be a brigadier general. Truman asked his aides whether he had the authority to do this; he was assured that he did. My father, having served briefly as a reserve second lieutenant in World War I, was impressed and commented to the President on how rapidly and easily he had risen in rank. Truman replied that he had felt the same way; in his case, he had gone from a captain in World War I to Commander-in-Chief without having done anything in the interim, he said, except serve as senator and vice president.

My father regarded the modest role he had played at the Emperor's request in the selection of the tutor for Crown Prince Akihito as the climax of the mission to Japan. He devoted several pages of his autobiography to this pleasant task, and Mrs. Vining has described it eloquently in *Windows for the Crown Prince* and *Quiet Pilgrimage*. The Stoddard children were very enthusiastic about the choice: we knew Mrs. Vining vicariously and favorably through her wonderful books for children. Mrs. Vining, my father wrote, "won the hearts of the Japanese people, high and low. She did not preach about the American way of life; she simply exemplified it at its best. Elizabeth Gray Vining, without portfolio, devoid of all pretension, became our most admired ambassador."

During his last few years, my father became greatly concerned about the future because of our "exponentially increasing power to destroy the human race."[4] In meeting this challenge, he noted,

> the hope of success among fallible human beings lies in a broad overlapping spectrum of idealism and self-interest. The time has come to unite these two incentives. Sacrifices of power and prestige are demanded. The grim alternative is a used-up planet, paradoxically both overpopulated and overkilled. At stake is the transformation of a cluster of war-infected nations into a decent sociopolitical structure devoted to survival. Toward this overriding issue we ask our leaders to turn their best thought and their deepest commitment. Morality of a high order is essential. The tensions that cause wars are not only related to the minds of men but also to their hearts—to their secret desires. When looked at from the moon, Earth seems to be a shining glory. The responsibility of all mankind is to make it so. . . . We must believe in our best selves and work courageously

with others to unite the world. The prophets of the Old Testament could scarcely have envisaged a more awesome mission. If alive today they would surely invest that mission with religious zeal; they would preach mightily to warn the unseeing.

The fourteen years that have passed since those words were written have not lessened our concern. Indeed, they have added to it a dangerous and ever more serious ecological dimension. Education is crucial: "The profession of education itself is a uniquely powerful force in the advancement of citizenship." Nowadays, George D. Stoddard—always the internationalist—would have written "*world* citizenship."

(*July 20, 1988*)

Notes:

1. George D. Stoddard, *The Outlook for American Education* (Carbondale and Edwardsville: Southern Illinois University Press, 1974), pp. 13–14.
2. Ibid., p. 14.
3. George D. Stoddard, *The Pursuit of Education: An Autobiography* (New York; Vantage Press, 1981), p. 80.
4. Ibid., pp. 270–271.

NOTES

Notes to Introduction

1. Willard E. Givens, Chairman of the Second U.S. Education Mission to Japan, called the Education Mission of 1946 "the First United States Education Mission to Japan" in his brief autobiography, "The Life of Willard Earl Givens," in the Archives of the National Education Association.

2. Hideo Sato, "Tainichi Beikoku Kyoiku Shisetsudan ni Kansuru Kenkyu" [A Study of the United States Education Mission to Japan], lecture on September 16, 1983, at the National Institute for Educational Research of Japan.

3. "The Life of Willard Earl Givens."

4. Letter to John E. Keough, Chief, Personnel Section, Office for Occupied Areas, Department of the Army, Washington, D.C., on September 27, 1950, from Willard E. Givens, Chairman, Second United States Education Mission to Japan, Box 38, Pearl A. Wanamaker Papers (Henry Suzzallo Library, Manuscripts and University Archives, University of Washington). In this letter, Givens wrote that "the members of the Second United States Education Mission to Japan have been glad to be of service to the Office for Occupied Areas of the Department of the Army. We hope that our report will be practical and useful."

5. GHQ/SCAP/CI&E, "Development in Japanese Education in terms of the Report of the United States Education Mission to Japan (A Working Document)" (Tokyo, August 1950). This document was drafted by 18 staff members, including Monta L. Osborne as the leader of the CI&E, for the Second Mission prior to its arrival. It includes the following sentence: "An enlightened electorate in Japan is certainly one of the greatest weapons against Communism in the Far East." This is quoted in the Final Report of the Second Mission.

6. When the State–War–Navy Coordinating Committee (SWNCC) was renamed the State–Army–Navy–Air Force Coordinating Committee (SANACC) after the Air Force joined (July 1947), the real power of decision making was transferred from

the State Department to the War Department. As a result, SWNCC was deprived
of its main function, and after 1948 the significance of the Occupation of Japan as
the military base for Far East strategy was established. Consequently, decision
making was taken completely out of the hands of SANACC and taken over by the
Joint Chiefs of Staff (JCS) and SCAP. Yoshizo Watanabe, "'New Dealer' no Taijo"
[Retirement of the New Dealers], in *Kyodo Kenkyu: Nihon Senryo* [Collaboration:
The Japanese Occupation] ed. Shiso no Kagaku Kenkyukai (Tokyo: Tokuma Shoten,
1972), p. 439.

7. Letter to Pearl Wanamaker, Superintendent of Public Instruction, State of
Washington, from Ivan Nelson, Vocational Education, CI&E Education Division,
June 19, 1950, Box 38, Wanamaker Papers.

8. Seiya Munakata, Akira Igarashi, and Eiichi Mochida, "Senryoka no Kyoiku
Kaikaku" [Education Reform Under the Occupation], in *Nihon Shihonshugi Koza:
Sengo Nihon no Seiji to Keizai* [Lectures on Japanese Capitalism: Postwar Japanese
Politics and Economy], vol. 2 (Tokyo: Iwanami Shoten, 1953), p. 345.

9. *Amerika Kyoiku Shisetsudan Hokokusho* [The Report of the United States
Education Mission], trans. Minoru Murai (Tokyo: Kodansha, 1979), pp. 152–
53.

10. Naiseishi Kenkyukai, *Kennoki Toshihiro Shi Danwa Sokki Roku* [Stenogra-
phic Record of Talks by Toshihiro Kennoki], second talk (April 10, 1973), p. 70.

11. Hiroshi Kida, ed., *Shogen: Sengo no Bunkyo Seisaku* [Testimonies: Postwar
Education Policies] (Tokyo: Daiichi Hoki, 1987), p. 20. This contradicts the historical facts by asserting that postwar education reform was accomplished by coercion
from the U.S. side. In relation to this, the memoir of a teacher contains the following inference: "We understood that the Report strongly indicated the state of
Japanese education. We agreed with the main substance of the Report, which is
based on observations of the prewar and wartime educational administration and
the world of education generally. It was so well informed that we thought, 'It
cannot have been written only by Americans. They must have had advice from
some Japanese teachers or scholars with a thorough knowledge of the actual conditions of Japanese education, and who also realized the difficulties.'" Tsuneo Shii,
Kyoshi ni Totte Guchoku to wa Nanika [What Is Simple Honesty for the Teacher?]
(Tokyo: Hitotsubashi Shobo, 1970).

12. Kazuo Kawai, *Japan's American Interlude* (Chicago: University of Chicago
Press, 1960), p. 188.

13. Televised speech of former Prime Minister Kakuei Tanaka, Fuji Television
Network, April 28, 1974. Masami Yamazumi and Teruhisa Horio, *Sengo Nihon no
Kyoiku Kaikaku 2: Kyoiku Rinen* [Postwar Japanese Education Reform 2: Educa-
tional Ideas] (Tokyo: University of Tokyo Press, 1976).

14. Hiroshi Sugo, Seiichi Miyahara, and Seiya Munakata, eds., *Amerika Kyoiku
Shisetsudan Hokokusho Yokai* [Study by Japanese Educators of the Report of the
U.S. Education Mission to Japan] (Tokyo: Kokumin Tosho Kankokai, 1950), p. 38.

15. Tokiomi Kaigo, *Nihon Kyoiku no Shinten* [Development of Japanese Educa-
tion] (Tokyo: University of Tokyo Press, 1951), pp. 18–19.

16. Shuichi Katsuta, "Sengo Kyoiku no Mondaiten" [The Problems of Postwar
Education], in *Nihon Kindai Kyoikushi* [The History of Modern Japanese Education]

(Gendai Kyoiku Gaku [Contemporary Pedagogy] 5) (Tokyo: Iwanami Shoten, 1962), p. 370.

17. It may be simplistic to illustrate the existence of Japanese initiative within the education reform by referring only to the abstract provision of the Potsdam Declaration in regard to "the ... strengthening of democratic tendencies." It should be noted, however, that the only official documents relating to the early period of the Occupation are the Potsdam Declaration and "The U.S. Initial Post-Surrender Policy for Japan." The latter conforms to the Potsdam Declaration, and its basic policy was drawn up by Gordon T. Bowles of the State Department. In this connection, it is necessary to point out that the Potsdam Declaration does not include a specific article on education, as the Potsdam Agreement does in the German case. Nevertheless, we should regard the basic subject matter of the Potsdam Declaration as providing encouragement for a Japanese initiative in the development of democratic education. This matter will be discussed in chapter 2.

18. I wish to thank Dr. Ernest R. Hillgard, Dr. Gordon T. Bowles, Dr. Herbert J. Wunderlich, Dr. Mark T. Orr, Dr. Pearl A. Wanamaker, Dr. John W. Taylor, Dr. Herman B Wells, and Dr. William G. Carr for their most generous assistance in this study. Errors of fact or interpretation are entirely my responsibility. I have summarized most of the quotations from these interviews. The Bowles interviews were held mostly in Japanese. For these reasons, at times the quotations may vary slightly from the exact words of the interviewees.

19. Tokumitsu Yagawa, *Nihon Kyoiku no Kiki* [The Crisis in Japanese Education] (Tokyo: Shin Hyoronsha, 1953), p. 34.

20. Eiichi Suzuki, "Beikoku Tainichi Kyoiku Shisetsudan Kenkyu no Kadai to Hoho" [The Subject and Method of a Study of the United States Education Mission to Japan], "Beikoku Tainichi Kyoiku Shisetsudan Hokokusho no Seiritsu Jijo ni Kansuru Sogoteki Kenkyu" [A Comprehensive Study of the Report of the United States Education Mission to Japan, with Particular Reference to the Preparation], ed. Eiichi Suzuki, Hideo Sato, Gary H. Tsuchimochi et al., *Bulletin of the Faculty of Education, Department of Education, Nagoya University* 31 (March 1985), p. 224.

21. Yamazumi and Horio, *Sengo Nihon no Kyoiku Kaikaku*, p. 223.

22. Masao Terasaki, "Senryo to Kyoiku Kaikaku" [The Occupation and Education Reform], *Sengo Nihon Kyoikushi* [The History of Postwar Japanese Education], ed. Takashi Ohta (Tokyo: Iwanami Shoten, 1982), pp. 79–81.

Notes to Chapter 1: The Organization of the Mission

1. *Report of the United States Education Mission to Japan* (Washington, D.C.: U.S. Government Printing Office, 1946), pp. 1–2.

2. Eiichi Suzuki, *Nihon Senryo to Kyoiku Kaikaku* [The Occupation in Japan and Education Reform] (Tokyo: Keiso Shobo, 1983), pp. 32–33. *Education in Japan*, by the CI&E, stated the functions of the CI&E as follows: "The functions of the Section are to make recommendations to effect the accomplishment of the informa-

tion and educational objectives of the Allied Powers ... to maintain liaison with the Japanese Ministry of Education [and] Educational Institutions ... to direct the initiation and production of such plans, materials and programs as are required to implement the information and education objectives of the Supreme Commander ... to make recommendations to insure the elimination of militarism and ultra-nationalism, in doctrine and practice, including military training, from all elements of the Japanese educational system, [and to insure] the inclusion of such new courses of instruction in school curricula as are necessary to accomplish the mission of proper dissemination of democratic ideals and principles.''

The CI&E was subdivided into Analysis and Research, Arts and Monuments, Religion, Planning and Special Projects, Information Dissemination (Press, Publications, Motion Pictures, Theater, Radio, and Reference Library), and Education divisions. The task of the Education Division was described as follows: ''The mission of the Education Division is to utilize the educational system of Japan as an instrument for accomplishing those reforms necessary to bring the basic pattern of Japanese thought, life, and actions into conformity with standards considered essential in a country which is to resume self-direction and a position of dignity in the community of nations.''

3. ''Memorandum to Col. Dyke: Mission of American Authorities to Assist and Advise the Civil Information and Education Special Staff Section of the Supreme Commander [of] the Allied Powers,'' Box 55, Trainor Papers (Hoover Institution Archives, Stanford University).

4. ''List of Advisers Suggested by the Education Ministry,'' Box 57, Trainor Papers.

5. ''Amerika Minshushugi: Zadankai'' [A Round-table Discussion: American Democracy], *Asahi Shinbun*, October 3, 1945. Elizabeth G. Vining, who was a private tutor to the Crown Prince at that time, testified: ''It is interesting that it was Mr. Maeda who suggested the Education Mission to General Fellers. He told me that he feared what military men might do to the schools and that he wanted the Occupation to have advice from the best American educators.'' Elizabeth Gray Vining, ''The View From the Other Side,'' *The Occupation of Japan: Educational and Social Reform*, ed. Thomas W. Burkman (Norfolk: The MacArthur Memorial, 1982), p. 206.

6. CI&E Education Division, ''Educational Advisers,'' *Weekly Reports*, October 8, 1945, Box 65, Trainor Papers.

7. ''Memorandum of Jiro Arimitsu, in Hiroshi Kida, ed., *Shogen: Sengo no Bunkyo Seisaku* [Testimonies: Postwar Education Policies] (Tokyo: Daiichi Hoki, 1987), pp. 175–76.

8. Interview with Herbert J. Wunderlich at his home in St. Maries, Idaho, August 13–15, 1984.

9. Mark T. Orr, ''The Reformers: Japanese Education During the Allied Occupation,'' Florida–Japan Seminar, University of Florida, May 3, 1980 (unpublished manuscript), p. 18. W. C. Trow wrote that his selection as a member was on Robert K. Hall's recommendation. William Clark Trow, ''Voices Down The Wind: Letters and Recollections of an Upstate New Yorker'' (unpublished manuscript, 1972),

p. 955. This memoir was obtained from Mrs. Trow. As a whole, it is based on Givens's diary, "Tokyo and Return," which is discussed later.

10. Postwar Program Committee, "Japanese: The Education System Under Military Government" (PWC 287a), November 6, 1944, p. 1, Box 144, Notter File (Modern Political History Materials Room, National Diet Library, Tokyo).

11. Gordon T. Bowles recalled the strained situation within the State Department as follows: "E. H. Dooman was one of the central figures in charge of postwar Japanese education policies in the Far Eastern Section of the State Department. When I joined their discussions later, I proposed two aspects from which to prepare the draft of policy documents for Japan, namely, that one should be discussed from the premise of the Japanese surrender and the other from the fact that Japan maintained military action in order to defend her territory up until the last moment. He insisted strongly that 'Japan never surrenders' and stressed that policies towards Japan should be the same as in the German case." Interview with Bowles at his home in Monterey, Massachusetts, February 13–15, 1983.

As a matter of fact, President Franklin Delano Roosevelt and the New Dealers in the White House adopted a conciliatory policy toward the Soviet Union but a punitive policy toward Japan, and they intended the same form of occupation for Japan as in the German case, that is, direct rule by military government. Watanabe, "'New Dealer' no Taijo" [Retirement of the New Dealers], p. 436.

12. "Office Memorandum to Mr. Benton: Status of Policies Relating to Education and Reeducation in Japan," Decimal File 894.50/10-545, Record Group 59, U.S. Department of State (U.S. National Archives).

13. The Subcommittee for the Far East, Ad Hoc Committee of SWNCC, suggested to Gen. MacArthur that one urgent task was the search for and support of Japanese who had had contact with Americans or had been educated in the U.S. prior to the war and who would cooperate with the aims of the Occupation. In this manner the necessity of establishing the Japanese Education Committee was implied. "Positive Policy for Reorientation of the Japanese," Revised Draft, September 3, 1945, Prepared by Borton and Bowles, SWNCC 162 Series (Top Secret), Roll 4, SFE/SWNCC Microfilm T-1205 (Modern Political History Materials Room, National Diet Library, Tokyo).

14. William P. Woodard, *The Allied Occupation of Japan 1945–1952 and Japanese Religions* (Leiden: E. J. Brill, 1972), p. 22.

15. "Education in Japan: Conclusions," Roll 4, SFE/SWNCC Microfilm T-1205.

16. Herbert Passin, *The Legacy of the Occupation: Japan* (Occasional Papers of the East Asia Institute, Columbia University, 1965), p. 4. An SWNCC document stated that "failure to prepare a positive and integrated program of reeducation and reorientation is a basic cause of the present chaos in Italy and has already invited severe criticism of our military government in Germany." "Positive Policy for Reorientation of Japanese" (SWNCC 162/D), July 19, 1945, Roll 4, SFE/SWNCC Microfilm T-1205.

17. Gordon T. Bowles, "Comments on Papers Presented at the Fourth Symposium on the Occupation of Japan: Educational and Social Reform," in Thomas W. Burkman, ed., *The Occupation of Japan: Educational and Social Reform* (Norfolk: The MacArthur Memorial, 1980), p. 517.

18. Letter from A. B. Chapman to John L. McClellan, 740.00119 Control (Japan)/10-3145, Documents of Department of State (U.S. National Archives).

19. Letter from James F. Brynes to John L. McClellan, 740.00119 Control (Japan)/10-3145.

20. Tamon Maeda, "The Direction of Postwar Education in Japan," *Japan Quarterly* 3 (1956), pp. 415–16.

21. Kazuo Kawai, *Japan's American Interlude* (Chicago: University of Chicago Press, 1960), p. 189.

22. Interview with James I. Doi in the Office of the Dean of the School of Education, University of Washington, February 8, 1983.

23. Harry Wray, "A Study of the First United States Education Mission to Japan, March 1946, and Its Significance for Educational Reform in Occupied Japan" (unpublished manuscript, 1981), p. 1.

24. The name in the Trainor Papers is "Gen. Marshall." This refers not to General George C. Marshall, Chief of Staff of the U.S. Army, in Washington, but to Major General Richard J. Marshall, Deputy Chief of Staff, GHQ/SCAP. (In the U.S. Army, "Gen." is commonly used as the abbreviation of "Major General.") It is not thought that the CI&E obtained approval directly from the General Staff Office in order to bypass SCAP or GHQ/USFPAC. Eiichi Suzuki, Hideo Sato, Gary H. Tsuchimochi et al., "A Comprehensive Study of the Report of the United States Education Mission to Japan, with Particular Reference to the Preparation" *Bulletin of the Faculty of Education, Department of Education, Nagoya University* 31 (March 1985), p. 241.

25. Robert K. Hall, "Memorandum to Chief of CIE, Notes on Presentation of the Plan for Bringing an Educational Mission to Japan," Box 56, Trainor Papers.

26. The initial plan in the State Department was for a three-man mission. However, Gen. MacArthur needed a Mission of about twenty members in order to resolve various problems the Occupation confronted prior to the start of the academic year. "Education Mission to Japan, January 23, 1946," Box 3, Stoddard Papers (Hoover Institution Archives, Stanford University).

27. "Memorandum: November 10, 1945," Box 56, Trainor Papers. This memorandum seems to be based on "Education in Japan: Conclusion," by SFE/SWNCC.

28. This study is found in neither the Library of Congress nor the Archives of the Carnegie Foundation. It can be conjectured that the CI&E, especially Robert K. Hall, produced it secretly to justify its selection of the candidates to Gen. MacArthur.

29. "Subject: Educational Mission for the United States," Box 56, Trainor Papers.

30. According to Edward R. Beauchamp, Conant was particularly hostile to Japan because his son had been wounded in a Japanese attack on the submarine on which he was serving near Tokyo Bay. Edward R. Beauchamp, "Educational and Social Reform in Japan: The First United States Education Mission to Japan, 1946," in Burkman, ed., *The Occupation of Japan: Educational and Social Reform*, p. 180. Although it is an interesting point, it does not seem a strong enough reason for Gen. MacArthur's disapproval of Conant as chairman of the Mission.

31. *The American People's Encyclopedia* (Chicago: Spencer Press, 1948), vol. 5, pp. 1019–20.

32. Iwao Ogawa et al., *Genbakutoka to Kagakusha* [The Atomic Bombing and the Scientists] (Tokyo: Sanseido, 1982), p. 52.

33. Interview with H. J. Wunderlich, August 13, 1984.

34. In the Trainor Papers the date is given as November 10, a discrepancy of nine days from Wunderlich's diary.

35. The original map, which the CI&E had marked with colors to indicate the geographical distribution of the candidates, was discovered in Robert K. Hall's home in Castine, Maine, on August 20–21, 1986.

36. Herbert J. Wunderlich, "Reminiscences of Occupation Japan, 1945–1946" (unpublished manuscript, 1984), p. 37.

37. "Education Mission to Japan, 1946," Box 3, Stoddard Papers.

38. "30 U.S. Educators Invited to Japan," *The New York Times*, January 5, 1946, p. 5.

39. Hideo Sato reported this in his lecture "Tainichi Beikoku Kyoiku Shisetsudan ni Kansuru Kenkyu" [A Study of the United States Education Mission to Japan], September 16, 1983, at the National Institute for Educational Research of Japan. This list of thirty candidates was handed over not only to the War Department but also to the Japanese Education Committee, which was organized later. This committee was in possession of the Mission members' biographical sketches, which were attached to the CI&E's fourth draft, and expected these thirty educators to be members of the Mission. "Biographical Sketches," 12 typewritten pages, *Sengo Kyoiku Shiryo* [Postwar Education Material], National Institute for Educational Research of Japan.

40. Interview with Gordon T. Bowles, February 13–15, 1983. Bowles also mentioned these circumstances in his memoir "Memorandum: U.S. Education Mission to Japan, March 1946" (unpublished manuscript, 1980; see Appendix D-1): "Sometime during the day the *New York Times* article appeared I received a call from Assistant Secretary Benton. After I had assured him I knew nothing about the proposed Mission, he assigned me the task of finding out whether or not it was a bonafide request and, if genuine, to ascertain what significance was attached to it by the Occupation Command and to make suggestions concerning the extent to which the Department of State might logically be involved." W. C. Trow also wrote about the report in *The New York Times* and the reactions to it in his diary "Japan, 1946" (Trow, "Voices Down the Wind"). On the basis of this diary he wrote an article on the Mission's stay in Japan, illustrated with photographs. William Clark Trow, "The Education Mission to Japan: Notes from a Travel Diary," *Michigan Education Journal* 23, no. 9 (May 1946).

41. "American Educators to Japan," Box 3, Stoddard Papers.

42. Confirmed in an interview with Gordon T. Bowles, August 9–11, 1984.

43. "Positive Policy for Reorientation of the Japanese" (SWNCC 162/D), July 19, 1945, Roll 4, SFE/SWNCC Microfilm T-1205.

44. Interview with Gordon T. Bowles, February 13–15, 1983.

45. "Positive Policy for Reorientation of the Japanese" (SWNCC 162/2), January 8, 1946, Roll 4, SFE/SWNCC Microfilm T-1205.

46. Letter from Kenneth C. Royall, to James F. Brynes, January 14, 1946, 894.42A/1-1946.

47. Letter from Dean Atchison to Kenneth C. Royall, January 19, 1946, 894.42A/1-1946.

48. Gordon T. Bowles, "Memorandum: U.S. Education Mission to Japan, March 1946" (unpublished manuscript, 1980), pp. 2–3.

49. "Procedure in Organization of Educational Mission to Japan, 28 January 1946," Box 3, Stoddard Papers.

50. This is not the CIC (Counter Intelligence Corps). See Yoshizo Kubo, *Tainichi Senryo Seisaku to Sengo Kyoiku Kaikaku* [The Occupation Policy Toward Japan and Postwar Education Reform) (Tokyo: Sanseido, 1984), p. 340. Gordon T. Bowles, who was concerned with this matter, stated: "So far as the question concerning the Memorandum relating to 'Procedure in Organization of the Educational Mission to Japan,' the answer is definitely that Item 5 should read 'The OIC representative ... etc.' Since I not only drafted the Memo but was the 'Officer in Charge' appointed later to the task, there is no question. I was never in any way associated with any aspect of 'Intelligence' gathering." Letter from Bowles to the author, February 6, 1985, in reply to a letter from the author, January 28, 1985.

51. Bowles, "Memorandum: U.S. Education Mission to Japan," p. 3.

52. The W. C. Trow papers were presented to the Group for Study of Existing Documents in the U.S. on Japanese Education During the Occupation Period, sponsored by the Japanese Ministry of Education, and are in the Archives of the National Institute for Educational Research of Japan.

53. Interview with G. T. Bowles, February 13–15, 1983.

54. RG 165, Records of the War Department, General and Special Staff, CAD 350 (Education) (U.S. National Archives). These are education policy papers of the Civil Affairs Division (CAD) of the War Department, which are included in the records of the War Department in the U.S. National Archives. With respect to the records of the War and State departments, see the author's "Taidoku Senryo Kyoiku Kaikaku ni Kansuru Zaibei Shiryo Jokyo" [Existing Materials in the U.S. on German Education Reform During the Occupation Period], in Research Committee on Rengokoku no Taidoku Senryo Kyoiku Seisaku ni Kansuru Hikaku Kenkyu [A Comparative Study of the Allied Powers' Occupation Policy Toward German Education], ed. *Rengokoku no Taidoku Senryo Kyoiku Seisaku ni Kansuru Hikaku Kenkyu* [A Comparative Study of the Allied Powers' Occupation Policy Toward German Education] (Tokyo: National Institute for Educational Research of Japan, 1986).

55. Letter from Edward F. McGrady to J. H. Hilldring, January 8, 1946, RG 165, CAD 350 Japan 1945–1946, January 8, 1946.

56. "Educators for Japan," *America* (January 19, 1946), pp. 435–36.

57. Roy Deferrari, *Memoirs of the Catholic University of America, 1918–1960* (Boston: St. Paul Editions, 1962), p. 382.

58. Letter from Irvin R. Kuenzli to J. H. Hilldring, January 11, 1946, RG 165, CAD 350 Japan 1945–1946, January 11, 1946.

59. Letter from Emily H. Hickman to President Harry S. Truman, January 22, 1946, RG 165, CAD 350 Japan 1945–1946, January 22, 1946.

60. "U.S. Education Mission to Japan, 30th January 1946," Box 3, Stoddard Papers.

61. Bowles, "Memorandum: U.S. Education Mission to Japan," p. 4.

62. "U.S. Education Mission to Japan, '46, Correspondence," Box 3, Stoddard Papers.

63. Letter from J. H. Hilldring to Edward F. McGrady, February 5, 1946, RG 165, CAD 350 Japan 1945–1946, February 5, 1946.

64. Letter from W. Benton to Emily Hickman, February 15, 1946, RG 165, CAD 350 Japan 1945–1946, February 15, 1946.

65. "Brothers to Japan," *Phi Delta Kappan* 28, no. 2 (October 1946), pp. 42, 73. According to Yoshizo Kubo, "Bowles said that the Mission had been organized by minor characters." Kubo, *Tainichi Senryo Seisaku to Sengo Kyoiku Kaikaku*, p. 349. Bowles gave a different opinion, however. He told the author that he thought that the Mission was well organized, despite pressure because of having to complete the organization of the Mission within one month and because the educators in SCAP's list of candidates were only available for a one-month stay in Japan. Interview with Bowles, February 13–15, 1983.

66. Interview with Bowles, February 13–15, 1983.

67. George D. Stoddard, "Frontiers for Youth," *School and Society* 56 (September 1942), pp. 225–30. In a speech on December 28, 1942, Henry Wallace, vice-president during President Roosevelt's third term, pointed out the necessity of reeducation by the Occupation in terms of German and Japanese education reforms. This proposal was an important starting point for American educators to express various opinions concerning the reeducation of the Axis Powers and resulted in controversy on the subject. Hiromi Akiike, "Amerika no Taidoku Saikyoiku Seisaku no Tenkai Katei to 'Saikyoiku' Kan no Seisakuka" [Development Process of the American Reeducation Policy Toward Germany and Formulation of the View of "Reeducation"], in *Rengokoku no Taidoku Senryo Seisaku ni Kansuru Hikaku Kenkyu*, p. 27.

68. Sadanobu Miwa and Toyokazu Urano, "Sengo Nihon Shihonshugi no Tenkai to Kyoiku" [Development of Postwar Japanese Capitalism and Education], in Taro Ogawa and Akio Igasaki, eds., *Koza Gendai Minshushugi Kyoiku* [Lectures on Modern Democratic Education], vol. 12 (Tokyo: Aoki Shoten, 1969), p. 194.

69. Yotaro Mohri, "Tainichi Kyoiku Shisetsudanin no Ronri: 'Stoddard G. D.' no Ronrikozo (1)" [The Philosophy of a Member of the Education Mission to Japan: The Case of G. D. Stoddard (1)], *Study Report of the Faculty of Education, Education Department, Yamanashi University* (1978), p. 124.

70. Toshio Nishi, *Unconditional Democracy: Education and Politics in Occupied Japan, 1945–1952* (Stanford: Hoover Institution Press, 1982), p. 190.

71. Letter from W. Benton to Dean Atchison, September 21, 1945, Benton Papers, Department of Special Collections, Joseph Regenstein Library, University of Chicago. According to the Stoddard Papers, the chairman of the American representatives was Archibald MacLeish, and the other members were G. D. Stoddard, Senator James E. Murray, Chester E. Merrow (a member of the House of Representatives), Harlow Shapley (Chief of the Observation Institute, Harvard

University), C. Mildred Thomson (Dean of Vassar College), and W. Benton. (George D. Stoddard, "Education and World Order," address at the American Association of Colleges, Cleveland, January 10, 1946, p. 6, Stoddard Papers.) At the inaugural meeting of UNESCO, which was held in London after three months after the atomic bombing, the necessity for scientific knowledge and its development and application was realized. Consequently, *S* for "Science" was added to the organization's name, between *E* for "Education" and *C* for "Culture."

72. George D. Stoddard, "The Emperor and I," in *The Pursuit of Education: An Autobiography* (New York: Vantage Press, 1981), p. 79.

73. Assistant Secretary of State Archibald MacLeish, who was a central figure in the forming of the reeducation policy of Germany, stated at the State Department's General Advisory Committee for Post-War Foreign Policy (GAC) in February 1943 that the United Nations was the most promising organization for conducting the "deintoxication" of the Axis nations, Japan, Germany, and Italy. James F. Tent, *Mission on the Rhine: Reeducation and Denazification in American-Occupied Germany* (Chicago: University of Chicago Press, 1982), p. 18.

74. Yomiuri Shinbun Postwar History Group, ed., *Showa Sengoshi: Kyoiku no Ayumi* [Postwar History of Showa: The Course of Education] (Tokyo: Yomiuri Shinbunsha, 1982), pp. 190–91.

75. Philip H. Stoddard, "George D. Stoddard and the U.S. Education Mission to Japan: A Brief Appreciation" (unpublished manuscript, 1988), p. 3. (See Appendix D-4.)

76. Interview with Philip H. Stoddard, son of George D. Stoddard, at his home in Bethesda, Maryland, July 18, 1985.

77. Telegram to George Stoddard from William Benton, February 6, 1946," Box 1, Stoddard Papers. Telegrams to the same effect, with "chairman of this group" changed to "a member of the group," were sent to the other candidates.

78. Telegram to William Benton from George D. Stoddard, February 7, 1946, Box 1, Stoddard Papers.

79. *Department of State Bulletin* XIV, no. 384 (March 3, 1946) pp. 345–46. Due to there being two Stoddards in the Mission, newspapers in Hawaii and Japan sometimes reported A. J. Stoddard as chairman of the Mission.

80. Charles Iglehart (1882–1969) was born in Illinois and went to Japan in 1907 as a Methodist missionary. He taught in the Senmonbu (College) and the Shingakubu (Theology Department) of Aoyama Gakuin from 1909 to 1919. From 1919 to 1927 he was a trustee, and devoted himself to reorganizing the school to include a Women's Department, which was inaugurated in 1927. After the war he returned to Aoyama Gakuin to teach again, and was a trustees from 1951 to 1953, when he finally retired and returned to the U.S. (This information was contributed by the Materials Center of Aoyama Gakuin Majima Memorial Hall.) According to Gordon T. Bowles, Iglehart cooperated with the Mission members as a consultant. The reason his name was withdrawn from the list has not been discovered. It can be assumed that his exclusion was based on the selection criteria of Gen. MacArthur. As mentioned above, he had lived in Japan and participated in Japanese education for a long time. For this reason we can consider him as almost half-Japanese and not as representative of American educators. Perhaps Gen. MacArthur excluded a

person with such extensive experience in Japan in order to give objectivity to the Report. (Interview with Gordon T. Bowles, February 13–15, 1983.) In a recent interview, Bowles said, "In forming our ideas about the Mission, we often asked Iglehart's opinion. He had been teaching in Aoyama Gakuin for a long time. Although he was not a Mission member, we often took his advice." "Moto Beikoku Kyoiku Shisetsudanin Gordon T. Bowles Hakase ni Kiku (Jo)" [Interview Dr. Gordon T. Bowles, Former Member of the U.S. Education Mission, Part 1], 1) *Naigai Kyoiku* [Education Worldwide], no. 3900, January 5, 1988.

81. "Advisory Group of Education to Japan, Roster," Box 3, Stoddard Papers.

82. Bowles, "Memorandum: U.S. Education Mission to Japan," p. 5.

83. Yomiuri Shinbun Postwar History Group, ed., *Showa Sengoshi: Kyoiku no Ayumi*, p. 200; interview with Gordon T. Bowles, February 13–15, 1983.

84. "Moto Beikoku Kyoiku Shisetsudanin Gordon T. Bowles Hakase ni Kiku (Jo)."

85. *Kyoiku Shinbun* [Educational Journal], June 30, 1975.

86. Ibid., July 21, 1975.

Notes to Chapter 2: Advance Preparations

1. Wray, "A Study of the United States Education Mission," p. 5.

2. Eiichi Suzuki, "Rengokoku no Tainichi Senryo Kyoiku Seisaku" [The Allied Powers' Occupation Education Policy Toward Japan], in *Koza Nihon Kyoikushi* [Lectures on the History of Japanese Education], vol. 4, *Gendai* [Contemporary] I/II (Tokyo: Daiichi Hoki, 1984), p. 230.

3. "PR–24 Preliminary, SWNCC, Politico–Military Problems in the Far East: The Post Surrender of the Military Government of the Japanese Empire, The Educational System," July 30, 1945, p. 12, Box 119, Notter File.

4. Office Memorandum from Hugh Borton to SFE 135/Miss Martin, Secretary of Ad Hoc Reorientation Committee, "Education in Japan," Dec. 6, 1945, Roll 7, SFE/SWNCC, Microfilm T-1205.

5. Yomiuri Shinbun Postwar History Group, "Borusushi Shuzai Noto" [Notes on Mr. Bowles] 3 (unpublished manuscript), pp. 16–19.

6. "Meeting of Advisory Group to Japan, Feb. 8th, 1946," p. 8, Box 55, Trainor Papers.

7. Ibid., p. 12.

8. Ibid., p. 7.

9. "Conference of Advisory Group on Education to Japan, 18th Feb. 1946," pp. 2–3, Box 36, Wanamaker Papers.

10. Telegram to CINCAFPAC from Washington (CAD), February 5, 1946, Box 57, Trainor Papers.

11. "Conference of Advisory Group on Education to Japan, 18th Feb. 1946," pp. 12, 14.

12. Joseph C. Trainor, *Educational Reform in Occupied Japan: Trainor's Memoir* (Tokyo: Meisei University Press, 1983), p. 73.

13. "Conference of Advisory Group on Education to Japan, 18th Feb. 1946," p. 13.

14. Interview with Gordon T. Bowles, February 13–15, 1983.

15. "Conference of Advisory Group on Education to Japan, 18th Feb. 1946," p. 3.

16. "Meeting in Mr. Vincent's Office, Tuesday—2/19," pp. 1–2, Box 3, Stoddard Papers. This note, which is separate from the records of the Washington meetings and the conference notes, summarizes discussions in the meetings. Stoddard's secretary (Smerling), who joined the Mission, dictated.

17. "Meeting in Mr. Vincent's Office, Wednesday—2/20," pp. 1–2, Box 3, Stoddard Papers.

18. Katharine Sansom, *Sir George Sansom: A Memoir* (Tallahassee: Diplomatic Press, 1972), p. 154.

19. Wray, "A Study of the First United States Education Mission," p. 6.

20. Emily Woodward, "Japan," pp. 1–2, Box 3, Woodward Papers, Robert W. Woodruff Library, Emory University.

21. Trow, "Voices Down the Wind," p. 958.

22. Bowles, "Comments on Papers Presented at the Fourth Symposium on the Occupation of Japan: Educational and Social Reform," p. 520.

23. Willard E. Givens, "Tokyo and Return," p. 2 (National Education Association Archives) (see Appendix D-3). "Tokyo and Return" is a journal which records in great detail the entire schedule of the First U.S. Education Mission to Japan. This 19-page journal is in the Archives of the National Education Association, of which Givens was a member. Incidentally, "Tentative Schedule of U.S. Education Mission," contained in the Trainor Papers, was prepared before the Mission's actual arrival in Japan and differs in some respects from the actual schedule, so that corroboration with Givens's journal is necessary. Givens subsequently went to Japan as chairman of the Second U.S. Education Mission in 1950.

24. Ibid.

25. "Meeting of Advisory Group to Japan, 2:00 P.M., 8 February 1946," p. 14.

26. See Appendix A: Brief Biographies of the Members of the Mission and Information on the Collections of Their Papers."

27. Ibid.

28. Wray, "A Study of the First United States Education Mission," p. 6.

29. Horton Papers (Archives of the Wellesley College). "Research Study of Existing Documents in U.S. on Japanese Education During Occupation Period," sponsored by the Ministry of Education in 1986, confirmed that the lectures are among the Horton Papers.

30. Edwin S. Dozier, "Memoranda on Japanese General Education."

31. Yukio Kimura, "Education in Japan."

32. Ernest S. Fujinaga, "Comments on Education in Japan."

33. Alberta Tarr, "Concerning Education in Japan."

34. Gilbert Bowles, "Notes on the Reconstruction of the Japanese Educational System."

35. E. V. Sayers, "Five Suggestions on Most General Policy for Educational Reconstruction in Japan."

36. Laura Thompson, "An Approach to the Problem of Education in Japan."

37. Oren E. Long, "Comments and Suggestions."

38. Carroll Atkinson, "Japanese Education is Getting Revised—a la America!" *School and Society* 64, no. 1,651 (August 17, 1946), p. 115. Carroll Atkinson, then a columnist for *The Honolulu Star-Bulletin*, also wondered about the members' qualifications: "With beautiful thoughts for the most part and here and there a down-to-earth observation, it is just about what one would expect to come from a group of traditional educators making a brief tour of the country. Few, if any, of these committee members knew a thing about the Japanese and their previous educational backgrounds and practices, except what possibly they may have read—and as yet there is not very much literature on the subject." Refuting his criticism, I. L. Kandel, a Mission member, stated: "The Mission was not invited by General MacArthur to impose American or any other educational theories on the Japanese, but to help the Japanese to reconstruct their own educational system." I. L. Kandel, "The Revision of Japanese Education," *School and Society*, 64, no. 1,652 (August 24, 1947), p. 134.

39. "Suggestions for the Educational Mission to Japan," n.d., date, Horton Papers.

40. "Japanese to Decide Own School Setup by Dr. Willard Givens," *The Nippon Times*, March 4, 1946.

41. "Part II: On Preparing the Report," p. 2, Box 3, Stoddard Papers.

42. Givens, "Tokyo and Return," p. 2.

43. "Part II: On Preparing the Report," p. 1.

44. Ibid., p. 2.

45. Ibid., p. 3.

46. Ibid., p. 5.

47. Ibid.

48. Ibid., p. 6.

Notes to Chapter 3: Activities of the Mission and Its Japanese Counterpart

1. Stoddard, "The Emperor and I," pp. 81–82.

2. Givens, "Tokyo and Return."

3. Woodward, "Japan," p. 4.

4. David H. Stevens, "Office Talk on Japan," p. 6. Stevens Papers, Record Group 2, 1946, 609, Box 348, Folder 2359 (Rockefeller Foundation Archives).

5. "U.S. Education Mission to Japan, Memorandum To: All Officers Education Division, 15 February 1946," Box 57, Trainor Papers.

6. Ibid.

7. Tetsuichi Sawato, "Beikoku Kyoiku Shisetsudan o Mukaete" [Receiving the U.S. Education Mission], *Monbu Jiho* [Review of the Ministry of Education], no. 827 (April 1946).

8. "Seinen Gakko ni Kansuru Shitsumon Yoko" [General Questions Concerning

Youth Schools], February 28, 1946; "Mondo" [Questions and Answers], March 4, 1946; both in Aruga Papers, Archives of the National Institute for Educational Research of Japan.

9. Box 5348, CI&E Records, Washington National Record Center, National Archives, Suitland, Maryland; Suzuki, *Nihon Senryo to Kyoiku Kaikaku* [The Occupation of Japan and Education Reform], p. 97. This "tentative brochure" was prepared for the Subcommittee of the Far East prior to its arrival. See Eiichi Suzuki, "The Occupation of Japan and Education Reform 1945–1952," paper presented at the 31st Conference of the Academy of History of Education, Hokkaido University, October 3, 1987.

10. Education Division, CI&E, SCAP/GHQ, *Education in Japan: 15 February 1946*, Box 36, Wanamaker Papers.

11. Tokiomi Kaigo, *Kyoikugaku Gojunen* [Fifty Years of Pedagogy] (Tokyo: Hyoronsha, 1971), p. 195.

12. The drafting of *Education in Japan* is described in Hiroshi Takuma, *"Education in Japan* no Kenkyu: Beikoku Kyoiku Shisetsudan to no Kanren" [A Study of *Education in Japan* in Relation to the U.S. Education Mission], *Bulletin of the Faculty of High School Affiliated to the Department of Education, Kyoto University of Education*, no. 23 (1978). Takuma verifies that *Education in Japan* was not written as a draft for the Report of the U.S. Education Mission to Japan but that "the CI&E raised points for the Mission to consider Japanese education in it."

13. Yomiuri Shinbun Postwar History Group, ed., *Showa Sengoshi: Kyoiku no Ayumi*, [Postwar History of Showa: The Course of Education] (Tokyo: Yomiuri Shinbunsha, 1982), p. 206; interview with G. T. Bowles, February 13–15, 1983. Orr testified that he and Major Robert MacAllen prepared *Education in Japan* for the Mission. See Eiiji Takemae, "Gendaishi no Shogen (6), Kyoiku Kaikaku no Omoide: GHQ Kyoiku ka M. T. Orr Hakase ni Kiku" [The Testimony of Modern History (6), A Memory of Education Reform: Interview with Dr. M. T. Orr, Education Division, GHQ] *Bulletin of Tokyo Keizai University*, no. 115 (March 1980), p. 139.

14. Education Division, CI&E, GHQ/SCAP, *Education in the New Japan*, vol. 1 (Tokyo, May 1948), p. 141.

15. "Brochure for Education Commission," Robert K. Hall Papers. (These papers are in the possession of Mrs. Hall, Castine, Maine. Concerning the drafting of the booklet and Lt. Fisher, Orr testified as follows: "There may have been a Cap. Barnard Fisher in CIE, but I don't recall him. However, he and Robert K. Hall were not involved in producing *Education in Japan*. In fact, that task was assigned to me and to Major Robert McAllen. We were co-editors. . . . There was also a Lt. Raburn J. Fisher, USNR, in CIE. He was assigned on the same orders with me (Nov. 7, 1945) but I don't recall anymore than that." Letter from Mark T. Orr to the author, March 13, 1992.

16. "Part II. Allied Control of Japanese Education," Box 3, Stoddard Papers.

17. "Nugent's Address to the U.S. Education Mission, March 7, 1946," pp. 2–3, 11–12, Box 57, Trainor Papers; Trainor, *Educational Reform in Occupied Japan: Trainor's Memoir*, p. 75.

18. Givens, "Tokyo and Return."

19. *Mainichi Shinbun,* March 9, 1946.

20. Interview with E. R. Hilgard at his office in the Department of Psychology, Stanford University, July 23, 1984.

21. Yoshishige Abe, *Sengo no Jijoden* [Postwar Autobiography] (Tokyo: Shinchosha, 1959), p. 73; Mieko Kamiya, *Henreki* [The Wandering] (Tokyo: Misuzu Shobo, 1980), p. 244.

22. "Response to Japanese Minister of Education, March 8th, 1946, by George D. Stoddard, Chairman, American Education Mission," Box 3, Stoddard Papers.

23. "Education Mission Organized into Four Committees," Box 5439, CI&E Records.

24. For details on the series of lectures by the staff of the Education Division of the CI&E, see Suzuki, *Nihon Senryo to Kyoiku Kaikaku,* pp. 166–78.

25. Lieutenant Commander Robert K. Hall, "The Mombusho: Japanese Ministry of Education," File: American Education Mission, IV—Annexes, Box 5439, CI&E Records.

26. Lt. P. M. MacBride, "Boys Middle School."

27. Lt. G. B. Gibson, "The Yochien and Kokumin Gakko."

28. Lieutenant Commander Alfred Crofts, "Higher Education in Japan."

29. Major Mark T. Orr, "Curriculum of Japanese Schools."

30. Capt. John W. Barnard, "Methodology in Japanese Education."

31. "Japanese Textbooks" (panel discussion).

32. Commander [Herbert J.] Wunderlich, "Critique of Textbook Problem."

33. Herbert J. Wunderlich, "The Japanese Textbook Problem and Solution" (Ed.D. dissertation, Stanford University, 1952).

34. Professor [Tokiomi] Kaigo, "The Development of Japanese Textbook," File: American Education, IV—Annexes., Box 5439, CI&E Records.

35. Captain [Harry E.] Griffith, "Reorientation of Teachers."

36. Harry E. Griffith, "Japanese Normal School Education" (Ed.D. dissertation, Stanford University, 1950).

37. Lieutenant Commander [R. K.] Hall, "Language Revision," File: American Education, IV—Annexes, Box 5439, CI&E Records.

38. Education Division, CI&E, *Education in Japan,* pp. 28–29.

39. [Masatsugu] Ando, "On Problems Concerning National Language and Its Character," File: American Education Mission, IV—Annexes, Box 5439, CI&E Records.

40. Major John W. Norviel, "Physical Education in Japan."

41. Captain Eileen Donovan, "Women's Education."

42. Helen Hosp Seamans, who was an adviser to MacArthur on women's higher education, also discussed the problems of women's education in "An Occupationaire Observes: The Progress of Japanese Women" (unpublished manuscript, 1984).

43. Interview with E. R. Donovan in Clearwater, Florida, September 5, 1986.

44. Stoddard, "The Emperor and I."

45. "Proposed Outline of the Report," Box 3, Stoddard Papers.

46. "Four Committees Meet: U.S., Japanese Educators Study School Problems," *Mainichi Shinbun*, March 19, 1946.

47. Concerning the audience and the selection of a tutor for the Crown Prince, see Gary H. Tsuchimochi, "Sengo Kyoiku Kaikaku to Kotaishi Katei Kyoshi no Jinsen Keii ni Kansuru Ichi Kosatsu" [A Study of the Postwar Japanese Educational Reform and the Selection of a Tutor for the Crown Prince], *Research Bulletin of Educational History of the Allied Occupation of Japan* no. 3 (June 1986).

48. "Notes on Conference with General MacArthur," March 20, 1946, "Rough Draft MacArthur," Box 1, Stoddard Papers.

49. This report was translated into Japanese under the title "Gakka Katei Kokugo oyobi Kyoikukan ni Kansuru Iinkai" before it was handed over to the Japanese side. The English original has not yet been discovered. Therefore, this passage has been translated back into English from the Japanese. For this reason, its wording is not identical with that of the original.

50. Givens, "Tokyo and Return." pp. 9–10.

51. Letter from P. A. Wanamaker to her secretary, March 11, 1946, Box 36/4, "Miscellaneous," Wanamaker Papers.

52. Shigeru Nambara, "University Men During and After the War," in "Short English Addresses" (Tokyo: University of Tokyo, 1949).

53. "Report of Committee II: Teaching and the Education of Teachers," Box 5395, GHQ/SCAP Records, Record Group 331 (U.S. National Archives); Box 57, Trainor Papers. (See Appendix C-2.)

54. "Discussion in Committee No. 2," in the Aruga Papers, which describes the Japanese Education Committee's debates, is also in the possession of E. R. Hilgard. For this reason, it seems to have been used as material for discussion on both the U.S. and the Japanese sides. A confirmation copy was received from E. R. Hilgard July 23, 1984.

55. Motohiro Ohashi, "Beikoku Tainichi Kyoiku Shisetsudan no Zainichi Katsudo to Hokokusho no Kiso Katei" [Activities of the U.S. Education Mission to Japan During Its Stay and Drafting Process of the Report], in Eiichi Suzuki, Hideo Sato, Gary H. Tsuchimochi et al., "Beikoku Tainichi Kyoiku Shisetsudan no Seiritsu Jijo ni Kansuru Sogoteki Kenkyu" [A comprehensive Study of the Report of the U.S. Education Mission to Japan, with Particular Reference to Its Preparation], *Bulletin of the Faculty of Education, Department of Education, Nagoya University* 31 (1984), p. 252.

56. Letter from E. R. Hilgard to the author, September 30, 1987.

57. Toshio Funayori, "'Beikoku Tainichi Kyoiku Shisetsudan Daini Iinkai Hokoku, Kyojuho to Kyoshi Kyoiku, 1946' no Sakusei Keii to Sono Naiyo: Sengo Kyoin Yosei Kaikakushi Kenkyu (Daiippo)" [A Study of Postwar Education Reform of Teachers, with Particular Reference to the Drafting Process and Details of the Report of Committee II of the U.S. Education Mission to Japan, Teaching and the Education of Teachers, 1946 (Report 1)], *Bulletin of the Faculty of Education, Hiroshima University*, no. 34 (1986), p. 74.

58. Interview with G. T. Bowles, February 13–15, 1983.

59. "Report of Committee III, USEM: Administration of Education in Japan at Elementary and Secondary levels," Box 36/15, Wanamaker Papers. (See Appendix C-3.)

60. "Statement of Japanese Committee No. 3 Concerning the Imperial Rescript of Education." Box 36/24, Wanamaker Papers. (See Appendix C-6.)

61. *Report of the United States Education Mission to Japan* (Washington, D.C.: U.S. Government Printing Office, 1946), p. 25.

62. "Imperial Rescript on Education," in "Recommendations of the Japanese Education Committee," Box 32, Trainor Papers.

63. Tokiomi Kaigo, *Sengo Nihon no Kyoiku Kaikaku* [Postwar Japanese Education Reform], vol. 1, *Kyoiku Kaikaku* [Education Reform] (Tokyo: University of Tokyo Press, 1980), p. 117.

64. Interview with G. T. Bowles, August 9–11, 1984.

65. Interview with E. R. Hilgard, July 23, 1984.

66. Eiichi Suzuki, "Beikoku Kyoiku Shisetsudan Hokokusho 40 Shunen o Mukaete" [The Fortieth Anniversary of the Report of the U.S. Education Mission], *Kyoiku* [Journal of Education], March 1986.

67. "Report of Committee III: Administration of Education in Japan at Elementary and Secondary Levels," Box 36/15, Wanamaker Papers.

68. Herbert J. Wunderlich, "Reminiscences of Occupation Japan, 1945–1946" (unpublished manuscript, 1984), p. 70.

69. Motohiro Ohashi, "Charles H. McCloy's Papers," in "The Report of the Overseas Research Project, Historical Materials Held in the U.S. Concerning Education Reform Under the Allied Occupation of Japan,"*Sengo Kyoiku Shiryo* [Postwar Education Reform Materials], vol. 6 (Tokyo: National Institute for Education Research of Japan, 1988), p. 81.

70. Eiichi Suzuki, "Emily B. Woodward's Papers," ibid., p. 89.

71. Letter from P. A. Wanamaker to her family, March 27, 1946, Box 36/4, "Miscellaneous," Wanamaker Papers.

72. Memorandum: "Report on Mission to Korea," March 2, 1946, Robert K. Hall Papers.

73. Hiroshi Abe, Eiko Seki, and Tsugio Inaba, "Kaihogo Kankoku no Kyoiku Kaikaku: Amerika Gunseiki (1945–48) o Chushin ni" [Education Reform After the Liberation of Korea, with Particular Reference to the U.S. Military Period [1945–48], *Kokuritsu Kyoiku Kenkyusho Kenkyu Shuroku* [Research Report of the National Institute for Educational Research], no. 10 (March 1985).

74. Givens, "Tokyo and Return"; Educational Policies Commission, *Learning the Ways of Democracy: A Case Book of Civic Education* (Washington, D.C.: National Education Association of the United States, 1940).

75. Yomiuri Shinbun Postwar History Group, ed., *Showa Sengoshi: Kyoiku no Ayumi*, pp. 259–60.

76. Ibid., p. 11.

77. Letter from G. T. Bowles to his wife, March 30, 1946, Bowles Papers.

78. "Memorandum To: A–B Mr. Benton, OIC Mr. Stone, ADO– Mr. Leverich FROM: ADO– Mr. Bowles/Subject: Education Advisory Group and CI&E Operations in Tokyo April 1, 1946." Bowles Papers.

79. "Memorandum To: Mr. Leverich From Bowles/Subject: Report on Trip to Japan (March 5th to June 1st, 1946)." Bowles Papers.

80. Letter to William Benton from G. D. Stoddard, April 4, 1946, Box 1, Stoddard Papers.

81. Telegram to the Chinese Liaison Office, Chinese Government, March 30, 1946, Box 3, Stoddard Papers.

82. Interview with G. T. Bowles, August 9–11, 1984.

83. "Memorandum To: A–B Mr. Benton, OIC Mr. Stone, ADO– Mr. Leverich FROM: ADO– Mr. Bowles/Subject: Education Advisory Group and CI&E Operation in Tokyo, April 1, 1946" (Bowles Papers). When Bowles and G. D. Stoddard met with Gen. MacArthur, the general described the CI&E staff as "daily counting their rosary of points." Bowles explained that by this metaphorical expression MacArthur had meant to suggest that the CI&E staff was so perplexed in trying to accomplish its task, that it had almost prayed to God for an angel from Heaven (the Education Mission) to help it. (Ibid., interview with G. T. Bowles, August 9–11, 1984).

84. Letter to Captain W. H. Beauchamp, Personnel and Training Branch, CAD, War Department, from Virginia C. Gildersleeve, May 25, 1946, Box 76, Gildersleeve Papers (Rare Books and Special Collections, Butler Library, Columbia University).

85. Givens, "Tokyo and Return."

86. Tamon Maeda, "Shusengo Gokagetsu Zaiju no Kiroku" [A Record of Five Months in Office Immediately After the War], *Monbu Jiho* [Review of the Ministry of Education], no. 824 (1946), p. 4.

87. Gary H. Tsuchimochi, "Senryo Shoki Amerika no Tainichi Kyoiku Seisaku ni Kansuru Nisan no Kosatsu: 'Shin Nihon Kensetsu no Kyoiku Hoshin' no Kiso Katei o Megutte" [A Few Comments on the Early U.S. Occupation Policy Toward Japanese Education, With Particular Reference to the Drafting Process of "The Education Policy for the Construction of a New Japan"], *Kokuritsu Kyoiku Kenkyujo Shuroku* [Research Report of the National Institute for Educational Research], no. 4 (1982).

88. The Diary of Jiro Arimitsu in the *Yomiuri Shimbun*, editorial date July 18, 1981, *Yomiuri Shimbun* Postwar History Group, ed., *Showa Sengoshi: Kyoiku no Ayumi*.

89. Taro Nakajima, *Sengo Nihon Kyoiku Seido Seiritsushi* [History of the Organization of the Postwar Japanese Educational System] (Tokyo: Iwasaki Gakujutsu Shuppansha, 1970), p. 8.

90. Robert K. Hall, *Education for a New Japan* (New Haven: Yale University Press, 1949), pp. 291–92.

91. Mark T. Orr, "Education Reform Policy in Occupation Japan" (Ph.D. dissertation, University of North Carolina, 1954), pp. 199–200.

92. GHQ/SCAP, *History of the Non-Military Activities of the Occupation of Japan*, vol. 11, *Social*, part A, "Education: 1945 Through Sept. 1949," p. 46; Education Division, CI&E, GHQ/SCAP, *Education in the New Japan* (Tokyo, May 1948), p. 136.

93. Macmahon William Ball, *Japan: Enemy or Ally?* (New York: Day, 1949). Ball, an Australian diplomat, represented the British Commonwealth on the Allied

Council for Japan from July 1946 through August 1947. He presented his analysis of the structure and operation of the Allied Occupation from its inception through 1948. In discussing the manner in which the Allied policies of demilitarization and democratization were implemented, Ball tended to be critical of the shifting positions of the American-dominated SCAP organization. See Robert E. Ward and Frank Joseph Shulman, eds., *The Allied Occupation of Japan 1945–1952: An Annotated Bibliography of Western Language Materials* (Tokyo: Nihon Tosho Center, 1990), pp. 192–93.

94. Ward and Schulman, eds., *The Allied Occupation of Japan 1945–1952*, pp. 16–17.

95. "The Reminiscences of Faubion Bowers" (unpublished manuscript, 1960), p. 30, Oral History Research Office, Columbia University.

96. James I. Doi, "Educational Reform in Occupied Japan, 1945–1950: A Study of Acceptance of and Resistance to Institutional Change" (Ph.D. dissertation, University of Chicago, 1952), p. 61. Doi's testimony is based on his own interviews with two officials of the Ministry of Education who later visited Chicago and who were involved in the drafting of the "New Education Policy."

97. Ray A. Moore, "Reflections on the Occupation of Japan," *Journal of Asian Studies* 38 (August 1979), p. 725.

98. Doi, "Educational Reform in Occupied Japan," p. 61.

99. "Japanese Postwar Education Policies," OSS Research and Analysis Report 3266, October 5, 1946, Interim Research and Intelligence, Research and Analysis Branch, Department of State (National Archives).

100. Eiji Takemae and Makoto Hino, "Sengo Kyoiku Kaikaku Josetsu (Jo): Amerika no Shoki Tainichi Kyoiku Kaikaku Koso (Takemae)" [An Introduction to Postwar Education Reform, Part 1: The Initial American Idea on Japanese Education Reform (Takemae)], *Bulletin of Tokyo Keizai University*, no. 105 (1978), pp. 14–15.

101. Hall, *Education for a New Japan*, p. 292.

102. Orr, "Education Reform Policy in Occupied Japan," pp. 126–27.

103. GHQ/SCAP, *Education in the New Japan*, p. 139.

104. Aruga Papers.

105. Suzuki, *Nihon Senryo to Kyoiku Kaikaku* [The Occupation of Japan and Education Reform], pp. 127–28; Kyoiku Kaikaku Doshikai, *Kyoiku Seido Kaikaku An* [Proposals on the Reform of the Educational System] (1937), pp. 29–31; "Committee of Japanese Educators, Appointed by the Japanese Ministry of Education to Meet with U.S. Education Mission" Box 3, Trainor Papers.

106. Sawato, "Beikoku Kyoiku Shisetsudan o Mukaete."

107. Aruga Papers. This is a Japanese translation; the original English interim report of Committee I is not available.

108. "Committee No. 2, Teacher Education and Methodology, First Meeting—9 March 1946," Box 36, Wanamaker Papers.

109. Givens, "Tokyo and Return."

110. Letter from P. A. Wanamaker to her family, March 10, 1946, Box 36/4, "Miscellaneous," Wanamaker Papers.

111. "Questions—Committee 4 (For Use of the Committee Only), March 9,

1946" and "Answers—Committee 4," Box 76, Gildersleeve Papers; "Digest of Discussions of Committee IV," Box 33, Trainor Papers.

112. Stevens, "Office Talk on Japan."

113. "Digest of Discussions of Committee IV," Box 33, Trainor Papers.

114. Ibid.

115. Ibid., Gildersleeve Papers.

116. Givens, "Tokyo and Return."

117. Shigeru Nambara, "Nihon ni Okeru Kyoiku Kaikaku" [Education Reform in Japan], in *Kyoiku Kihonho no Seitei* [Establishment of the Fundamental Law of Education], ed. Eiichi Suzuki (Tokyo: Gakuyo Shobo, 1977), p. 24.

118. Yamazumi and Horio, *Sengo Nihon no Kyoiku Kaikaku*, vol. 2, p. 242.

119. Interview with G. T. Bowles, February 13–15, 1983.

120. Department of State, Office of Research and Intelligence, No. 3836, "The Japanese Education Committee Part II: Report to the Education Ministry, Washington, June 7, 1946," Box 47, Far Eastern Commission (Modern Political History Material Room, National Diet Library). It is assumed, however, that by about this time the CI&E had also confirmed the existence of the report of the Japanese Education Committee. See "Memorandum to: Major Orr, from Lt. Comdr. Trainor, Subject: Report of Japanese Education Committee, 27 May 1946," Box 31, Trainor Papers.

121. Shigeru Nambara, "Gakusei Kaikaku no Keika" [The Process of Education Reform], in *Kyoiku Kihonho no Seitei* [Establishment of the Fundamental Law of Education], ed. Eiichi Suzuki (Tokyo: Gakuyo Shobo, 1977), p. 235.

Notes to Chapter 4: The Mission's Report and Reform of the Japanese Language

1. Two documents on the draft of reform on *romaji* are kept in the Stevens Papers at the Joseph Regenstein Library, University of Chicago. One is a six-page document entitled "Language Reform," on which "The second draft by Stevens and Counts," is handwritten. The other is also a six-page document, entitled "Language," and is labeled "The third draft by Stevens and Counts," which has also been handwritten. These drafts indicate that the drafts of "Language Reform," by the Special Committee on Language, were prepared by Counts, as chairman, and Stevens, as a member of the committee. Both drafts have more or less identical contents. If one compares them to the final Report, however, the structure of the contents is closer to the second draft. Therefore, it can be assumed that it was the second draft that was actually submitted to the Chairman of the Mission. (See Appendix C-1.)

Initially, the CI&E and the Mission used, the term "Language Revision," not "Language Reform," although it is uncertain whether they intentionally made any distinction between these terms. Perhaps they envisioned a more concrete reform rather than Japanese language reform in a broad sense. The Japanese translations of these terms by the Ministry of Education also vary. The mixing of terms indicates how the Occupation confused the problem of the national language with the national script. (Masao Terasaki, "Shiryo: Tokyo Daigaku Kyoiku Seido Kenkyu Iinkai Kiroku" [Materials: The Record of the Research Committee on Education System at Tokyo]," *Tokyo Daigaku Shi Kiyo*, Vol. 7, March 1989.)

2. 894.402/7-345 Robert K. Hall, "The Exclusive Use of Katakana As Official Written Japanese" (23 June 1945, S-5 Education, CASA, Presidio of Monterey) (U.S. National Archives).

For a previous study in this area, see "Senryo Gun no Nihongo Seisaku ni Tsuite (Sono 1)" [The Occupation Policy for the Japanese Language: Part 1], by Harry Wray and Kanji Katsuoka, in *Research Bulletin of Educational History of the Allied Occupation of Japan* (Educational History of the Occupation, Research Center, Meisei University), Vol. 3, 1986.

3. 894.402/7-345, Letter from John H. Hilldring to Eugene H. Dooman, July 3, 1945 and from Eugene H. Dooman to John H. Hilldring, July 6, 1945.

4. Marlene J. Mayo, "Psychological Disarmament: American Wartime Planning for the Education and Re-education of Defeated Japan, 1943–1945" in *The Occupation of Japan: Educational and Social Reform*, ed. Thomas W. Burkman (Norfolk: The MacArthur Memorial, 1980), p. 70.

5. Herbert J. Wunderlich, "Reminiscences of Occupation Japan, 1945–1946" (unpublished manuscript, 1984), p. 33.

6. Ibid., pp. 7–8.

7. Robert K. Hall, *Education for a New Japan* (New Haven: Yale University Press, 1949), pp. 354–55.

8. "A Tentative Study: Japanese Written Language Revision Study, March 1946, Tokyo, Japan." Trainor Papers, Box 37.

9. "Memorandum To: Lt. Cmdr. R. K. Hall from D. R. Nugent, Lt. Col., Acting Chief, CI&E Section." Trainor Papers, Box 37.

10. Interview with Mrs. William C. Trow, Ann Arbor, Michigan, on August 1, 1986, and also with Dr. Donald B. Trow (a son of Dr. William C. Trow), Binghamton, New York, on August 4, 1986.

11. Letter from Herbert J. Wunderlich to the author, dated January 18, 1985.

12. "Part II on Preparing the Report." Stoddard Papers, Box 3, p. 5.

13. Subcommittee No 1 of the Japanese Education Committee, "The Committee on Curriculum, Language and Educational Views—An Interim Report" (in Japanese), Sanji Aruga Papers, (Archives of National Institute for Educational Research of Japan).

14. "U.S. Education Mission to Japan, 1946, Personnel." Stoddard Papers, Box 3.

15. "Proposed Outline of the Report." Stoddard Papers, Box 3.

16. "Beikoku Kyoiku Shisetsudan ni Kyoryoku subeki Nihongawa Kyoiku Iinkai no Hokokusho" [Recommendations of the Japanese Education Committee for Cooperation with the U.S. Education Mission] (22 pages typewritten in Japanese). (Archives of National Institute for Educational Research of Japan). An English translation of the Recommendations was also made by the Japanese Education Committee, entitled, "Recommendations of the Japanese Education Committee," Trainor Papers, Box 32.

17. *Tokyo Daigaku Hyakunenshi—Tsuushi 3* [Centenary of the University of Tokyo: General History] ed. Tokyo Daigaku Hyakunenshi Committee (Tokyo: University of Tokyo Press, 1986), pp. 18–28.

18. *Sengo Nihon no Kyoiku Kaikaku 1 Kan, Kyoiku Kaikaku* [Postwar Japanese Education Reform, Vol. 1—Education Reform], p. 115.

19. Nambara, "Gakusei Kaikaku no Keika [The Process of the Educational Reform], pp. 239–40. Within the cultural movement for the New Republic of Turkey, great emphasis was laid on the abolition of inappropriate Arabic characters within the Turkish script and the adoption of a new 29-character Turkish alphabet based on the Roman alphabet. The Turks had used the Arabic script for a long time, like many other Muslim civilizations. However, Arabic was neither sufficient for expressing the subtitles of the Turkish mind nor easy to understand, thus creating an obstacle to the spread of literacy, education, and science. (The rate of literacy in 1923, when the Republic of Turkey was established, was 10 percent). In other words, Turkish language reform was essential in promoting the policy of modernization in Turkey. As of January 1, 1929, publications in Arabic were prohibited, and national schools were opened all over the country to faciliate the teaching of the new Turkish alphabet. This adoption of a new alphabet did not only lay the foundation for the spread of education and the improvement of the literacy rate, but also greatly contributed to the rise of Turkish nationalism. Hironao Matsutani, *Toruko Gengogakugairon* [An Introduction to Turkish Linguistics] (Tokyo: Tairyusha, 1980), p. 28.

It seems that R. K. Hall was so enthusiastic about language reform that he intended to carry out the Japanese language reform in the light of the Turkish experience. However, the Japanese situation was entirely different from that in Turkey. The literacy rate in Japan was not low, as Hall asserted, and the Turkish case was not applicable to Japan.

20. Letter from Gordon T. Bowles to the author dated May 16, 1988.

21. Gordon T. Bowles, "Comments on the Education Mission's Language Reform Recommendation" (unpublished manuscript, September 1988).

22. Interview with Herbert J. Wunderlich, Education Division of CI&E Section, St. Maries, Idaho, on August 14, 1984.

23. Letter from Bowles, dated May 16, 1988.

24. "Tsuyokkata Nihon Gawa Kyoikuka Iin no Eikyo—Sengo Kyoiku Kaikaku de Kicho na Shogen, Moto Beikoku Kyoiku Shisetsudan 'Gordon T. Bowles' Hakase ni Kiku (Ge)" [The Strong Influence of the Japanese Education Committee—An Important Testimony on the Postwar Education Reform, Interview with Dr. Gordon T. Bowles, Former Member of the U.S. Education Mission (Part II)], *Naigai Kyoiku* (Jiji Tsushin), No. 3901 (January 8, 1988), p. 4.

25. Gordon T. Bowles, "Reflections on the March 1946 U.S. Education Mission to Japan" (unpublished manuscript, April 1987). (See Appendix D-2.)

26. Hall, *Education for a New Japan*, pp. 355–56.

27. Mayo, "Psychological Disarmament," pp. 69–70.

28. 894.42A/5-146 Letter, Wilson Compton to William Benton, May 1, 1946.

29. Trow, "Voices Down The Wind."

30. Hall, *Education for a New Japan*, p. 358.

31. With regard to *romaji* education, it is necessary to point out that spelling was also a problem. *Romaji* spelling of the names of railway stations, cities and roads, in official gazettes, and in documents relating to the Occupation, were all based on the Hepburn system, the adoption of which was introduced by SCAP in September 1945. However, Japan was already using the *Kunrei* system, in accordance with the Cabinet instruction "Concerning the Romaji Spelling of the Japanese Language." Therefore, under the Occupation, the Committee of the Vice-Minister decided to adopt the Hepburn system for the names of railway stations, etc., and the *Kunrei* system for domestic subjects. Although the Romaji Education Council proposed the solo adoption of the *Kunrei* system, there was opposition from a group supporting the Hepburn system. Eventually, the Japanese Education Reform Committee decided that the *romaji* system in compulsory education should be based on the *Kunrei* system initially, but that the Hepburn system should be used as an alternative. In fact, *romaji* textbooks published by the Ministry of Education were based on both these two systems, the choice of which to use being left to the discretion of those in charge. In addition to these two systems, a previously invented system, slightly different from the *Kunrei* system, was also in use. Consequently, *romaji* textbooks were published using any one of these three systems by nongovernmental publishers. The discrepancies existing among these systems often created confusion and prevented the promotion of *romaji* education. (Yoshiaki Takebe, "Kokugo Kokuji Mondai no Yurai" [The Origin of Problems of the Japanese Language and Script], in *Iwanami Koza, Nihongo 3 Kokugo Kokuji Mondai* [Iwanami Lectures: The Japanese Language 3, Problems of the Japanese Language and Script] (Tokyo: Iwanami Shoten, 1978), pp. 293–94.)

Notes to Chapter 5: The Mission's Report and Reform of the School System

1. Givens, "Tokyo and Return." Pearl Wanamaker's personal letter to her family of March 22, 1946, also endorses the entry in Givens's diary, by writing that on that day Committee III devoted the entire day to drafting their report, and that on the next day, Saturday the 23rd, they were going to submit it to the general meeting of the Mission. (Letter from P. A. Wanamaker to her family, March 22, 1946. Wanamaker Papers, Box 36/4, "Miscellaneous.")

2. On the discovery of the Wanamaker Papers, refer to Gary H. Tsuchimochi, "Sengo Kyoiku Kaikaku no Genten to 'Wanamaker' Bunsho" [The Starting Point of the Postwar Education Reform and the Wanamaker Papers], in *Naigai Kyoiku* (Jiji Tsushin) No. 3593, November 16, 1984. The interview with Wanamaker was made possible through the assistance of Bowles (Letter from Bowles to Wanamaker, August 11, 1984). Concerning the Wanamaker Papers, refer to: *The Report of the Overseas Research Project: Historical Materials Held in the U.S. Concerning Education Reform Under the Allied Occupation of Japan*, by the National Institute for Educational Research of Japan, March 1988. These important primary histori-

cal materials are also kept in the Archives of the National Institute for Educational Research of Japan.

3. "Report of Committee III: Administration of Education in Japan at Elementary and Secondary Levels," Wanamaker Papers, Box 36/15.

4. Interview with G. T. Bowles, August 9–11, 1984.

5. Letter from Bowles to Wanamaker, August 11, 1984.

6. Interview with Pearl Wanamaker, August 16, 1984, at her home in Seattle, Washington.

7. Eiji Takemae and Akira Amakawa, *Nihon Senryo Hishi (Jo)* [The Untold History of Occupied Japan, Vol. 1] (Tokyo: Asahi Shinbun Sha, 1977), p. 149. For details of this matter, see "GHQ and CI&E, Recommendations on the Reform of Japanese Education," *The Sankei*, September 12, 1975.

8. "Projected Staff Studies—Subject: Compulsory Education," Robert K. Hall Papers.

9. CI&E, *Education in Japan*, pp. 11–12.

10. "University of Michigan—CATS, Far Eastern Area. Education In Japan Lectured, by Huntley, May 7, 1945," Eileen R. Donovan Papers.

11. GHQ/CI&E, Education Division, "Weekly Reports (Oct. 1945–July 15, 1946) 2 Feb. 1946," Trainor Papers, Box 65.

12. Ibid., 1 March, 1946. The moves made by the Japanese were translated into English by the CI&E Media Analysis Division in great detail, and furthermore were reported to the U.S. when necessary, by the Political Advisor to Gen. MacArthur (POLAD), who had been sent by the State Department. The Media Analysis Division had inserted a magazine article which welcomed the implementation of the prewar 6–5 school system. (894.42/3-2246, Subject: Recent Japanese Magazine Articles on Education, Office of the U.S. Political Advisor, Tokyo, Japan, March 22, 1946—Publication Analysis, 21 February 1946.)

13. Aruga Papers.

14. Interview with G. T. Bowles, August 9–11, 1984.

15. Interview with E. R. Hilgard, July 23, 1984, at his office at Stanford University.

16. "Special Report by Shigeru Nambara, President, Tokyo Imperial University and Chairman of the Japanese Committee, to G. D. Stoddard, March 21, 1946," Wanamaker Papers, Box 36/17. (See Appendix C-4.)

Later, Nambara stated: "The substance of the Report which the U.S. Education Mission studied and drew up from their own observations and standpoint, was coincidentally in accord with our opinions in the Japanese Education Committee, in general principle." (Shigeru Nambara, "Nihon ni Okeru Kyoiku kaikaku" [Education Reform in Japan], in Eiichi Suzuki, ed., *Kyoiku Kihon Ho no Seitei* [Establishment of the Fundamental Law of Education] (Tokyo: Gakuyo Shobo, 1977), p. 24.

17. Gordon T. Bowles, "Reflections on the March 1946 U.S. Education Mission to Japan" (unpublished manuscript, 1987).

18. Nambara, "Nihon ni Okeru Kyoiku Kaiaku" [Education Reform in Japan], p. 25.

19. Wray, "A Study of the First United States Education Mission," p. 14.

20. Stevens, "Office Talk on Japan," p. 3.

21. Seiya Munakata and Sadanobu Miwa, *Abe Shigetaka—Kyoiku Kaikaku Ron*

[Shigetaka Abe—The Theory of Education Reform] (Tokyo: Meiji Tosho, 1971), p. 20.

22. Yasuo Akatsuka, *Shinsei Chugakko Seiritsu Shi Kenkyu* [A Study of the History of the Establishment of the New Junior High School] (Tokyo: Meiji Tosho, 1978), pp. 42–44.

23. Aruga Papers.

24. *Kaigo Tokiomi Chosaku Shu* [A Collection of Tokiomi Kaigo's Works]. Vol. 9 of *Sengo Kyoiku Kaikaku* [Postwar Education Reform] (Tokyo: Tokyo Shoseki, 1981), p. 529.

25. Ibid., pp. 254–56.

26. "Report of Committee No. 3 Concerning Youth Schools Et Al," Wanamaker Papers, Box 36/16. (See Appendix C-5.) The author and date of this report are unknown. However, the bases for presuming that this report was compiled by the Japanese are that its contents correspond to the functions assigned to Committee No. 3 of the Japanese Education Committee; the fact that the author was well acquainted with the state of things in Japan; the style of English; and the use of the first person singular. In fact, Gordon T. Bowles, who read the original, assumed that the report was definitely not authored by a Mission member, but by someone on the Japanese side. Because the report is included in the Wanamaker Papers, it is assumed that it was presented to the Mission by Committee No. 3 of the Japanese Education Committee. Interestingly, Bowles conjectured that this report could have been written by Tano Jodai, a trustee of Nihon Joshi Daigaku.

Tano Jodai was a trustee of the university at the time the Mission was visiting Japan, and was inaugurated as its sixth president in 1956. She obtained a Master of Arts degree from Wells Women's University in New York State before the war, and after returning to Japan became a professor of English literature at Nihon Joshi Daigaku. According to Bowles, she was on close terms with Pearl Wanamaker, a member of Committee III of the Mission; and they worked together. Jodai was not a member of the Japanese Education Committee; however, Bowles said that she cooperated with the Mission members as an independent consultant. Additionally, Bowles wrote in his letter to the MacArthur Memorial that Jodai gave particularly important advice on education and the language reforms. It is noticeable that many Japanese educators cooperated with the Mission who were not actually official members of the Japanese Education Committee. (Interview with G. T. Bowles, August 9–11, 1984. Letters from Bowles to the author, May 16, and June 3, 1988. Letter from Bowles to the Archives of the MacArthur Memorial Hall, May 19, 1982. For a brief history of Jodai, refer to the exhibition material, "Joshi Koto Kyoiku Shinten no Toki—Jodai-Ariga-Do Gakucho no Jidai" [The Period of Development of Women's Higher Education—In the days of President of Jodai-Ariga-Do], Naruse Memorial Hall, Japan Women's University.

27. Eiji Ushiyama, "Gakko Kyoiku Seido Kaikaku Shiken" [Personal Opinions on the School Education System Reform], March 1946, in the Aruga Papers (the Archives of the National Institute for Educational Research of Japan).

28. Taketoshi Yamagiwa, "The Problems of Elementary School Education," in "Notes—Meeting of the U.S. Education Mission and Japanese Committee: At 9:00—11:00 Monday, March 25, 1946," Trainor Papers, Box 57.

29. "Education Reform—Official Version of the Japanese Education Committee," 25 March 1946, 16:00, in Higher Education 1946–1947, Trainor Papers, Box 29.

30. It should be noted that Committee II's draft's recommendation is "to retain" the normal school system and reorganize it into a four-year university course, as follows: "We believe that the normal schools system should be retained. However, normal schools should be reorganized on a higher level so as to offer better professional preparation and broader and more adequate liberal education. In short, the normal schools should become higher schools or colleges for the preparation of teachers. Four full years beyond the middle school should be offered by all the normal schools, although it may be necessary to certificate primary teachers at the end of two years. Later opportunities should be provided for these two-year graduates to complete the four-year course." The statement that "the normal school should be abolished," must therefore be in line with GHQ and the Japanese Education Committee itself, rather than the Mission's own idea.

31. The reform plan which is mentioned here was proposed by Kyoiku Doshi Kai in 1937. [Refer to: Eiichi Suzuki, "Sengo Kyoiku Kaikaku ni Okeru Kyoiku Kihon Ho to 6–3–3 sei—Tokuni Nihon Gawa no Shutaisei ni Tsuite" [The Fundamental Law of Education and the 6–3–3 System in the Postwar Education Reform—in Particular Reference to the Japanese Initiative] in *Kokumin Kyoiku* (Rodo Junpo Sha), Vol. 64, May, 1985), p. 112.]

In China, the American 6–3–3 school system had been adopted since 1922. (Refer to: Ministry of Education, Research and Statistics Division, *Gendai Chugoku no Kyoiku Jijo* [The Educational Situation in Present China], 1949, p. 19.)

32. *Education in the New Japan*, p. 139.

33. "Recommendations of the Japanese Education Committee." Trainor Papers Box 32. (See Appendix C-8.)

34. "The Education Report" in *Nippon Times*, Tokyo, Thursday, April 11, 1946; Gildersleeve Papers, Box 76.

35. Shigetaka Abe, "Gakko Keito Kaikaku no Shian" [Personal Suggestions for School System Reform], in *Abe Shigetaka Chosaku Dai 6 Kan* [Abe Collection, Vol. 6] (Tokyo: Nihon Tosho Center, 1983), p. 18. Worth noting is the prewar friendship between one of the Japanese Education Committee members, Teizo Toda (Dean, Faculty of Literature, Tokyo Imperial University, and Professor of Sociology, 1887–1955), and Abe. Toda mentioned the implementation of the 6–3–3 school system by saying: "If Abe was still alive, it would have been carried out by him. As he died young, I have to do it instead." Here we can see expressed the genealogy of the education reform theory, from Abe to Toda. (See Yasuo Akatsuka, *Shinsei Chuggako Seiritsushi Kenkyu* [Studies on the History of Formation of the New Junior High School System] (Tokyo: Meiji Tosho, 1978), pp. 68–78.

36. Naohisa Ichimura, *Amerika 6–3 Sei no Seiritsu Katei* [Formation Process of the American 6–3 System] (Tokyo: Waseda University Press, 1987), pp. 20–21. This work, concerning secondary education reform in the U.S., particularly the formation process of the 6–3 system, is an important paper for examining the Japanese postwar 6–3 school system.

37. Interview with Hilgard, July 23, 1984. This is a translation of a summary of an interview, by the author.

38. Interview with Bowles, August 9–11, 1984.

39. Report of the U.S. Education Mission to Japan, pp. 25–26.

40. "Recommendations of the Japanese Education Committee," Trainor Papers, Box 32.

41. According to Secretary Kaigo's records of the proceedings of the Research Committee on the Education System, at Tokyo Imperial University, at the 6th committee on April 1, Chairman Toda stated: that "The president expects us to discuss the whole education system. Outside opinions on the reform of the education system should be included. The committee, on the Japanese side in the Education Mission, is going to complete its report." And it also records that "There are both the 6–2–4–4 plan and the 6–3–3–4 plan." *Tokyo Daigaku Hyakunen Shi— Tsushi 3* [Centurary History of the University of Tokyo—General History 3] (Tokyo: University of Tokyo Press, 1986), p. 33.

42. Gordon T. Bowles recalls the circumstances of those days as follows: "Within the Mission, there were a few who were against the recommendations on the 6–3–3 system and the language reform, made in the final Report. Chairman Stoddard respected their opinions, and proposed that they make a report based on them. This was the so-called "Minority Report," and was presented at our general meeting by Counts, as a representative of this opposition. I remember it as consisting of not more than one or two pages, and the contents may have been mainly about romanization and may have included the 6–3–3 system. It was probably difficult to make recommendations in the Report, on what had been opposed by some of the other members. Properly speaking, it might have been desirable, from a democratic point of view, to produce the Report with the opposing opinions included. However, Dr. Stoddard thought it would create confusion for the Japanese side, to receive it in that form, and also that it would weaken the coherence of the Report. The main point of the opposition was not concerned with the subject matter, but rather with the form of its expression in areas of emphasis. Eventually, the Chairman, together with the opposition, discussed the matter and decided not to include the "minority opinions" in the final Report." (Interview with Bowles, August 9–11, 1984.)

43. In regard to this matter, Horio compares the differences between prewar and postwar educational ideals. He states, "The idea of the prewar reform of compulsory education could have been conceived as a means for 'training the nation for Empire,' or creating a false consciousness of 'national unity,' in order to prepare the populace for patriotic devotion to war. On the other hand, the postwar system of reform incorporated and guaranteed education as 'the right of the nation.' In so far as these two reforms are concerned, it must be said that there are decisive differences between them." (Yamazumi and Horio, *Sengo Nihon no Kyoiku Kaikaku 2—Kyoiku Rinen* [Postwar Japanese Education Reform 2—Educational Ideals], p. 398.

44. *Tokyo Daigaku Hyakunen Shi—Tsushi 3* [100th Anniversary of the University of Tokyo—General History 3], pp. 18–28.

45. Ibid.

46. Ibid.

47. "Appendix to Minutes of Committee No. 4: Talk by Dr. George D. Stoddard, Chairman of the U.S. Educational Mission to Japan, Before the Special Sub-Committee on Education of Committee No. 4: Strengthening of Democratic Tendencies of the Far Eastern Commission, 8 May 1946" Far Eastern Commission, Box No. 47, FEC (B)—0217 (Modern Political History Materials Room, The National Diet Library, Japan). It is interesting that the title of this subcommittee was in accord with the spirit of the Potsdam Declaration, which is "strengthen democratic tendencies."

48. Isaac L. Kandel, "Reorienting Japanese Education," *Educational Forum* IX (November 1946), p. 17.

49. "Letter to J. Dixon Edwards from Mrs. Mildred McAfee Horton on May 12, 1950," Stoddard Papers, Box 1, p. 3.

50. Interview with Bowles, February 13–15, 1983.

51. *Education in the New Japan*, p. 143.

52. Interview with Hilgard, July 23, 1984, and his letter to the author dated 30 September, 1987. As a matter of fact, when he returned from Japan, he wrote a paper on the friendly attitude of the Japanese, which was entitled "The Enigma of Japanese Friendliness," *The Public Opinion Quarterly* (Fall, 1946).

53. Interview with Bowles, August 9–11, 1984.

54. Letter from Borton to the author, dated January 22, 1985.

55. Frank N. Freeman, "Educational Problems of Japan," *Phi Delta Kappan*, Vol. XXVIII, Oct. 1946, Number 2, pp. 72–73.

56. Kandel, "Reorienting Japanese Education," pp. 16–17.

57. "How Can We Re-Educate the Conquered" by Charles S. Johnson in *Speeches of Charles Spurgeon Johnson*, Vol. Twelve (Fisk University Library), p. 9.

58. "Educating Japan for Democracy" by Charles S. Johnson at the South Central Forum, Chicago, Illinois, February 17, 1948 in the *Speeches of Charles Spurgeon Johnson*, Vol. Twelve (Fisk University Library), p. 3.

59. Wunderlich, "Reminiscences."

60. Stoddard, "The Emperor and I" in George D. Stoddard, *The Pursuit of Education: An Autobiograph* (New York: Vantage Press, 1981), p. 94.

61. Bowles, "Reflections on the March 1946 U.S. Education Mission to Japan," p. 6.

Notes to Chapter 6: The Mission's Report and the Reform of Higher Education

1. "Part II, On Preparing the Report," Stoddard Papers, Box 3, p. 5.

2. "Digest of Discussions of Committee IV," Trainor Papers, Box 57.

3. "Draft Report of the Subcommittee on Higher Education," Stevens Papers. "Report of Committee IV: The Aims and Freedom of Higher Learning" (see Appendix C-7).

4. Tokiomi Kaigo and Masao Terasaki, *Sengo Nihon no Kyoiku Kaikaku 9 Kan, Daigaku Kyoiku* [Postwar Japanese Education Reform, Vol. 9—University Education] (Tokyo: University of Tokyo Press, 1976) p. 69.

5. *Tokyo Daigaku Hyakunenshi—Tsushi 3* [Centenary History of the University of Tokyo—General History 3] ed. Tokyo Daigaku Hyakunenshi Committee (Tokyo: University of Tokyo Press, 1986) pp. 14–15.

6. "Digest of Discussions of Committee IV," Trainor Papers, Box 57.

7. As has been pointed out in the previous chapter on the reform of the school system, GHQ compiled the CI&E's proposal plan concerning the education system reform in the spring of 1946, prior to the Mission's arrival. In this plan recommended the 8–3–4 single-track school system. It also recommended abolition of the Imperial universities, which had became education institutes for the bureaucracy, and of boy's higher schools, which had became preparatory schools for universities. In other words, the CI&E was behind the reorganization of the Imperial university structure. ("GHQ & CI&E, Recommendations on the Reform of Japanese Education," in *The Sankei*, September 12, 1975).

8. Joseph C. Trainor, *Educational Reform in Occupied Japan: Trainor's Memoir* (Tokyo: Meisei University Press, 1983), p. 222.

9. Alfred Crofts, "Universities of Japan," The Social Science Foundation of the University of Denver in Cooperation with the Rocky Mountain Radio Council, Volume IX, Number 32, pp. 226–227. Mildred McAfee Horton Papers (The Margaret Clapp Library, Wellesley College)

10. Wray, "A Study of the First United States Education Mission," p. 13.

11. Crofts, "Universities of Japan," p. 227. Crofts himself told the author that he assumed office as the first president of Keijo Imperial University, in an interview on September 17, 1986. However, it is recorded in the 30th Annal of the University of Seoul and the History of the Republic of Korea, that the first president was Harry B. Ansted.

12. "Special Report by Shigeru Nambara, President, Tokyo Imperial University and Chairman of Japanese Committee to G. D. Stoddard, March 21, 1946," Wanamaker Papers, Box 36/17.

13. Carl L. Becker was born in Iowa on September 7, 1873, and died in New York on April 10, 1945. He was a Professor Emeritus at Cornell University. The quote is taken from Chapter Three, "Freedom of Learning and Teaching."

14. Refer to: Gary H. Tsuchimochi, "Senryoka Doitsu no Kyoiku Kaikaku—Amerika Taidoku Kyoiku Shisetsudan Hokokusho to Koto Kyoiku Kaikaku" [Education Reform Under American Occupation in Germany—United States Education Mission to Germany and Reform of Higher Education), *Daigaku Ronshu*, Vol. 19 (March 1990).

15. Kaigo and Terasaki, *Sengo Nihon no Kyoiku Kaikaku 9 Kan, Daigaku Kyoiku*, p. 70.

16. Refer to: Gary H. Tsuchimochi, "Beikoku Gakujutsu Komondan Hokokusho to Sengo Nihon no Koto Kyoiku Kaikakuan—Adams Dancho Bunsho o Chushin ni" [The Report of the U.S. Scientific Advisory Group and Postwar Japanese Higher Education Reform—with Particular Reference to the Papers of Chairman Adams] *Daigaku Ronshu*, Vol. 20 (March 1991).

Roger Adams was the former special adviser to Lt. Gen. Lucius D. Clay, Deputy Military Governor of the American Zone of Occupation, and was also chairman of the U.S. Scientific Advisory Group to Germany in 1946.

Masao Terasaki, "Daiichiji Beikoku Kyoiku Shisetsudan Oyobi Beikoku Gakujutsukomondan no Teigen" [Proposals of the First U.S. Education Mission and the U.S. Scientific Advisory Group], in *Sengo Nihon no Kyoiku Kaikaku 9 Kan, Daigaku Kyoiku*, ed., Kaigo and Terasaki, is insightful and the only previous study in this area.

17. Orr, "Education Reform Policy in Occupied Japan," p. 93.

18. "Digest of Discussions of Committee IV."

19. "Special Report by Shigeru Nambara, President, Tokyo Imperial University and Chairman of Japanese Committee to G. D. Stoddard, March 21, 1946."

20. "Education Reform—Official Version of Japanese Education Committee," 25 March 1946, 16:00 in Higher Education 1946—1947, Trainor Papers, Box 29.

21. "Recommendations of the Japanese Education Committee" Trainor Papers, Box 32.

22. Kaigo and Terasaki, *Sengo Nihon no Kyoiku Kaikaku 9 Kan, Daigaku Kyoiku*, p. 62.

23. Trainor, *Educational Reform in Occupied Japan: Trainor's Memoir*, pp. 222, 226.

24. Harry Wray, "Change and Continuity in Modern Japanese Educational History: Allied Occupational Reform Forty Years Later," *Comparative Education Review*, Vol. 35, No. 3, August 1991, p. 475.

25. Hisashi Yasujima, "Sengo Gakusei Kaikaku to Kyoiku Chokugo ni tsuite" [Postwar Reform of the Education System and the Imperial Rescript on Education], *Sengo Kyoikushi Kenkyukai Tsushin* [The Newsletter of Education History of the Occupation, Research Center, Meisei University], No. 2 (April, 1991).

26. Kaigo and Terasaki, *Sengo Nihon no Kyoiku Kaikaku 9 Kan, Daigaku Kyoiku*, p. 19.

Notes to Chapter 7: The U.S. Education Mission to Germany: A Comparison

1. Hoei Fujisawa, "Amerika Senryo Kyoiku Seisaku no Henbo Katei" [The Transformation Process of the American Occupation Policy on Education], in Akira Nakano and others, *Sengo Doitsu Kyoikushi* [History of Postwar German Education] (Tokyo: Ochanomizu Shobo, 1966), p. 35.

2. John W. Taylor, *Youth Welfare in Germany: A Study of Governmental Action Relative to Care of the Normal German Youth* (Nashville, Tenn.: Baird-Ward Company, 1936). This is a publication of his Ph.D. dissertation, which was submitted to Columbia University in 1936.

3. James F. Tent, *Mission on the Rhine—Reeducation and Denazification in America-Occupied Germany* (Chicago: University of Chicago Press, 1982), p. 24. In the process of writing this book, Tent made free use of historical material, and it

is full of important suggestions. The author was given the opportunity to interview Tent at his home in Birmingham, Alabama, on August 26 and 27, 1989.

4. Harold Zink, *The United States in Germany, 1944–1955* (Princeton: Princeton University Press, 1957), pp. 194–95.

5. *Report of the United States Education Mission to Germany* (Washington, D.C.: United States Government Printing Office, 1946), p. 44.

6. Interview with John W. Taylor at the Union League Club in Chicago, July 28, 1986.

7. Herman B Wells, *Being Lucky—Reminiscences & Reflections* (Bloomington: Indiana University Press, 1980), pp. 302–4; also interview with H B Wells at Owen Hall of Indiana University, July 30, 1986.

8. Tent, *Mission on the Rhine*, p. 20.

9. The members of this committee were Reinhold Niebuhr, Edmund E. Day, Frank Graham, John W. Taylor, and Archibald MacLeish, David Harris, Gordon T. Bowles, and E. N. Anderson from the State Department. [U.S. National Archives, Record Group 59, U.S. Department of State, Decimal File 862.42 (Reeducation of Germany), File 862.42/6-1345, Secretary's Staff Committee.]

10. SWNCC/SANACC 1944—1949, Roll No. 24 (Modern Political History Materials Room, The National Diet Library, Tokyo).

11. U.S. Department of State, *Germany, 1947—1949, The Story in Documents* (Washington, D.C.: U.S. Government Printing Office, 1950), p. 49. This article, concerning education in the Potsdam Agreement, is similar to that set forth by the U.S. as a guideline for Gen. Eisenhower in April of 1945. In the "Directive to Commander-in-Chief of United States Forces of Occupation Regarding the Military Government of Germany, April 1945," Part I: "General and Political," Article 14, "Education," includes the following similar statement: "A coordinated system of control over German education and an affirmative program of reorientation will be established designed completely to eliminate Nazi and militaristic doctrines and to encourage the development of democratic ideas." [U.S. Department of State, *The Axis in Defeat: A Collection of Documents on American Policy Toward Germany and Japan* (Washington, D.C.: U.S. Government Printing Office, 1948), p. 48.]

12. Arthur Hearnden, *Education in the Two Germanies* (Oxford: Basil Blackwell, 1974), p. 29.

13. George F. Zook, "The Educational Mission to Japan and Germany," *International Conciliation*, No. 427 (Jan. 1947), p. 5.

14. Robert K. Hall, "The Battle of the Mind: American Educational Policy in Germany and Japan," *Columbia Journal of International Affairs 2* (Winter, 1948), p. 64.

15. Allied Control Authority Directive No. 54, *Germany, 1947–49*, p. 49. Hoei Fujisawa, "Fasshizumu no Hokai to Sengo Kyoiku o Meguru Jokyo" (The Collapse of Fascism and the Situation of Postwar Education) in Akira Nakano and others, *op. cit.*, p. 10. "Allied Control Council Directive 54" was issued June 25, 1947. Its contents are as follows: 1. There should be equal education opportunity for all. 2. There should be free tuition in all public schools: free textbooks and materials and school maintenance grants for those who need them.   3. Compulsory full-

time school attendance should be required for all between the ages of six to fifteen and part-time compulsory attendance from sixteen to eighteen years of age.   4. Schools for the compulsory periods should form a comprehensive educational system to serve all youth. The two-track system and all overlapping of elementary and secondary schools will be abolished. The terms elementary and secondary shall mean two consecutive levels of instruction.   5. All schools should lay emphasis upon education for civic responsibility and a democratic way of life, both by means of the curriculum and by the organization of the school itself.   6. School curriculum should promote international good will and understanding in every way possible.   7. Professional, educational, and vocational guidance should be provided for all.   8. Health supervision and health education should be provided in all schools.   9. All teacher education should be on the university level. 10. The administration of the schools should be democratic and sensitive to the wishes of the people.

16. Hearnden, *Education in the Two Germanies*, pp. 31–41.

17. Zink, *The United States in Germany, 1944–1955*, p. 193.

18. Fujisawa, "Amerika Senryo Kyoiku Seisaku no Henbo Katei," p. 31.

19. "Senryoka Doitsu no Kyoiku Josei" [The Situation of German Education under the Occupation], *Chosa Shiryo* 92 [Research Material of the Ministry of Education] (April 1948), p. 6.

20. According to an internal State Department memorandum, W. G. Carr of the National Education Association first suggested sending the Mission to Germany. (862.42/5-1446, Memo, Speier to Anderson, Attached materials, "Background Material on Mission") (U.S. National Archives).

21. 862.42/6-1445, Letter, Willard E. Givens to Henry L. Stimson.

22. 862.42/7-345, Report on the Re-education of Germany.

23. 862.42/8-945, Letter, Julius E. Lips to J. W. Riddleberger.

24. 862.42/5-3145, Memorandum for the President, Subject: Appointment of Chief of Education and Religious Affairs Section, C. C. Germany.

25. RG 165, Civil Affairs Division, U.S. Department of War, File CAD (Education), Letter, Hilldring to Benton, 23 January 1946 (National Archives).

26. 862.42/5-346, Letter, James M. Read to James F. Byrnes.

27. 862.42/5-646, Letter, William G. Carr to David Harris, 6 May 1946.

28. Ibid., Letter, David Harris to William G. Carr, 10 May 1946.

29. Radio Program, "The State of the World Program," May 22, 1946, Frederick G. Hochwalt Papers (Department of Archives and Manuscripts, The Catholic University of America, Washington, D. C.).

30. OMGUS, 308-1/5, Letter, O. P. Echols to Clay, 17 April 1946 (U.S. National Archives).

31. OMGUS, 308-1/5, Memo, Taylor to IA&C Division for Clay, 29 April 1946. This long memo over Taylor's signature was not actually sent to the War Department, but was kept in OMGUS as an internal document. It is assumed that the memo was not approved in full by Gen. Clay.

32. OMGUS, 307 2/5, ER&A Minutes, 10 December 1945.

33. OMGUS, 308-1/5, Cable from AGWAR Echols to OMGUS Personal for Clay for Education and Religious Branch IA&C, 5 May 1946.

34. OMGUS, 308-1/5, Recommendation on "Report of U.S. Education Mission to Japan," John W. Taylor, 7 May 1946.

35. OMGUS, 308-1/5, Cable, OMGUS to AGWAR Echols, 8 May 1946.

36. Although OMGUS officially requested of the War Department that the Education Mission should consist of only a small number of members, they actually discussed a larger-scale Mission at the same time. According to a draft telegram to Echols, the list included the following names as candidates: P. M. Limbert, G. F. Zook, R. Niebuhr, E. J. McGrath, H. H. Hill, and T. V. Smith (who actually became members); W. E. Givens, G. S. Counts, T. V. Smith, and M. M. Horton (who were members of the Mission to Japan). Also included were Robert M. Hutchins, President of the University of Chicago, William F. Russell of Columbia University, and Mrs. Eleanor Roosevelt. However, OMGUS finally organized a smaller group. (OMGUS, 308-1/5, Draft Cable Proposed Answer, from OMGUS to AGWAR for WARCAD Personal for Echols), date unknown.

37. 862.42/5-1446, Memo, Speier to Anderson.

38. 862.42/7-1046, Memorandum of Conversation, Education Mission to Germany.

39. 862.42/7-2046, Telegram, OMGUS, Berlin, Germany, to War Department.

40. 862.42/7-3046, Memo, Benton to Stone.

41. 862.42/7-2546, Letter, Benton to Edmund E. Day.

42. 862.42/7-3046, Telegram, Edmund E. Day to Benton, July 29, 1946.

43. CAD 350 (Education), Telegram, War Department to OMGUS, 1 August 1946.

44. Ibid., Telegram, OMGUS to War Department, 6 August 1946.

45. Ibid., Telegram, War Department to OMGUS, 10 August 1946.

46. 862.42/8-746, Letter, Benton to Zook.

47. Letter from John W. Taylor to the author, dated November 15, 1984. He testifies that "I suggested to General Clay that he (ask) the War Department to ask Dr. Zook (then President of the American Council on Education) to form a Mission. I wanted a qualified group of educators to review what my group had done."

48. Helen C. White Papers (Division of Archives, University of Wisconsin–Madison)

49. CAD 350 (Education), Memo Prepared for the Secretary of War, 19 August 1946.

50. Department of State for the Press, "The Education Mission to Germany," August 20, 1946; No. 584, Helen C. White Papers.

51. RG 165, WDSCA 350 (Education), Memo Department for the Secretary of War, 19 August 1946: Telephone Conversations, 22 August 1946, General Echols called Col. McRae, Re. Education Mission.

52. A draft of "Long-Range Policy Statement for German Reeducation," drawn up by the Advisory Committee on Germany Reeducation on May 28 and 29, 1945, was adopted as a SWNCC policy document. Its first article is quoted in *The Report of the Education Mission to Germany*, as follows: "The reeducation of the German people can be effective only as it is an integral part of a comprehensive program for their rehabilitation. The cultural and moral reeducation of the nation must,

therefore, be related to policies calculated to restore the stability of a peaceful German economy and to hold out hope for the recovery of national unity and self-respect." At the drafting stage, "a peaceful" is not included. A copy of this document is included in the Helen C. White Papers. For this reason, it appears that it might have been handed to the Mission members as part of their basic materials.

53. "Proposed Itinerary for American Education Mission to Germany, 26 August to 26 September 1946," Helen C. White Papers. This was a tentative itinerary and changed in the course of the Mission's progress. Although the submission of the Report was scheduled for September 21 in the Mission's interim schedule, it appears that September 20 was the actual date of submission. ("Report of the United States Education Mission to Germany," from George F. Zook, Headquarters Education to Germany, Berlin, September 20th, Deputy Military Governor, Office of Military Government for Germany. OMGUS, Box 133).

54. "The Briefing in Berlin," Helen C. White Papers

55. "Very Tentative Outline of Report," Helen C. White Papers and T. V. Smith Papers (University of Chicago, The Joseph Regenstein Library, Rare Books and Special Collections).

56. Letter to Major Robertson, Civil Affairs Division, War Department, from Earl J. McGrath, October 5, 1946, Earl J. McGrath Papers (University of Iowa Libraries). In this schedule, the Mission's programs between September 20, 1946 (submission date of the Report) and September 26 (return to the U.S.) are not presented and have not been revealed by previous studies.

57. "Austria's Schools Purged of Nazism—6 U.S. Educators Felt Vienna is Capable of Setting up a Democratic System," *New York Times*, September 27, 1946, p. 14.

58. Letter to George F. Zook from Robert P. Patterson, Secretary of War, October 8, 1946. Letter to the Honorable Robert P. Patterson, Secretary of War, from George F. Zook, October 15, 1946. Earl J. McGrath Papers.

59. CAD 350 (Education), Telegram, War Department to OMGUS, 8 October 1946. Subject: "Suggest Changes be Inserted Re. to [sic] Report of Education Mission."

60. Letter from B. Braude to the author, March 6, 1988.

61. "Broad Program is Outlined for Germany's Re-Education," *Nippon Times*, Tuesday, November 12, 1946. Benton's opposition was criticized by educators in the U.S. For details of this matter, see Gary H. Tsuchimochi, "Senryoka Doitsu no Kyoiku Kaikaku—Amerika Taidoku Kyoiku Shisetsudan Hokokusho to Koto Kyoiku Kaikaku" ["Education Reform under American Occupation in Germany—Report of the United States Education Mission to Germany and Reform of Higher Education"], *Daigaku Ronshu*, No. 19 (March 1990).

62. Letters of Transmittal, Department of State, *Publication 2664, European Series 16* (Washington, D. C.: U.S. Government Printing Office).

63. Letter to Dr. George F. Zook from John W. Taylor, Chief of Education and Religious Affairs Branch, International Affairs and Communications Division, Office of Military Government for Germany (U.S.), January 3, 1947, Helen C. White Papers.

64. Report of the United States Education Mission to Germany, p. 23. With regard to the introduction of the Social Sciences in postwar Germany, see Gary H. Tsuchimochi, *Senryoka Doitsu no Kyoiku Kaikaku—Amerika Taidoku Kyoiku Shisetsudan to Amerika Taidoku Shakaika Iinkai* [Educational Reforms under American Occupation in Germany—U.S. Education Mission to Germany and the U.S. Social Studies Committee to Germany] (Tokyo: Meisei University Press, 1989).

65. "Comment of Report of U.S. Education Mission to Germany," from the Office of the Military Government for Germany (U.S.) to Major General O. P. Echols, Director, Civil Affairs Division, War Department. OMGUS, Box 133, p. 35.

66. Letter to Dr. George F. Zook from John W. Taylor, Chief of Education and Religious Affairs Branch, International Affairs and Communications Division, Office of Military Government for Germany (U.S.), January 3, 1947, Helen C. White Papers.

67. SCAP/GHQ/CI&E, Education Division, Japanese Education Reform Committee, "Reorganization and Decentralization of the Japanese System of Education," Trainor Papers, Box 31.

68. Letter to Mrs. Pearl Wanamaker, Superintendent of Public Instruction, State of Washington, from Ivan Nelson, CI&E Education Division, Vocational Education, June 19, 1950. Wanamaker Papers, Box 38.

69. Interview with G. T. Bowles, August 9–11, 1984.

70. J. W. Taylor testifies that he wanted a qualified group of educators to review what his group had done. Letter from J. W. Taylor to the author dated November 15, 1984.

71. Interview with G. T. Bowles, August 9–11, 1984.

72. Gary H. Tsuchimochi, "Amerika ni okeru Senryoki Nihon no Kyoiku Kaikaku ni kansuru Kenkyudoko—Gakuironbun o chushin ni" ["American Trends in a Study of Postwar Japanese Education Reform During the Occupation Period—Doctoral Dissertations as the Main Focus"], *Kokuritsu Kyoiku Kenkyusho Kenkyushuroku*, [Research Report of the National Institute for Educational Research], No. 3, 1982.

73. Zook, "The Educational Mission to Japan and Germany," p. 5.

74. Ikutaro Shimizu, "Konnichi no Kyoiku Tetsugaku" [Philosophy of Education of Today], *Shiso* (April 1951). This article is an interesting comparative and analytical study of the Report of the Education Missions to Japan and Germany. For another comparative study of the two Missions, see Masao Terasaki, "Senryo to Kyoiku Kaikaku" [The Occupation and Education Reform] in Takashi Ohta, ed., *Sengo Nihon Kyoikushi* [History of Postwar Japanese Education] (Tokyo: Iwanami Shoten, 1978).

75. Zook, "The Educational Mission to Japan and Germany," pp. 3–6.

76. Letter from the National Association of Education to the author, June 21, 1984. Letter from William G. Carr to the author, September 29, 1984.

77. Letter from Henry J. Kellerman to the author, March 21, 1988.

78. Fujisawa, "Amerika Senryo Kyoiku Seisaku no Henbo Katei," p. 40.

79. Letter from B. Braude to the author, October 20, 1986.

80. *Taidoku Amerika Kyoiku Shisetsudan Hokokusho* [The Report of the U.S. Education Mission to Germany], "Foreword" by Masaharu Amano.

Notes to Summary and Conclusions

1. Akio Igasaki and Koichiro Yoshihara, eds. and commentators, *Beikoku Kyoi-ku Shisetsudan Hokokusho—Sengo Kyoiku no Genten 2* [The Report of the U.S. Education Mission: The Original of Postwar Education 2] (Tokyo: Gendaishi Shuppan Kai, 1975), p. 41.

2. Kaigo, *Sengo Nihon no Kyoiku Kaikaku 1—Kyoiku Kaikaku* [Postwar Japanese Education Reform 1: Education Reform], p. 103.

3. Bowles, "Reflections on the March 1946 U.S. Education Mission to Japan."

4. Tsuguhisa Tamaki, *Okinawa Senryo Kyoiku Seisaku to Amerika no Kokyoiku* [The Occupation Policy for Okinawa Education and American Public Education] (Tokyo: Toshin Do, 1987), pp. 22–23.

5. Hideo Sato, *Kyoiku to Joho* [Education and Information] (June 1991).

6. Harry Wray, "Change and Continuity in Modern Japanese Educational History: Allied Occupational Reforms Forty Years Later," *Comparative Education Review*, Vol. 35, No. 3 (August 1991), p. 475. This article describes the pattern of Japanese cultural borrowing as follows: "No country in the world has borrowed so freely and on such an extensive scale or kept as much of the old as Japan. . . . In the Meiji period, the Japanese borrowed heavily but selectively and modified most of what they had borrowed to fit their culture. . . . In the 4 decades since the Occupation, the same selective borrowing process and tendency has taken place" (Ibid., p. 471).

INDEX